This work is an innovative and controversial study of how the best-known Jews writing in Russian in the early Soviet period attempted to resolve the conflict between their cultural identity and their place in Revolutionary Russia. Babel, Mandelstam, Pasternak and Ehrenburg struggled in very different ways to form creative selves out of the contradictions of origins, outlook and social or ideological pressures. Efraim Sicher also explores the broader context of the literature and art of the Jewish avant-garde in the years immediately preceding and following the Russian Revolution. By comparing literary texts and the visual arts the author reveals unexpected correspondences in the response to political and cultural change. This study contributes to our knowledge of an important aspect of modern Russian writing and will be of interest to students and scholars in Slavonic and Jewish studies, as well as anyone concerned with the construction of cultural and ethnic identity.

JEWS IN RUSSIAN LITERATURE AFTER
THE OCTOBER REVOLUTION

CAMBRIDGE STUDIES IN RUSSIAN LITERATURE

General editor MALCOLM JONES

Editorial board: ANTHONY CROSS, CARYL EMERSON,
HENRY GIFFORD, BARBARA HELDT, G. S. SMITH,
VICTOR TERRAS

For a complete list of books in the series, see the end of this volume

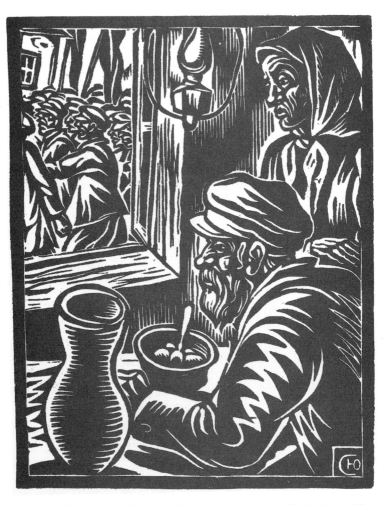

Solomon Yudovin, *First Days of the Revolution*, linocut *c.* 1921 (Tsilia Menjeritsky
Collection, Israel Museum, Jerusalem). © Israel Museum, 1991

JEWS IN RUSSIAN LITERATURE AFTER THE OCTOBER REVOLUTION

Writers and Artists between Hope and Apostasy

EFRAIM SICHER

Associate Professor, Abrahams-Curiel Department of Foreign Literatures and Linguistics, and the Centre for Russian Studies, Ben-Gurion University of the Negev

CAMBRIDGE
UNIVERSITY PRESS

Published by the Press Syndicate of the University of Cambridge
The Pitt Building, Trumpington Street, Cambridge CB2 IRP
40 West 20th Street, New York, NY 10011-4211, USA
10 Stamford Road, Oakleigh, Melbourne 3166, Australia

First published 1995

Printed in Great Britain by Woolnough Bookbinding Ltd, Irthlingborough, Northants.

A catalogue record for this book is available from the British Library

Library of Congress cataloguing in publication data
Sicher, Efraim.
Jews in Russian literature after the October Revolution:
writers and artists between hope and apostasy./Efraim Sicher.
p.   cm. – (Cambridge studies in Russian literature)
Includes index.
ISBN 0 521 48109 0 (hardback)
1. Russian literature – Jewish authors.
2. Babel', I. (Isaak), 1894–1940– Criticism and interpretation.
3. Mandel'shtam, Osip, 1891–1938 – Criticism and interpretation.
4. Pasternak, Boris Leonidovich, 1890–1960 – Criticism and interpretation.
5. Erenburg, Il'ia, 1891–1967 – Criticism and interpretation.
6. Russian literature – 20th century – History and criticism.
7. Soviet Union – History – Revolution, 1917–1921 – Literature and the revolution.
I. Title.   II. Series.
PG2998.J485 1995
891.7'098924 – dc20   95–956 CIP

ISBN 0 521 48109 0 hardback

1004322014

Dedicated to the living memory of Max Hayward

Contents

Illustrations

Preface

> *Espero* – hope. We hoped that soon the forces fighting for
> the brotherhood of all men – for communism – would
> triumph throughout the world. And we believed that in our
> country ... a national forum of different peoples and races
> had already been realized... Precisely for this reason our
> native land had become *the fatherland of the laborers of the whole
> world.*[1]

A joke dating from Soviet times tells of a school class in *politgramota*
(ideological indoctrination). The teacher asks a Jewish pupil who
his father is. 'The Soviet Union,' comes the correct reply. To the
question who his mother is, little Abram obediently answers, 'The
Party'. 'And what do you want to be when you grow up?' asks the
teacher. 'An orphan,' replies the little Jewish boy.[2] Many years
later that little boy was indeed orphaned, from both the Party
and the Soviet Union. The collapse of the Soviet Union and the
emigration of large numbers of Jews to Israel, however, have
made all the more topical questions that have been simmering for
two centuries: Russian national identity, the cultural identity of
Russian-speaking Jews who have assimilated and lost contact with
the Jewish heritage, and finally, the destiny of those Jews who will
remain in Russia. The Jews who started fleeing to Israel in 1989,
choosing between no bread and no work, mostly came to Israel
with a cultural identity forged out of a blind faith in the
humanism of Pushkin and Dostoevsky, believing in what one
'repatriate' intellectual bluntly called the superiority of the
Russian language over falafel and houmus. Jews in Russia, they
find themselves Russians in Israel.[3] Some of their Russian
neighbours accused them of desertion (since so many Jews were

active in the dissident movement), others of Russophobia and
treachery (since so many Jews were directly involved in the
Revolution and the Communist system). The Jews have been a
traditional scapegoat in Russia and were all the more so when
Russianness was at the centre of debate over Russia's political
future and national identity. Igor Shafarevich's tract, 'Russophobia' (1989), gave voice to the paranoiac fear of the world
Zionist conspiracy which, along with the West. was supposedly
responsible for Russia's spiritual and economic crisis. In particular, Shafarevich believed in the subversive influence of Jews at
work in culture, naming Bialik, Babel, Galich, Grossman, Heine,
Kafka and others who were alleged to be destroying Russian
national and religious values.[4] In opposing the 'rootlessness' of
the Jews to Russian *pochvennost'* – a healthy Russia attached to its
soil – such chauvinist or neofascist views managed to revive both
Tsarist anti-Semitism and Stalinist anti-cosmopolitanism in an
attempt to exclude Jews from Russian culture.

Apart from the adulation of Russian socialism which had a
strong influence on the kibbutz movement, Israelis have always
respected Russian literature for its role in the *Haskalah*, the
secular Jewish enlightenment of the nineteenth century, and its
influence on the first generations of pioneer settlers and immigrants, which in turn contributed significantly to modern Hebrew
poetry.[5] The decline of socialism did not weaken the vivid interest
in things Russian and in Russian affairs. Russia was the birthplace
of several Zionist leaders, among them David Ben-Gurion and
Zeev Jabotinsky, and the history of modern Zionism could not
be understood without the historical events that shook Russia
between 1861 and 1917. The regaining of access to the lost Jewish
heritage in Russia under *perestroika*, resulting in major exhibitions
in Russia and Israel (of particular note, the early Chagall and An-
sky), coincided with a rediscovery of the East European roots of
modern Israeli identity. The radio presents excerpts from Osip
Mandelstam's 'Kamen'' ('Stone') while Educational TV devotes
an hour and a half to Boris Pasternak.

In his biography of Khaim Nakhman Bialik, universally recognized to be the national Hebrew poet, whose name is almost
synonymous with the renaissance of Hebrew literature in the

modern period, David Aberbach emphasizes the Russian influence: 'He is unmistakably a Russian poet, with the energy, the moral sincerity and torment, the chiaroscuro moods, the love of the Russian landscape and the changing seasons, which characterize Russian poetry. Russia is as much the subject of Bialik's poetry as Zion or his inner world.'[6] Bialik lived in Russia until his emigration in 1921, and it was Russia and Russian Jewry which provided the landscape of his poetry. However, during the Soviet period Hebrew literature was more or less unknown in Russia. The Russian language and Russian culture predominate in the identity of the Jews who came to Israel in the waves of exodus in the seventies and after 1989. Outside the room where I type these lines, students from the former Soviet Union sit on long benches in a dim corridor, waiting for the Russian-speaking registration advisor; in the street and in government offices hang signs and notices in Russian, and electronic billboards and public service announcements flash messages with no Hebrew translation. The Israeli television channels compete with the Russian stations available on cable TV by offering news and features programmes in Russian, as well as simultaneous translation of newscasts. My electrician swears obscenities in Arabic and pidgin Russian at his Soviet-trained apprentice. Captain Khokhlov is at the moment steering the *MS Dmitri Shostakovich* on course for Haifa with a passenger-load of immigrants following the same route as their forefathers a hundred years ago, though driven less by idealism than by radioactive contamination from the Chernobyl reactor and uncertain prospects, as well as hyperinflation, in the Ukraine and other republics of the CIS. Soon a fifth of the population will be Russian-speaking, the largest immigrant group after the Moroccans. On the one hand, the incredible awakening of Jewish consciousness; on the other, mixed families resulting from widespread exogamy, and the tenacious hold on anything Russian in a strange land.

The contemporary Jewish author writing in Russian may consider Jewish themes a sensitive chapter in his corpus, but since 1989 Israel has become a viable alternative homeland, though not necessarily a preferred homeland or a literary homeland. The playwright Aleksandr Gelman, for example, expressed views on a

visit to Israel that typify the Russified Jew who has committed his
pen to satirizing Russian society but can also use his political
influence to lobby on Jewish issues.[7] As for Feliks Roziner and
David Markish, they are part of a 'third wave' of émigré literature
of Jews writing in Russian in Israel and the United States for whom
the Russian language is still a homeland, even if Russia is not.[8]

In a fantasy story called 'Strange Kike' Grigorii Gerenshtain
once formulated the metaphysical, surreal identity of the Soviet
Jew who becomes aware that he is one of those who gets taken
away in the middle of the night. That strange name learnt from
graffiti and insult endows him with a fragile existence that can be
realized only where he can be free from time and space: 'My
future had come, because time lost its goals [...] I had stopped on
the border between the sky and the earth, on the shores of time
and space. I listened to their tense silence and understood their
language.'[9] Cut off from any meaningful Jewish identity and
denied anything but alien status in Russia, Grigorii Svirsky,
former dissident and Soviet Jewish activist, proclaimed that since
he had been made a Jew by Point Five in the Soviet internal
passport he now wished to be a Jew without Point Five:

Even if I don't know Hebrew, and probably will never be able to learn
it well enough to write books in it, even if I always remain a man of
Russian culture, with all the symptoms of homesickness known to
civilization, I shall say – no, not say, but shout aloud – if I still have any
human dignity left, 'I am a Jew!'[10]

Notwithstanding the uncertain political situation in the Russia of
the first half of the 1990s, there were sufficient signs of a
reawakening among Jews for us to conclude that the culture of
the next generation is likely to be very different. The two-
hundred-year history of the Jews in Russia is at an end and, as the
literary critic Lev Anninsky graphically described it in the
Moscow *Nezavisimaia gazeta*, the Russian stepmother might well
shake her crutch and curse the departing Jews, but Russians
would miss the indispensable Other in their make-up, and Jews
would have to stop rejecting their own culture as alien.[11]

Jewish culture in the Soviet Union was repressed and lay
dormant but it was never killed. Alongside ideological or cultural

apostasy Jewish artists and writers continued to create against all odds in the hope of a synthesis of Russian and Jewish culture. This book does not, however, pretend to be a history of Jewish culture in the Soviet Union. Such a history sorely needs to be written.[12] Rather, these are discrete essays on how Isaak Babel, Osip Mandelstam, Boris Pasternak and Ilia Ehrenburg created art out of their accommodation with the Revolution and with themselves. Since the examples are so varied and because I want to focus on the texts I have not tried to give an exhaustive treatment or tried to answer all the questions. My selection of what might be loosely called 'poetic autobiography' or 'autobiographical fiction' does not reflect the wealth of material (in particular the poetry of Mandelstam and Pasternak) and for a number of reasons I have focused on prose. Moreover, the problem of the integrity of the artist is too complex for a straightforward account in any culture and especially in one where the medium of art, language, is itself in question. I have therefore prefaced these case-studies with a general discussion of the writing self against the background of acculturation and apostasy among Russian-speaking Jews in Russia before and after the Revolution – a discussion which interrogates a number of texts and authors, not all of them typical or of equal weight, in order to investigate the diversity and range of literary responses to modernity and revolution. The traumatic destruction of Jewish communal life and the breakdown of traditional values under the impact of pogroms, war and revolution provide a prologue to the specific example in the second chapter of the use of Jesus and the crucifix, a most vivid case of personal and ethnic crisis which also shows the complex inter-relationship with the European avant-garde at a time of exciting experimentation in collaboration between the arts. The book then progresses from the ironical portrayal of split identity by Babel, through cultural apostasy in Mandelstam's self-presentation of the poet and spiritual apostasy in Pasternak to the enigma of ideological apostasy in Ehrenburg and the puzzle of his true identity.

My approach to the tensions of writing and identity is illuminated by Bakhtin's notion of polyphony, and the semiotic theory of the Tartu-Moscow school helps to explore the binary relationship of the discourse of Self and Other. I have applied an interdisciplinary method to draw attention to the intertextuality of some key texts in the visual arts, some of which relate directly to the questions of identity and to the authors I am discussing. My differences from Simon Markish and Alice Nakhimovsky, who have written much about writing by Jews in Russian, will be apparent. I argue that the Revolution and the events leading up to 1917 in art and in the social history of the Jews caused a complete break with the old Russian-Jewish literature.[13] These are individual portraits of the artistic self in conflict with time and history. If they have anything in common it is a birthdate in the bygone age of the 1890s, a commitment to Russian and West European culture, a writer's fate born of the Russian Revolution and a declaration of love for Russia which (with the notable exception of Babel) negates a Jewish language. Mandelstam and Pasternak were far less familiar with the Jewish world than was Babel, but their obsession with Russianness was no less a conflict of self and art. At the same time the context of Yiddish and Hebrew modernism in Russia must no longer be ignored. I will show shared concerns and shared images in the Jewish artists and writers of the revolutionary years. The Christian nature of some of those images, particularly the crucifix and the apocalypse, were relevant in a disturbingly modernist manner to the destruction of East European Jewry.

The end of modernism coincides with the beginning of the first Five-Year Plan, forced collectivization and the dimming of artistic freedom under Stalin. It will be seen that Ehrenburg's self-identification in *Liudi, gody, zhizn'* (*People, Years, Life*) is largely determined by the Holocaust and the Stalinist anti-Cosmopolitan campaign which followed it. A brief epilogue therefore brings my story to a close with some examples from Vasily Grossman's novel *Zhizn' i sud'ba* (*Life and Fate*) which show some of the ways in which the Holocaust was a turning-point in the discourse of the Soviet Jewish author. The delayed impact of the Holocaust on Jews in Russia found its expression in films such as Aleksandr Borshchagovsky's *Damskii portnoi* ('The Ladies' Tailor') or official events such as the commemoration by the Ukrainian government of the fiftieth anniversary of Babi Yar. Alice Nakhimovsky devotes the second half of her book *Russian-Jewish Literature and Identity* (Baltimore: Johns Hopkins Press, 1992) to writers such as Grossman and Galich who wrote after the Holocaust, and Grossman may carry great weight here, because of his own fate as a writer and because of the bombshell effect of his writing twenty years after his death, when Stalinism was being reassessed under Gorbachev and the national conscience was at last being probed openly. Anatoli Rybakov is a comparatively lesser talent but has also done much in *Tiazhelyi pesok* (*Heavy Sand*) and *Deti Arbata* (*Children of the Arbat*) to restore both Stalinism and the Holocaust to the forefront of Russia's collective memory. The poets Margarita Aliger, Yunna Moritz, Pavel Antokolsky, Boris Slutsky and Nobel Laureate Joseph Brodsky likewise belong to the postwar situation. Yunna Moritz was born in Kiev in 1937, which made her lucky to avoid the fate of Kiev's Jews at Babi Yar, and has translated Yiddish poetry. Born of an assimilated family, Margarita Aliger enjoyed the opportunites offered by the Revolution and came to know the suffering of Stalinism and Hitler's invasion of Russia. Her lyrics dealing with survival express her concern that the generation which survived Stalin was misunderstood, and in one poem of 1946–56 she complained that 'people do not forgive me my mistakes'. Like Ehrenburg, she was both very close to the literary establishment (she lived with Fadeev) and deeply affected by the fate of such non-conformists as Marina Tsvetaeva. In 'To the Portrait of Lermontov' she confesses she has paid the price of bearing the unendurable and asks, 'What weighs more, heavy blows the living feel, or / grass that's growing overhead?'[14] Evgenii Evtushenko wrote that Aliger had 'the pure light / and pride of / someone who was both Jewish woman / and Russian poet'.[15] By and large, however, these poets make little reference to their Jewish origins, except in the sense of a shared experience of Stalinism and war. Joseph Brodsky in particular represents Mandelstam's ideal of the man of world culture who eschews any self-conscious ethnic identity even as he continues a Russian literary tradition. Brodsky and Yulii Daniel, author of the short-story collection *This is Moscow Speaking* who wrote under the Russian pseudonym of Nikolai Arzhak, properly belong to a discussion of the dissident movement of the Brezhnev years.

Daniel has a poem which is relevant to the fate of any Russian or
Jewish poet,

> O how impossible it is for the poet
> To escape the lassoo, the sliding slip-knot
> When the law's fangs are at his throat,
> [...] And yet how light his thorny crown
> Compared with glory after death.[16]

It is, however, the Jew who has had to face the contradiction
and sometimes the synonym of Jew and writer. Either or both of
these might have to be paid for in martyrdom or oblivion.
Ronald Hingley has debated the notion of the martyrdom of the
Russian poet, pointing out that suffering was for long a condition
of life in Russia, not a condition of writing, though Pushkin and
Lermontov both came into conflict with the authorities and after
the Russian Revolution Osip Mandelstam spoke of the 'nightingale fever' of one who could not stop singing. Yet Mandelstam,
Akhmatova, Tsvetaeva and Pasternak were not in any way
actively committed to political opposition; rather their tragedy
was to be caught up in a totalitarian system of which they were
among many victims and which did not tolerate those who
refused to sing the right songs, or who fell silent.[17] Tsvetaeva
herself wrote of Pushkin's Negro origins as a sign of the writer's
otherness: 'What poet, dead or living, is *not* a Negro? What poet
has *not* been murdered?'[18] This was a variant of Tsvetaeva's line
that 'all poets are Yids' in 'Poema Kontsa' ('Poem of the End'), a
line to which we will return in the discussion of Mandelstam's and
Ehrenburg's self-presentation as Jew-Poet. As Donald Fanger has
shown, however, the public myth of the poet as martyr both
continues and challenges the model of the Russian writer as
vehicle of ethical and social conscience, his role of 'a sort of
second government' to quote a character in one of Solzhenitsyn's
novels. When Andrei Siniavsky borrowed the pseudonym Abram
Tertz from a song about the Odessa Jewish underworld he
referred to the mythic status of Jew as dissident and to a marginal,
criminal language in order to bypass conscription of the poet by
the State,[19] the sort of conscription which made it possible for
Pushkin's pro-Decembrist rhetoric to serve Party propaganda.

Pushkin had subscribed to the divine authority of the poet in

'Prorok' ('The Prophet'), but the secular authority of the poet in his self-presentation, which paralleled that of Church and State, usurped a complex vocabulary that combined sainthood with martyrdom, chivalric nobility with Christ-like humility. Only in public myth, in the martyrologies penned by Herzen (*Du Développement des idées révolutionnaires*), after the deaths of Griboedov, Pushkin, Lermontov and Ryleev, and by Roman Jakobson ('The Generation That Squandered its Poets'), after the deaths of Maiakovsky and Esenin, did the institution of poet become canonically associated with actual martyrdom and, together with the discourse of revolutionary martyrdom, infuse the poet's self-presentation.[20] Modernism, however, seriously modified the moral imperative of the writer, and that Western influence reached the Russian avant-garde before the State was overturned by revolution, so that these years prove to be of particular interest for the literary construction of poetic identity.

This book was researched and written at various times beginning in 1977 in Moscow and Oxford, but its completion and final revision were interrupted by teaching and family responsibilities, as well as by the launching from Western Iraq of Soviet-made Scud missiles, all of which gave pause for thought. My teaching and lecturing duties have also placed me in the position of defending my ideas without covering fire in a confused *Kulturkampf*. To all those who listened and to those who encouraged me I am grateful. Among those who read my work and commented on it I should mention Mordecai Altshuler (Hebrew University), Christopher Barnes (Toronto), Jan van der Eng (Amsterdam), Jonathan Frankel (Hebrew University), Maurice Friedberg (Illinois), Jane Gary Harris (Chicago), Simon Markish (Geneva), Arnold McMillin (London), Alice Stone Nakhimovsky (Colgate), Shimon Redlich (Ben-Gurion University) and Seth Wolitz (Texas at Austin). Chapter 4 is indebted to the work of Kirill Taranovsky and Clarence Brown, Chapter 5 to that of George Gibian, Christopher Barnes and Lazar Fleishman. Wherever humanly possible I have recorded these and other debts in the footnotes; for any sins of omission I beg forgiveness. To the archivists of the IMLI and TsGALI (now RGALI) state archives in Moscow and Yad Vashem in Jerusalem I owe the debt of acknowledgement for perusal of unpublished documents, and to numerous librarians in Moscow, London, Oxford, Jerusalem and Beer-Sheva must go the unsung glory of helping to locate rare material and obscure information. Conversion of word-processing applications was assisted by the BGU Macintosh-support guru Rami Peles, of blessed memory, who died of cancer before publication of this book. The research benefited from the support of the Memorial Foundation for Jewish Culture in New York and a Basic Research Grant from the Israel Academy of Sciences, and the cost of publishing the illustrations was defrayed by the Research Committee of the Faculty of Humanities and Social Sciences of Ben-Gurion University.

In transcription from Russian I have followed the Library of Congress system, but have preferred non-compliance to incomprehensibility and have attuned Hebrew and Yiddish transcription to this system. Proper names are in most cases given in their best-known form in the West, for example Budyonny, Tolstoy, Yosif, Yakov. The symbol ′ represents the 'soft sign', ″ the 'hard sign' and ‛ the glottal stop. No distinction has been made between sin and samekh or kaf and quf. I have rendered Russian *x*, Hebrew khet and khaf all by kh; similarly sh stands for that sound in Russian, Hebrew and Yiddish. Transcription from Hebrew follows the Modern Hebrew (Sefardic) pronunciation. Scriptural references are to the Masoretic text of the Hebrew Bible. For the benefit of readers with no Russian or with no Hebrew and Yiddish I give sources in English translation. In general I refer to the complete unexpurgated texts based on archival manuscripts or early editions, which may differ from the versions used by previous scholars. Dates follow the Western 'New Style'.

CHAPTER I

Burning embers

Moi roman s revoliutsiei gluboko neschasten.
Viktor Shklovsky, letter to Gorky, 15 April 1922

THE POLITICS OF LANGUAGE

Language has often been deemed a determining factor in the definition of culture, something which in the nineteenth century presumed the correspondence of natural with linguistic boundaries, a Romantic view that drew on Schiller and Fichte. But a nation does not live by language alone and distinctive cultures can take root across linguistic, political and ethnic borders. The legitimacy of the new Literatures in English across the far-flung British Commonwealth is more recent than the recognition of the Francophone cultural empire in Africa, yet it is a phenomenon that draws attention to the shifting norms of Englishness more than it unites a varied crowd of Australians, Irishmen and others.

In the countries where Jews have been exposed to the host culture and where they have been accorded a modicum of tolerance they have contributed in their own languages (Hebrew, Yiddish, Ladino) or in the local vernacular to an extraterritorial corpus of Jewish song, rites, poetry and metaphysical prose. In the modern period, after civic emancipation and the erosion of traditional patterns of Jewish community, it is debatable whether Kafka, Svevo or Bellow have anything in common as Jews. One might well ask if mixed parentage counts, as in the case of Proust. Yet the claim exists for a Jewish culture beyond borders or a common linguistic and political discourse. However, most Jews writing in non-Jewish languages would not think of themselves primarily as Jewish writers. Bellow certainly thinks of himself as American, which does not contradict his memory of the Jewish world or some affinity with it. Kafka said he found little in common with himself let alone with others, and the French modernist Proust can hardly be said to show exclusive interest in Jewish themes or symbols.

Isaac Deutscher has spoken of the 'non-Jewish Jew', George Steiner of 'metarabbis'. Albert Memmi and others have written copiously about the secular Jewish intellectual. Freud, Einstein, Buber and Memmi himself have become the subjects of books about their Jewishness. I suppose there are varying degrees of truth in these prognoses. However, the artist who invests in his creative persona the anxieties of being and becoming is for various reasons considered characteristic of the aesthetic and literary issues that will be immediately familiar to readers of T. S. Eliot, Pound, Joyce and Rilke. Kafka's existential anxiety of being – the anxiety of rootless man outside time and space, at home everywhere but safe nowhere – is typical of the fictive autobiography that is a confessional mode of poetical becoming (or nonbecoming). In his explanation of the 'Kafka syndrome' Gershon Shaked has tried to understand why Kafka's vivid interest in Judaism and Zionism is not matched by obvious Jewish references in his fiction. Shaked explains the discrepancy in the transformation of anxiety about identity and dissatisfaction with the assimilationist position into a parable of the Jew's exiled situation which runs through Kafka's writing.[1] Edmund Wilson's discussion of the myth of Philoctetes as a parable of human character could be relevant in another way to this writing out (in the sense of both erasure and exorcism) of Jewishness. The disease and unease which render the artist abhorrent to the rest of society paradoxically make the artist a master of a superhuman art that commands respect. In Gide's version of the myth of Philoctetes there is an undeveloped implication that 'genius and disease, like strength and mutilation, may be inextricably bound up together'.[2]

For centuries Russianness had been a linguistic and spiritual heritage implanted in the subjugated peoples of the Tsarist empire by means of edict, colonization or inducement to better employment and social mobility. For the Jews who became the unwanted and mistrusted subjects of the Russian autocracy in the Partitions of Poland, Russianness was a stick-and-carrot to assimilation, to the big cities, to the wider vistas of Western culture and particularly the literature of so-called world-wide and progressive values. Ironically, Pushkin or Turgenev, who were the last word in a humane, liberal standpoint for those straining to escape the confines of the Pale of Settlement, did not know their Jewish readers except through romanticized myth and anti-Semitic stereotype. In general the landed gentry viewed at best with suspicion anything as commercial and un-Christian as the average *shtetl* dweller. The Jew was perceived as a mythical stereotype who spoke bad Russian.[3]

For their part, the People of the Book, who had given the world moral and prophetic inspiration, had been exiled from their land and no longer spoke the language of the Bible. Unlike the *maskilim*, the Jewish reformers in Germany who followed Moses Mendelssohn, the majority of Jews in Tsarist Russia spoke Yiddish and clung to ancient traditions. They maintained well-established educational, judiciary and welfare networks in close-knit communities largely cut off from the surrounding inhospitable host society, at a time, moreover, when most Russians were illiterate serfs with little or no access to schooling, medical services or justice. It was surely ironic that Jews should want to forsake their traditions in order to enter secular schools and undergo Russification in the hope of gaining civic rights. The model of the Jewish enlightenment in Germany, the *Haskalah*, did, however, encourage the hope that Jews could be equal citizens, if only they would throw off medieval Jewish garb and practices and if they could at the same time overcome the barriers of misunderstanding that seemed to prevent their becoming full and useful members of society.[4] To 'attack and to defend' was how one Russian-Jewish writer, Lev Levanda, phrased his strategy, and this might loosely define the *raison d'être* of the Russian-Jewish press that appeared from the 1860s, first in Odessa, then in St Petersburg.[5] Its popularity derived from the hopes raised by the emancipation of the serfs and other reforms, including some concessions to the Jews, in the first part of the reign of Alexander II. One of the centres of the new Jewish culture was Odessa, and Steven Zipperstein has shown why modernity characterized the Jews of Odessa more than any other city of the Russian Empire and made possible the unique flowering of a secular Jewish culture there in Russian, Yiddish and Hebrew.[6] The writing of Osip Rabinovich, Lev Levanda or Grigorii Bogrov was mainly publicist, and their fiction furnished the gentile reader with a critical presentation of the Jewish world and the plight of the Jew in Russia, as well as promoting the aims of the *Haskalah* on Russian soil alongside the journals and novels in Hebrew.[7] The fact that Russian-Jewish authors had in mind two readerships, one largely indifferent or hostile, the other a narrow-interest group lacking social power, necessarily limited their impact, and they were further hampered by the restraints of censorship. For instance, the Odessa Russian-Jewish newspaper *Den'* closed down rather than cover the Odessa pogrom of 1871 with the lie of official silence.

Levanda, a fervent proponent of the *Haskalah* in Russia, was acutely aware of the feelings of the assimilated Jew who was to all appearances not Jewish but who felt Jewish at heart and had to witness hatred of his people. Among the sketches of Jewish life in *Ocherki proshlogo* ('Sketches of the Past', 1875) attacking blind faith, arranged marriages and adherence to ancient customs, there is one of a thinly disguised Czech Jew pretending to be a Catholic in order to make a living, which I quote as a demonstration of the complex discourse of the Self inwardly torn but outwardly on the defensive against hostility towards a cultural, ethnic and religious difference which he claims does not exist. For all the self-hatred and the egoism which has replaced communal allegiance, Levanda pleads his defense of cosmopolitanism:

As a citizen of the world, nothing civic, i.e. rational, in any nationality can be alien, hostile or inimical to me; I may in some way indeed be he for whom I am taken, and the mistake concerning me is only in the outer semblance, but not what [the non-Jew] presumed was beneath that outer semblance. If you ask about patriotism, I will answer that cosmopolitanism does not at all exclude patriotism.[8]

The tendentious Russian-Jewish polemicist claimed a supranational identity of humane Western values, but in fact this was axiomatically subsumed in Russianness, which was itself in the throes of a controversy raging between the Slavophiles and the Westernizers. Moreover, to endorse the European Enlightenment agenda of Reason was implicitly to agree that while Christianity could be a religion of reason, Judaism could not. In any case, the Jew was aware that to stand a chance of acceptance he had to become virtually transparent among Russians. There must be no trace of an 'accent' in his language, and no reference to the culture of the Other except in 'objective' criticism, a statement of what he claims not to be.

The polemical adoption of hostile stereotypes by Levanda and other Russian-Jewish authors thus lands them in the double bind of self-hatred defined by Sander Gilman in his study of self-hatred among German-Jewish authors:

On the one hand is the liberal fantasy that anyone is welcome to share in the power of the reference group *if* he abides by the rules that define that group. But these rules are the very definition of the Other. The Other comprises precisely those who are not permitted to share power within the society. Thus outsiders hear an answer from their fantasy: Become like us – abandon your difference – and you may be one with us. On the other hand is the hidden qualification of the internalized reference group, the conservative curse: The more you are like me, the more I know the true value of my power, which you wish to share, and the more I am aware that you are but a shoddy counterfeit, an outsider.[9]

In Russia the situation was more complicated than the German model analysed by Gilman, because Russia had since Peter the Great been drawn to the West but lacked Western-style institutions and concepts of change, while the Slavophiles rejected the Western model and proclaimed the moral superiority of Orthodox Russia over capitalism and liberal democracy. The late historian of Russian Jewry Shmuel Ettinger nevertheless commented in terms that would fit Gilman's analysis: the fact that 'an enlightened Jew who wished to make a way for himself in Russian society had to stress his aversion to Judaism, either by religious conversion or by taking part in the criticism of Judaism' invariably alienated the secular Jewish reformer *(maskil)* from the bulk of the traditional Jewish public.[10] Worse, as Paul Mendes-Flohr has shown in a different perspective on assimilation, the self-image of the self-hating Jew acquired a life of its own, like someone locked up in a Hall of Mirrors who would end up believing in the 'phantasmagoric images refracted by the mirrors as true'.[11]

Russian cultural identity was still maturing at the time of Pushkin and had been formed through the late development of a literary language. Russian literature was conscious of its mission as the major vehicle of social criticism in an autocratic state and the bearer of the Russian idea. The Russified Jew therefore had to make considerable efforts to disassociate himself from the Ostjude or 'bad' uncultured Jew who had little or only 'bad' Russian and whose way of life in the *shtetl*, the traditional religious small-town or village community in Russia and Poland, was diametrically opposed to the concept of literature, particularly one in which the Jew was usually portrayed as a hostile alien.[12] Writing, insists Gilman, is crucial to the identity formation of the Jew, and it was the acquisition of culture that allowed the Jew to erase his difference, except that paradoxically in so doing he pointed it out. The comic language of the *shtetl* Jew was mocked by the first generation of Russian-Jewish writers, who would supply extensive footnotes to explain the barbarous practices of the Jews for the enlightened Russian reader. However, by the end of the century the process of Russification had advanced so far that Jewish words and customs would have to be explained to Jewish readers. Semyon An-sky (pen-name of Solomon Zanvil Rappoport) could ironically distance himself in his novel *Pionery* ('The Pioneers', 1905) from the earlier attempts of *maskilim* to acculturate, while he saw the pressing need to reclaim a lost culture by documenting it in his sketches and his reworking of lore and legend.

BE A MAN!

To be a Jew at home and a man on the street was the catchword of the followers of Moses Mendelssohn adopted by the Hebrew poet Yehuda Leib Gordon who appealed in a poem of 1863-64 'Hakitsa, 'ami' ('Awake, My People, How Long Will You Sleep?'):

To the treasury of the state bring your wealth
Bear your shares of its riches and bounty
Be a man in the streets and a Jew at home
A brother to your countryman and a servant to your king.

Moses Leib Lilienblum led a prevailing misinterpretation of this dictum as demanding the repression of Jewish identity in public. What Gordon believed in was Russification as an entry ticket to European culture, while introducing to it the treasury of the Hebrew heritage. Gordon was in fact making a distinction between the sacred and the profane in his reading of the verse in the penultimate chapter of Deuteronomy, where Moses gives his valedictory blessing, 'Rejoice O Zebulun in thy going out, and Issachar in thy tents.' However, 'In the pathological course leading from *Haskalah* to assimilation to self-hatred, Gordon's dictum early on epitomized the psychic damage inflicted on the modern Jew by the specious distinction between man and Jew.'[13]

Autocratic Orthodox-Christian Russia was of course not Prussia, and the policies of the Tsars during the nineteenth century wavered between apparent liberalization and harsh measures such as enforced conscription of Jewish children (abolished in 1856) or decrees directed against Jewish religious practices. The change came in the 1860s with the reforms of serfdom and some civil disabilities. The efforts to eliminate Jewish difference by secularization and removal of the Jews from their traditions were initially welcomed by some *maskilim*, but the absence of any real progress towards emancipation disappointed the hopes of many who had broken with traditional Jewish life. Education and qualifications were of no use without opportunities, and the new government schools had taken Jews away from the *kheder* (the elementary Jewish religious school) and the *yeshiva* (the rabbinical seminary), so that the result was often a cultural limbo.

Faced with economic strangulation thousands voted with their feet after the pogroms which followed the assassination of Tsar Alexander II and the 1882 May Laws. The Western border was open, declared Count Nikolai Ignatiev, the Minister of the Interior. So was the American melting-pot. Yet not everyone agreed that in the absence of full emancipation the only answer was emigration, and the hope persisted among those who had already committed themselves to Russianness that the Russian people were not at heart anti-Semitic and that emancipation would come in time. The Russian-Jewish press reflected the crisis: *Russkii evrei* called on the Jews to wait patiently for recognition of their civic rights, while *Voskhod* opposed a policy of emigration. Only *Rassvet* advocated mass emigration, though initially clinging to the idea of Russia as the fatherland of Russian Jewry. Out of the despair were born the seeds of political and cultural nationalism. The year 1882 saw the publication in Berlin of Leo Pinsker's *Autoemancipation*, in which Pinsker, a former advocate of assimilation, switches to the argument that Jews must normalize their national status and establish a territorial homeland, for the non-territorial anomaly of the Jews is what has brought about anti-Semitism. Zionism made inroads into the despair of Russian Jewry and attracted such ardent supporters of the *Haskalah* as Moses Lilienblum and Lev Levanda. Levanda actually attacked the assimilationists after the Balta pogrom and wrote that he saw no hope of a solution to the Jewish problem in Russia. The pogroms of 1881 were a watershed in Jewish politics, as Jonathan Frankel has shown,[14] and after the pogroms even apostates were moved to revisit the synagogue. However, the numbers seeking conversion did not diminish, whether out of faith in Jesus and self-hatred (like the notorious Brafman), for reasons of career and entry into a profession, out of desperate poverty and sheer opportunism, or simply because, as Daniel Chwolson quipped, 'it is better to be a professor in St Petersburg than a *melamed* in Eyshishok'.[15]

The various revolutionary movements offered another desperate hope, though some Russian populists condoned the pogroms as expressing the legitimate wrath of the Russian peasants. To change the world and in so doing to free the Jews from mental as well as economic bondage appealed nevertheless to young radicals as a heady and daring formula. Between Tsardom and freedom the choice was clear. Years before, in 1864, the convert Vladimir Vasilevich Fedorov (born Tsvi Hirsh Grünberg), who was a government advisor in Kiev, had warned that uprooting Jewish youth from their traditions and exposing them to Reason would not make them patriotic citizens but would convert them to nihilism.[16]

The founding of the Bund in 1897 provided a specifically Jewish framework for socialist aspirations towards the unity of all workers, while the Zionist workers' party Po'alei Tsion sought to implement socialist ideals in the ancient Jewish homeland, then under Ottoman rule, where Yiddish would be one of the national languages alongside Hebrew. In fact, the Russian component in the agricultural resettlement was to leave an unmistakable imprint on the new Hebrew culture, but only a small number of the Jews fleeing Russia after 1881 braved the swamps, malaria and bureaucratic Turkish autocracy.

THE LANGUAGE WAR

The language issue in the debate over Jewish national identity is typified by the Czernowitz conference of 1908. The conference was the brainchild of Nathan Birnbaum, who was determined to rescue Yiddish from ignoble shame and restore it to the status of a language of culture, notwithstanding accusations that he did not himself have full mastery of the language. Czernowitz was in Bukovina, part of the multinational Austro-Hungarian empire where Jews were not the only cultural minority, and it was sufficiently close to the Russian Empire, where the vast majority of Jewry lived, but where government restrictions made the convening of such a conference difficult to say the least.[17] Delegates did not represent either scholarly institutions or communal bodies, but they did reflect the widest spectrum of ideological and conceptual views, from the Bundist to the Zionist, so that there was little possibility of the conference resulting in a solid consensus or engendering some organizational movement. The conference nevertheless gave voice to the sharpening conflict in the Jewish world on the status of language in ethnic and national identity on the eve of a rebirth of Jewish consciousness and against the background of rampant assimilation. Yiddish offered a secular and modernist alternative to the religious tradition without risk of losing national identity. The conference declared Yiddish to be 'a national language of the Jewish people' rather than '*the* national language', the formulation proposed by the Bundist leader from Vilna, Esther Frumkin. For the Bundists

Yiddish was a means to reach out and educate the Jewish masses, whereas the renowned Yiddish writer Y. L. Peretz distinguished between national and folk culture, calling for the young generation of writers to reacquaint themselves with the Bible so they would not lose touch with their national heritage.

The war of languages hotted up when Akhad Ha'am, in his famous essay on the language controversy, urged the adoption of Hebrew as the language of national revival and the only language in which the national culture could be transmitted to the next generation. Here he joined battle with the Hebrew novelist and thinker M. Y. Berdichevsky, who had far more radical ideas.

The Yiddishists derided the Zionist position, since Hebrew was not a living language and mass resettlement of the Land of Israel seemed such a utopian pipe-dream. As for the Orthodox religious community, Yiddish had for centuries been the language of the studyhouse *(bet midrash)* and of the market-place, the language of the women's Bible translations, while Hebrew was held sacred for prayer and religious books.[18] They rightly feared the influence of the new secular forces.

Meanwhile, in Russia dissenting voices were heard in the wake of the reaction after the 1905 Revolution. The Russian poet and critic Kornei Chukovsky declared that Jews writing in Russian would never succeed in creating anything of lasting value because they ignored the principle that a national spirit could not be expressed in another language.[19] Chukovsky's mentor and fellow-Odessite, Vladimir Jabotinsky – who had already established himself as a Russian-language journalist and was to become a popular fiction writer in several languages – thought of Russian as no more than a stepping-stone to the revived language of a Hebrew nation; but, as the Revisionist leader whom other Zionists loved to hate, he was later to look back more critically on his own dual cultural identity in his autobiography and in the novels *Samson Nazorei* (translated into English as *Prelude to Delilah*) and *Piatero* ('The Five', 1932), a story of the decay of an assimilated Jewish Odessa family against the background of the 1905 Revolution.[20] Stepping into the furore around Chukovsky's remarks, Jabotinsky asserted in a 1908 essay on Jews in Russian literature that the ethnic content of any text depended on its implied reader and varied according to the author's spiritual and cultural concerns. In his eyes, the Jewish writer could not be blamed for seeking entry into the wider vistas of Russian literature, for preferring Rome to the provinces, but it was desertion all the same at a time when the 'Jewish street' lacked leadership.[21]

When An-sky spoke the same year of the Czernowitz conference, in a lecture to the Jewish Literary Society in St Petersburg, he advocated the cultural parity of Russian, Yiddish and Hebrew on the grounds that a sizeable portion of the Jewish intelligentsia now spoke Russian. According to the 1897 census only 3% of Jews in the Russian Empire did not have Yiddish, but a third of male Jews had a command of Russian and 9% were already declaring Russian as their native tongue. An-sky is himself a good example of the complex inter-relationship of cultures and languages: like many *maskilim*, he turned away from Judaism after reading Lilienblum's Hebrew memoir, *Khatot ne'urim* ('Sins of Youth', 1876) and worked under cover to undermine the faith of traditional observant youth in provincial communities in Lithuania and Russia. Then, under the tutelage of Gleb Uspensky, he 'went into the people' among the peasants and coal miners of South Russia, who gave him the name Semyon Akimovich. From 1902 An-sky played an important role in the Social-Revolutionary Party under the cover name of Z. Sinnani, according to one account a Russian reference to his mother ('syn Anny'), under which name he published the revolutionary tract *Kampf un kempfer* ('Struggle and Strugglers', London, n.d.). In Paris he acted as Lavrov's personal secretary. An-sky had sought the source of poetry in Russian literature, and it was Russian which served him for his return to his people, a return mapped out in his Russian sketches and stories which David G. Roskies believes to be paradigmatic of the life-story of the Jewish intellectual of the time.[22] Publication of one of his stories was translated back into Yiddish for Y. L. Peretz's *Di yomtev bletter* ('The Festival Pages', 1895–6), and after 1905 he turned more and more to the Jews and to Yiddish under the impact of pogroms and Bloody Sunday. Having moved from the Rusian populism of the *narodniki* to the Social-Revolutionaries, An-sky now reapplied his political beliefs to the popular culture and oral lore of the *shtetl*. In 1912–14 he headed an ethnographic expedition to salvage the artistic heritage of East European Jewry, an expedition which, as will be seen in the next chapter, was to be important for the rediscovery of the folk culture that would be adopted by Yiddish modernism and the Jewish avant-garde. During the First World War, An-sky was frantically involved in rescuing Jewish artifacts as part of emergency relief work among the Jewish communities, whose destruction he recorded in a monumental documentation of what he entitled the 'Destruction of Galician Jewry' (Warsaw, 1921).[23] His play *The Dybbuk*, a masterpiece of Jewish folk-lore reworked into a modern secular drama, was first written in Russian and translated into Hebrew from Yiddish by Bialik, then translated back from Hebrew into Yiddish after An-sky lost the Yiddish version. Leonid Pasternak did an oil painting of An-sky reading from his play at the home of Stiebel, the editor of the Hebrew journal, *Hatekufah*, in which Bialik's translation appeared in Moscow in 1918; but, despite their friendship, the artist was touched no more than briefly by An-sky's ideas on Jewish culture, as will be seen in Chapter 5. It was the Russian theatre director Stanislavsky who suggested introducing the figure of the Messenger prior to the Moscow Art theatre première, which was cancelled because of Stanislavsky's illness and the revolutionary upheavals. Evgenii Vakhtangov produced the play at Habimah, the Hebrew theatre in Moscow, to an audience which mostly did not understand Hebrew. Originally entitled *The Dybbuk: Between Two Worlds*, the play epitomized An-sky's own dual position, as well as the synthesis of bygone traditions and secular modernity which he advocated at the end of his life. That paradoxical synthesis was reflected in the music by Iu. D. Engel and the combination of expressionist staging (in Natan Altman's design) with Hasidic melodies. Indeed, the play became the centre of a debate over the identity of Jewish culture both in East Europe and in the Land of Israel. However, An-sky did not see the fulfilment of his ideals; he had to flee revolutionary Russia, disguised as a priest, and died, a broken man, in Poland.

The choice of Hebrew, Yiddish and/or Russian could be complex, as in the different Hebrew and Yiddish voices of Mendele Moikher-Sforim, who expressed his bitter affection for the Jewish masses in his fiction. In transforming five of his novels from Yiddish into Hebrew, Mendele played with the language of the Bible and prayer to point out Divine injustice in treatment of the Jewish poor. Such sophisticated intertextuality has been studied by Menakhem Perry and David G. Roskies, who have demonstrated its role in the development of Hebrew modernism, while David Aberbach has shown that the duality of Mendele's language could be a tool to undermine all authority.[24] A different example is the Yiddish poet Semyon Frug, who wrote Russian verse full of pride in his national identity:

> I am the Aeolean harp of my people's fate,
> I am the echo of my people's suffering.

In fact Jewish culture or Jewish themes were not necessarily incompatible with the medium of Russian. This was the case well before Russian became the exclusive first language of the majority of Soviet Jews after the October Revolution. The viability of Jewish culture in the Diaspora was indeed a fundamental belief of Simon Dubnov, the Jewish historian who perished in the Holocaust,[25] a faith which lives on today among Russified Jews in Russia and among supporters of local nationalism in the Ukraine or the Baltic states. Yet the post-Revolutionary generation, cut off from the Jewish heritage and ignorant of the achievements of modern Hebrew, felt the need to justify their self-identity with Russian culture, as if only Russian culture was a world culture and a culture of humane values.

The Bolshevik coup d'état swept away the old Russian intelligentsia, to which Russian-Jewish authors had sought admission. The Jewish readership, too, had changed: the former Pale of Settlement had been dissolved, the traditional communal network was abolished and the survivors of war and pogroms within the new borders of Soviet Russia (excluding the independent Baltic states and Poland) underwent rapid urbanization, secularization and Russification. The new Jewish proletariat and the intellectuals of Jewish descent had very little in common with the Russian-Jewish *littérateurs*. Most of the latter died or went into emigration within a few years after the Revolution. Mikhail Gershenzon is a case in point. A respected critic of Russian literature, Gershenzon felt that he had been stripped bare by the Revolution which he saw as a new beginning. In a polemical correspondence literally between two corners, in a Soviet hostel for writers in the summer of 1920, he found it difficult to agree with the Symbolist poet Viacheslav Ivanov who saw clearly the vacuum in his spiritual and cultural identity.[26]   In a brief report on Jews in Soviet Russian literature Valentin Parnakh, an enigmatic figure whom we will meet again in Chapter 4, declared Gershenzon, who had died the previous year (1925), to be representative of the Russified Jew, a Jew in love with Russian poetry and gentile beauty.[27]

As Mark Slonim wrote in a 1944 survey of Soviet Jewish writers in Russian, the changeover of generations had pushed the old gods offstage.[28] The old social and geographical distribution of readers of Russian-Jewish literature no longer existed, nor did the aim of amelioration of the Jewish position. A writer's allegiance to Soviet literature was expected to derive from class consciousness, not ethnic identity. The relatively large number of Jews who were well-known in Russian literature in the Soviet period came from an entirely different social and cultural background. Some, for example Ehrenburg, Mandelstam, Boris Pasternak and Babel, had made their first debut in Russian literature before the First World War. They were remote from traditional life and only Babel stands out as being intensely concerned with Jewish themes. Isaak Babel's stories of pre-Revolutionary Odessa do have their pre-Revolutionary antecedents in Gorkyan sketches by Karmen (Korenman) and stories by Semyon Yushkevich, but we will see in Chapter 3 how different is Babel's prose style. The majority of Jews who wrote in Russian were 'point five' Jews, Jews only by definition of their Soviet passports. They had, in their own eyes, broken out into the 'expanse' of Russianness, and if they are moved by memories of childhood to refer in any way to Jewishness, then it is significantly by differentiation of language, by referring to Yiddish as the language of the Other, and by distancing in time and space.

BREAKDOWN AND BREAKOUT

The Yiddish modernists who were active from around 1908-11 were writing at the time Marinetti was proclaiming his manifesto in Italy and the Russian futurists were slapping the face of public taste and dethroning the idol of Pushkin. The Yiddish modernists in New York, Vilna and Kiev took note of the modernist experimentation with language and used Yiddish to express their own transition to the urban world of modern technology and cosmopolitan values. The inversion or negation of traditional values and literary conventions was a linguistic rebellion against their forefathers as well as an attempt to parallel developments in the gentile world of art and literature. This was arguably Yiddish modernism but also modernism in Yiddish.

Nor did Khaim Nakhman Bialik and Shaul Chernikhovsky present a familiar Jewish world. These were new voices in the Hebrew poetry of Russian Jewry who heralded a renaissance of modern Jewish literature at the beginning of the twentieth century. Jewishness suddenly bore an independent pride and could feel at home in both the natural and pagan universe, could respond other than passively to the unending misery and despair brought by pogroms and economic attrition. The destruction of *shtetl* life in the centre of the combat zone in the First World War and later in the pogroms and Civil War that followed the Russian Revolution resulted in a final breakdown in the relationship between the self and the past. M. Z. Feuerberg's question, in the title of his novella *Lean?* (*Whither?*, 1899) suggested that escape from the constricting enclosure of the *shtetl* had not necessarily led anywhere, except to a madman's call for Zionist colonization; nevertheless the spiritual and artistic crisis did lead to a search for a new language in which to express that disorienting alienation, as well as to mark the break with the old mournful voice by the waters of Babylon, the 'lachrymose view of Jewish history' (in the phrase of S. W. Baron) which could see no hope for the future beyond a Wailing Wall. Significantly, the new poetry of Bialik was translated into Russian for the Jewish intelligentsia that had no Hebrew and was much appreciated by such prominent Russian writers and critics as Maksim Gorky and Mikhail Gershenzon. Gershenzon saw in the poetry of Bialik and Chernikhovsky a claim to a new spirit of freedom, distinct, however, from the Nietzschean freedom vindicated by the Hebrew novelist M. Y. Berdichevsky.

Chernikhovsky's 'return' to the pagan gods of light and life did not just express the Odessa poet's preference for Hellenism but was an attempt to detach himself from the traditional pattern of *shtetl* life, associated with the collective memory of pogroms, and to think in terms of a non-monotheistic Hebrew culture, later formulated by Yonatan Ratush and others in the 1930s as part of a new Canaanism. In Chernikhovsky's 'Lenokakh pesel apolo' ('In Front of the Statue of Apollo', 1899) the poet takes off the straps of the phylacteries, which in obedience to the Biblical commandment the Jew binds on his arm and for a sign between his eyes, a sign of the covenant which binds him to God; the poet binds with them the statue of the pagan god, thus unbinding himself from the imprisoning confines of the Jewish faith of the *shtetl* and transferring the enslaving bonds to the Hellenist god of light ('veasuruhu beretsu'ot shel tefilin'). This breaking out of the binding confines and binding precepts of Judaism is a daring revolt against the Divine Covenant, since Hellenism had long been considered the archetypal adversary of Jewish mono-theism.[29]

Bialik too had abandoned the Holy Ark of the Jewish Law for literature. Writing out of deep feelings of personal as well as national bereavement, he described the narrow confines of the studyhouse as a decaying, lifeless past, a twilight world with no future. In 'Lifnei aron hasfarim' ('In Front of the Book Cup-board', 1900) the poet returns to his lost childhood in the rotting, faded pages of Diaspora Judaism in the delapidated old study-house (just like the narrator of Isaak Babel's 'Gedali') and wonders whether he has not lost a language. The poet returns from *outside* to find his past self dead and alien. Similarly it is the dead world of the walled-in study-house that the poet observes from his position as an ambivalent outsider in the narrative poem 'Hamatmid' ('The Talmud Student', 1884–5). In mourning the wasting away of the student's soul in the studyhouse, the poet is lamenting his own loss, loss of youth and love, and expressing the urge to escape. The bitter-sweet tune of the Talmud is the language of his former self which he rejects. In that poem there is no hope invested in what Bialik calls the 'burning embers' of traditional Jewry, and the Hebrew-Aramaic language of the

Talmud is introduced as a refrain differentiating and distancing it from the poet's modern Hebrew discourse, a discourse which inverts or negates the meaning of the texts to which he alludes and questions their viability in the crisis of national survival and their centrality to the experience of modernity.

The opposition of outside and inside inverts the binarism of raw:cooked which Lévi-Strauss observed in primitive cultures. From an anthropological viewpoint, the inside is rejected as 'non-culture' and contrasts with the open space outside the window, even though the narrator is painfully aware that the closed space of the interior world houses the fragile memory and lost language of his childhood. Yet neither Bialik nor Chernikhovsky forgot their deep love for the Jewish people, to which they were tied by the choice of Hebrew and a poet's consciousness of national destiny, as in Bialik's poems on the Kishinev pogroms and Chernikhovsky's later elegy for the community of Worms ('The First Dead').[30]

If the outside had hitherto shone with the light of the secular enlightenment centred in Berlin and Odessa, the external space of Russia now menaced the Jew with barbarity and violence. One can see this in Solomon Yudovin's static domestic scene (reproduced as the Frontispiece) of the old Jews who watch through the framing device of the window as a revolutionary crowd surges forward. This example of the semiotic opposition of inside:outside contains much ambivalence and irony: the Jewish figures are foregrounded, not the revolutionary marchers, and the post-revolutionary date of composition immortalizes an ancient wisdom that has survived utopian dreams and untold disasters. The Russian semiotician Yurii Lotman has pointed out that it is a universal principle of every culture that the world is divided into internal and external space, although the interpretation of the boundary is subject to the typology of each culture.

One of the primary mechanisms of semiotic individuation is the boundary, and the boundary can be defined as the outer limit of a first-person form. This space is 'ours', 'my own', it is 'cultured', 'safe', 'harmoniously organized', and so on. By contrast 'their space' is 'other', 'hostile', 'dangerous', 'chaotic'.[31]

The spatial modelling of universality is commonly associated with boundlessness, though often the markers of spatiality may be non-spatial referents, such as *familiar* and *understood* corresponding to *near*, or *incomprehensible*, *alien* corresponding to *distant*. The oppositions *heaven:earth* or *left:right* have theological and cultural meaning. In Lotman's analysis of up:down oppositions in the poetry of Tiutchev and Zabolotsky, spatial modelling is not mimetic of another system and its non-fulfilments are as meaningful as its fulfilments of systemic functions.[32] The spatial model generated in the structure of the text realizes more general spatial oppositions, but at the same time conflicts with them and de-automatizes the language in which they are perceived. Here Lotman looks back to the Russian formalist Viktor Shklovsky's concept of the literariness of the literary text and makes estrangement (*ostranenie*) relevant to the perception of spatial models in narrative discourse. The portrayal of multiplane space is achieved by the specific language of the text, much as composition controls perception in the visual arts. In this way the space of the text is structured in an evaluative hierarchy by means of two- or three-member sets of oppositions that operate not merely on the basis of an equation of vertical polarity (up:down) with sociological, moral or ideological judgement (good:bad), but also by an approximation of distance (near:far) to familiarity and belonging (home:away). Elsewhere I have applied this semiotic model to the modern literary text, applying the principle in Propp's analysis of the magic folk-tale that boundaries are functional in plot development and character development;[33] now I would like to depart from accepted readings of some canonic texts in Jewish literature to demonstrate the binary oppositions of spatial organization in a paradigm of the alienation of the Jewish intellectual who, as in the examples from Bialik and Chernikhovsky, breaks out from the confining Jewish world.

In his lament on the primal Jewish national crisis, the Destruction of the Temple, which has been archetypal for poets and believers through the ages, Jeremiah links the idea of the downfall of Israel and the descent into exile with the metaphors of spatial descent and constriction. In the first chapter of Lamentations, Jeremiah describes the dire straits (*ben hamitsarim*) in which the people of Israel find themselves, a phrase that came into common use for the Three Weeks of Mourning between 17 Tammuz, when the first breach in the walls of Jerusalem was made, and the final disaster on 9 Av when the Temple was destroyed. However, the phrase can also be read homiletically to refer not just to spatial and temporal constraint, but also to the spiritual and psychological constraint of exile, familiar from the foreign bondage in Egypt (*mitsraim*, a strikingly similar form in Hebrew to *mitsarim*, 'straits'). Either way the metaphor of containment invokes spiritual descent and social decay which result in linguistic and cultural alienation. In the admonishment spoken by Moses in Deuteronomy (Chapter 28) exile was to be a punishment of dwelling among a foreign people and adopting a strange language and strange gods.

The condition of exile is to be seen in terms of a non-normal and destabilized state of national fragmentation. Indeed, the root of the Hebrew word for crisis, *shvr*, is etymologically connected with breakage: Israel underwent panic and pitfall, ravage and ruin; the prophet's eyes shed unceasing streams of tears for the ruin of his people (*Pakhad vefakhat haya lanu haset vehashaver. Palgey mayim/tered 'eyni 'al shever bat-'ami*, Lamentations 3, 47–8). The violation of sacred boundaries in the breaching of Jerusalem's city walls and the destruction of the Temple remained a deep trauma in Judaism. In Cabbalistic terms, the Divine Presence had gone into exile with His people and redemption from exile in space and time required gathering the dispersed divine sparks of holiness. Immediately after the Destruction of the Second Temple, however, the boundaries of the sacred had been reinstated spiritually, their continuation ensured at Yavneh where the Sanhedrin was reinstated, and henceforth every Jewish home and studyhouse was to symbolize a microcosmic sanctuary. The rabbinical teaching, 'make a fence for the Torah' (Ethics of the Fathers 1, 1) to safeguard it, reminded the faithful of the metaphysical boundaries of the commandments. The Giving of the Commandments at Sinai was itself commonly represented as taking place in a fenced-off space (Figure 1) to illustrate the prohibition of trespassing on the holy site. The modernists' revolt against the constraints of exile was consistent

Figure 1.   'Giving of the Law'. Woodcut from *Sefer haminhagim* (Amsterdam, 1723). Jewish National and University Library, Jerusalem.

with this semiotic model and it was represented as breaking out, with the Nietzschean overtones of a criminal act.[34] 'One who breaks through the fence' *(porets gader)* is the common term of condemnation for a Jew who breaks away from Torah law by not keeping the traditions or infringing rabbinical decrees, and at first sight it seems that this breaking of the boundaries of Judaism fits the semiotic model outlined above. Yet the encounter with the open gentile world outside the boundaries did not necessarily mean a complete abandonment of peoplehood. One feels, for example, an extraordinary awareness of the rival boundaries of Jewish and gentile territories in Bialik's *Meakhorei hagader* ('Behind the Fence', written 1908-9), except that after the Jews push out the gentile residents to the rural *expanse* out of town and take over a suburb it is the enclosure of old Shkurifinshchikha's yard which is the fenced-in enclave under siege. The boundary is still closed and it remains as a reminder of the hostile and belligerent relations of Jew and gentile. The attraction of the Polish girl Marinka whom Noah befriends through the chinks in the fence cannot cancel out the dangers and contradictions of being a Jew in a non-Jewish world, a forbidden, unedenic garden of ritual impurity, with Freudian implications.[35] The story ends with Noah marrying a nice Jewish girl according to all the traditional rites, while Marinka looks on from behind the fence holding her baby.

The term 'behind the fence' designates the unconsecrated burial ground reserved for outcasts and apostates, so that there is no way to return to hearth and home once one has stepped outside the enclosures of Jewish space. Hence the tragic irony of the title of Bialik's poem 'Bitshuvati' ('On My Return', 1891–2), playing as it does on the sense of repentance in return and its impossibility in the stinking stasis of the old world. Another poem, 'Levadi' ('Alone', 1902), declares in its non-closure the tormented indecisiveness whether or not to remain in the studyhouse – a place both of desolation and refuge – after everyone has been swept away by the 'wind' of the Jewish secular enlightenment and drawn to the 'light' of the secular, Western world. Breaking out of the enclosed Jewish world meant escaping the narrow streets of the *shtetl*, but it also provided a far-reaching metaphor for the dilemma of that generation as they moved into modernity and into literature.

AFTER THE REVOLUTION: REFERENCE AND REJECTION

The metaphor of breakout found its most poignant expression after the fragmentation of traditional Jewish life, when the bonds to Jewishness were held by no more than childhood memory. The February Revolution released the Jews from centuries of Tsarist repression, discrimination and persecution, and it released them more immediately from the wartime prohibition on the Hebrew and Yiddish press, imposed by a xenophobic and paranoiac administration out of fear of espionage. However, the Bolshevik coup in November 1917 (the October Revolution in the old calendar) put an end to the sudden proliferation of Jewish publications[36] and made clear the choice facing Jewish artists between unquestioning communism and the old world of rabbis and *shtetl* shop-keepers, now class enemies together with the Church and the bourgeoisie. The Revolution turned upside down the values and traditions of the Jewish community:

> The combined forces of emancipation, on the one hand, and the state persecution of Judaism, on the other, generated a pace of secularization, acculturation, and alienation from the Jewish tradition unparalleled in modern Jewish history. In western and central Europe, the emancipation of the Jews had involved an implicit bargain ... that the Jews would shed most or nearly all of their cultural particularism in exchange for their newly granted status. But in the Soviet Union, the emancipation bargain was articulated explicitly by the state, and its terms were extreme and rigid. The new Soviet man of Jewish origins was a full member of society, and could advance to the upper echelons of all its institutions; Judaism, on the other hand, ... would not be tolerated.[37]

A contemporary witness succinctly described the rapid and dramatic transition of a Belorussian *shtetl* to the new order when he wrote in approving terms of the generational divide between old and young, fathers and sons, and observed that the atheist youths were tolerated and became objects of pride, even when they requisitioned their own fathers' working tools.[38]

November 1917 also saw the Balfour Declaration, which excited hopes for a Zionist future,[39] but the communist regime ruthlessly repressed Zionist organizations and declared Hebrew *lingua non grata*. Incredibly, Hebrew literature continued to be written in the Soviet Union against all odds and produced its own 'nightingale without a nest' in the person of Khaim Lensky, who was not deterred by the worst conditions of a labour camp.

> Language of Ancients, of Hayman, Halevi,
> Some miracle made you mine, gentle-voiced Queen.
> Your cadences kindled my soul, and your words
> Burnt my lips like the kisses of passionate lovers.
> From the shores of Euphrates and Jordan, you summoned
>   your legions

... From the Don and the Neva and the Nieman, my river
I brought over your cohorts – and I their commander.
So bring home my name across the waters of Lethe
Like the names of the ancients, like Hayman, Halevi.[40]

One of the last Soviet publications in Hebrew, bearing the symbolic title *Bereshit* ('Genesis'), was published in 1926 with a cover design by the avant-garde Jewish artist Yosif Tchaikov (Figure 2 a–b). Significantly, it included translations of stories from Isaak Babel's *Konarmiia* (*Red Cavalry*, 1926) which focus on the dilemma of the intellectual torn between commitment to Communism and a violent revolution, between acceptance by the heroic Cossacks and a nostalgia for the dying Jewish past with its Judaic command not to kill. Most of the contributors to *Bereshit*, however, voiced the naive belief in the feasibility of the ideal of Babel's fallen hero, Ilia Bratslavsky, of fusing Hebrew and Communism. They claimed ideological conformism by mimicking the style of Blok and Maiakovsky, while claiming theirs was a new Genesis, completely cut off from their Jewish past and from the Hebrew national poetry of Bialik. The futile attempt to write verse about the modern city or the class struggle in a language of a small cultural elite resonant with the Biblical and ethnic references of the past proved to be a short and tragic adventure for many of the Hebrew communists.[41]

To embrace Communism meant equal opportunities in the urban centres of a revolutionary society, an immediate panacea to the stigma of centuries of persecution and inferiority. Moreover, the incompatibility with any remaining allegiance to Judaism did not seem apparent to many even after the dismantling of Jewish communal organizations soon after the Revolution and the repression of political opposition (including the Social-Revolutionaries and the Bundists). The promise of a Soviet Yiddish culture, 'national in form, socialist in content', seemed sufficiently attractive in the 1920s to persuade a number of Yiddish writers to settle in the Soviet Union or return from emigration. Yet the delusion soon became apparent. Attacked by the *apparatchik* Moshe Litvakov for depicting only Jewish revolutionaries in his novel *Brider* ('Brothers', 1929), Perets Markish declared – to the consternation of the Party newspaper *Der Emes* –

Figure 2a

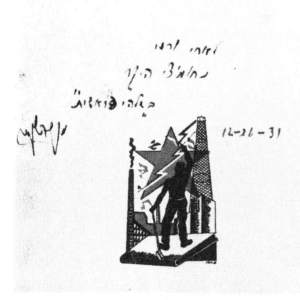

Figure 2b

Figure 2 a–b.   Yosif Tchaikov, Cover of *Bereshit* (Leningrad-Moscow, 1926)
and inscribed inside page with publisher's logo by B. Shubin. The inscription
reads 'To my friend and brother, dear Nakhumitsi, "on the verge of Genesis" ';
though headed volume 1, no further issues of this rare Soviet Hebrew publication appeared. Reproduced by kind permission of Mr Toby Holtzman.

that nobody would make such an absurd criticism of a Russian
revolutionary novel which described only Russian revolutionaries.
The farce of having to pretend that Yiddish was devoid of any
collective memory, and was free of attachment to a particular
people or immune to writers and influences abroad, encouraged a
hypersensitivity aggravated by guilt feelings and varying degrees of
regret for the destruction of the *shtetl* which had nurtured the
Yiddish language. A parable of the intolerable position of the
Soviet Yiddish writer is related in Der Nister's *Unter a ployt* ('Under
a Fence', 1929), a complex symbolist confession in the strange
manner of the fables told by the eighteenth-century Hasidic mystic
Nakhman of Bratslav. Here to be buried 'behind the fence' is to be
buried as a writer, dead to the Jewish community and dead to the

world, to have one's Yiddish words and therefore one's identity erased without monument.[42] The year 1929 was the year of the Kvitko affair, which, like the Zamiatin and Pilniak affairs in Russian literature, sounded dread warning to mystical symbolists like Der Nister, who wrote under the influence of the Serapion Brothers, and others who were scathingly abused as fellow-travellers. Some, like the poet Itsik Feffer or the artist Yosif Tchaikov, made the transition to Socialist Realism more easily, but some, like the artist Solomon Yudovin, converted on the surface to Socialist Realism while nursing their Jewish roots in their hearts.

If Jews had previously been unwanted guests in Russian culture, after the Revolution they rushed to fill the vacuum left by the old Russian intelligentsia. However, they soon learned to be hypersensitive to accusations of 'nationalism', especially if they had a Bundist or Menshevik past to conceal. Now they tried to achieve a new transparency to differentiate themselves from the old ('bad') Jew and to claim status as a new ('good') Jew who had cut himself off from his own past and had learned the lesson of pogrom experience, according to Party propaganda a phenomenon of the feudal Tsarist system, which taught that national difference was 'bad' and that anti-Semitism would disappear along with the capitalist bourgeoisie. Opting for Russian became a statement of ideological identity (since Yiddish and Hebrew reverberated with the continuity of Jewish national existence). Alternatively, Russian could be coded with the covert language of the Other for those Jewish readers who were bilingually proficient in 'double book-keeping' and who were painfully aware that the large representation of Jewish names in the Communist Party or in Soviet cultural institutions and the popular association of the Jew with the entrepreneur in the NEP (the temporary retreat to limited capitalism) meant no end to 'Jewish troubles'.

The distance travelled from the Jewish past by the Soviet Jew writing in Russian is exemplified by the 'Komsomol poet' Mikhail Svetlov's 'Stikhi o rebe' ('Verses About the Rebbe', 1923). The narrator guards the future and when he turns to the East, towards Jerusalem, the traditional direction of Jewish prayer, it is only to see if his Komsomol comrade is coming. The rebbe and the priest are alike doomed to die with the old world. They are both branded with the stereotyped accusation of financial speculation, that is to say, economic sabotage and anti-communist, disloyal behaviour. The sunset splashes the *shtetl* and its dark, empty synagogue with the red of the Red Flag and the faded Talmud is rejected after the Revolution. In 'Khleb' ('Bread', 1929) a new kinship is discovered between the pogrom-scarred Jew Samuel Liberzon and the Russian former *pogromshchik* Ignatius Mozhaev: the class solidarity of fathers who have lost sons fighting for the new regime. Svetlov at least remembered the Jewish past with some melancholy and pain and described the Jewish revolutionary martyr as a new Moses on a Soviet Sinai, a proud descendant of the Maccabees. By comparison, Yosif Utkin is much more satirical in his 'Povest' o ryzhem Motele, gospodine inspektore, ravvine Isaie i komissare Blokhe' ('Tale of Red-headed Motele, the Tax Inspector, Rabbi Isaiah and Commissar Bloch', 1924–25). By blending Yiddish in his Russian rhyme and metre, Utkin achieves a linguistic interference that reflects the cultural and ideological transformation of *shtetl* Jew into communist commissar. The former victim of the Kishinev pogrom can sew a shroud for the Tsar, a poetic vengeance which marks an end to the standard resignation to their fate of the powerless Jews. The Soviet critic A. Lezhnev commented that the stylization of Yiddish works only because it is in a *Russian* text. In the context of the Revolution, which has signalled the death of the milieu to which it refers, it casts doubt on the credibility of the depicted Jewish world.[43] The election of Yiddish to an equal, if jocular, partnership with Russian speaks for a new hopeful pride, as in Utkin's 'Miloe detstvo' ('Sweet childhood', 1926–33) when the boy rejects his aunt's wish to dedicate him to God and a trade, but tells his Russian comrade he is not a Yid, he is a Jew. However, the aspiration for a secular Yiddish identity, tainted as it was with the *shtetl* and the underworld, drowned in the Russification of the urbanized Jewish professional classes and had to be forgotten in the reign of fear and increasing chauvinism under Stalin.

Eduard Bagritsky, a poet from Odessa, went so far as to curse his Jewish parentage in 'Proiskhozhdenie' ('Origins', 1930) and made the typical break with Jewish rituals which had lost their meaning for the revolutionary Jewish youth. Again the only way to survive is to break out of the stifling Jewish basement (the constraint and descent of exile) and to deny the heritage of parents whose only idea of escaping poverty is to get rich. One of Isaak Babel's memories of Odessa childhood is called 'V podvale' ('In the Basement', 1931) and describes a similar attempt to escape the closed world of the Jewish basement (inside, down below). Significantly, the escape of Babel's boy narrator is initially attempted through fantasy, Shakespeare and, in a connected story, 'Probuzhdenie' ('Awakening', 1932), through a frustrated initiation into Russian literature and nature. The boy finally achieves an epiphany when he is enlightened at the end of another childhood story, 'Di Grasso', by the statue of Pushkin, a literary inspiration that also points to cultural choice, as we will see later in the cases of Samuil Marshak and Osip Mandelstam.

There is little that is specifically Jewish in Bagritsky's favourite themes of hunting and fishing, though the Civil War hero of his epic poem *Duma pro Opanasa* ('The Lay of Opanas', 1926) is a Jew called Yosif Kogan. His heroic death at the hands of Makhno's partizans is a martyrdom envied by the Red soldier at the end of the elegy, and it serves as an example of unswerving loyalty and dedication, with no trace of the irony and ambiguity of the death of the failed Jewish revolutionary Ilia Bratslavski which closes the first edition of Babel's *Red Cavalry*, published the same year, 1926. Kogan is one of several token Jews among the countless Civil War heroes in Soviet literature of the 1920s. This token Jewish presence is perceived as 'positive' because all traces of Jewishness have been washed out from it. If the recent pogrom experience is mentioned, as it is in Nikolai Ostrovsky's Civil War classic *Kak zakalialas' stal'* ('How the Steel Was Tempered', 1935), this is simply one more reason to fight the counter-revolutionary forces, rather than poetic justice that the Jew is fighting his former enemies. When it came to defining a collective memory for the next generation, Bagritsky referred in his 'Razgovor s synom' ('Conversation with My Son', 1931) to the archetypal image of feathers flying in a pogrom, but the hope which he bequeathed to the next generation was of an internationalist universe where such things did not happen. The dream of universal social justice remained far off, and meanwhile Bagritsky, a professing atheist caught up in the romanticism of the Revolution, remained nostalgic for his native shore. In 'Vozvrashchenie' ('Return', 1924), and, in a posthumously published long poem 'Fevral'' ('February', 1933–4), he marvelled at how a sickly Jewish boy like himself had become a poet with a love for nature and for women. He does not hide his circumcision, and does not jibe, like the Yiddish poet Itsik Feffer, 'so what if I'm circumcised?' More obliquely, Bagritsky's translation of 1927 from Itsik Feffer's long poem 'Dnieper' evokes the poet's native Ukrainian landscape and does not fail to record the children thrown into the river during the Civil War. Isaak Babel, Bagritsky's friend and fellow Odessite, eulogized him after his death from tuberculosis in 1934 as combining the spirit of the Komsomol and 'Ben Akiva'.[44]

The examples of Svetlov, Utkin and Bagritsky are illustrative of the 'hidden language', to use Gilman's phrase, of the Soviet Jewish Communist who had to prove his loyalty to international communism and the Soviet state by demonstrating negation of anything remotely 'nationalistic', that is to say Jewish. But to sever oneself from one's own memory of past and family did not solve the problem of identity. Jews who changed their names to 'neutral' Russian or demonstratively Russian revolutionary names still had to prove their hatred for their ethnic past more than their non-Jewish comrades (which did not help them when, during Stalin's 'anti-Cosmopolitan' campaign, many writers and critics were 'exposed' in the press by having their original names published in the attacks on them). The Evsektsiia, the Jewish section of the Soviet Communist Party, showed extra zeal in persecuting all forms of religion and was instrumental in repressing Jewish cultural institutions before being liquidated itself.[45] In recent years Jews have been singled out by anti-Semitic detractors who held them guilty for the damage done to Russian churches, as well as for the famine in the Ukraine caused by enforced collectivization, since so many Party leaders and activists were identified as Jews.

However, in the first decade after the Revolution it was easier for Jews to deal with anti-Semitic stereotypes in Russian litera-ture, since discrimination had been officially eliminated with the old order; but it was harder to deal with continuing traditional anti-Semitism among the masses. A short novel by an otherwise conformist writer Mikhail Kozakov, *Chelovek, padaiushchii nits* ('The Man Who Prostrated Himself', 1928), records the painful experience of anti-Semitism that persisted despite official Party policy and propaganda. In his well-known 'Istoriia moei golubiatni' ('Story of My Dovecote', 1925) Babel testifies through the estranged view of a boy seeking entry to the *gimnaziia* (Russian grammar school) how instrumental was the memory of anti-Semitism in the make-up of identity. The avoidance of cliché in this vivid description renders more effective the introduction at the end of the story of the word 'pogrom'. The hysteria and bookishness induced by the experience of growing up a Jew in Tsarist Russia make that experience still relevant after the Revolution, and the boy's story concludes with the words, later deleted for obvious ideological reasons, of the sequel to this story 'Pervaia liubov'' ('First Love', 1925), 'And now, remembering those sad years, I find in them the beginning of the ailments which torment me and the cause of my terrible premature fading.'[46]

During the harsh years of War Communism the Bolsheviks tolerated and actually fed a number of intellectuals who could in some way or other be useful to the regime or who benefited from Gorky's still powerful patronage. The climate of the early years of the Revolution encouraged a heated debate among a remarkably wide range of literary and artistic standpoints, even while the Cheka was arresting and executing 'counter-revolutionary' elements (the poet Nikolai Gumilev was shot in 1921, for example). One of several literary groupings was that of the self-styled Serapion Brothers, named for a character of E. T. A. Hoffmann. Their literary mentor was Evgeny Zamiatin, who practised 'neo-realism', a modernist prose adapted to the chaotic post-Revolutionary times. Their credo was emulation of the West and the priority of poetry over ideology. One of the Serapion Brothers was a young Russified Jew called Lev Lunts, whose life was tragically cut short in a Swiss sanatorium in 1924 at the age of twenty-three. In two short pieces which deal with Jewish themes, Lunts expressed his awareness of the situation of the Europeanized Jew writing in Russia in the form of parable. 'V pustyne' ('In the Desert', 1921) was included in the Serapions' first anthology in 1922. It retells the Biblical story (Numbers 25, 1-9) of Phineas ben El'azar the priest, who struck a blow for monotheism and the rule of Moses when he speared a copulating couple, piercing their genitals and pinning them to their bed. The threat to Israel's spiritual and national survival posed by the Midianite women and the idolatrous worship of Ba'al Pe'or is elaborated in Lunts's midrashic version, with some blasphemous additions, to draw a clear parallel with the upheavals of the Russian Civil War and to suggest a similar whoring after false gods. The Promised Land of utopian milk and honey is far off in both cases and there is no food and water for the people, who wish to return to the fleshpots of Egyptian slavery. The disappointment with Communism and the hardships of daily life are matched by the depravity that affects all levels of society and the general demoralization. The story closes ambivalently with a stylized refrain which speaks of God's long patience with the sinful people.

A more personal parable is 'Rodina' ('Homeland', 1922) dedicated to Lunts's friend and fellow Serapion Brother, Viniamin Kaverin. It was published in a Soviet Jewish anthology of Russian-language material on Jewish themes in 1923.[47] It is a parodistic fantasy which questions the self-identity of the author looking at his reflection in a mirror in the revolutionary capital Petrograd (St Petersburg), which is both native and foreign for him ('rodnoe no chuzhoe'). He distinguishes himself, a secular non-believer who writes in a foreign tongue (*chuzhoi iazyk*), from his father, the traditional *Polish* Jew praying for the restoration of Jerusalem, who bewails his son's cultural apostasy (drinking homemade vodka on the Sabbath). Yet like his father he longs to see the banks of the Jordan and he berates his friend Viniamin Kaverin (whose real name was Zilber) for playing the self-hating Jew, urging him to reidentify with the Biblical story of the Jews and to revive in himself their prophetic spirit.

Petrograd is decadent Babylon and it is to ancient Babylon, the Jews' first exile where they prayed to the West (the direction of Jerusalem) and where they forgot their fathers' names, that the author dream-travels dressed in his ancient Hebrew-Yiddish name, Yehuda-Leib, together with Binyomin (Kaverin), who, like the other Serapion Brothers, also turns to the West. Language and naming were considered by the sages of the Talmud to be two of the factors in the preservation of Jewish identity in Egyptian bondage and its loss in Babylonian exile; language and naming were subject to intense Russification in Lunts's own day. This is a tale of bereavement, psychological wounds and self-alienation, a parable which turns on the author's conscious rejection of the road which leads to the new Jerusalem. At the same time he comes to a painful knowledge that he cannot take the road to the old Jerusalem in a strange land, which is nevertheless his native land, but denies him his identity as writer and as Jew.[48] That impasse will serve as a useful paradigm for the self-identity with which many Russian Jews could not live easily.

SELF-HATE AS MEANS TO BECOMING

The *Haskalah* had preached a low profile on external signs of Jewishness as part of the campaign to make Jews seem more acceptable to their neighbours and to curb what the reformers viewed as medieval superstition and ignorance. An-sky was not alone in erasing his Jewish name, language and dress when he abandoned the *shtetl* and his family for the Russian peasants and the Populist movement. By the early years of the twentieth century Russified Jews found themselves looking as outsiders at their own people. Even a nationalist like Jabotinsky, attacking the trend of assimilation in 1903, confessed that during a time of pogroms he and his comrades had instinctively affected a Moscow accent and tried to look Russian in order to melt into the crowd.[49] Seeing a pious Jew, whose Jewishness was God-given and genuinely unself-conscious, he realized that his mask of non-Jewishness made his own identity one that was imposed upon him by others and devoid of any inner freedom. In his article on Jews in Russian Literature, Jabotinsky regrets the fact that Jews writing in Russian spoke of Jews as 'they' and Russians as 'we'.[50] By making Russian culture, which was Christian in roots and temperament, one's own, any reference to Jewish themes became a reference to the *other*, to the non-Christian and therefore foreign and dangerous culture, with the satanic implications of territory beyond boundaries.

An archetypal case in Russian culture of the alien associations of outsiders is found in the Russian Primary Chronicle, which speaks of the heathen Slavic tribes outside the borders of civilized Rus'. Rus' adopted the 'true' faith of Christianity in 988 after rejecting emissaries of Judaism (from the Khazars) and of Islam. Russian space is sacred and cultured in binary opposition to the hostile barbaric non-Russian space.[51] In *Taras Bul'ba* Gogol paints a hilarious scene when the Jew Yankel tells the Cossack chief that his son has gone over to the other side (the Poles); being a Jew, Yankel fails to understand what is so bad about crossing to the other side and putting on *alien* dress.[52] The Jew who crosses the boundary of the *shtetl* or the Pole cannot see his otherness in the eyes of the Russian but soon discovers the otherness of his language on alien soil.[53] The word, as Bakhtin conceived it in his *Problems of Dostoevsky's Poetics,* is by definition partly another's *(chuzhoi)* and becomes one's own *(svoi)* by becoming appropriated through assimilation to the speaker's intention and accent. To make an application of the notion of double-voicing to the Jew writing in Russian, a language not 'one's own', we might say that the Jew writing in Russian was so hypersensitive to the valuation of himself as Other that he sought to appropriate Russian cultural texts as his own and to attenuate the difference of his discourse from that of the Other. It will be seen in following chapters how this effects the reinvention of self and, especially in the case of Mandelstam, the concept of *logos.*

When the Jewish people is threatened by anti-Semitism, however, even the poetic discourse which displays its sense of being at home in Russian culture can reveal affinity with the Other. The famous Russian poet and *narodnik* (supporter of the Populist movement), Semyon Nadson, who died in 1887 aged twenty-five and whose only claim to Jewish identity is a baptized father, wrote of Jews as *chuzhoi,* foreign and alien:

> I was born alien to you, rejected people
> and not to you did I sing in moments of inspiration.
> The world of your traditions, the burden of your grief
> are foreign to me, as are your teachings.[54]

Nadson finds nothing with which to identify in the Jewish heritage, but as long as the word 'Jew' invites humiliation and persecution, the poet wants to stand in the ranks of the warriors of the Jewish people. This Christianized idea of the Jews as martyrs will be met again in the person of Ilia Ehrenburg. Of course, such self-alienation of the apostate was not confined to those baptized into the Orthodox Church but was also shared by those who had made Russianness their destiny in the large cities, and who had fused themselves with the Russian intelligentsia.

Self-alienation was essential to the act of becoming a writer in Russian. Writing about the popular, but now forgotten, short-story writer David Aizman, Alice Stone Nakhimovsky comments:

> By choosing to write in Russian and about Jews, a writer is taking on a tradition that runs counter to the kind of unconscious self-identification that others working in their national literatures take for granted. Working in Russian, he becomes both Russian and Jew; a revisionist, a sympathizer, a self-hater.[55]

That kind of inner contradiction is indicated in Aizman's description of a situation close to his own in his story 'Na chuzhbine' ('In a Foreign Land', 1901). The all-consuming longing to return to Russia felt by a Jewish doctor and his pharmacist wife in the French provinces can be diagnosed as a chronic case of that typically Russian melancholy, *toska*, verging on mystical longing; but it is dictated also by a Marxist conviction that pogroms are of no consequence when one can be of use to the masses of one's native land. For Aizman's generation, that kind of emotional and ideological attachment was strong in the absence of any sense of belonging to a Jewish community. In another story, 'Zemliaki' ('Fellow Countrymen', 1902), a lonely Russian woman from a provincial Deadville working as a housekeeper in rural France strikes up a friendship with a Jewish hatter that negates the recent past of violent pogroms. The common denominator which helps Shapiro and Varvara Stepanovna overcome their mutual prejudices is specifically Russianness, but it is an encounter which takes place on Jewish territory, at a Sabbath eve meal. Even old sightless Shapiro must realize that his stubborn hope for a reconciliation between the two nations, the dream of his grandchildren living as human beings in Russia, remains something of a delusion.

Sight is retrospective, and the reconstruction of identity when hopes have been more soberly appraised is a form of narrative which inscribes self-alienation with the signature of authorship. Jerome Bruner concurs with Paul Ricoeur and Hayden White that telling of events lived in past time requires a narrative which may take autobiographical form, but in any portrait of an artist or a figure in search of identity it is difficult for the artist to avoid some aspect of self-portrayal. Conversely, for Goethe autobiography was as much poetry as truth.[56] Life imitates art as much as the other way round (a view to which we will return in the chapter on Pasternak). The poetic construction of a life meshes real events with an imaginative retelling to continually reinterpret experience. Bruner counts self-criticism, tell-tale omission, verbal aspect and tense, preference for passive or active verbs and prolepsis among responses to self-identification in the miniature culture of the family and in society at large. These are devices influenced by the culturally determined paradigm of life-story telling and they try to make sense of identity in a metaphysical and historical context. Literary autobiography, moreover, achieves an 'epiphany of the ordinary', in Joycean terms, in order to explore and at the same time to create the ontogenesis of the poet.[57]

The life of the artist, at least at the beginning of the twentieth century, is inseparable from his work. James Olney cites Yeats's rhetorical question 'How can we know the dancer from the dance?' in support of his Jungian approach to invention of self, stressing how difficult it is to divide the living of life from the pattern of life.[58] In describing the *rite de passage* into manhood and into poetry, an artist's biography is as much performance as is his art, attracting the public attention that gives life to a myth. The complex and sometimes agonized relationship between autobiography and *Ich-Erzählung* gives birth to a poetic identity, an artistic and temporal becoming of the writing self, at the same time as it moulds a public myth not always loyal to biographical truth, itself relative and evasive. The narratives to be discussed in this book – whether fictions in the guise of autobiography or diary in the case of Babel's stories or Mandelstam's and Pasternak's poetic confessions and Ehrenburg's *apologia pro vita mea* – are privileged but reflexive stories. The linguistic predicament of the autobiographical act is that the author is his own represented subject.

The narrative of self, being reflexive, can never escape indeterminacy and it is impermeable to verification. Perhaps that is why modernist prose is well suited to an enterprise which is ultimately endless, 'an endless prelude'.[59] William Wordsworth's own *Prelude* is a prelude to poetry and to being which he revised, with the necessary revisions in self-identity required by the disappointment of the hopes invested in the French Revolution and the post-1815 reaction, after his turn to conservatism and the bestowing of cultural status. The deconstructionist critic Paul de Man, in his brilliant discussion of Wordsworth's essays on epitaphs, describes autobiography as a 'defacement' caused when language attempts to restore mortality, to create a 'monument' to the immortal name of the author.[60] Of particular interest to us is the relevance of Romantic theory in modelling a narrative of poetic identity and especially in the context of a Revolution. But for Mandelstam and others, living in the twentieth century required the rejection of the nineteenth-century autobiographical conventions of Tolstoy and Aksakov and a new writing of oneself into time and history, which for Mandelstam meant also writing himself into language.[61]

The need after the Russian Revolution to pass ideological control in order to publish meant, under state monopoly, the self-censorship and rewriting of identity in order to maintain the ontological and professional status of a writer. A typical example is the autobiography of Samuil Marshak, *V nachale zhizni* (*At Life's Beginning*, 1961). Marshak was a well-known children's writer and translator, fulfilling the Jew's traditional role as international cultural broker and mediator between Russia and the West. He conformed, at least outwardly, to ideological demands, though he did not escape criticism. But as Kornei Chukovsky said, Marshak had several faces, and after the Revolution it was expedient to conceal his previous Zionist identity. So his autobiography, which bears the restraints as well as the freedoms of the Thaw, downplays the background of Jewish pogroms (though they are not ignored entirely) and focuses on the author's claim to Russian culture, through Lev Tolstoy and Vladimir Stasov, who took the young poet under his wing, through Russian poetry and the world of St Petersburg. Marshak could – like Babel and many others – legitimately name Gorky, whose Russianness is indisputable, as a safe guarantor of ideological and cultural credentials.[62] The chronological parameters are the revolutions of 1905 and 1917, not the pogroms and the Balfour Declaration. But, as in Mandelstam's *Noise of Time*, memory has its wellspring in the Dreyfus affair of the 1890s, which pushed Herzl and many others toward Zionism, although this is described (in accordance with the rules of public discourse in communist Russia) as Marshak's first impulsive solidarity with the forces of radicalism and student rebellion. And when the boy's father stands up to a policeman who wishes to exploit his legal non-status as a Jew visiting outside the Pale he is presented as defying Tsarist authority.

The family seems thoroughly assimilated, distanced from the grandparents' old world of Vitebsk where even the horses understand Yiddish. The non-glossia of the maternal grandparents, who have no Russian, reminds us again of Mandelstam's *Noise of Time*, and in the precarious pair of mirrors hanging in the grandparents' house can be seen the topsy-turvy mimesis of what for the boy is an alien world, small and constricting, whose historical and psychological fragmentation is symbolically reflected when the boy breaks the mirror. From that 'incomprehensible' dead world he is happily expelled. This paradigm of breakout from the Jewish home, or rather non-home, takes a new turn in the modern period, since it is a break with an alien world that has no language, and therefore no culture, in preference for Russianness to which the boy naturally aspires as the only culture of ideological and social acceptance. Memory is located firmly in the Russian past, in provincial towns where the boy plays among urchins and holy fools. That the boy goes further than his parents may be guessed from the hint of guilt at eating with the peasants or the showing of his poetry (self-exposure) to the half-undressed student in a hotel room, an ethnic and class identification with almost homosexual overtones.

Like the boy in Babel's 'Story of My Dovecote', Marshak's autobiographical self must declaim Pushkin with greater enthusiasm than the Russian boys, indeed does so with a passionate frenzy, in order to pass the entrance exam into the Russian *gimnaziia*, the key to entrance into Russian society and a decent living, if not a career. The boy does not, however, rail bitterly against his Jewish disability, which bars him despite his brilliant cultural and linguistic performance. In fact he remembers his Hebrew tutor, a traditional *melamed*, with warm affection, though he claims he learnt nothing of that language (like Ehrenburg and others who claimed to have 'forgotten' Yiddish). As in Babel's story, the Jewish mother's neurotic anxiety and her pogrom wisdom are proven right and the coveted school badge must be put away in deference to the incomprehensible discriminatory percentage which kept many Jews out of Russian schools. 'People like me,' notes Marshak cryptically, 'did not pass into the gimnaziia'. The boy's response to his rejection is to buy the schoolmasters (in effigy from the photographer's shop, not in bribery as was more often the case) and to iconize them in literary form in his memoirs. When the boy cuts up the photographs he amputates the schoolmasters' legs, surely expressing a Freudian fear of castration; indeed, it is quite clear that the barring of entrance to Russianness actually means not attaining manhood and losing the chance to succeed where his father has failed despite his cultural proficiency. It is astonishing how the traditional confirmation of a Jewish boy at the age of thirteen, through the performance of a sacred text, is time and again transmuted by Marshak and other writers into the performance of canonical non-Jewish texts (particularly classics of Russian literature). When the boy in Marshak's revisionist memoir is finally admitted to the *gimnaziia* he has to excel in his performance of Latin. He also displays a compassion for the underdog more Christian than that of the Christians. That compassion is dressed up as revolutionary solidarity, but we cannot help noticing that initiation into poetry, when it comes, is axiomatically an initiation into the values of the Russian writer who is both Christian and male.

The pattern of negation of Judaism by opposition of closed to open space, where the enclosed Jewish territory is alien and strange *(chuzhoi)*, is seen here and will be repeated in the cases of Mandelstam, Pasternak and Ehrenburg. Their rewriting of personal history fabricates their past in a poetic invention of the writing self. Their claim to a literary persona meant making Russian culture their own and crucifying their rejected projected selves.

The crucifix was a loaded image for Jews, signalling a threat to their physical existence (icons are carried in the procession prior to the pogrom in 'Story of My Dovecote'), and the cross negated their spiritual existence (the Christians claimed to have displaced the Jews as a chosen people and condemned them to the historical status of a fossil, that is to national non-status); they were universally stigmatized as collectively responsible for the crucifixion, or at least for not accepting what Christians believed to be the true faith. So potentially the adoption of the cross as value and as image could eliminate the 'Jew' in the projected self. The cross is the ultimate icon of apostasy in Jewish eyes. However, the writing of cultural apostasy is more complex and more interesting. It is not just that the Jew's 'anxiety' at not having sufficiently mastered the language of the non-Jew and having to display constantly his non-identitification with the Other forced him to show himself more Christian than the Christian. The 'hidden language' of the Jew had to adapt to the fundamental change in cultural values in the period of modernism, and particularly to shifts in the evaluation of religious imagery. Then war and revolution destroyed the already decaying fabric of Jewish life in Eastern Europe, while bringing the promise of a new messianism in the wake of an apocalypse. The next chapter will therefore examine the appropriation of the crucifixion by Jewish avant-garde artists and writers in response to the Revolution and to the pogroms which swept through Russia, the Ukraine and Poland in 1918–20, paying particular attention to the textualization or iconization of old identity conflicts as well as pointing to new options for identity formation.

CHAPTER 2

Modernist responses to war and revolution: the Jewish Jesus

Out from under the knout, from the wounds that still bleed -
O Messiah, come now on your silvery steed.

Abraham Reisen

... only the blood doesn't seethe any more and the blood
   doesn't cry
and hands in the villages close around hats
when a cross passes by or a picture of Mary
and their lips are trembling and their hearts are silenced
praised be king Jesus-
forever -
amen

Melekh Ravich

MODERNISM AND CATASTROPHE

As David Roskies has shown in his study of Jewish modernism,[1] traditional paradigms of cultural response to catastrophe broke down in the face of the pogroms and the Holocaust of the twentieth century. The title of Bialik's famous poem on the Kishinev pogrom, ''Al hashkhita' ('On the Slaughter', 1904) undermines the religious formula for animal slaughter, while the midrashic response to the Ten Martyrs put to death by the Romans, 'Aseret harugei hamalkut, which speaks of a divine sacrifice of the souls of the righteous on a heavenly altar,[2] seems no longer adequate to relate the slaughter of innocents on the earthly altar to concepts of divine justice:

And cursed be the one who says: Avenge!
Vengeance such as this, vengeance for the blood of a little child,
Satan has not yet created –

Let the blood pierce the depths!
Let the blood pierce the depths of darkness
And consume in the darkness and there undermine
All the rotting foundations of Earth!

The violence of pogroms, revolutions and wars in the early twentieth century elicited a personal response from the assimilated Jewish avant-garde, while modernism suggested possible strategies and metaphors which subverted both Jewish and Christian conventions. One striking example is the Jewish modernist appropriation of the crucifixion as an expression of suffering in the perspective of pogroms and revolution. Distinct from the crucified Jew, there also emerges a messianic figure who articulates the often ambiguous, sometimes sceptical hopes for a secular salvation in Russia, especially after the Russian Revolution.

The secularization of Jesus began with modern Bible critics, Jews and Christians, who each had their own theological axe to grind. Among others, David Friedrich Strauss, in *Das Leben Jesus* (1835), and Ernest Renan, in *Les Origines du christianisme* (1863–1883), had done much to separate the historical personage from theological doctrine. Theodore Ziolkowski has mapped the 'fictional transfiguration' of Jesus in modern literature[3] and I do not wish to go over this ground once more. The Christ-figure of Romantic poetry became a familiar archetype and the Passion is memorable in Goya's portrayal of political execution in *Third of May, 1808* (1814). Needless to say, the image of Jesus is central to symbolist apocalyptic mythology in Russia prior to the First World War and the Revolution, for example in the poetry of Merezhkovsky and Ivanov and in the thought of Rozanov and Solovyov. Bely, like other symbolists, saw the Revolution at first as a mystical event, a second coming. The figure of Jesus leading the revolutionaries in Blok's *Dvenadtsat'* ('The Twelve', 1918) is well known. Discussion of the crucifixion in symbolist eschatology or in decadent art is beyond the scope of the present discussion, as is the no less relevant context of the Slap in the Face of Public Taste, when the futurists revolutionized the various visual and plastic arts and blasphemed the icons of the bourgeois past. Examples of modernist profanation of sacred images can be taken from several movements across Europe, such as the German expressionist Max Ernst's avant-garde treatment of a Renaissance convention in his 'The Virgin Slaps the Infant Jesus in Front of Three Witnesses' (1926). But in Russia, revolution and war made the Christian story of the apocalypse especially meaningful in both the modernists' and the revolutionaries' use of Orthodox iconology, whether in Goncharova's 'Mystical Images of War' (1914) or in the Soviet novelist A. N. Tolstoy's application of Calvary to the Civil War in his well-known trilogy.

The crucifixion was additionally a *topos* of the First World War, either as a legend of enemy barbarity or a poetic image of the common soldier's burden.[4] This is how Wilfred Owen, the English war poet and infantry officer, spoke in a letter of 1918 of the common soldier's burden as that of Jesus on the way to crucifixion:

For 14 hours yesterday I was at work – teaching Christ to lift his cross by numbers, and how to adjust his crown; and not to imagine he thirst till after the last halt. I attended his Supper to see there were not complaints; and inspected his feet that they should be worthy of the nails. I see to it that he is dumb, and stands to attention before his accusers. With a piece of silver I buy him every day, and with maps I make him familiar with the topography of Golgotha.[5]

George Grosz has Jesus wearing a gas mask on the cross in 'Maul halten und weiter dienen' (Figure 3), an image borrowed by Friedrich Emmler in his film *Oblomok imperii* ('Fragment of an Empire', 1929). That kind of satirical use of the image of Jesus for pacifist propaganda, as in Boardman Robinson's cartoon 'The Deserter' (1916), was politically controversial,[6] but it did not risk the kind of modernist desacralization of myth that we find in Joyce's *Ulysses* or Nikos Kazantzakis's *The Last Temptation*.

For Jewish artists the problem was more complex, since so much Jewish blood had been shed in the name of Christianity, which condemned the Jewish race as guilty for the crucifixion of Jesus; the cross was too often a hated symbol of persecution. In the face of political anti-Semitism in the 1870s some Jewish artists nevertheless used the figure of Jesus, but stressed his Jewish

Figure 3. George Grosz, 'Maul halten und weiter dienen', from his *Hintergrund* (1928)

features,[7] as did the sculptor Mark Antokolsky. His *Ecce Homo* (1873) expressed a message of brotherly love and suffering that was not always acceptable to either of the two faiths. Echoing the earlier view of the father of the *Haskalah*, Moses Mendelssohn, developed by historians Heinrich Graetz and Abraham Geiger, that Paul had distorted the true teaching of the Jew Jesus, Antokolsky stated that if Jesus were to return, he would be horrified by the Christian persecution of the Jews. In particular, as Antokolsky's letters to Vasily Stasov in 1873 show, the renewed anti-Semitism (starting with the 1871 Odessa pogrom) awakened childhood memories of forced military conscription of Jewish children for purposes of conversion.[8]

Traditional Jewish art, whose orientation was essentially narrative, was inimical to the figural art which in the Eastern and Catholic churches tended to make the saints an object of worship.

For all the reciprocal influences of Islamic and Christian art, the semantics of Hebrew Bible illumination, ritual or synagogue decoration and numismatics remained consistent with Jewish monotheism and the messianic belief in redemption.[9] It was in keeping with their revolt against traditional values that modern Jewish artists reclaimed Jesus as legitimate artistic material, a symbol of the Western culture to which they wished to belong, yet a symbol totally alien to the world of their fathers which they had forsaken.

At the beginning of the century the figure of Christ became an object of sympathetic contemplation as a new relationship emerged, conditioned by historical insight and Enlightenment; artists dealt in a secular way with ideas hitherto repressed or forbidden. Christ is addressed by the newly emancipated Hebrew poet as a brother who will in the future return to his people, wrapped in the traditional prayer shawl.[10]

Maurycy Gottlieb holds the most interest for his autobiographical use of Jesus as his own relationship changed with the Jewish community.[11] The earlier figure of Jesus preaching at Capernaum in a Jewish prayer-shawl is transformed into the self-portrait in the well-known *Day of Atonement* where a Hebrew inscription *in memoriam* records the artist's forthcoming death (Figure 4).

Gospel scenes appear in Chagall's early work, usually accompanied by a subtext that comments on the Christian legend with an irony apparent to those who knew the Yiddish proverbs and the pogrom experience to which the painter referred. These are 'in-jokes' like those found in the paintings of Henri Rousseau, Pablo Picasso and Marcel Duchamp, but, over and above the intimately personal significance and Chagall's love of mystification, they refer to a coded dual language, decipherable only by Jews from the same cultural background in the Jewish Pale and therefore rendered inoffensive to the host culture.[12] Chagall would thus be referring in a self-mocking way to his own identification with the Jewish world while caught between being a Jew in Russia and a Russian in Paris. The ambivalence towards both Judaism and Christianity is evident in *Calvary* (1912) (Figure 5), which displays the influences of cubism and

Figure 4.   Maurycy Gottlieb, *Jews Praying in the Synagogue on the Day of Atonement*, 1878.

other forms of European modernism, as well as Russian icons. Later, in 1977, Chagall claimed, 'For me Christ has always symbolized the true type of the Jewish martyr. That is how I understood him in 1908 when I used this figure for the first time ... It was under the influence of the pogroms.'[13] Back in Russia,

Figure 5.   Marc Chagall, *Calvary*, 1912.

where he was caught up with the rest of the Jewish population in war and pogroms, Chagall depicted in a pen-and-ink drawing, 'War' (1914), an old Jew against the cross of a window-frame showing a scene of war. Like Babel's Gedali, Chagall's old Jew is beyond historical time and bears the suffering of all ages. However, only following the anti-Jewish incidents in Nazi Germany did the crucifixion become a specifically Jewish image in the series beginning with *White Crucifixion* (1938) (Figure 6). Significant here is Chagall's use of the ladder, a convention associated with the Ascension and, in Byzantine iconography, with the torture of the crucified Jesus, whereas in Jewish art, apart from Jacob's ladder, it represents the ascent of Moses to receive the Law on Mount Sinai.[14] For Chagall the ladder is, together with the boat, a motif of flight and exile, a literal means to rescue

Figure 6.   Marc Chagall, *White Crucifixion*, 1938.

the Jews from their burning homes, but it also suggests a giving back of the Covenant by a people contending that their suffering was undeserved.[15] In the 1918 Pogrom Series of another Jewish artist of the period, Issachar Ber Rybak, the scene of a desecrated synagogue similarly suggests returning the Law against the historical and autobiographical background of Jewish suffering in the pogroms. Rybak's father was killed by Cossacks in a pogrom, and one of the murdered Jews in the Pogrom Series appears partly bound like Isaac, partly crucified (Figure 7). Since the

Figure 7.   Issachar Ber Rybak, from the Pogrom Series, 1918.

Holocaust the crucifixion of the Jew has become as much an
indictment of the Church for its official silence as a blasphemous
symbol of despair, but for the assimilated Jewish intellectual in
the period we are discussing – 1905–30 – this was primarily an
expression of an inner conflict.

The crucifixions of Chagall and Rybak's Pogrom Series are not
only reactions to Ephraim Moses Lilien's martyrology of the
Kishinev victims, but also draw on familiarity with Russian icons
and the current of primitivism and folk-art in Russian modernism.
These are artists thoroughly grounded in the Jewish world and
sceptical towards the gentile world they have entered. Interest
was awakened in traditional Jewish folk-art by An-sky's expedition
of 1912–14, sponsored by the Jewish Ethnographic Society, which
also sponsored the discovery by Rybak and Lissitzky of the
Mohilev synagogue with its impressive painted wooden ceiling in
1916. The outbreak of Revolution caught Jewish artists in a
debate that had raged over a decade before in Russian art on the
paradoxical marriage of modernism with folk-art, and it freed

them from all conventions and institutions. Reviewing An-sky's book *Evreiskaia narodnaia khudozhestvennaia starina* ('Jewish Folk-Art'), which brought the expedition's findings to public attention and contributed to a minor renaissance of Jewish art, the critic Abram Efros called on Jewish modernists on the Left to help Jewish art mature by drawing on the newly rediscovered traditional Jewish forms.[16] The revolutionary attempt to impose one's own canon, as recommended by Efros, was one way to absorb modernist aesthetics in the void created by the destruction of the Jewish community and in the absence of an integral Jewish artistic tradition that would be meaningful outside the context of the Jewish community. The slogan 'modernist in form, national in content' was a bid for both survival and acceptance by the world of art in terms that could accommodate the new secular Jewish identity with its celebration or memory of a dynamic and eternal spirit that held its own against outside influences. The encounter a few years later with constructivism and experience in the theatre universalized the Jewish content of these traditional art-forms, most notably in the work of Lissitzky.[17] Thereafter the slogan changed to 'national in form, socialist in content', while the non-territorial status of Jewish nationality under communist policy and the increasingly difficult political and working conditions in Russia cut short the experiment in a Jewish art. The rise of the Proletkul't and hard-line Marxists in the arts, the coming of Socialist Realism and Party control in the thirties and the repression of modernism under Stalin finally stifled any remaining modernist as well as ethnic instincts.

Modernism was a mode peculiar to the new Yiddish-speaking secular culture in that its imagery and language represented the crisis of the Jewish community facing the overwhelming forces of assimilation, urbanization and secularization at the beginning of the century, and it expressed the shock of the violent anti-Semitism which traumatized the maturing Jewish artist who had abrogated ties with that community. Primitivism in Rybak's Pogrom Series conveys the view of the uncomprehending child-like bystander who sees the looting and rape as a carnival or circus, rather like the child's view in Babel's 'Story of My Dovecote' and 'First Love', while the Cossacks on the rampage and apocalyptic scenes of desecration recall *Red Cavalry*. The erasure of a Jewish perspective on these events and the use of a non-Jewish language deautomatize habitual responses and question the identity of the artist who has left his people but now witnesses their crucifixion.

REVOLUTION AND APOCALYPSE

Christian themes are not absent from Jewish literature, as is evident in the best-known Yiddish folk-tales, not least in the sixteenth-century collection *Di maise bukh*. There is also a long rabbinical tradition of polemical literature about Jesus as a demon or heretic, as well as a tradition of false messiahs, or the Messiah of the House of Joseph, such as the drama of that name, *Meshiakh ben Yosef*, by Beinish Shteiman, killed during a civil war pogrom. The pogroms and revolutionary movement in Russia in particular inspired rival messiah figures, such as the beggar-saviour in H. Leivick's *Der golem* ('The Golem', 1920, produced by the Habimah Theatre in Moscow, 1924) or similar figures in the stories of the symbolist Yiddish prose writer Der Nister.

In the modern period the theme may express Jewish self-vindication, partly in response to persecution. A poem 'The Last Words of Don Henriques' by Zalman Shneour (1887–1959) assimilates the crucifixion to Jewish experience in the *auto-da-fé* of the Inquisition and invokes the historical Jesus, as Dostoevsky does in 'The Legend of the Grand Inquisitor'. 'The Legend of the Madonna' by Ber Horovits (1895–1942) goes a step further in turning the Christian blood libel into a vindication of the Jews, but the miracle of the Madonna who appears to a Jewish woman leaves the Jewish community, who are thereby saved, feeling most awkward. Sholem Asch's *The Nazarene* (1938–43), which angered many readers because it restored Jesus as a Jewish saint, came much later, but I might mention his *String of Pearls* (1916), a drama set in the Russian war zone, which relates Jewish martyrdom to a symbolic messianism, and *Kiddush hashem* ('Sanctification of the Name', 1919), which compares the Ukrainian massacres of 1918–19 with those of Bogdan Khmelnitsky in 1648.[18]

In his 1909 essay on 'The Crucifix Question' An-sky credited Der Nister with breaking the taboo on Jesus in modern Yiddish literature as early as 1907, and Roskies has characterized two modernist responses to the crucifixion based on two stories that appeared in 1909, Sholem Asch's 'In a karnaval-nakht' ('The Carnival Legend') and Lamed Shapiro's 'Der tselem' ('The Cross'). In the former the cross symbolized an ecumenical ideal of Jesus identifying with Jewish suffering and asking forgiveness; in the latter it symbolized a primitive violence that negated all ideals. A third group (including Asher Barash and Nobel laureate S. Y. Agnon) confirmed the age-old enmity between Christianity and Judaism. These three groups represented three stages in Jewish history between 1848 and 1948, the Bolshevik Revolution forming an apocalyptic crisis midway along the road to redemption and statehood.[19] It should not be surprising that in their rebellion against religious life and against nineteenth-century realism the Jewish modernists usurped and blasphemed the icons of all religions but the pogrom experience became a living out of apocalyptic myths more terrible than mythology. The Hungarian Hebrew novelist Avigdor Hameiri has described an actual crucifixion in his *Hashiga'on hagadol* ('The Great Madness', 1929) perpetrated before his eyes by Cossacks on the Galician front. Hameiri's novel, incidentally, is a classic of fiction of the First World War considered on a par with Remarque's *All Quiet on the Western Front*.[20] If Bialik's elegy for the Kishinev victims 'Be'ir haherega' ('In the City of Slaughter', 1904) presumed some kind of communal integrity that would survive, or if Chernikhovsky and others reactivated the historical heroes and martyrs of the Jewish nation, then the 60,000 victims of the massacres in the Ukraine in 1918–20 following the devastation of world war and civil war seemed to preclude the possibility, implicit in the use of sacred archetypes, that the *shtetl* would flourish again.[21]

The destruction of Jewish communities in Russia and the Ukraine reached such proportions that a primeval scream of atheistic nihilism could not suffice to express the collective anguish. The personal experience of the Yiddish and Hebrew expressionist poet and self-styled heir of Bialik, Uri Tsvi Greenberg (1894–1981), on the Serbian front and in a Polish pogrom in 1918 took on mythological proportions in his *Golgotha* (1920): 'Each morning I am nailed up again on the burning red crucifix.' As for Chagall

and others, the crucifixion becomes an autobiographical statement of artistic and ethnic identity. Jesus joined other false
messiahs in the poet's new historiography of the Jewish people
which rejected Europe as the 'Kingdom of the Cross' where the
dead Jews were so many crucifixions.[22] His one-man protest took
the typographical form of a cross 'Uri Tsvi farn tselem' ('Uri Tsvi
in Front of the Cross', 1922),[23] while his feet acted on the poet's
call to a new destiny in the Land of Israel. That option was
rejected by those who remained in Bolshevik Russia or, like
Lamed Shapiro and another Yiddish modernist, Moshe-Leib
Halpern, emigrated to America.

The hero of Shapiro's 'The Cross' discovers that the pogrom
has literally left the mark of the cross on the victim who was
liberated from the *shtetl* through violence and rape. 'The Cross'
narrates the story of how a young revolutionary acquired the sign
of the cross between his eyes. The sign between the eyes is a
modernistic parody of the phylacteries which are signs of the
Jew's faith, the 'sign between your eyes' prescribed in the Bible.
The primitive brutality with which the sign of the cross is cut into
his flesh marks his own transformation into a *ba'al-guf*, a man of
action more independent than the Benia Kriks or the tough guys
on Sholem Asch's *Kola Street*, a bestial creature who vengefully
rapes his Russian revolutionary comrade and finds riding the roof
of the railroad through the wild expanses of America an appropriate expression for the brute strength that for him can be the
only way to rebuild a destroyed world. The modernist theme and
style was felt sufficiently appropriate for a Russian translation to
appear in the same post-Revolutionary anthology of Jewish
culture, *Evreiskii mir*, in which Abram Efros published his call for a
Jewish modernism in a programmatic review of An-sky's book on
folk-art, alongside Vaisenberg's iconoclastic story of the 1905
revolution, *A Shtetl*, and An-sky's messianic tale of the Four
Towers in Rome.

Halpern also looked back on the destruction of the Old
World as so total that there seemed nothing left to redeem. His
poem *A nakht* ('A Night', 1916; revised 1919) transforms the
historical nightmare of the First World War into a personal
schizophrenia. The pogrom is relived as a vaudeville show in

which the poet overturns all the idolatrous messianisms of a bankrupt and self-destructive civilization. Unlike traditional Jewish lamentation or Bialik's outcry after the Kishinev pogrom in 'City of Slaughter', writes Ruth Wisse, 'Halpern's vision denies religious and national meaning to the current devastation, which exposes the mendacity of earlier inflated messianic claims.'[24] In his unperformed drama 'In New York', written with his friend Moshe Nadir, Halpern satirized the American Jewish response to war and pogroms in Eastern Europe and attempted to redeem Jesus from the Christians who killed Jews in his name:

We dreamed up a messiah for the world. The world is blind. We must open its eyes. Don't kill in the name of the cross ... If you carry the ax along with the cross we will take the cross away from you – because he who hangs on the cross belongs to us. He is ours, our martyr, the sacrificial victim of our messianic dream ...

Since when did Christ become yours? He is our flesh and blood. When you killed him he became yours. You claim all the Jews once you have put them to death. Jesus my brother! Drunken goyim cheapen your faith. Strangers disgrace you and your own people doesn't recognize you. I swear: let the whole world hear – I swear that you are ours.[25]

The Jew here appears closer to the Christian concept of compassion and pacifism than the Christian. In venting his anger at the Christians, however, Halpern was annihilating the memory of the past and establishing an iconoclastic identity that wavered between hope and scepticism toward the new messianism of the Bolsheviks.

The theological impact of the pogroms is felt acutely in the long poem *Di kupe* ('The Heap', 1921) by Perets Markish. This is an obscene montage of the *'akeda* (Binding of Isaac), Golgotha, and giving back the Tablets of the Law at Mount Sinai, as in one of Rybak's Pogrom Series of 1918. The stinking heap of bodies at Horoditsh on the day after the Day of Atonement 1921 overshadows all images. The Jews prayed for Divine mercy, but in the blood that is spilt the next day the poet sees neither the redemption of the paschal sacrifice nor the covenantal blood of circumcision. The Jews killed in the name of Jesus are sold, as Jesus was, for a purse of silver: 'Come! cross yourself and count them. / A shekel a head, / A shekel a head.'[26] The irresolvable paradox is that this *kaddish*, which anticipates the modernity of Allen Ginsberg's unorthodox mourners' prayer, is addressed to a God whose godliness is denied.[27] The aesthetics of modernism fragmented the mythological texts into a new poetic sense of language and existence in a post-apocalyptic world, where, as in T. S. Eliot's *The Wasteland* (1922), theology could be both destructive and deconstructive.

The negation of the divine sacrifice legend, to which I referred at the beginning of this chapter, reminds us of another story set in the years of war and revolution, Lamed Shapiro's well-known 'Vaise khala' ('White Sabbath-Bread', 1919), which is told through the eyes of a demented Russian peasant Vasily. The shock and horror at the desecration of the ultimate divine image *(tselem elokim)* – man – is reinforced by the human sacrifice at the end of the story, a Communion of the Host as the *pogromshchik* bites into a Jewish woman – bread and flesh – but it also achieves a travesty of the midrash of the heavenly altar on which the victims were sacrificed. Such an atavistic burst of animal Passion (*sic*!) symbolized for Shapiro the final meaning of the pogroms; in other stories by Shapiro, too, instead of heroic acts of revenge by Jewish revolutionaries there is bestiality and suicide.

The deliberate shift of perspective from that of victim to that of perpetrator recalls Isaak Babel's stories 'The Letter' and 'Betrayal' which use the *skaz* technique of free indirect discourse to convey the mentality of semi-educated Cossacks. Another example, this time in the Yiddish prose of a leading modernist of the Kiev group, Dovid Bergelson (1884–1952), is the *skaz* view of two Russian partisans Botchko and Zeek which is central to his novella set during the massacres of Ukrainian Jewry in 1918–20, 'Civil War' (1922–27), published in his *Shteremteg* ('Storm Days', 1928). The primeval, brute force of the Cossacks caught up in the apocalypse which sweeps Russia is here disturbingly taken out of the context of Jewish suffering. As for the underground Bolshevik leader Lezerke, his Jewishness is immaterial to the class struggle and serves only to emphasize the rift of hatred that exists between him and the petty bourgeoisie of the dying *shtetl*.

REVOLUTION AND REDEMPTION

One way in which avant-garde Jewish artists responded to anti-Semitism was to invoke Jesus as a 'Crucified Jew', the title of a 1927 book by Max Hunterberg. Leib Kvitko's *1919* contains a lyric which shows a crucified Jesus wandering in shame through the Ukrainian towns hit by the pogroms, tearing down his image and marking black crosses on the walls of priests' houses; later, in Perets Markish's Holocaust epic *Milkhome* ('War', 1948), the hero Gur-Arye has a vision of Jesus as a crucified Jew like himself. Such identification underlined the contradiction between the humane teachings of Jesus and the anti-Semitic incitement of many priests. At the same time, as part of their modernist revolt against the Jewish traditional world that was crumbling, the Jewish modernists were ready to adopt New Testament images of the revolutionary apocalypse which they were witnessing.

The Jewish national revival and the Balfour Declaration spurred the messianic hopes of Jews in Russia and East Europe for a realization of the Hebrew prophets' millenarian visions of social justice and harmony. For some, this was to be expressed in the return to Zion; for others, the Bolshevik takeover promised, at least for a while, a radical social experiment in utopia. The modern Hebrew novelist Haim Hazaz (1898–1973) published in 1923–25 three stories of the Revolution which he saw as a major event in the messianic outcome of Jewish history. The Revolution is presented in terms of Ezekiel's vision of apocalypse, but the young generation rebels against tradition. Reb Simkha's daughter, Henia, has Motl Privisker arrested for hiding contraband, while pogroms and the disarming of the Jewish brigade put in doubt any hopeful outcome.[28] In the second volume of Perets Markish's *Dor in, dor ois* ('Generation Comes, Generation Goes', 1929) another secular redeemer, Ezra, is the revolutionary hero who rejects the passivity of the older generation, although in *The Heap* the idealism of both Jesus and Marx was rejected.

A renegade Jewish intellectual who has opted for the Bolshevik version of redemption appears in Isaak Babel's *Konarmiia* (*Red Cavalry*, 1923–25, first edition 1926). He may be placed in the

Jewish tradition of Elijah the prophet who, it is believed, will return to herald messianic times that will bring peace and justice to the world. Yet the imagery is christological. This Elijah (Ilia) profanes the Sabbath by smoking, he has the 'emaciated face of a nun' and the 'forehead of Spinoza' – that other Jewish heretic – and the Hasidim round him are likened to 'fishermen and apostles'. Later, at the end of *Red Cavalry* in 'Syn rabbi' ('The Rebbe's Son'), he renounces his mother (reminding us of Matthew 12, 46–50) in the name of a new messianic ideology, the Red Cavalry. Nevertheless, Babel is writing within the Jewish messianic tradition. It is, as Maurice Friedberg has pointed out,[29] surely no accident that Ilia is surnamed Bratslavsky, for the Bratslav Hasidim are among the most messianic of Hasidic sects. The fact that they had had no *rebbe*[30] since the death of Nakhman of Bratslav in 1811 seems to suggest Babel was consciously emphasizing Ilia's messianic role. Babel would possibly have known Nakhman's story 'The Rabbi's Son', a tale of frustrated messianism, in Martin Buber's rendering, but the Hasidim whom he met during the Soviet-Polish war were apparently not followers of Bratslav.

Who, then, was the revolutionary hero from a Hasidic family? The Israeli poet Meir Bosak has discovered a prototype in real life for Babel's Ilia Bratslavsky. The Zhitomir *rebbe* belonged to the Twersky family of the Chernobyl dynasty, and it is note-worthy that Babel recorded his meeting with the Zhitomir *rebbe* in his Diary for 3 July 1920, although he could not make out the name of the *rebbe*.[31] It turns out that in the battle for Novograd-Volynsk, mentioned in the first story of the *Red Cavalry* cycle, 'Perekhod cherez Zbruch' ('Crossing the Zbrucz'), there fell in action on the Bolshevik side a son of the *rebbe* of Markov. The *rebbe* of Markov was among the offspring of the founder of the Chernobyl dynasty, Nakhum, whose son Motele fathered eight Hasidic *rebbeim* who became very popular in the Ukraine and carried on the name of Chernobyl. Motele is the name given to the *rebbe* in Babel's story. The granddaughter of the Markov *rebbe*, Malkah Twersky, who now lives in Israel, has testified that her maternal grandfather had a son called Froike who was indeed a revolutionary and did meet a tragic death in the street. He was also a poet, which might explain the 'crooked' lines of verse in Hebrew script found among Ilia's last possessions in 'The Rebbe's Son'. These would then be the lines in Yiddish, or maybe in Hebrew, of a young poet who could be counted among the fallen heroes of Russian Jewry in the Revolution and Civil War.[32]

If Ilia is a failed Elijah whose death questions the viability of the dream of the Jewish communist, or at least underscores the irresolvable paradoxes, we are left with the figure of the Jewish narrator who goes by the un-Jewish cover name of Liutov and who cannot resolve the stormy conflicts between Judaism and Communism raised in his ancient memory. The Jewish narrator whose self is negated by the contradictions around him appears in a book by another Jew who happened to be serving on the Polish side of the front in 1920, Israel Rabon's *Di gas* (*The Street*, 1928). The demobbed Polish Jewish soldier roams the streets, feverishly haunted by the absurd futility of those postwar years in the circus and movie-house where sick fantasy and brutal reality become mixed, rather like the nightmarish world of Italo Svevo and Bruno Schulz. No fantasy, however, is the recollection of almost freezing to death on the battlefield. Crawling out of the womb of a dead horse, where he has sheltered for the night, the Jew stands frozen to the spot as a bloody crucifix, the ultimate negation of self: 'I stood in the empty waste like a frozen tombstone with the cross of myself on it.'[33] The autobiographical self is crucified in this living death and literally stands as an icon of the crucified Jew. Very different from this incarnation of a symbol to be found by every roadside in Catholic Poland, and which instilled superstitious dread in Rabon's narrator as a child, is Babel's imaginative transformation of the crucifix into artistic metaphor.

Babel presents the crucified Jew through the art of an invented artist, Pan Apolek, a drunken Pole (derogatively *a polak* in Yiddish) who makes a living by painting church interiors and whose heretical views incur the wrath of the ecclesiastical authorities. A statue of Jesus, a bleeding, suffering, persecuted Polish *shtetl* Jew, in 'U sviatogo Valenta' ('At St Valentine's Church'), frightens a Cossack soldier in the Polish–Soviet war whose comrades and forbears have persecuted so many Jewish communities:

At the back of the uncovered niche, against the cloud-furrowed sky, there ran a bearded figure in an orange cloak, barefoot, with a torn and bleeding mouth. At that moment a hoarse cry pierced our ears. In disbelief we stepped back from the face of terror, the terror caught up with us and its dead fingers probed our hearts. I saw hatred pursuing the man in the orange cloak and an unseen mob catching up with him. He was warding off a blow with his hand, from which flowed a purple stream of blood. The Cossack standing next to me shouted and, lowering his head, started to run away, but there was nothing to run away from, for the figure in the niche was only Jesus Christ – the most extraordinary image of him I have ever seen in my life.

The saviour of Pan Ludomirsky was a curly-haired little Yid with a tousled beard and a low wrinkled forehead. His sunken cheeks were painted in carmine, his eyes were closed in pain and above them arched fine ginger eyebrows.[34]

This epiphany comes as part of a sacrilegious desecration by the Cossacks which recalls the Destruction of the Temple, a central image in Jewish martyrology and commemorative ritual, and it relates to the subtext in *Red Cavalry* of the cyclicity of Jewish suffering from Roman times to the present, at the hands of Khmelnitsky and Budyonny. The scene is based on the ransacking of a church, described in Babel's Diary, and its transformation tells us much about Babel's recognition of the power of myth to make supernatural or historical events relevant to the present day, an aesthetic concept which the author places at the centre of the art of that mythical myth-maker, Pan Apolek, and which is without doubt modelled on the masters of the Renaissance. The result is a new and unexpected historical perspective in which the historical is seen as real and the real as legendary.

Apolek realizes in ordinary folk, with all their human vices, their potential for spirituality and epic deeds. Above all Apolek brings out the aesthetic beauty of human flesh, which he colours like a 'tropical garden'. Lush and sensuous, Apolek's paintings beatify mundane existence as if mythical, while the mythical is revitalized to reveal hidden truths. Apolek's scenes of the Nativity resemble Babel's impressions of the religious paintings of Rembrandt, Murillo, and the Italian masters which he saw in a Polish

church in Beresteczko and described in an entry in his Diary
dated 7 August 1920:

wonderful Italian painting, pink priests rocking the infant Jesus, a
wonderful mysterious Christ, Rembrandt, a Madonna after Murillo or
perhaps a real Murillo, and the main thing is these saintly, well-fed
Jesuits, a weird Chinese figure behind the veil, in a raspberry cloak, a
bearded little Jew, the little store, the broken shrine, the figure of St
Valentine. The beadle trembles like a bird, cowers, mixes up his
Russian with Polish, I mustn't touch, he sobs. The beasts, they came to
ransack, it's so clear, the old gods are being destroyed.[35]

The hint at the pre-Christian and pagan origins of the Church in
the 'Chinese carved rosary' which the Novograd priest holds as
he blesses the infant Jesus in Apolek's painting is also clear here.

Aleksandr Flaker has tried to uncover the historical model for
Apolek's painting and has related it to baroque or rococo,
suggesting that Babel may have had in mind the erotic and
secular Madonna of Caravaggio, whose *Death of the Virgin* shocked
the Church. However, it might be pointed out that Caravaggio,
unlike Apolek, did no frescoes. Besides such innovations as
Caravaggio's *John the Baptist* and *Crucifixion of St Peter* and the
general desacralization of the Caravaggio school, Babel would
also have encountered the wandering baroque artists of the
eastern borderlands of the Rzeczpospolita. Murillo Madonnas
would have been imitated by local artists not only in the
seventeenth and beginning of the eighteenth centuries but also
well into the twentieth century. The Trinity Church at Beresteczko did indeed house the relics of St Valentine and contained
a copy of a Murillo; more interestingly, its murals and the
sculptural pieces around the altar were the work of the Vienna
artist Josef Pregtl in the middle of the eighteenth century.
Apparently his is the Bethlehem scene which Babel mentions,
transferring to the low baroque church in Novograd-Volynsk the
naivety and illusory light of the Beresteczko church.[36]

In the diary which Babel wrote while on the Polish-Soviet front
in 1920 and which served as raw material for the later *Red Cavalry*
stories there is no word of a Polish painter, but in the ruins of
Catholic churches and in the home of Leopold Tuzinkiewicz (the
priest of Beresteczko) with its ancient tomes and Latin manuscripts

Babel stumbles upon the Catholic mystery, which provides him, a Jew from Orthodox Russia, with a startling revelation.

The narrator of *Red Cavalry* first comes across the art of Pan Apolek in the story 'Pan Apolek'. In his introduction to the story the narrator takes vows to the aesthetic ideal of Apolek's art, a 'gospel hidden from the world', and writes with hindsight that the saintly life of Pan Apolek 'went to his head like old wine'; it later transpires that Apolek is a drunken heretic. The invented aesthetic model of the Polish painter expresses in characteristically visual imagery Babel's concept of art and history. It is an ideal, moreover, which awakens a sense of destiny and a sense of his own failings in the mind of the alienated Jewish intellectual torn between his roots in his doomed ancestral past and the Revolution. It is an ideal that juxtaposes the real and the ideal. The narrator chats to Apolek about the romantic past of the Polish gentry and about Luca della Robbia, the fifteenth-century sculptor who created a spiritual beauty in his church art, but the treatise on Apolek's artistic ideal ends with the narrator returning to the gruesome reality of his plundered Jews, lonely, homeless and filled with impossible idealism.

The first of Apolek's *chefs-d'oeuvre* to be exhibited is his portrait of St John. This is a portrait of St John the Baptist, for his head lies on a clay dish after his execution; but at the same time it is of St John the Apostle-Evangelist, for out of the mouth issues a snake, a reference to the legend in which a snake saved the Apostle's life by extracting the venom from a poisoned chalice. The dead St John's face seems familiar to the narrator and he has a presentiment of the truth: the severed head is drawn from Pan Romuald. Pan Romuald, we recall, was the treacherous viper of 'Kostyol v Novograde' ('The Novograd Church'), the runaway priest's assistant who was later shot as a spy. His venomous character is introduced in that story by the image of his cassock snaking its way through the dusk ('gde-to v zmeinom sumrake izvivalas' sutana monakha'), and his soul is merciless, like a cat's. Incidentally, the association of Romuald with the serpent and the cat makes him both the natural and the mythological enemy of Apollo the mouse god and slayer of the python. The monkish eunuch Romuald, like the ascetic yet decadent theology of the established Church (in which he would have become a bishop had he not been shot as a spy) stands in direct contrast to the aesthetic and doctrinal heresy of Apolek.

The narrator finds himself half-way towards solving the riddle of Apolek's iconography when he spots the Madonna hanging over the bed of Pani Eliza, the priest's housekeeper, for it is she who is portrayed as a rosy-cheeked Mary. Apolek first came to Novograd-Volynsk thirty years before, as the narrator relates in his apocryphal rendering of the coming of this questionably 'holy fool' who sparked off a long and bitter war with the established Church. Like Michelangelo in the Sistine Chapel, Apolek climbs along the walls of the Novograd church and paints into his frescoes a psychological, though ahistorical, truth. The lame convert Yanek is depicted as Paul – who is disabled with blindness in the story of his conversion (Acts 9, 1-19). The scene of the stoning of the adulteress (John 8, 3-11) is referred to as the stoning of Mary Magdalene, who is appropriately depicted as the Jewish prostitute Elka, for all three are 'fallen women'. Apolek's heresy is to elevate ordinary folk into mythical heroes with the haloes of saints, while bringing the divine, supernatural myths to the level of comprehension of mortals. In the same way that Renaissance painters flattered their patrons, Apolek wins a smile and a glass of cognac from the old priest who recognizes himself among the Magi, and he peoples the homes of the local population with peasant Josephs and Marys. For an extra ten zloty their enemy can be depicted as Judas Iscariot. Apolek even offers to paint the narrator as St Francis of Assisi, with a dove or a goldfinch on his sleeve, an ironical indirect reference to the horse's head insignia on the sleeve of the narrator's Red Cavalry uniform.

Apolek's reweaving of the Gospel stories transposes the sacred and the profane, rendering the supernatural grotesquely earthy and the everyday almost super-human. As the fence and cemetery watchman Witold declares in Apolek's defence to the church dignitary investigating the local outbreak of blasphemy, Apolek's art conveys to the sinful, ignorant masses the sort of truth which was as unpalatable to the authorities at the time of the Gospels as it is now. And is there not more truth, he asks, in Apolek's paintings, which ennoble the spectator, who is also depicted as participating in them, than in the angry and condescending words of the clergy? Italian prelates and Polish priests, it would seem, are not at all out of place in nativity scenes set in the Renaissance, painted in the 1890s and viewed by the narrator in 1920 when the Roman Church was being sacked by Slav hordes. However, this is only one side of Babel's art of contrasts; the other side is much darker, with corpses strewn among the thirsty roses and death waiting in ambush.

The readings of the Gospels are irreverent and ironic, since, unlike Bely or Blok for whom the Revolution was a new Calvary, Babel would not have been able to see a transfiguration scene on the Polish front in Russian and Christian terms. The crucifix remains for him an antipathetic sexual symbol, as it is in 'Guy de Maupassant' (1920–2, first published 1932). In this story the assimilated Jewess Raisa appears as the most seductive crucifix ever, against a decadent setting of Roerich paintings and Slavic-style carved furniture. Yet the narrator finds that in the Christian tradition sex brings morbid guilt and fear of mortality, as exemplified by the complexes of Tolstoy and the fate of Maupassant. The semen-oozing seductive crucifixes of the decadent Polish Catholic Church, described in 'Church at Novograd', corrupt young virgins. In a poetic Communion which neatly inverts the blood libel, the narrator tastes crucifixion in Pani Eliza's biscuits and senses treachery among the Jesuits. Besides the priest's love letters, the Bolshevik search party finds a hidden cache of gold.

By contrast, Jesus is portrayed as an unmessianic, earthly figure, as aesthetically sensual and human as the 'winking Madonnas' are ascetic and inhuman. Apolek's parable of Jesus and Deborah, in 'Pan Apolek', demonstrates Babel's love of the apocryphal. Apolek not only demythicizes Jesus, but rewrites the Gospels, relating that the wedding night of the Israelite virgin Deborah ended in tears of shame when she took fright at her approaching bridegroom and vomited. Jesus takes pity on her by dressing in the clothes of her bridegroom, just as it is Jesus who sends the angel Alfred to Arina in 'Iisusov grekh' ('The Sin of Jesus', first published as early as 1921).[37] The all-embracing love of Jesus in Apolek's parable is specifically a union of the flesh. Lying in adultery with Deborah, Jesus proves his compassion more just than the law. When the drunken Apolek credits him with a bastard son, who was hidden by the Church, Christianity is exposed as a pagan mystery religion predating Jesus, its gospels a lie. Deborah is Hebrew for a bee, and it is the 'pchela skorbi' (bee of sorrow) which stings Jesus: 'A deathly sweat broke out over his body, and the bee of sorrow stung his heart.'[38] Stung by post-coital remorse, Jesus leaves unnoticed to join John in the desert. The sacrilegious confusion of the Wedding at Cana, the description of the messiah as a 'bridegroom', the scene in the Garden of Gethsemane and other episodes in the Gospels may be compared to Marc Chagall's irreverent uses of Christian themes such as the Madonna and Child.[39] John Donne had given an erotic reading of the Passion in his love lyrics and 'Holy Sonnets', as had Shelley in 'Epipsychidion', and modern writers have played on the meanings of passion and Passion in metaphors of the writer and the writing act. However, Babel's travesty sounds sceptically Jewish in its literal reading of the Christian myths as *boba-maises* (old wives' tales).

The bee may hint at the deadliness of human passion if we compare the bestial desire of Dvoira, the Yiddish form of Deborah, who drags off the bridegroom at the end of 'Korol'' ('The King', 1921) looking at him like a cat holding a mouse. However, the bee also figures prominently in Afonka Bida's parable of the crucifixion in 'Put' v Brody' ('The Road to Brody'). The bee, who is by extension of the Christian virtue of industriousness essentially a proletarian creature, refuses to sting Jesus on the cross out of class solidarity, for Jesus came from a carpenter's family. The context, of course, is ironic, as the narrator is mourning the Cossacks' destruction of the Volhynian beehives and the 'daily atrocities' committed by the soldiers. It has been suggested by Zsuzsa Hetényi that Afonka Bida's parable of the bee and of the drunken Cossack officer anticipates the death of his own horse, whose head is described as crucified ('raspiataia').[40] Ironically, too, the Jews in the synagogue scene in Babel's play *Zakat* (*Sunset*, 1928) are stung by the bee of grace ('pchela blagodati').

The propensity for suffering and compassion are the attributes of Jesus which are brought out in the syphilitic shepherd Sashka Koniaev, whose meekness earns him the nickname 'The Christ'.

It is by explicitly sexual compassion and an earthy acceptance of sin that Sashka, like Jesus in Apolek's parable, becomes himself something of a Jesus figure. His stepfather Tarakanych is a carpenter, like Mary's husband Joseph. Sashka begs his stepfather to be allowed to become a shepherd, because 'all the saints' were shepherds, but Tarakanych mocks the idea of a saint with syphilis. That night Sashka has a vision from heaven in which he sees himself in a rosewood cradle hanging from the sky on two silver cords. A syphilitic Russian peasant, he too has aspirations to be supernaturally born. There is, however, an implicit irony in Sashka's exchange of his mother's sexual purity for permission to join the shepherds.

Babel's appropriation and subversive retelling of Christian myth reorientates it to the perspective of Russia in war and revolution, to the brutality of the Cossack and Russian masses. Bolshevik propaganda did portray the heroes of the Revolution as modern saints, but we cannot be sure how to take the presentation of Cossack soldiers as New Testament apostles – Zsusza Hetényi counts twelve of them in *Red Cavalry*.[41] For example, Matvei Pavlichenko, whose rather unsaintly *zhizneopisan'e* (hagiography) is related in *Red Cavalry*, differs from his patron saint in not listening to Jesus' teaching about turning the other cheek (Matthew 5, 38–9). His cheek burns with personal as well as revolutionary vengeance and in retribution he tramples his former master to death.

At the same time, the crucifixion held a grotesque aesthetic attraction for Babel. In the 1918 sketch for Gorky's newspaper *Novaia zhizn'* , 'Mozaika' ('Mosaic') a crucified Jesus rises in the sky lit by electric lamps, and the raspberry glimmer of the icon in 'Sviateishii patriarkh' ('The Holy Patriarch', another *Novaia zhizn'* piece of that year) similarly fascinates the Jewish outsider in Revolutionary Russia where all icons were being turned upside down and converted to Communism, as they are in the story 'Konets sviatogo Ipatiia' ('The End of St Hypatius', 1924).

The comparison between the imagery of Babel and that of Chagall is striking in the reversal of the colours of the sky and grass in 'Beresteczko', but more remarkable is the comparison between their use of artistic language to depict a barely recognizable, carnivalized world turned upside down by pogrom and revolution, as Chagall depicted it in his later *Revolution* (1937):[42] a world in which the Jewish intellectual found himself uprooted and homeless, caught between conflicting values and loyalties. In Chagall's *The Holy Coachman* (1911–12) the central figure is rotated on an axis that alternately inverts Jewish and Christian space, the cross and Yiddish writing. *Self-Portrait With Seven Fingers* (1912–13) (Figure 8) dramatically expresses the artistic self's conflict between, on the one hand, the picturesque, whimsical memories of Vitebsk's Russian church and its anecdotal Jewish characters, their precarious existence suspended in the air, and, on the other hand, Paris, modernist city of light and art, framed with the Eiffel Tower in the window behind him. The picture on the easel is Chagall's own *To Russia, Asses and Others* (1911–12) and incorporated into the painting is the Yiddish text 'Russia-Paris'. Chagall rebuts interpretation of what he terms plastic elements and cubist-like use of pictorial space, but his evasions here and elsewhere are disingenuous considering his confirmation of the autobiographical intertext of his fantasies.[43]

The geographical question-mark in this painting echoes the one in Lissitzky's illustration of Ehrenburg's 'The Steam-Ship Ticket' in his 'Six Tales about Easy Endings ' (1926) (Figure 9). The Jewish avant-garde artist is pulled between the dying Jewish community in Russia and the modernity of America, where Lissitzky's father had emigrated, only to be called back by his wife who had decided not to join him after taking rabbinical advice. The superimposed hand is cabbalistic but also the artist's own; the Hebrew RIP stands for Lissitzky's own art (an idiosyncratic acronym for ProuN – the Project for the Affirmation of the New).[44] The hand and the eye, both cabbalistic amulets, also figure at the centre of Lissitzky's *Self-Portrait: The Constructor* (1924), a splendid example of Jewish motifs in constructivist language at the intersection of autobiography and ideology after the artist had apparently incorporated communist ideology into his poetics. Photomontage dismantles and reconstructs values and hierarchies,[45] but the statement made in this case is fundamentally ambiguous about the identity and status of the artist's self (the

Figure 8.   Marc Chagall, *Self-Portrait with Seven Fingers*, 1912-13.

hand and eye of the artist) in the utopian space of the technological and revolutionary future.

If we compare the different versions of the lithographs Lissitzky did in 1917 and 1919 for the *Khad Gadya* series (Figures 10 and 11) we can see the changing metaphorical meaning given to the Revolution in this allegorical tale of Jewish history sung at the close of the retelling of the Exodus in the Passover Haggadah.

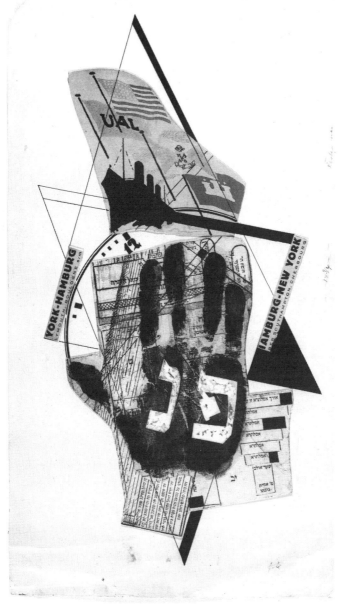

Figure 9.   El Lissitzky, illustration for 'The Steamship Ticket' in Ilia
Ehrenburg's 'Six Stories about Easy Endings', 1922.

Figure 10.   El Lissitzky, illustration for *Khad Gadya* No. 10, 1917.

The song, an Aramaic 'House that Jack Built', describes how God vanquishes the destructive forces of history, killing the Angel of Death himself in the final redemption. In the 1917 version the Angel of Death is dying, as the Tsarist reactionarism and pogroms come to an end; but two years later, in a fundamentally constructionist revamping of the drawing, the Angel of Death is

Figure 11.   El Lissitzky, illustration for *Khad Gadya* No. 10, 1919.

dead, as the Bolsheviks have won victory.[46] Haia Friedberg points to the resemblance of the Divine hand in *Khad Gadya* to the hand of the Revolution breaking the chains of slavery and oppression on Soviet stamps, as well as to Lissitzky's dressing the Angel of Death in Russian folklore depiction of the Tsarist crown, and comments, 'Lissitzky tries to persuade the Jewish public of the justice of the communist way by using traditional language, symbols and characteristic Jewish values.'[47] The Revolution promised not just redemption but also retribution for past persecution, as hinted in Lissitzky's famous poster, *Beat the Whites with the Red Wedge*, which reverses the Black Hundred slogan 'Beat the Jews and Save Russia'.[48] However, in the text from Ezekiel in Chagall's 1917 painting of the Jewish cemetery the artist cast doubt on immediate redemption of the burial ground of Russian Jewry. Babel's miniature pen-portrait of a typical East European Jewish cemetery ('The Cemetery at Kozin', 1923) with its traditional symbols and verse eulogies likewise speaks of the unredeemed wandering Jews ('Beduin') in a relentless cycle of unavenged pogroms from Bogdan Khmelnitsky to the present day:

To one side, under an oak tree struck by lightning, stands the tomb of rebbe Azriel, killed by Bogdan Khmelnitsky's Cossacks. Four generations lie in this sepulchre, poorer than a water-carrier's hovel, and the inscriptions, green with mould, sing of them in a Beduin's eloquent prayer.

> 'Azriel, son of Ananias, mouth of God.
> Elijah, son of Azriel, a brain that combatted
>   oblivion.
> Wolf, son of Elijah, a prince taken from Torah study
>   in his nineteenth spring.
> Judah, son of Wolf, Rabbi of Cracow and Prague.
> O, death, o covetous one, o greedy thief, why did
>   you not spare us just once?'[49]

This elegy for Russian Jewry echoes the rhetorical question of the pregnant Jewess at the end of 'Crossing the Zbrucz': why has death not once spared the Jews?

Chagall's Russian churches and crosses, like Babel's use of the icon and the figure of Jesus, give a remarkable and unexpected illustration of modernist responses to war and revolution by the Russian Jew in search of art, self and identity. Immersed in West European culture, the Jewish intellectual rediscovered Jewish roots and had to reassess the future of Jews in Russia in the perspective of the pogroms, in particular the mass killings of 1918–19. Nowhere is that inner turmoil more extreme than in what Roskies (in a phrase once applied to Beckett) has termed the 'cruci-fictions' painted against the background of war and revolution by Babel and Rabon, Chagall and Rybak, Hazaz and Greenberg, Halpern and Markish, Asch and Shapiro.[50]

CHAPTER 3

The Jewishness of Babel

Who was Babel? Where did he come from? He was an accident. We are all such accidents. We do not make up history and culture. We simply appear, not by our own choice. We make what we can of our condition with the means available. We must accept the mixture as we find it – the impurity of it, the tragedy of it, the hope of it.

Saul Bellow

A JEW ON HORSEBACK

Simon Markish has called Babel a fount of Russian-Jewish literature in the Soviet period,[1] yet Babel's prose style is easily distinguishable from the censorious tone of earlier Russian-Jewish authors, such as Osip Rabinovich. Their dual position, divorced from Jewish cultural sources yet addressing themselves to a Jewish readership, negating a Jewish voice yet not totally accepted in Russian literature, was already felt to be untenable by the 1880s.[2] For Babel Russian was not a conscious choice, but the natural environment in which he had grown up. No doubt because he had never had to make a choice he was not estranged from Yiddish.

If Babel refers in any way to Russian-Jewish literature he does so ironically. In a 1916 sketch, 'Deviat'' ('The Nine'), one of the characters awaiting the editors' beneficence is the Jew Korb who suffers from pains in the head as a result of wounds sustained during a pogrom. During the First World War he joined the Foreign Legion and was evacuated back to Russia after being wounded. Now he has written a drama which begins 'Ring the

71

bells, Judea has perished!' The only Russian-Jewish author praised by Babel (in a conversation reported in Konstantin Paustovsky's memoirs) is the émigré satirist Sasha Cherny.[3]

It was pointed out in Babel's own day that what was of anecdotal or ethnographic significance in Russian-Jewish literature was transformed by Babel into an expressive, convincing work of art of wide appeal. Babel was acclaimed as the first Jewish writer to write from *within* Russian literature and to give the Jewish milieu colour and depth.[4] Russian-Jewish literature boasted no Heine, and one could scarcely measure its writers on the same scale as the Yiddish masters Mendele Moikher-Sforim (usually known simply as Mendele), Sholom Aleichem or Y. L. Perets; whereas, in the opinion of at least one contemporary critic, Babel and other Soviet Jews writing in Russian could aspire to the class of Turgenev and Tolstoy.[5] Babel might be regarded as no different from other assimilated European Jewish writers like Leon Feuchtwanger and Max Brod for whom 'the Man on Horseback ... is more vital than the student, the rabbi ...'.[6] In his day Babel was cited as an example of a 'true product of fire and sword'.[7] However, the image of Babel as a Jew on horseback who celebrates the Jew as a man of action, empowered by the Revolution and free of inhibitions about violence is, as we shall see, far from accurate; but it is true that the Jewish tough guys had already made their way into Jewish literature (as in stories by Sholem Asch and Khaim Nakhman Bialik), and in Babel's Odessa stories the gangsters belong unashamedly to the Jewish world, as does Liubka the Cossack, nicknamed 'the Cossack' in Yiddish for her unmotherly and rough behaviour. The Odessa Jewish underworld had already made an appearance in Semyon Yushkevich's *Leon Drei* (1908),[8] but the new generation's revolt against the patriarchal magnate's philistinism and his imperviousness to the suffering of fellow Jews in Yushkevich's drama *Korol'* ('The King', 1908) provides a useful contrast with the rebellion of Benia 'The King' against the vulgar, cruel regime of his father Mendel 'The Pogrom' in Babel's play *Zakat* (*Sunset*, 1928), if only because the old Odessa was already a matter of nostalgia for a dead past, and the Revolution had swept away traditional Jewish life along with the old order.

Though at first glance it might be taken as a typical statement by an assimilated self-hating Jew, Isaak Babel's 'Avtobiografiia' ('Autobiography') is a brilliant piece of mystification which claims suitable Soviet credentials for the writer, for example giving the false impression that it was Gorky who first published him, or insinuating that he only learned Hebrew and Talmud 'at his father's insistence'.[9] Already in his literary manifesto of 1916, 'Odessa', Babel had questioned the primacy of Gorky and had prophesied that Russia's literary messiah would be a Maupassant from Odessa who would overcome the fog of Gogol's Petersburg and the mist of Turgenev's country estate.[10] Being an Odessa Jew Babel could easily accommodate Maupassant and modernism, Chekhov and Sholom Aleichem. There is a touch of Tolstoyan wisdom in some of Babel's Cossacks, and Gorky compared them to the Cossacks in Gogol's *Taras Bul'ba*. Babel's admiration for Tolstoyan realism is reflected in some of his less flamboyant pages. The grotesque imagery of Gogol's Petersburg Tales mingles with the hyperbole of Yiddish folk humour. But it is to Yehuda Halevi, one of the great figures of the Golden Age of Hebrew poetry in medieval Spain, a time of fertile symbiosis of Jewish and Arabic philosophy and culture now being reevaluated in the Hebrew literary revival, to whom Babel refers in 'Doroga' ('The Journey', 1932). This is a story of the Jewish narrator's archetypal journey of flight from embattled Kiev, through the gauntlet of vicious partisans looking for Commissars and Jews, to the eerie nightmare of the capital, St Petersburg. Yehuda Halevi had lamented that he was in the West while his heart was in the East; but he was killed, according to legend, at the portals of Jerusalem. Unlike the Jewish teacher Yehuda, killed on the train, and the Hebrew poet Yehuda, Babel's narrator gets to the Promised Land of Bolshevik headquarters and joins the Cheka: he arrives in both senses of the word. But the cliché ending belies any surety that the new Jew who enjoys some of the power stripped from his former oppressors will be truly happy or will succeed in the symbiosis of his two cultures.[11]

Whatever ambivalence or disquiet Babel may have felt about the future of a writer in the Soviet Union, he could not possibly have resigned himself to becoming a taxi-driver in Paris, where his first wife had lived since 1925. There Babel's daughter Nathalie was born in July 1929. Babel lived in Paris in 1927–8. He thought émigré literature sterile, the only exception being Vladimir Nabokov, whose writings seemed to him to be 'about nothing'.[12] Babel could hardly be expected to find sympathy for monarchist and anti-Semitic periodicals, and he pitied Chaliapin, Bunin and Kuprin for the depths to which they had been reduced. Nor were Western publishing houses any more sympathetic to his laborious and uncompromising method of writing than was the Soviet system. He had hoped to bring his family back together again in Russia, but October 1928 found him alone in Kiev, arranging the affairs of his deceased father-in-law: 'I feel fine on my native soil. There's poverty here, much that is sad, but it is my material, my language – something that is of direct interest to me.'[13] The Russian language was Babel's native language, as English was to be for Saul Bellow and Philip Roth, but uniquely it was also a Jewish language with all the ensuing conflicts of Self and Other embedded in the word itself.

One reason for this can be found in Babel's biography and particularly his birth in Odessa, a cosmopolitan Russian port in the Ukraine, whose population consisted of a large proportion of Jews – over 34% according to the 1897 census. Babel's grandparents spoke Yiddish, and his parents also knew Yiddish, but they talked with their children in Russian. This is a familiar pattern of acculturation in a fairly assimilated middle-class Jewish family that was urbanized and aspired to social mobility. Isaak Babel was nevertheless and quite naturally tutored at home in Hebrew, Yiddish, the Bible and Talmud. From the age of six he was sent to *kheder,* and, according to his sister Meri, was keen on his Jewish studies. So Babel, though brought up speaking Russian, had a command of Yiddish as well as some knowledge of Hebrew.[14]

Odessa was a relatively new and modern city where traditional Judaism was less deep-rooted than in the *shtetl* and where the ideas of the *Haskalah* had found fertile ground in the second half of the nineteenth century.[15] The Odessa of the early twentieth century was an important cultural centre of East European Jewry. Here at one time or another the leading lights of the new modern

Jewish culture worked and published: Akhad Ha'am, Pinsker, Klausner, Jabotinsky, Bialik, Sholom Aleichem and Mendele. Babel met Mendele on several occasions before the death in 1917 of the 'grandfather' of Yiddish literature.[16] In later years Babel translated Sholom Aleichem into Russian, and in the twenties he wrote the sub-titles for Gricher's silent film adaptation of Sholom Aleichem's Menakhem Mendel stories, *Jewish Luck* (1925), starring Mikhoels, whose great friend and fan he was. His film script based on Sholom Aleichem's novel *Vagabond Stars* came out in 1926. We may believe that Sholom Aleichem always remained close to Babel's heart, despite the deprecatory preface to the published screenplay which was a defence against ideological attacks on such 'unsuitable' material.[17] In 1936 Babel was commissioned by the Soviet publishing house Academia to edit the works of Sholom Aleichem, whose stories he had previously edited in a two-volume translation by Semyon Hecht.[18] He spent many hours in his last years reading Yiddish and translating from Yiddish purely for pleasure. Babel, we know, often had to give up work on his own stories to undertake translating and editing work for financial reasons, but his devotion to Yiddish literature was genuine.

The break with tradition and the motif of escape from the stifling Jewish home into the outside world link the boy in Babel's series of Childhood stories and the intellectual in *Red Cavalry* with the romanticized heroes of *Haskalah* literature who were depicted as breaking out of the stifling restraints of the outdated Jewish home. However, after the pogroms and the disappointment of the 1905 Revolution, in spite of turning his back on the Jewish past and becoming 'Russian', the Jewish intellectual failed to be fully accepted in Russian society. In an ironic variation on the identity crisis discussed in Chapter 1, the assimilated Jewish intellectual in Babel's 'Gedali' returns nostalgically to the Jewish *shtetl* only to find it ruined, doomed, just as the life has gone out of the unchanging old Jews in Bialik's 'On My Return'. In 'Alone' or 'At the Threshold of the Studyhouse' there remained little but dark despair in traditional Judaism. Now the Bolshevik Revolution claimed the loyalty of the Russian-speaking Jew, for whom, after the destruction of *shtetl* life, there was no return and no way out.

Feuerberg's question in the title of his novella *Whither?* (1899) assumed new tragic proportions. Yet before the Revolution Bialik's 'In the City of Slaughter' and other poems on the pogroms had inspired Babel's generation with the flame of resistance and a new national pride. In 'Pervaia liubov'' ('First Love', 1925) Babel's ten-year-old narrator fantasizes that he is a member of a Jewish self-defence group during a pogrom. Being a Jew in his house and a man in the street is what makes Benia Krik king of the gangsters of Jewish Odessa. Not only can he sleep with a Russian woman and satisfy her, says Arye-Leib in 'How It Was Done in Odessa', but he also meets the Russian world on his own terms: the gangsters shoot back at the *pogromshchiki*. Babel's Odessa stories may seem a departure from conventional portrayals of the passive Jew, but the burly Jews in Sholem Asch's 'Kola Street' count among the antecedents of Babel's rough Odessa Jewish carters, not to mention Gnessin's 'The Fight', Shneour's 'Noah Fanderah' and Yitskhak Shinhar's 'Flesh and Blood'. The Jewish underworld had already been immortalized by Sholem Asch in *Motke the Thief*, by Yosef Opatoshu in *Romance of a Horse Thief* and later by Oyzer Varshavsky in *Smugglers*, not to mention Sholom Aleichem and Mendele. The positive Jewish hero who uses brawn as well as brain was a secular and modernist expression of national consciousness and the search for human dignity in Russia .

In marked contrast to other writers discussed in this book, Babel was probably active in Zionist groups[19] and worked for a Jewish welfare organization in Odessa.[20] His profound interest in the 'Jewish Question' can be seen in most of his stories and is evident in the first story known to us, 'Staryi Shloime' ('Old Shloime'), published in Kiev in 1913.[21] In this contribution to a regular column on the 'Jewish Question' a senile Jew chooses suicide rather than see his son convert and assimilate into Russian society under economic and social pressure following anti-Jewish measures. While there is no approbation of apostasy or assimilation, there is no hope for the future or a return to the Torah of Shloime's father. In Kiev Babel took a course in business studies from 1911, the year the Beilis blood-libel trial took place in that city, and he mixed with the *nouveaux-riches* of the assimilated Jewish intelligentsia whom he was to caricature in a later story,

'Guy de Maupassant'. At the home of Boris Gronfein, a business acquaintance of his father, Babel met his future wife Evgeniia, a painter, who shared his dedication to art and West European culture. She no doubt took his Tolstoyan refusal to wear a coat in the thick of winter to be a passing bohemian fad; and his embarrassing tendency to gobble cream cakes in public might have seemed far less shocking than the behaviour of avant-garde artists who dressed and behaved to shock public taste.[22] But later it became apparent how incompatible was Babel's mischievous humour, his love of secrecy and of wandering, with her love of art and of comfort.

On the outbreak of war the institute in Kiev was evacuated and Babel continued his studies in Saratov, where he wrote the first or prototypal story in a series on Jewish childhood, which survives in a manuscript titled 'Detstvo. U babushki' ('Childhood. At Grandmother's', November 1915). The series was later conceived as a book entitled *Istoriia moei golubiatni* ('Story of My Dovecote'), which was not strictly autobiographical but freely used the facts of Babel's own life to present the estranged viewpoint of a boy growing up in a Jewish family in Russia before the Revolution. 'Childhood. At Grandmother's' powerfully conveys the constriction of the Jewish home and the boy's urge to escape. The tension becomes electric when the boy imagines the swish of Vladimir's whip striking Zinaida's cheek in Turgenev's *First Love*, which he has been reading to his illiterate grandmother who speaks only a broken Russian. The boy feels the erotic violence on his own body, a sexual as well as cultural violation of Jewish boundaries. The clarity of Turgenev's Russian prose, as well as the lure of Russian belonging and Russian nature outside the poverty of the Jewish home, are a recurrent opposition to Jewish space and Jewish language. In the later stories in the Childhood series, 'Probuzhdenie' ('Awakening', 1931) and again in 'Di Grasso' (1937), the world outside is the unfamiliar and coveted world of art. Babel becomes a writer by writing about the breakout into art and literature, but he does not stop being a Jew and can look ironically at the neuroses of the alienated Jewish intellectual.

In 1915 Babel moved to Petrograd and enrolled at the Psycho-

Neurological Institute, whose doors were open to Jews. According to surviving records, Babel was not involved in the revolutionary activities which went on there.[23] Although he liked his readers to think he hid from the police because he had no residence permit, this was not the case and he was living not uncomfortably with the family of a Jewish engineer called Slonim. In 'Ilia Isaakovich and Margarita Prokofevna' (1916), one of the sketches and stories he published in Petrograd periodicals at this time, Babel describes how an Odessa Jew dodges arrest for not possessing a residence permit by spending the night with another victim of the Tsarist system, the Russian prostitute Margarita Prokofevna. He teaches her his homely and optimistic Jewish outlook on life, his Tolstoyan belief that men are good but have been taught to do evil, and Margarita Prokofevna is so moved that she sees Hershkovich off at the station with a farewell gift of greasy pies. Jewish compassion shines through in a fragment of another story which Babel never finished, but on which he seems to have continued working after the Revolution. 'Three O'Clock in the Afternoon'[24] tells the story of a Russian priest whose son is imprisoned. The unlikely saviour of Father Ivan is his Jewish lease-holder Yankel. Babel appears to be saying that it is the self-confident Jew who has much to offer the Russian, and that inherent anti-Semitism and persecution will not daunt his spirit.

The Revolution seemed to offer opportunity to realize such hopes. On Babel's return in March 1918, after brief service on the Romanian front, to revolutionary Petrograd, he contributed to Gorky's anti-Bolshevik newspaper *Novaia zhizn'*. There is in these sketches of incompetence and negligence, of starvation and violence, a bitter irony mingled with a hopeful idealism. The opening of a maternity home, for example, gives rise to thoughts that will later be associated with Gedali: 'Slinging a rifle on your back and shooting each other may sometimes not be a bad idea', but it's not all there is to revolution and might not be revolution at all.[25] Babel does not declare any political allegiance, though one can surmise he was not far from the Menshevik position of *Novaia zhizn'*. He also published a Russian version of the Hershele Ostropoler story 'Shabos-Nakhamu'[26] in a Social-Revolutionary newspaper in which several other young intellectuals were writing, including Osip Mandelstam. In the Yiddish folk-tale the eighteenth-century Jewish prankster Hershele tricks an inn-keeper's wife into giving him a hearty meal by telling her he is 'Shabos Nakhamu', the Sabbath of Consolation following the annual period of mourning for the Destruction of the Temple, when the more hopeful chapters are read from Isaiah. In a later *Red Cavalry* story the narrator tells the Zhitomir rebbe he is putting Hershele's adventures into verse, to which the rebbe replies, 'the jackal whines when it is hungry, every fool has sufficient foolishness for despondency and only the wise man can tear the veil of being with his laughter.'[27] For Russian readers in starving Petrograd, who were probably as cold and hungry as Hershele proverbially was, the social and political analogy was not difficult to discern. For Jewish readers, the Yiddish story reminded them ironically of their own hopes regarding the Russian Revolution and provided a splendid example of Yiddish interference in Babel's Russian prose, whose subtext was often humorously at variance with the plain meaning of the Russian.[28]

A fellow Odessite, the Russian novelist Konstantin Paustovsky, attested to Babel's sensitivity to anti-Semitism by quoting him as saying, 'I didn't choose to be a Jew . . . I am a Jew, a Yid. At times I think I can understand everything. But one thing I will never understand and that's the reason for that filthy treachery which goes by the humdrum name of anti-Semitism.'[29] The short story 'Story of My Dovecote' (1925) records the painful impres-sion made by pogroms on the occasion of the 1905 Constitution. In the story which follows 'Story of My Dovecote', 'Pervaia liubov'' ('First Love'), the boy joins his parents, who are sheltering at the house of their Russian neighbours, but cannot resolve the contradiction between the reality of his father debasing himself in the mud before a Cossack officer, while his own portrait is thrown out of his father's store, and the fantasy of his passion for the Russian Galina. In early editions the father is named 'Babel', thus emphasizing the split identity in the portrayal of the narrator.[30] Babel defamiliarizes that 'humdrum name' in order to render all the more effective its inhuman brutality and stupidity, and that is why the word 'pogrom' is mentioned only at the end of 'Story of My Dovecote'. Babel was one of the few Jewish authors to portray pogroms in Russian after the Revolution, besides Mikhail Kozakov ('The Man Who Prostrated Himself', 1930), the children's author Lev Kassil (*Shvambraniia*, 1933) and Aleksei Svirsky (*Story of My Life*, 1935). In 1930 Babel's 'Story of My Dovecote' was still being coopted by official Party propaganda against anti-Semitism, but gradually any mention that anti-Semitism still existed in Soviet Russia was prohibited.

Although Babel told Michael Gold in Paris in 1935 that there was no longer a 'Jewish Question' in Russia,[31] this is not borne out by his published writing. His 'Story of My Dovecote' leaves an unforgettable impression of what it meant for a Jewish boy in Tsarist Russia to grow up into the adult world of sexuality and violent pogroms. 'The Journey' and 'Beresteczko' describe the atrocities of the Civil War period. Rather than presenting a Marxist standpoint and portraying the pogrom as the work of reactionaries, as does Valentin Kataev in 'Lone White Sail' or Nikolai Ostrovsky in *How the Steel Was Tempered*, Babel depicts the violence done to Jews before and after the Revolution as their natural lot. In 'Story of My Dovecote' the cripple Makarenko, seeing he is getting nothing but bonnets from the looting, strikes the Jewish boy, squashing his newly purchased doves, a Biblical symbol of peace and sacrifice. His rage is matched by Katiusha's venom: 'Their seed should be wiped out ... I can't stand their seed and their stinking men' (45). The trauma threatens Jewish and sexual identity; but it is a formative, cathartic experience in the maturation of the artist, as in that of the boy in Joyce's 'Araby'.

Like many secular Jews, Babel adhered to the humanitarian ideals and some traditional customs of Judaism, rather than to religious law. For him God had been officially de-deified in 1917, though he tried to buy *matzos* for Passover and sent greetings for the Jewish New Year to his family abroad. In a letter of 1935 he speaks of rediscovering God and praying for his mother's recovery from illness,[32] but the same day he was still joking about the 'former God' punishing him for leaving Odessa.[33] His attitude is summed up in a letter he wrote in 1938. It was time, he remarked, to forget Jewish ailments, bitter memories and anxieties: 'We must decorate our houses with gaiety not with *tsores* [troubles]. But how can one convince people of that?'[34]

Babel knew the sun had set on Russian Jewry. The sunset metaphor appears frequently in Babel's writings and nowhere more obviously than in the play *Zakat* (*Sunset*, 1928) which is based on an earlier short story of the same name. We recall that in Y. L. Perets's dramatic poem 'The Golden Chain' the Hasidic Rabbi Shloime wants to hold on to the Sabbath as long as he can, but his son restores the mundane order of this world; nevertheless, the hope for final redemption lives on. In Babel's play, Mendel Krik seeks to evade the sunset of his terrible reign and to cheat his sons Benia and Levka of their inheritance by selling his carter's business and running off to Bessarabia with the gentile Marusia. However, in the words of the local oracle, Rabbi Ben Zechariah, Mendel has repeated the 'mistake' of Joshua the Prophet, who 'stalled the setting of the sun' (Joshua 10, 12–15) and Jesus of Nazareth, who 'stole' the sun.[35] All his life Mendel wanted to bask in the midday sun, to delay the coming of the Sabbath at sunset: 'But God has policemen on every street, and Mendel had sons in his house. Policemen come and make order. A day is a day, evening is evening. Everything is in order, Jews. Let's drink a glass of vodka …!'[36] The inevitability of social and historical change – the play is set in 1913 – is emphasized by the allegory of King David, told by Arye-Leib, the *shames* (synagogue beadle), after the downfall of Mendel under a blood-red sunset. Mendel and David both faced attempts by their sons to usurp power; both strayed from the strict path of morality. As a parable of Mendel's story Arye-Leib tells of King David's rise to power, his wealth and fame, and of how he took Batsheva, the beautiful wife of Uriah the Hittite. The sunset of the Jewish world would be historically justified as a prelude to the messianic Sabbath, the utopian age of socialism, except that the argument is that history is cyclical and that Ecclesiastes was wise enough to know that there was nothing new under the sun.

Benia Krik is Ben Tsion, Son of Zion, and is modelled on the real-life gangster Misha Yaponchik, who helped to defend Odessa's Jews from the Whites but was afterwards killed by the Reds, as is Benia in Babel's film of the Odessa stories, *Benia Krik*

(1926). Benia is liquidated as a danger to the Revolution and the film ends with the revolutionaries poring over production plans. True, despite his mock-epic speech in 'How It Was Done in Odessa', in which he speaks of Joseph Muginshtein as a scapegoat for 'the whole working class', Benia the King institutes no new social order. However, the red dawn does not shine brightly in any of Babel's works, although the hope of a happy future for the new proletarian generation is voiced at the end of the play *Mariia* (published in 1935, but repressed while in rehearsal at the Moscow Vakhtangov and Jewish theatres). Babel's readers knew the Stalinist reality all too well. The exotic adventures of the Odessa gangsters gave way to melancholy for the old Odessa lost after the Revolution ('Froim Grach', 'End of the Old Folks' Home'). There was to be no place in the new order for the old, or for an independent Jewish response to the Revolution.

Themes of the Civil War and the ambivalence of the post-Revolutionary intellectual were topical in Russian literature in the early 1920s, as were underworld heroes. But Babel's stories, with their distinctive Jewish point of view, also dealt with issues that occupied contemporary Yiddish authors such as Dovid Bergelson, Der Nister, Perets Markish and Dovid Hofshtein of the Kiev group. Like Babel, they were attacked by the proletarian critics for lamenting too much the passing of the *shtetl* and not drawing uncritical portraits of 'positive' socialist heroes. Their acceptance of the Revolution was not unambivalent. Markish, Bergelson, Kvitko and Hofshtein left the USSR for a while, and their tragic fates during Stalin's last years put paid to the desperate hopes after October when East European Jewry lay devastated by war, revolution and pogroms.[37] Babel's stories were published by the Kiev Kultur-lige in 1925, though by then its originators had gone to Warsaw and it was infiltrated by communists.[38] A close friend of Dovid Bergelson after his return in 1933 from emigration, Babel translated Bergelson's New York story 'Giro Giro' and Bergelson translated Babel's play *Sunset* into Yiddish for the Moscow Jewish State Theatre (though it was apparently not performed.)

Babel was too much of an individualist to toe the line, and in the 1930s, although it became increasingly dangerous to keep silent, fewer and fewer of his works were published. He was never a Party member and, apart from the obligatory references to Stalin, was doubly cautious when making rare pronouncements on literary issues. He tried to legitimize his 'silence' by claiming that he was obediently studying the construction of socialism around Russia, and invoked the interests of the proletariat when defending a cultured, humanitarian position. Needless to say, Babel was under much pressure to sign denunciations during the purges,[39] but even after his arrest in May 1939 he quickly retracted the 'confession' extracted under torture which implicated some of his best friends in a 'writers' plot'. Certainly Babel was aware of the difficulty of publishing his own accounts of collectivization (only one part of *Velikaia Krinitsa* appeared), industrialization (in the lost story of a reformed gangster in the Donbass mines, *Kolia Topuz*) and Kabardino-Balkariia, whose leader Betal Kalmykov was purged, a fact that obviously forestalled any thought of stories in which he made a prominent appearance. The novella *Evreika* ('The Jewess'), on which Babel worked in the late 1920s, dealt with the final demise of the *shtetl* and it remained unpublished for many years. Like the Yiddish 'fellow travellers', Babel could not ignore the suffering and fate of the *shtetl* when depicting those who devoted their lives to socialist ideals. He did not give a full portrayal of a socialist hero, except for the steel-hard smith Baulin in 'Argamak', and he made clear the painful dilemma of the Jewish intellectual in post-Revolutionary Russia.

Unfortunately, the fact of Babel's Jewishness has been almost totally ignored by both critics and scholars.[40] Nevertheless, F. Levin, a Soviet scholar and critic, writes: 'Portraying Gedali, the Bratslaver rebbe Motele and other Jews, Babel conveys in their speech a specific blend of the style of the Talmud and the actual colloquial speech of the inhabitants of the Jewish *shtetl*, with its aphorisms and humour.'[41] Galina Belaia, writing after freedom of speech had been restored in post-Soviet Russia, sensed that 'Jewish culture determined a lot in his work: it is found in the epic-lyrical intonation of his stories, in the wealth of parable in his prose, in his tendency toward aphorism and euphemism, in the joyous, occasionally frank eroticism ... in the requirement that a person live in joy and avoid sadness'.[42] Likewise E. Dobrenko points to Hasidism as one pole in the cultural dialectic of *Red Cavalry*.[43]

Babel's stories sound Jewish partly because the exposition of the plot resembles a Talmudic discourse. This is how Arye-Leib tells his story: 'Arye-Leib began, as always, with allegories and parables that crept up from afar and towards an aim that not all could perceive' (301). Such is the tortuous, insidious path of Talmudic logic. A question is answered by another question. The object of analysis and eventual comprehension is isolated and the problems blocking the mind's way to full understanding are delineated and enumerated:

Let's talk about Benia Krik. Let's talk about his lightning beginning and his terrible end. Three black shadows block the paths of my imagination. There is the one-eyed Froim Grach. The russet steel of his deeds – can it really not bear comparison with the strength of the King? Here is Kolka Pakovsky. The simple-minded fury of that man contained everything necessary for him to wield power. And couldn't Khaim Drong make out the brilliance of a new rising star? Why then did Benia Krik alone climb to the top of the rope ladder, while all the rest were left swaying precariously on the lower rungs? (246)

However, Babel's laconic prose, the exuberant metaphors of the Odessa stories and *Red Cavalry* and the *joie de vivre* of his writing style are features characteristic of much modernist prose. Here is the outsider's acute awareness of language that T. W. Adorno has attributed to Heine and Steiner has attributed to Kafka. As an Odessite Babel was a natural cosmopolitan who might be placed among an entire group of Odessa writers who came to prominence in Moscow in the mid-twenties, though under Stalinist conformism the idea of a distinct Odessa voice in Soviet literature, represented by the satire of Ilf and Petrov or the verse of Bagritsky, Inber and Selvinsky, became heretical (Viktor Shklovsky was forced to recant after proclaiming a South-Western school). Rather, the 'Jewishness' of Babel's style can be explained by its unparalleled and unself-conscious reference to Jewishness and to Judaism, as well as by reference to Yiddish.

Benia Krik is surnamed *geshrei* ('yell') and he 'raises a yell' in

Odessa. When he addresses the mourners at the funeral of Yosef Muginshtein, the clerk shot by the gangsters in the stomach (as his Yiddish surname suggests), Benia 'the King' speaks from on high like Moses, complaining to God about the condition of Jews in Russia. In his eulogy he adapts a saying found in the Midrash (Bereshit Rabah): 'There are those who can drink wine and those who cannot drink wine', but adds, 'the former get pleasure from sorrow and joy, while the latter suffer for all those who don't know how to take their vodka' (254). He then leads the mourners to the fresh grave of Savely Butsis, rubbed out for being drunk on the job and shooting the poor clerk. Stylization of Yiddish speech resurrects a bygone age, and linguistic interference resists the destruction of History.[44] Like Bialik in Hebrew,[45] Babel naturalizes Yiddish in his Russian prose, playing on words and realizing idiom in anthropomorphisms, creating amusing resonance and ironic subtexts. Murray Baumgarten has applied to Babel the words of Michel Serres, 'Il faut lire interférence, comme interréférence'; in this case to introduce interference of a Jewish language and Jewish texts is to refer to a condemned culture.[46]

Babel's prose abounds in references and allusions to the Hebrew Bible, Prophets and later holy scriptures, to what George Steiner has called the 'textual homeland' of the Jewish world. Indeed, the Yiddish of East Europe is inconceivable without the intertextual references of scripture and Bible commentary, of Talmud and medieval poetry, even after militant communists decreed the de-Hebraicization of Yiddish. Arye-Leib, who expounded Rashi's standard commentary to the Song of Songs on a Soviet stage in 1928, might have been one of Sholom Aleichem's interlocutors. The humour is Yiddish in the Odessa stories. In texts that were worked on almost to perfection this can sometimes be sensed only in nuances of the subtext, but it is felt in the very style of Babel's Russian prose with its devices of repetition and refrain. A. B. Murphy sees Biblical overtones dominating even a story narrated by a Cossack, 'Sol'' ('Salt').[47] Stylization has the effect of evoking the epic, but it also on occasion draws attention to parable. By referring to myth and using it in a transferred or distorted sense the end result obtained is actually a *demythicization* of the often stereotyped Jewish world.[48]

Levka Krik, on leave from the Tsarist cavalry in the play *Sunset*, declares that a Jew who has mounted a horse has ceased to be a Jew and has become a Russian; but, for all their attraction to the open, gentile world of physicality and nature, the Jewishness of Babel's Jews is indispensable – unlike that of Levinson, the Jew on horseback in Fadeev's 'The Rout' (1927), or Libedinsky's Mindlov in *Commissars* (1926). The Russian classics tended to treat the Jew as little more than a mythical enemy, not as a real phenomenon of Russian life – though the picture is not all black, of course, as evidenced by the contributors to Gorky's *The Shield* and others who championed the Jewish cause in Tsarist Russia. Jews who were smugglers and who made rowdy scenes in taverns were indeed not unknown, but to take an example, Kuprin's treatment of Biblical motifs ('Shulamit') and of East European Jewry ('The Coward', 'A Wedding') lacked an inside view of Jewish life and Yiddish folk-lore. The *shtetl* is seen through the eyes of a Russian officer. The novelty of Babel's contribution to Russian literature was its very Jewishness. The stance of an outsider does not hide the attachment of Babel's Jewish narrators to the Jewish world they wish to abandon, and they do not find it so easy to break free from their Jewishness.

THE 'JEWISH COSSACK'

As a war correspondent attached to Budyonny's First Cavalry (*Pervaia konnaia armiia*) from May until September 1920, Babel adopted the pseudonym Liutov and passed himself off as a Russian. The name Liutov itself speaks for the ironic contrast between its connotation of fierceness in Russian and Babel's meek appearance. Babel found himself a Jew among Cossacks whose animosity toward the Jews was as awesome as their ferocity and horsemanship. If we now examine the conflict of Russian and Jew in the writer's identity, we will see how Babel came to form his image of the post-Revolutionary Jewish intellectual, torn between Judaism and Communism, alienated from his past and unable to come to terms with the future.

The legendary First Cavalry had been formed in November 1919 out of Cossack and peasant horsemen in the Red Army. Its command, under Semyon Mikhailovich Budyonny (1883–1973), grew out of Stalin's faction which had defied Trotsky at Tsaritsyn. After a phenomenal march through Makhno country of 750 miles in a month, the First Cavalry crossed the Dnieper on 6 May 1920, in time for the opening of the Soviet counter-offensive in the Ukraine.[49] Babel accompanied them as a war correspondent for the South Russia Telegraph Agency during the Polish campaign of summer 1920, but was apparently never a regular soldier in a combat unit. He talked with many Jewish local residents who had been subjected to pogroms and extortion under a number of occupying powers including Reds, Whites, Poles, supporters of Petliura, anarchists and peasant bands. Much of the fighting was waged in the heart of the former Pale of Settlement, territory disputed for centuries by Russians, Poles and Ukrainians. Yet, despite his assumed Russian identity, Babel's true sympathies for the victims of looting and pogroms are revealed in his Diary and in the articles he wrote for the front-line propaganda news-sheet, *Krasnyi kavalerist*.[50] His testimony is unusual for two reasons. First, Babel was a chance witness in areas under Bolshevik control (unlike for example, the members of the international investigating commission which had visited Poland in 1919). Second, Babel intended to use his experiences for literary purposes, and in the Diary which he kept he writes as an objective bystander, even though he himself records his deeply emotional affinity with his Jewish brethren.[51]

In 1921–1922 Babel was working on the drafts of stories about the First Cavalry[52] and in 1923 the completed stories began to appear in the Odessa Party newspaper *Izvestiia* and then in Moscow literary journals. They were later included in a controversial and extraordinary collection, *Konarmiia (Red Cavalry)*, which was published by the State Publishing House in Moscow in 1926. The published stories merge and transform the plotlines in the drafts and occasionally they revert to the material in the Diary. It seems that Babel returned to the Diary after abandoning about half the plots in the drafts,[53] despite his promises to his editor Dmitri Furmanov, author of the Civil War epic *Chapaev,* that he would introduce in the completed book more of the masses and militant communists.[54] A comparison of the Diary entries with the fictional stories helps explain the position of the diarist vis à vis the Cossacks, the local Jews and his own historical situation as a Jew.

Written by hand in an accounting book, Babel's 1920 Diary was preserved by friends in Kiev during his years of wandering and it thereby escaped confiscation with the rest of Babel's papers when he was arrested by the NKVD on 15 May 1939. It is clear from several instructions to himself to 'remember' or 'describe' that Babel had in mind a literary work which would be based on the material he recorded; there is no trace of the 'voennyi zhurnal' (military journal) which he mentions in the Diary. Some fragments and draft versions of short stories on Red Cavalry themes were written on pages torn from the Diary, so that the manuscript may be more complete than has previously been thought. In addition, pencil and red ink marks were made over Diary entries, probably at a later date, as part of the transfer of material to literary form. The Diary is written in elliptic phrases, aides-memoire not intended for publication, and its hurried style makes obvious that it was written during the campaign at the time of the events which it describes. Each entry is headed with a date, mostly also with a place name; however, it should be noted that the date and place given at the end of the stories in their early published versions, and retained in several cases in *Red Cavalry*, do not always relate to those in the Diary but were added to enhance the illusion of authenticity and the journal style of some of the stories.

The personal tone of the Diary conveys Babel's bitter cynicism from the first weeks of his stay in the First Red Cavalry, as well as his shrewd assessment of the military situation and of the behaviour of the Soviet rank and file. By September he is ill and hates the war. It is worth quoting at length from an unsent personal letter of mid-August 1920, found between the pages of the Diary, to get an idea of Babel's mood and his attitude to the Revolution, as well as to his writing:

Today's heading should read, Forest Clearing North-West of Starye Maidany. Since morning the divisional staff has been here in the forest with the squadron command ... For days on end we ride from one brigade to another, watch the fighting, compose dispatches, spend the night at ... [one word indecipherable] in the woods, run away from the aeroplanes which drop bombs on us. Above us are captivating skies, a cool sun, around us it smells of pine trees, hundreds of Steppe horses snort, this is where to live but all our thoughts are on killing. These words of mine sound trite, but war is actually sometimes beautiful, though in every case destructive.

I have gone through here two weeks of complete despair; this was because of the brutal cruelty which does not let up for a moment here and because of my clear realization of how unfit I am for the business of destruction, how difficult it is to wrench myself away from the old times, from ... [indecipherable]; from what was perhaps bad, but for me breathed with poetry like a hive with honey, I am going away now, but so what, – some will make the revolution, and I shall, I shall sing of what is to be found to one side, what is to be found deeper; I have felt that I can do this, and there will be a time and a place for this. ... [indecipherable] woke up, one hundred horsepower throbbing in my chest, I again start athinking and two demons, that is, two bombs which went off half-an-hour ago a hundred paces from us, cannot disturb me.

I often write to you but there is no answer, I live in tense anxiety, they say there are some letters and telegrams for me wandering around, that means trouble; with what close ties [here the MS breaks off].[55]

Although Babel was aware of the irreparable decay of the East European *shtetl*, these petty-bourgeois Jews were his 'kin' and he opened his heart to them (Diary, 5 July 1920). The first entry in the Diary mentions the pogrom by the Poles at Zhitomir, in which 43 Jews had perished and two were buried alive.[56] Babel suffered from no illusions that the Jewish population could expect any better treatment from the Cossacks:

The Zhitomir pogrom was initiated by the Poles, later, of course, by the Cossacks.

After the appearance of our advance guard the Poles came into the town for 3 days, Jewish pogrom, they cut off beards, that's usual, they assembled 45 Jews on the market square, they led them away to the cattle slaughterhouse, tortures, they cut off tongues, wailing all over the square. (Diary, 3 July 1920)

Babel had to travel quickly in order to catch up with the divisional command, owing to the rapid Soviet advance after the breakthrough of 5 June at Zhitomir, and he visited a number of

Jewish communities. On the way to Równe he spent the night in
Hoszcza. Despite the dissuasion of Russian soldiers Babel insisted
on staying with a Jewish family, the Ucheniks. Their six-year-old
daughter was not slow to guess their guest was a Jew and Babel
told them something of his family, saying he had a Jewish mother.
Throughout the campaign Babel tried to maintain the guise of a
Russian who did not understand Yiddish, though he realized his
Jewish hosts were not easily fooled, while his heart was bursting
from emotion at the plight of his brethren. The Jews' apprehen-
sions are justified: the soldiers' intentions are clear towards the
women of the house and Hoszcza is pillaged in the dead silence of
night, 'chistaia rabota' (a professional job). Not even crying can
be heard (Diary, 5 July 1920).[57] Eavesdropping on a Jewish family
in Równe after the arrival of a Cossack brigade, Babel hears of
the robberies committed by Budyonny's men (Diary, 6 July 1920).
A number of Jews believed that their livelihood was threatened
by Soviet restrictions on free trade, an understandable fear
considering the precarious economic structure of *shtetl* life, and
Babel noticed the pervasive fear of rape and requisitions.

Support for the Bolsheviks is found only among the Jewish
youth (a column of Jewish 'midgets' appears in the drafts and we
recall the Jewish *ataman* with the face of a Talmud student in
'Afonka Bida'); the old Jews are indifferent. The local Jews are,
however, oriented toward Russian culture and have little love for
the Poles, especially after the recent pogroms. Babel quotes the
saying that it is better to starve under the Bolsheviks than eat
white bread under the Poles. It should be remembered that
joining the Reds afforded a chance of revenge for the pogroms
and that the Bolsheviks had overturned the old order responsible
for Jewish suffering, promising a new social justice for all.

The general picture in the Diary of the destruction of a once
bountiful Jewish life full of tradition is confirmed by Babel's visit
to Brody (30 July 1920, 31 July 1920). After the successful Polish
defence of Warsaw – the 'Miracle on the Vistula' – there is little
change in the picture; at Laszków Babel hears the 'usual stories'
of the degradation of rabbis (9 August 1920). In the four-hundred-
year-old *shtetl* of Korec Babel finds the synagogues and other
buildings in ruins. The graves give mute testimony to the Jews

who fell in the First World War. No atrocities are recorded here, although the Cossacks empty a local store (21 July 1920). Dubno passes from hand to hand in July 1920, but does not seem to Babel to have been the scene of looting; on his arrival there, however, he finds the synagogues wrecked (23 July 1920). At Sokal' (26 August 1920) Babel is witness to organized looting but he finds time to visit the local synagogues, observing the two-hundred-year dispute between Hasidim and the anti-Hasidic *mitnagdim*, between followers of the Husiatyn and Belz rebbes (the latter had fled to Vienna). The dispute is featured in the story 'Eskadronnyi Trunov' ('Squadron Commander Trunov') and it suggests to Babel the unchanging and unshakable traditional Jewish way of life that continues despite war and revolution.

In Demidowka the Red Cossacks force the local Jews to desecrate the Sabbath by digging potatoes. A Jewish dentist resists. The fact that it is the eve of the Fast of the Ninth of Av increases the tragedy in Babel's mind, for on this day Jews read the lament of Jeremiah and sit on the floor in mourning for the destruction of the Temple in Jerusalem; now they must relive that destruction:

Ninth of Av. An old woman sobs, sitting on the floor; her son, who adores his mother and says that he believes in God to make her feel good, sings in a pleasant tenor and explains the story of the Destruction of the Temple. The terrible words of the prophets – the people eat dung, the maidens dishonoured, the men killed, Israel destroyed, angry melancholy words. The lamp smokes, the old woman howls, the young man sings melodiously, girls in white stockings; outside the window is Demidowka, night, Cossacks, everything as it was when they were destroying the Temple. (24 July 1920)

The prophecies of Isaiah and Jeremiah have always been part of the Jewish response to national and communal calamities, commemorated on the Fast of Av by a liturgy of communal repentance and prayers for spiritual as well as historical redemption. The Destruction of Jerusalem was the archetypal paradigm of the catastrophes of Jewish history that renewed the meaning of the Ninth of Av, especially instances of martyrdom in the Crusades and the Khmelnitsky massacres; in fact, some Polish communities used to prepare for the Fast by reading Hannover's elegy for Khmelnitsky's victims, *Yeven metsulah*. In the First World War, just a few years before, Cossacks had pillaged and wrecked Jewish homes in these and adjacent areas of dense Jewish population. When An-sky toured Galicia in a Russian uniform as representative of the State Duma committee to aid war victims, the Destruction of Jerusalem was very much in his mind. At Sadgora in 1917 he found an icon placed in the Holy Ark of the synagogue, *tselem beheikhal* ('an idol in the sanctuary'), just as in the Talmudic narrative of the desecration of the Temple.[58] In Babel's drafts we read: 'Ninth of Av – Destruction of Jerusalem ... Lament of Jeremiah ... about the Ninth of Av – to structure [the story] on the correspondence of the prayers and what is on the other side of the wall.' Babel began writing a story about the *shtetl* of Demidowka which centred on the national tragedy of the Jews symbolized by the destruction of the Temple and the prophecy of Jeremiah, but he gave it up, apparently in favour of a more subtle approach that would not require a Jewish literary focus yet would retain the importance of the experience at Demidowka, whose centrality is indicated in a number of drafts on the subject.

The shift in focus is reflected in 'The Cemetery at Kozin', a brief miniature quoted at the end of the previous chapter, which is based on impressions in the Diary of overgrown Jewish cemeteries where the victims of Khmelnitsky were now joined by those of another Cossack hero, Budyonny: 'Everything is repeating itself; now this story – Poles – Cossacks – Jews – is being repeated with striking accuracy; what is new is Communism' (Diary, 18 July 1920). In the stories Babel stresses that nothing has changed for the three centuries of victims of Poles and Cossacks, but he does this surreptitiously, by flanking the description of the graves of the *unavenged* Jews in 'The Cemetery at Kozin' with two stories of horrifying Cossack vengeance.[59]

Babel makes no mention of the Bolshevik Party line, which discriminated between the Jewish bourgeoisie and the Jewish proletariat, and we know from other sources that often the Cossacks on the Bolshevik side made no such distinction.[60] In the stories 'Sol'' ('Salt') and 'Izmena' ('Treason') the Cossacks think of the Jews as non-fighting intellectuals; Balmashev goes as far as to

defend Trotsky (the Minister of War) from the charge of being a
'zhid' by identifying him as the son of the governor of Tambov
province who went over to the workers![61]

A Putilov worker sees little point in dragging prisoners along
only to put their lives into the hands of the convoys (Diary, 30
August 1920), and one may presume that these carters who
transported prisoners to headquarters for further investigation
meted out the sort of rough justice described in 'Ivany' ('The Two
Ivans'). One healthy prisoner was wounded by two bullets
without any provocation whatsoever (27 July 1920). Babel notes a
massacre of prisoners (17 August 1920) and records another
incident in which ten prisoners perished (30 August 1920). Drafts
entitled 'Ikh bylo deviat'' ('There Were Nine') and 'Ikh bylo
desiat'' ('There Were Ten') describe in detail the shooting of
Polish prisoners who had undressed before capture in order to
conceal the identity of their officers. A pitiful scene in 'There
Were Nine' is one in which a beaten Jewish prisoner, Adolf
Shulmeister, a Łódź shop-assistant, recognizes the narrator as a
fellow-Jew and begs for his life. The narrator tears himself away
with some difficulty:

He kept pressing up against my horse and stroked and caressed my boot
with trembling fingers. His leg had been broken with a rifle butt. It left a
thin trail of blood like that of a wounded dog, and sweat, glistening in
the sun bubbled on his cracked, yellowish bald pate.

'You are a *Jude*, sir!' he whispered, frantically fondling my stirrup. 'You
are – ' he squealed, the spittle dribbling from his mouth, and his whole
body convulsed with joy.

'Get back into line, Shulmeister!' I shouted at the Jew, and suddenly,
overcome by a deathly feeling of faintness, I began to slip from the
saddle and, choking, I said, 'How did you know?'

'You have that nice Jewish look about you,' he said in a shrill voice,
hopping on one leg and leaving the thin dog's trail behind him. 'That
nice Jewish look, sir.'

His fussing had a sense of death about it, and I had quite a job fending
him off. It took me some time to come to, as though I had had a
concussion.[62]

In the story 'Squadron Commander Trunov' the incident is incorporated into the more ironic context of the martyrdom of Trunov at the hands of American bomber pilots, while the narrator (who quotes Trotsky's orders not to shoot prisoners) cannot join him. More subtly, the raid on the beehives, mentioned in the Diary in connection with the massacre of prisoners, is transferred in *Red Cavalry* to 'Put' v Brody' ('The Road to Brody') where it introduces the unending litany of death and the 'chronicle of daily atrocities'.

The capture of an American pilot provided Babel with an indication of the anti-Semitic image of the Bolsheviks disseminated on the Polish side. The pilot, who had enlisted in the Kosciuszko Squadron of the Polish Air Force, pretended to be a Jew called Frank Mosher in the hope that he could thus enlist the sympathy of the Bolsheviks, who were thought to be predominantly Jews. The Soviet armies were virtually defenceless against the reconnaissance and bombing raids of the Polish aeroplanes, whose pilots included a group of Americans who had volunteered for an adventure in Poland rather than return home from the Western Front.[63] Babel, who was pretending *not* to be a Jew, interrogated the captured pilot, and displayed special interest in the pilot as a representative of Western culture. From him, and from a letter found on him written by Major Fauntleroy, Babel learned details of the unstable political situation in Poland and of the Poles' exaggerated idea of Bolshevik strength, as well as their belief in communist intentions to 'annihilate' (*sic!*) national minorities and their customs (14 July 1920). Nothing further is recorded of the American pilot in the Diary, but the planes of his commanding officer, Major Fauntleroy, are the ones in action in the story 'Squadron Commander Trunov'.

Babel considers Bolshevik propaganda to have a much greater effect on the Cossacks than the sentimental patriotic Polish appeals, and an unspecified number come over to the Soviet side (15 July 1920). However, the low level of understanding among the Cossacks of the aims of the Revolution is quite evident; but now that they have been organized by the Soviets they present a formidable sight, professional yet also bestially cruel. They regard the local population as a natural target for looting and they make use of the opportunity for unleashing their promiscuity. Babel regards the Cossacks as scavengers (he calls them 'barakhol'shchiki') and also remarks: 'A terrible truth – all the soldiers suffer from syphilis' (28 July 1920). The moan of peasants who have been robbed of their pigs and chickens or given emaciated nags in exchange for their healthy mounts (16 July 1920) is described in the story 'Nachal'nik konzapasa' ('The Remount Officer'). The Cossacks are not at all impressed, as they cross into Galicia, by the order from South-West Command which tells them to treat the local population well because they are not coming as a conquering army but in order to assist the Galician workers and peasants in the establishment of Soviet power (18 July 1920). A commissar warns Babel not to take anything from 'our region' during forced requisitioning in a Czech colony (12 July 1920); a commissar who remonstrates with soldiers in one of the drafts for the stories is met by obscene abuse from the soldiers who justify pillaging. Instead of Bolshevik 'salvation' the bewildered Jews are greeted by Cossack whips and shouts of 'zhidy'; they tell the 'usual stories' of pillage. They are, of course, not the only ones to suffer: horses and fodder are forcibly taken from peasants and Czech colonists. Babel sums up, 'Budyonny's men are bringing Communism, an old peasant woman cries' (14 July 1920).

On his visits to the Zhitomir rebbe or to Hasidic synagogues Babel ponders his own fate, and he has no illusions about the significance of the Revolution for the battered Jewish communities. By the end of August the Soviet forces are in retreat and Babel complains in his Diary of his illness and depression. The Jewish New Year finds him in Kiwercy, homesick, hungry and weary. He finds a Jewish housewife, a proverbial 'eshet khayil', Woman of Valour, who gives him bread: 'I am moved to tears; here only my tongue helped; we talked for a long time' (13 September 1920). 'My tongue' can equally be 'language', meaning Yiddish, the common tongue of the Odessa Jew and the *shtetl*, and this gives a clue to the conflict of self on the part of a Jew in a Revolution that was hastening the destruction of the *shtetl*.

It might be thought that Babel wished to become a Cossack and that this ridiculous form of self-hate explains the nonchalance towards Cossack acts of brutality in *Red Cavalry* and in such stories as 'First Love'. The Diary suggests a rather different conclusion. During the Polish campaign Babel was deeply interested in whatever remnants he could find in Poland of Western culture, whether in bookshops or the Catholic churches. However, his sympathy for the Jewish families with whom he billets overrides all other sentiments.[64] 'How everything strikes a chord in my heart,' he remarks in Zhitomir when he talks to local Jews, including a philosophic shopkeeper, who says of both Revolution and Counter-Revolution that each side pillages and who wishes that there was one government that was good (3 July 1920). This idealistic shopkeeper was to be the prototype of Gedali in the *Red Cavalry* story that bears his name, the imaginary founder of the Fourth International of Good People.

Babel's Diary represents anti-Jewish incidents as part of the lot of Russian Jewry, not just sporadic outbursts of anarchic elements or the inevitable effects of the war. The personal agony of the writer is unmistakable, for he was only too aware of the historical symbolism of the incursion of semi-literate, barbaric Cossacks to the heart of the former Jewish Pale of Settlement, to those same areas decimated by their heroic forbear Bogdan Khmelnitsky in 1648 and recently subjected to brutal pogroms by Ukrainians, Poles and other warring factions. This was not merely the 'back garden' of two armies, as might be thought from Budyonny's wrathful outburst of 1924 when he accused Babel of bawdy babbling about women's breasts in some kitchen in the rear.[65] Jews were a common enemy of Poles and Cossacks, an easy, defenceless target for quick retribution and an immediate outlet for low morale, as well as for the more corrupt and base instincts of the semi-literate professional Cossack soldiers, who did not usually share the ideological motivation of the foot-slogging revolutionary volunteers. Retribution against the Jewish population from all sides involved in the conflict was extraordinarily swift, even when fighting was still in progress. Zamość was the scene of a pogrom perpetrated during the battle for the town in the days from 30 August to 1 September 1920; it was to be described in the *Red Cavalry* story 'Zamość'. Dragged in his sleep by his horse to the front-line, the narrator can hear clearly the screams of the Jews in Zamość. A peasant soldier on the Soviet side comments approvingly to his visitor, whom he apparently takes for a Russian intellectual:

'Everything is the Jew's fault, for what has happened to us and to you. There will be a very small number of them left after the war. How many Jews are there in the world?'

'Ten million,' I replied and began to bridle my horse.

'There'll be two hundred thousand left,' the peasant shouted and touched my arm, afraid I might go away. But I managed to climb into the saddle and galloped to the place where staff headquarters were. (210)

During the Polish campaign Babel posed as a Russian, an identity which had come naturally during the Revolution when he wrote of 'our fighters' in Gorky's anti-Bolshevik *Novaia zhizn'* ('About the Horses') or presented himself as a Russian ('Finns'). But here he was among his own people, and it would not have been as natural for him to pretend to be a non-Jew as it was for Ehrenburg in *Viza vremeni* ('Visa of Time') to represent himself as Russian vis à vis the Polish Hasidim. These were his kith and kin (*rodnoe*), whereas among his comrades-in-arms, 'our lads' (*nashi*), he felt forever 'alien' ('ia chuzhoi,' he writes on 26 July 1920). Nevertheless he steeled himself to go through with the ordeal. After his horse went lame, for example, he chided himself for being 'too weak' (29 August 1920). Somehow he managed to stand by and watch defenceless Jews being harassed or mal-treated, 'And I am silent, because I am a Russian' (24 July 1920).

On entering the *shtetl*, Babel had warned himself to 'be on my guard' and had tried to restrain Prishchepa, a communist Cossack whose terrible vengeance on his home village is immorta-lized in the story bearing his name. Now Babel notes the pain of the situation in which he is an involuntary accomplice to the desecration of the Sabbath and – of all days – the Fast of Av: 'They all hate us and me' (24 July 1920). However, as he had done when his conscience was similarly affected three days previously during the ransacking of a Jewish shop in Korec, he told the poor tormented Jews yarns of the communist utopia ('nebylitsy o bol'shevizme', 24 July 1920). Babel applied what he

called 'the usual system' and his fantastic stories of a better future
were heard eagerly by the local Jews, whom Babel pitied for their
credulity (23 July 1920). He preferred to 'pour balm' (as he put it
in the Diary entry for 21 July) on the wounds of the pogrom
victims, telling them of the socialist utopia in Moscow, and he
apparently did nothing when Cossacks attacked Jews and prisoners, looted Jewish and other local property, or desecrated
synagogues and Polish churches.

If the avoidance of direct involvement was dictated by self-
preservation, in the *Red Cavalry* stories the observer's distancing of
self becomes an aesthetic device which exposes the brutality
natural to the Cossacks, as well as parodying the alienated Jewish
intellectual who thought he could live among them. The admiration for the Cossacks' professionalism contradicts the integrity of
the self who identifies with their Jewish victims. In the story called
'Beresteczko' the town is the setting for a callous execution 'for
spying' of an old Jew by Soviet Cossacks:

Right in front of my windows a few Cossacks were shooting an old
silver-bearded Jew for spying. The old man was wriggling and
screaming. Then Kudria from the machine-gun team grabbed his head
and hid it under his armpit. The Jew quietened down and spread his
legs. With his right hand Kudria drew a knife and carefully cut the old
man's throat, taking care not to splash himself. Then he knocked on the
shuttered window, 'If anyone's interested,' he said, 'they can come and
get him.' (168)

The narrator watches, apparently dispassionately, as the Cossacks
turn the corner, but the absence of comment underlines the
personal trauma akin to that of the boy in 'First Love' watching
his father's victimization by Cossacks in a pogrom. In both cases
our attention is diverted to the professional confidence of the
Cossacks. It could be that the fascination with the aesthetics of the
perpetrators conceals a repressed guilt for impotence in not
preventing a violent act which also threatens his own ethnic and
artistic identity. However, sufficient irony is contained in the
Cossacks' epic march from the nearby village of Chotin, past the
watchtower where Bogdan Khmelnitsky was routed by the Poles,
for us to notice the unspoken authorial message. The town greets
the 'heroes' with silent, barred windows, and at the end of the

story the pillaged Jewish burghers elect a Revolutionary Committee, which supposedly puts all power in their hands. The election is held in the garden of the castle of the mad Polish countess, a description based directly on the Diary entry, and, although the Diary does not record the execution, it confirms that the suspicion of espionage fell on the Jewish population with the entry of Soviet as well as Polish forces.

The Diary records that Babel could not help thinking seriously about his own destiny in view of what he experienced in Galicia (26 July 1920), but he nevertheless maintained his false identity even though he knew that the Cossacks would never accept him, an intellectual in spectacles and a Jew. Such deception raises serious questions concerning Babel's stance as a Jew and a writer.

To achieve artistic self-restraint can be both physically and psychologically dangerous. We know from the 1920 Diary and from his private correspondence of later years how much it exhausted Babel. Indeed, curiosity has been known to kill the cat, though in this case it gave birth to an *alter ego*, the fictional Liutov of the *Red Cavalry* stories. Liutov is a composite figure who was apparently added at a late stage of composition to embody a Jewish intellectual distinct from the authorial voice who adopts differing standpoints in relation to other protagonists. He appears most obviously in confrontation with the Cossacks in 'Squadron Commander Trunov' and during the retreat of the Bolshevik forces in 'Zamość' when he assaults his Polish landlady. Liutov can also be identified with the bespectacled law graduate in 'My First Goose', who is at first rejected by the Cossacks, and with the unnamed Jewish intellectual who yearns for his Jewish past in the ruined Jewish quarter of Zhitomir in 'Gedali' and 'The Rebbe'.

At the beginning of 'Gedali' the narrator sadly recalls his childhood when the Sabbath candles were kindled and his grandfather would read the Bible commentator Ibn Ezra: 'On these evenings my child's heart rocked like a little ship on enchanted waves.[66] Oh, the rotted Talmuds of my childhood! Oh, the heavy melancholy of memories!' (125). He wanders around the former market of Zhitomir – the thematic and biographic association with Bialik is striking – in search of a 'shy star' that marks the beginning of the Sabbath, a 'Jewish glass of tea' and a bit of that 'retired God' in the glass of tea.[67] The narrator's search brings him to the junk store of old Gedali who has witnessed the cruelty both of the Poles and the Bolsheviks. With Talmudic logic Gedali examines the warring camps, but neither offers him salvation. The Revolution cannot accommodate Jewish values: ' "To the Revolution we say 'yes', but are we to say 'no' to the Sabbath?" Thus Gedali begins and winds round me the silken straps of his smoky eyes. "Yes, I shout to the Revolution, yes, I shout, but the Revolution hides from Gedali and sends forth naught but shooting..." ' (126). The narrator retorts in Bolshevik propaganda slogans that the Revolution will open closed eyes and the story ends with the narrator returning to the brightly lit propaganda train. However, Gedali's eyes have been closed by *pogromshchiki*, not by ideological blindness or hostility to Communism. On the contrary, he believes in the coming of Messiah and universal justice, like all devout Jews who read Maimonides' Thirteen Principles daily. The 'straps' he winds around the narrator are the phylacteries which ought to bind him to Judaism and the Jewish people (a neat reversal of Chernikhovsky's iconoclastic image mentioned in Chapter 1). The straps are 'silken' rather than leather perhaps because Gedali is a *zadener mentsh*, a 'silken man', exceptionally learned, and Gedali's words recall those of Moses in Deuteronomy relating the redemption story of the Exodus from Egyptian bondage: 'And we all, learned people [*anashim nevonim*] we prostrate ourselves and cry out loud: woe to us, where is the sweet revolution?' (126). If the Revolution kills and requisitions private property (his gramophone, for example) then it cannot be the real revolution. Since Gedali is a petty-bourgeois shopkeeper who does not believe that pogroms are a symptom of the class struggle, he is an enemy of the Revolution, so that most commentators have failed to see that it is the Jewish communist who does not resolve the contradiction of violence and revolution, Jewish identity and Communism.

A similar dilemma was faced by many Jewish intellectuals who had forsaken Jewish life and pledged allegiance to the Revolution, but could not be totally indifferent to the destruction of the *shtetl* and its values. Nor could they ignore the bestial violence unleashed in the Revolution and Civil War or the common soldier's frequent ignorance of Marxism. It is not by chance that Babel's stories, including 'Gedali', were the only translations to be included in the short-lived Soviet Hebrew journal *Bereshit*.[68] The dilemma is presented by Babel with subtle irony. Gedali, who has studied the Talmud and loves Rashi and Maimonides, departs for the synagogue, a lone figure in the setting sun which symbolizes the end of the *shtetl*, but which also heralds the inauguration of the Sabbath – day of rest and foretaste of the messianic age. As he departs in the setting sun, Gedali dreams of an 'International of Good People' who will distribute first-class rations to all.

The subjective first-person narrator of 'Gedali' recalls his Jewish childhood when he wanders around Zhitomir on a Sabbath eve searching for symbols of the Jewish past and his own identity. He recalls his grandfather's yellow beard and the old woman's almost occult ritual of lighting candles. This typological model of ethnic-cultural identity places Judaism on an estranged distanced plane, a generation removed, coloured in an oppressive black and yellow melancholy, lifeless and doomed like the *rotted* Talmuds of the narrator's childhood. Yellow is the colour of the grandfather's beard which brushes the open pages of Ibn Ezra, the culture of the medieval Jewish past, and yellow are the 'indifferent' walls of the 'ancient' synagogue. The narrator's return to his grandparents' past continues as a search for that same point in time which began the story, the Sabbath eve, for the 'shy star' that will inaugurate the day of rest, a Jewish space of communal identity and belief. The search and the return culminate at sunset in the shop of a ridiculous old *shtetl* philosopher, a microcosm of the outdated values of the enclosed Jewish world and the impasse which it represents for the narrator. The spatial metaphors and the attributes, especially those of colour and smell, accruing to the enclosed areas underscore the recurrent typology of constriction and repulsion. Gedali's shop is hidden away in the tightly closed stalls of the dead town market. The shop is a 'labyrinth' of all kinds of useless junk and dead things, secluded from the real world and closer to the spirit of Dickens's *Old Curiosity Shop* than the present day. A hunter's rifle is dated 1810. Gedali is blind, his hands are white, his beard is narrow and grey;

he wears a black top hat and a green coat. There is a slight rotting smell.

Yet if the narrator enters Gedali's store armed with the hostile stereotypes of Judaism as repulsive, dying and confining, he soon encounters a revelation which undermines his position and questions his apparent non-identification with his Jewish brethren, a revelation foreshadowed in 'Crossing the Zbrucz' and here by the metaphorical and not so metaphorical blood of sunset. The narrator answers Gedali's complaint that the Revolution sends forth only shooting with a Party line retort that 'we' will rip open eyes that have closed to the sun. Yet in a whisper the old man reveals that his eyes were closed not by ideological error in blindness to the truth but by anti-Semitism in a pogrom, an event which identifies both Gedali and the narrator as Jews. The dialectic rages between the narrator and his Jewishness, between his writing 'I' and the collective 'we,' not between Gedali and the Revolution. The Revolution is supposed to bring justice to the world and it is dealing retribution to the anti-Semitic Pole, yet it requisitions Gedali's gramophone. Where then, asks Gedali, identifying himself with the culture of the narrator's grandfather, with Rashi and Maimonides, where is the just Revolution welcomed by God-fearing Jews? The narrator must awake to the irreconcilable contradiction between the violent Revolution and humane Judaism. As the sun sets over Zhitomir and over Jewry, the narrator turns to Gedali, the dreamer of a Fourth International and a believer in the messianic Sabbath, and he asks to share Jewish experience with him. But it is too late. The Jewish cake and the Jewish glass of tea, in which there is 'a little of that retired God', are not to be had. The ravages of war and revolution have devastated the Jewish population, long resigned to their tragic fate.

The Sabbath begins and Gedali departs for the synagogue alone, although the narrator will also go there as the bystander and detached observer of 'The Rebbe'. However, interposed between the two stories, 'Gedali' and 'The Rebbe', is 'My First Goose,' an ironic comment on the inability of the narrator to reconcile his Judaism with the hostile outside world of violence and maturity, war and revolution. The topology of 'My First

Goose' is consistent with the opposition between enclosed Judaism and the outer space of aspired acceptability. Savitsky, the Cossack commander, expresses the violence with which spatial barriers must be broken open when he does not simply stand in the middle of the hut but rather splits it in two. His *raspberry* hat links him with the men of action of the Odessa stories, the Jewish gangsters who sport raspberry waistcoats, while Savitsky's astonishing physicality and his explicitly feminine sexuality arouse the narrator's envy. The semi-literate Cossack does not rate very high the chances of the bespectacled intellectual's survival among the Cossacks ('specs get your throat cut around here'), and he consigns him to the quartermaster who warns the young Jew he will be accepted only if he breaks the Judaic humanitarian code: 'But you mess up a lady, the cleanest lady, then the boys will be kind to you' (130).

The road is round and yellow 'like a pumpkin', images of lifeless vegetation and alienation. The sun is dying. The first act of the Cossacks is to kick the intellectual's suitcase of manuscripts, his synecdochal identity, out of the courtyard, a transitory space between home and the non-bounded outside. In an obscenely offensive way one young Cossack disrupts his reading of Lenin's speech to the second congress of the Comintern. The narrator responds by taking up the quartermaster's challenge and symbolically raping a virgin: he abuses a fellow-victim, the bespectacled landlady, and defiles a *white*-necked goose. As I have noted elsewhere in my analysis of estrangement in this story,[69] he first takes someone else's (*chuzhoi*) sword and, lured by the homely smoke of the *unkosher* pork in the Cossacks' cooking-pot, he commits an act of violence in order to win the admiration of the Cossacks as well as acceptance into their ritual communion. Only then do they allow him to resume the role of intellectual and to read them Lenin's speech.

Yet despite the dreams of women and the warmth of the Cossacks' bodies, that might be interpreted as surrogate sexual fulfilment of the earlier envy of Savitsky, the narrator's Judaic conscience cannot be at peace with wanton killing. The contextual setting of maternal Nature, and the semantic as well as rhythmic repetition of the description of the killing of the goose, suggest that this 'first kill' has violated something within the narrator: 'Only my heart, crimson with killing, squealed and bled' (132). The tension between the past tense of the Jewish home (*svoi*) and the alluring outer space of the Cossacks (*chuzhoi*) creates a dramatic conflict in the estranged vision of the intellectual between what he is and what he cannot be.

'The Rebbe' opens with Gedali speaking of Hasidism as an immortal, if battered, building at the crossroads of history. Judaism, he is saying, will weather the storm. In the story 'The Rebbe' the narrator seems to have found his 'shy star', and Sabbath peace has descended on the crooked roofs of Zhitomir. The rebbe's room is stone-built and empty 'like a morgue' (in the Diary the surroundings were ordinary, bourgeois, and even spacious). The rebbe has a yellow beard and sits at his table surrounded by 'fools and madmen', attended by the eccentric deformed beggar, the ragged Reb Mordecai (details absent from the Diary). The imagery of constriction is reinforced by the sudden glimpse of the rebbe's son, Ilia Bratslavsky, a sort of recaptured fugitive from 'prison'. The messianic role of Ilia, which was mentioned in the previous chapter, is thwarted by images of emaciation and impotence: Ilia's face is compared with that of an emaciated nun, a simile with strong Christian associations as incongruous as the likening of the Jews to 'fishermen and apostles', while the attribute of impotence (*chakhloe*) links Ilia with the Jewish ataman in 'Afonka Bida'; later it describes the dying Ilia's genitals in 'Syn rabbi' ('The Rebbe's Son'). The New Testament allusion, Ilia's 'powerful forehead of Spinoza' and his desecration of the Sabbath clash with the rebbe's blessing (the Sabbath *kiddush*, normally pronounced over wine) which praises the Creator for singling out the Chosen People from all the nations.

The silent enclosedness of this doomed world is juxtaposed with the hostile noises of war outside, the wilderness beyond the window-frame: 'The desert of war yawned outside the window' (135). The window-frame is the imprisoning frame of the Jewish space threatened by the violent outdoor gentile world, by war and by anti-Semitism. The window is a framing device as well as a threshold between the hostile exterior, where the alienated Jew would like to belong, and the enclosed interior of Judaism where his sympathies secretly lie but from which he has attempted to sever his roots.

The narrator of 'The Rebbe' is the first to leave the rebbe's house and returns to his unfinished task of writing an article for *Krasnyi kavalerist*, the Russian propaganda newspaper. He returns to the bright lights and the machinery of the Propaganda Train, an antithesis of his Judaic heritage in imagery but also in cultural and linguistic values. The 'I' rejoins the collective, but he makes no friends or allies, apart from Grishchuk, a former prisoner-of-war and a fellow-victim. As becomes apparent in 'Smert' Dolgushova' ('Death of Dolgushov') and 'Posle boia' ('After the Battle'), he fails to acquire the Cossacks' 'simplest of abilities': to kill. Here Babel might be mocking Tolstoyan non-resistance, but the ability to kill can be simple only for the Cossack. The Judaic prohibition of murder is absolute and unconditional, just as the disrespect for a father (in addition to anti-Semitic prejudices) is most evident to a Jewish sensibility when the Cossack lad in 'Pis'mo' ('The Letter') enquires after his horse before casually relating his tale of parricide. Liutov's acceptance of the taunt of 'Molokan', a sectarian who will not shed blood, is merely yet another example of self-mocking narration which serves to fore-ground the complex questions of violence in the name of a better future.

'Crossing the Zbrucz' – the opening story of *Red Cavalry*, often translated as 'Crossing into Poland' – will serve to illustrate the device of the detached narrator used to pinpoint the menace of anti-Semitism while calling into question the ethnic and ethical identity of the narrator. The first-person narrator separates himself from the rearguard in Novograd-Volynsk and billets with a Jewish family. What meets his eye is the disgusting filth in which the Jews live – a typical stereotyped perception from a non-Jewish point of view – but when the third sleeping Jew turns out to be a horrifying corpse the reader must correct this perspective. Here is the aftermath of a pogrom carried out by the Poles. Just as in the ironic lyricism describing the march, when the sky reflected the bloody deeds of men, here too Nature proves a more impartial witness. The moon is homeless, like the Wandering Jew. The story ends with the same plea for justice and mercy which closes 'The Cemetery at Kozin': why has the Angel of Death never spared the Jews?

If Babel had had any doubts it was now clear to him what was the price in blood of war and revolution. He could not avoid seeing the impossibility of wedding Judaism to Communism, of welding together the ideals and traditions juxtaposed in the last effects of the dying Ilia Bratslavsky in 'The Rebbe's Son':

Here everything was thrown together – propaganda manifestos and the jottings of a Jewish poet. The portraits of Lenin and Maimonides lay next to each other. Lenin's knotted iron skull and the dull silk of the portrait of Maimonides. A lock of a woman's hair was placed in a copy of the Resolutions of the Sixth Party Congress and in the margins of communist leaflets were crowded the crooked lines of Hebrew verse. They descended on me in a sad and tedious rainfall, pages from the Song of Songs and revolver cartridges. (229)[70]

This story is addressed to someone called Vasily, who has not previously been introduced as an interlocutor. This would suggest that the narrator's memories of the Friday evening with Gedali and the Rebbe (inaccurate memories, incidentally) and his lament over Ilia, the last prince of a Hasidic dynasty turned revolutionary, are directed to a Russian audience. It is to his aspired-towards Russian identity that the narrator turns at the end of *Red Cavalry* to explain his own attachment to the 'ancient body' of Judaism and Jewish culture (Maimonides, Hebrew poetry) while he is writing in Russian. By the time *Red Cavalry* was written it was clear how irreconcilable were Lenin and Maimonides, love and Party resolutions, Hebrew verse and communist propaganda, the Bible and war. The paradox is that among the hordes of typhus-ridden peasantry, 'monstrous Russia, incredible like a swarm of fleas' (228), the Jewish renegade Ilia is the only one to stretch out an emaciated hand for Trotsky's leaflets, and that he dies having failed to win the battle for the Revolution.

As the failed Jewish revolutionary lies dying, the narrator recognizes him as his spiritual brother, a similar type of dreamer who has severed his roots in the dying Jewish past, which nevertheless remains nostalgically and poisonously attractive. Ilia is Elijah, the prophet who will herald the messianic age, and he also brings to mind his namesake Elijah the Vilna Gaon, the staunch opponent of Hasidism in the eighteenth century, whose name is shouted by the *mitnagdim* at Sokal' in 'Squadron Commander Trunov'. The narrator – who himself can barely contain within his ancient Judaic consciousness the 'storms' of his imagination – thus ends *Red Cavalry* with an ambivalent portrait of the Jewish intellectual who wished to reconcile love and violence, Judaism and Communism. Only in 'Argamak', the later addition to the cycle in 1933, does Liutov succeed in riding a horse without attracting the hostile stares of the Cossacks, though not before making more enemies. Nevertheless, the dialectic of Jewish intellectual and Revolution, Jew and Cossack, remains unresolved.

THE END OF ODESSA

Any residual hope for the synthesis suggested by the last effects of Ilia Bratslavsky dims with the final destruction of the *shtetl* in the 1920s and the disappearance of Jewish tradition under economic, cultural and ideological pressure. The final Odessa story, 'Karl Yankel' (1924–9, published 1931), is set against the background of the anti-religious campaigns of the 1920s. Naftula, red-haired *mohel* (circumcizer) of old Odessa, finds himself in the dock at a show trial. The father, anxious about his application to join the Communist Party, cuts a ridiculous figure, and the public prosecutor Orlov (born Zusman) was himself once circumcized by the defendant. For all the slogans of the Friendship of the Soviet Peoples (a Kirghiz suckles the Jewish child) and the promise that the unfortunate baby will be an airman – the spirit of the new age! – Naftula embodies for the narrator the irretrievable past of Odessa Jewry, while the unlikely and unholy union of the Jewish and Marxist patriarchs in the name of the unfortunate babe suggests a hope for a better future: 'I grew up on these streets, now it is the turn of Karl-Yankel, but no one fought over me as they are fighting over him.' The narrator concludes the story with equivocal optimism by whispering to himself, 'It cannot be that you will not be happy, Karl-Yankel ... It cannot be that you will not be happier than me' (316–17).

The hope that might have been maintained by the fellow-traveller despite the terrible human price of Stalinism is daunted by the stark reality of forced collectivization expressed by powerful understatement in 'Kolyvushka' and 'Gapa Guzhva' (chapters from the apparently aborted book *Velikaia Krinitsa*, 1929–30).[71] Even the enthusiasm for construction of a new socialist society in 'Neft'' ('Oil', 1934) does not – in the story's unexpurgated version – gloss over the trials of the specialists and grossly exaggerated production targets in industry.[72] Yet the achievements of the only socialist society in the world are nevertheless impressive when seen by someone who would have had no place in Russian society before the Revolution and can now contribute a Jewish faith in life and sense of family responsibilty to the vision of the future.

The ironies of the Jew on horseback are muted in the incomplete novella 'The Jewess', when a Jewish widow leaves forever the Jewish *shtetl*, now in its last death throes, to join her Red Army officer son Boris in Moscow. Boris shares none of Liutov's disabling complexes about war and justice or violence and poetry. He was a commissar in a Ukrainian Cossack regiment and has made a successful career. The heritage of an isolated and persecuted people makes him sensitive and zealous in friendship, loyal to a regime which fought Petliura and proud of the Russia he has helped to build. There can be no return for Boris to his Jewish home town, none of the nostalgia Liutov felt for the Jewish past or the painful homesickness which Babel expresses in his Diary, but, apart from the ominous trouble caused by the smell of *gefilte fish*, there is no way to know the outcome of the Ehrlichs' move to the Soviet capital, for the rest of this manuscript of Babel's longest piece of prose fiction is lost.[73]

In the wake of Babel's rehabilitation after the Twentieth Party Congress and the republication of his *Izbrannoe* ('Selected Works', 1957) with a preface by Ehrenburg, Liutov was equated with Mechik in Fadeev's *Razgrom* (*The Rout*), an intellectual stock-type incapable of fully accepting the Revolution,[74] while other Soviet scholars defended Babel as a sincere, if somewhat misguided, Bolshevik.[75] Liutov is sometimes described as an embodiment of doubts, held by the intellectual or by Babel himself, which must be swept away by the dialectic forces of the Revolution, and Western scholars have usually followed the varying Soviet views. James Falen, for example, states that Liutov is more or less a portrait of Babel as he saw himself in 1920 and that he was appalled by the lethargy and backwardness of the Jewish 'ghetto'.[76] Patricia Carden is more sensitive to the ironies of Babel's elusive narration, but speaks of the Cossack ethos that Liutov 'lacks and that he longs to appropriate for himself'.[77] The violence of the Cossacks is attractive to the young Odessa Jew because it is a quest for justice, and this supposedly longed-for adaptability to Cossack ways necessitates a complete break with Judaism,[78] a recognition by the intellectual of the Freudian 'discontent' of society, which idealizes the noble savage. This, at least, is how Lionel Trilling explained why he thought the Tolstoyan idealization of the Cossack more attractive to Babel than the traditional Jewish stereotypes of the harbingers of destruction.[79]

The seeing eye of the narrating 'I' who records as if impassively events which touch him intimately (literally so when a Polish soldier's brains spill on him in 'Squadron Commander Trunov') may confuse the reader inattentive to modernistic manipulation of point of view. The voyeuristic view of a raped Jewish woman in 'At Batko Makhno's' is not an extreme statement of a Jew's self-hatred, but shares the voyeurism of 'Through the Fanlight' (an early version of which appeared as early as 1917) and a peep into a Cheka police station in the *Novaia zhizn'* sketch 'Evening' (1918).

It should not be forgotten that Babel came to a part of the world that had been until recently the thriving centre of Hasidism as an assimilated Odessa Jew, and the difference in look and outlook between the two communities could not be more obvious. Babel remarks on it in his Diary (21 July 1920) and at the end of the story 'Uchenie o tachanke' ('Discourse on the Tachanka'):

Narrow-shouldered Jews loiter sadly at the crossroads. And the image lights up in my memory of the southern Jews, jovial, pot-bellied and bubbling over like cheap wine. You cannot compare with them the bitter arrogance of these long and bony spines, these yellow and tragic beards. There is no fat and no pulsation of warm blood in their passionate, tormented features. The movements of the Galician and Volhynian Jew are impetuous, jerky and uncouth, but their sorrow is filled with a sombre grandeur and their secret contempt for the Polish lord is limitless. Looking at them, I understood the poignant history of these parts, the tales of Talmud scholars who kept taverns, rabbis who lived off money-lending, and young women who were raped by Polish soldiers and fought over by Polish magnates. (140–1)

The discovery of traditional Jewish life did not result in radical repentance as it had for Jiří Langer, a friend of Kafka from Prague, who had visited the Belz Hasidim in this same area six years before and who had immortalized the experience in his *Nine Gates*. Yet it was impossible for Babel to look impassively on the destruction of his past. It required tremendous self-restraint to be able to convey in his matter-of-fact record the mentality of men who were making history and to do this without giving himself away, not to mention the personal risk among hostile Cossacks and in a communist propaganda unit that was without doubt under ideological scrutiny.[80]

If Levka Krik thought that a Jew on horseback had ceased being a Jew and become a Russian, Babel's Diary shows that Babel was far from being either a 'Jewish Cossack' or a loyal Bolshevik. The difference between the Diary and the drafts, on the one hand, and the published stories, on the other, involves not so much historical accuracy as the artistic kaleidoscoping of disparate events into a meaningful experience that at the same time maintained the fragmentary, episodic immediacy of a witness account. Babel discarded thematic or chronological for structural unity, much as the historian must disregard strict chronology when reordering the sequence of events into a narrative of the causes and effects of History. Babel's approach is true to the midrashic approach, which fills in the 'gap' in official historical records with homiletic tales of everyday incidents that get at the essence of historical and moral meaning. The problem was to render the historical injustice done to the Jews in a way that would be artistically effective and publishable in the Soviet Union of the mid-twenties, to portray the cruel paradox of the delusion of the intellectual torn between his Jewish past and the

Revolution when these were incompatible. In the Diary Babel is still trying to make some sense out of the war and the Revolution; *Red Cavalry* is a consciously open-ended dialectic of contradictions and indicates an acute awareness of the situation of the Jewish intellectual in Soviet Russia after idealistic hopes had been dashed.

CHAPTER 4

The 'colour' of Judaism: Osip Mandelstam's 'Noise of Time'

Les couleurs de Gargantua feurent blanc et bleu, comme cy dessus avez peu lire, et par icelles vouloit son pere qu'on entendist que ce luy estoit une joye celeste; car le blanc luy signifoit joye, plaisir, delices et resjouissance, et le bleu choses celestes.   François Rabelais, *Gargantua*.

THE SEMIOTICS OF MEMORY

In *War and Peace*, Natasha thinks of Boris as narrow and grey, while Pierre Bezukhov is contrasted as round, red, and blue (Book VI, Chapter 13). Indeed, for many of us individual personalities, places, or occasions are coloured in various arbitrary and subjective hues. Yet the experiential associations or intuitive reception of the reader turn out not to be a fail-safe guide to their decoding in a literary text. Elsewhere I have argued that colour words in the prose of Isaak Babel of the 1920s are organized according to the structural context of the represented fictional world,[1] not according to any symbolist theosophy, as in the case of Bely.[2] In the lexicon of the semiotic modelling system which constructs the spatial coordinates of Time in the work of art, selection and non-selection of evaluative markers can have more significance than their mere relevance to biographical fact.

Before beginning any analysis of the coloration of Mandelstam's view of Judaism, it is worth contrasting that view with the way in which, in the previous chapter, we saw the Jewish world represented by Babel. Mandelstam apparently did not take too seriously the discourse of the communist who fretted over conflicts between his identity as a Jew and as a 'Cossack'.[3] Indeed, comparison of Babel and Mandelstam may seem at first glance unfounded, despite Narbut's attempt to get Babel admitted as an Acmeist or neo-Acmeist.[4] Yet there are unexpected points of similarity in their use of synaesthesia and synecdoche to juxtapose evaluative markers in the recapitulation of time past. Both are poets whose prose reverberates with rhythm and association, though Babel's subtext does not match what has been called Mandelstam's 'poetic anamnesia'. Both transfer the anxieties of modernity and of ethnic-cultural identity to a peripatetic self that remains strangely peripheral even when recounting personal experience: 'Art is a means by which the poet tries to bind chaos. It stands between him and reality. To attain the illusion of order and harmony he must remain something of an outsider, he must, as Mandelstam says, "keep his distance"'.[5] On the face of it, Babel and Mandelstam could not be further apart in their attitudes to their Jewish origin and we do not find in Mandelstam's work the intensity of the Jewish experience that is so central to Babel's short stories. On the other hand, the sensory metaphors that form the lexical markers of the narrator's past in *Red Cavalry* have a curious affinity to the 'colour' of Judaism in Mandelstam's *Shum vremeni* (*Noise of Time*) beyond the tragic implications of their shared destiny as writers and as Jews.

Almost invariably in the dialectic of *Red Cavalry* we saw that the old world of traditional Judaism, like the spiritual arena of Polish Catholicism, was perceived by Babel's alienated narrator to be enclosed and enclosing. The Jewish home stifles the narrator who wishes to escape, though he has nowhere to escape to except transitional areas (the Bolshevik propaganda train, the front line) and from these he will return time and again. If we now apply the semiotic oppositional model outlined in Chapter 1, we can see that inherent in the systematic ordering of artistic space is the tension between the rejected *svoi* (one's own) of the home and the rejecting *chuzhoi* (other, alien) of the outside. Each area is designated as bounded or non-bounded by evaluative markers, while the border (doors, windows, courtyards, walls) between them is a crossing point of plot action. The binary oppositions of the evaluative markers function dynamically and not as a mechanistic imagery of negative versus positive, yet schematically the sets of oppositions in the narrative space of *Red Cavalry* would look something like Table 1.

The narrator of *Red Cavalry* seeks to escape from the binding enclosedness of the Jewish home, which nevertheless remains his own home *(svoi)*. Yet he finds himself ultimately incompatible with the outside space of the Cossacks, whose historical entity, values and behaviour are in conflict with the doomed ruins of the Jewish home, although the Cossacks' physicality and professionalism allure the alienated Jewish intellectual aspiring to acceptance. For example, the smoke of the Cossacks' cooking-pot in 'My First Goose' attracts the alienated Jewish intellectual like a 'native home' *(rodnoi dom)*, and in the transitional area of the courtyard he must deny the Judaic humanitarian code by assaulting a woman and defiling her sexual surrogate, a pure-white goose, before joining the Cossacks' ritual communion and eating non-kosher pork.[6] Enclosedness expresses such concepts of socialization and identity as home or homeland *(rodnoi)*, while unenclosedness is associated with the cold, hostile outside *(chuzhoi)*. The opposition of bounded and non-bounded areas, moreover, demarcates a boundary whose impenetrability delays or prevents resolution of the protagonists' plot function. In the prose of Babel and Mandelstam the first-person narrator must resolve the problem of the boundary if he is at all to integrate his own writing personality with self and with Time, to 'bind chaos'.

MANDELSTAM'S JUDAIC CHAOS

The chaos in *Noise of Time* is specifically the Judaic one, in binary opposition to Russian culture. The integrity of Russian culture is a question of language as well as a question of aesthetic balance *(ravnovesie)*, so important in Mandelstam's poetry. *Noise of Time* was written in 1923 at the Crimean spa of Gaspra at the suggestion of Isai Lezhnev, the author of a conventional, ideologically 'correct' discourse, the memoir of the poor Jewish youth who accepts Marxism; Lezhnev rejected Mandelstam's unorthodox version.[7] Mandelstam is, strictly speaking, not writing in an autobiographical mode: 'My desire is not to speak about myself but to track

Table 1:   *Binary oppositions in Babel's Red Cavalry*

BOUNDED	NON-BOUNDED
home *(svoi)*	alien *(chuzhoi)*
culture	non-culture
closed	open
putrefaction	vitality
white, green, yellow, black	red, raspberry, crimson
irregular surfaces	hyperbolic forms
asceticism	violence
impotence	sexual exuberance

down the age, the noise and the germination of time. My memory is inimical to all that is personal.'[8] Mandelstam, writes Jane Gary Harris, seeks to bridge the 'hiatus' of family history by displacing it with links to Russian history and culture: 'The object of Mandelstam's autobiography ... becomes the recovery of a sense of time through an examination of analogies or parallels between his individual destiny and Russia's cultural history.'[9] His teacher Gippius provides an alter ego and a literary home, while subtextually Pushkin's 'Feast During the Plague' offers a model aesthetic conscience for dealing with a new winter of Russian history, and Kautsky and Tiutchev throw a cover over the 'abyss'. This is the story of a poetic becoming of a *raznochinets*, an uprooted intellectual.

Noise of Time focuses on the tranquil decay of the 1890s, and it is built upon the clearest juxtaposition of contrasting impressions of time past. It opens with the remarkably obsessive talk of the Dreyfus Affair over morning tea, reminding us of the social and psychological pressure of anti-Semitism that forms a similar background to Proust's *A la recherche du temps perdu*. The madeleine which recalls Combray and the sounds or textures which colour memory are also characteristic of the impressions of music and feelings that form a *durée* in the time and space of *fin de siècle* St Petersburg.[10] The traumatic significance of anti-Semitism moved Mandelstam, who, as Nadezhda Mandelstam tells us, was later to suffer his own 'Dreyfus Affair', even if anti-Semitism is played down here and transfused into the general *fin de siècle* smell of decay and anxious introspection: 'It was as if, having acquitted

Dreyfus and settled accounts with Devil's Island, that strange century had lost all meaning' (70).[11]

In the concerts at the Pavlovsk railway station restaurant the poet senses not the imminent collapse of empire but the centrality of some 'Elysium' into which streams all St Petersburg. A similar aesthetic and historical illusion of centrality characterizes the festive and sacred world of granite Petersburg peopled by an imaginary military parade. The ecstatic child feels that something very solemn and splendid is about to happen:

All this mass of militarism and even a kind of police aesthetics may very well have been proper to some son of a corps commander with the appropriate family traditions, but it was completely out of keeping with the kitchen fumes of a middle-class apartment, with father's study and its heavy odour of leathers, kidskin and calfskin, or with Jewish conversations about business. (74)

Such craving for spectacle parallels the deluded Great Expectations of the narrator's father who hammers on the locked bathroom door in Babel's 'Awakening'. In both cases the smells and colours of the indoor and anti-aesthetic Judaic disorder and its defunct time are in opposition to the order and progressive nowness of Russian time which is the narrator's perspective. It is worth quoting at length to note the self-conscious deliberateness of Mandelstam's synaesthetic and chronotopic opposition of the two value-systems:

All the elegant mirage of Petersburg was merely a dream, a brilliant covering thrown over the abyss, while round about there sprawled the chaos of Judaism – not a motherland, not a house, not a hearth, but precisely a chaos, the unknown womb world whence I had issued, which I feared, about which I made vague conjectures and fled, always fled.

The chaos of Judaism showed through all the chinks of the stone-clad Petersburg apartment: in the threat of ruin, in the cap hanging in the room of the guest from the provinces, in the spiky script of the unread books of Genesis, thrown into the dust one shelf lower than Goethe and Schiller, in the shreds of the black-and-yellow ritual.

The strong, ruddy, Russian year rolled through the calendar with decorated eggs, Christmas trees, steel skates from Finland, December, gaily bedecked Finnish cab-drivers, and the villa. But mixed up with all this there was a phantom – the new year in September – and the strange, cheerless holidays, grating upon the ear with their harsh names: Rosh Hashanah and Yom Kippur. (76–7)

The space of Judaism is constricted, glimpsed through the 'chinks' of the stony interior, and is not even a homely habitation, nor even a ruin to which the alienated Jewish intellectual might return in a moment of nostalgia, as in *Red Cavalry*. The Jewish womb-home is an abyss, a chaos which undermines acceptance into Russian culture. The threat of Jewish destiny intrudes when some unfortunate relative from the Pale of Settlement importunately seeks aid and protection from the ravages of pogroms, discrimination and economic crisis. Mandelstam does not mention the privileged status of the family, who lived in the Imperial capital despite the restrictions on Jewish residence.

The Judaic calendar is quirky in its temporal progression, having nothing of the joy of the Orthodox year. Its ritual lacks the integrity of Russian culture. The 'shreds' of Judaism suggest the ragged poverty of the Jews in *Red Cavalry*, while the black-yellow colour may represent a discoloured and torn prayer shawl, like the 'cherno-zheltyi shelkovoi platok' (blackish-yellow silk shawl) which the narrator's grandfather forces on the squirming boy who can barely mutter the requisite prayer.[12] The fossilized shreds of the antiquated Judaic blackish-yellow ritual ('klochkami cherno-zheltogo rituala') are immediately contrasted by the healthy and non-alien image of the ruddy Russian year ('Krepkii rumianyi russkii god'). A similarly alliterative identification of Russian time and space appears in Isaak Babel's 'Otets' ('The Father', 1924), when Katiusha heats up for the Jewish gangster Benia Krik her ruddy Russian paradise ('raspisnoi, svoi russkii i rumianyi rai.').

It should be noted, though, that yellow is also the colouring of Petersburg in the Russian literary myth of that most abstract and phantasmagoric city, the colour of brothels and madhouses, as well as the unhealthy pallor of biliousness *(zhelch')*.   Kirill Taranovsky has given examples from Annenskii's 'Peterburg' (1910), Blok's 'V eti zheltye dni' ('In Those Yellow Days', 1909) and 'Unizhenie' ('Degradation', 1911), not to mention Mandelstam's own 'Peterburgskie strofy' ('Petersburg Strophes', 1913).[13]

Yet the yellow of Mandelstam's Petersburg shines resplendently against the darker shades of Judaism's *blackish* yellow. In the first chapter of *Noise of Time* the new express trams on Nevsky Prospekt are painted yellow and they outpace the old dirty wine-coloured vehicles, colours which match the respective velocities of Progress and Antiquity. Yellow and black are the colours, too, of the Tsarist standard, and in yellow there is envy: 'Only two colours in the world have not faded / In yellow is envy, in red – impatience'.[14] There is likewise the yellow and black of the goldfinch in the later poem about that bird, but these are not the blackish-yellow of Judaism.

Judaism, recalling the whiff of death in 'Gedali', also *smells* of decay: 'As a little bit of musk fills an entire house, so the least influence of Judaism overflows all of one's life. Oh, what a strong smell that is! Could I possibly not have noticed that in real Jewish houses there was a different smell from that in Aryan houses? And it was not only the kitchen that smelled so, but the people, things and clothing' (77). The sickly sweet Jewish smell 'swaddles' the narrator in the internment – both womb and tomb – of the Judaic timespace which belongs primarily, as in the case of Babel's narrator, to the grandparents' house. The commercial aroma[15] of the father's leatherskins reeks of the all-pervasive environmental determinants of the father's drab, petty-bourgeois surroundings: 'My father's study at home was itself unlike the granite paradise of my sedate strolls; it led one away into an alien world, and the mixture of its furnishings, the selection of the objects in it were strongly knitted together in my consciousness' (77).

The bookcase in the father's study categorizes the culture/non-culture opposition which, according to Mandelstam, accompanies a person throughout his life and which determines the colour, height, and arrangement of his value-system. The conscious cultural geology of the bookcase contrasts the narrator's genealogy through his mother with the heritage, or rather non-heritage, of his father. The lower, lowly strata comprise the Judaic chaos of Jewish history, the neglected 'ruins' of Jewish literature. The father, however, himself abandoned Judaism and imitated so many followers of the Jewish secular enlightenment before him, autodidactically fighting his way out of the Talmudic 'wilds' into German Romanticism and making the inevitable pilgrimage to Berlin, shrine of the citizens of Mosaic faith, as the followers of Moses Mendelssohn styled themselves.[16] The second stratum up, therefore, is that of Goethe and Schiller, as well as Shakespeare. The superior, highest level is the mother's, the pure Russian of Pushkin. Satirizing Rimbaud's 'idiotic alphabet of colours', Mandelstam eulogizes Pushkin as colourless, clothed in the brownish-black cassock of the Isakov edition. Lermontov stands in military greenish-blue next to the vanished tranquillity of Turgenev and the prohibitively 'heavy' Dostoevsky.[17] Next, interestingly for Mandelstam's origins and affinities, comes the Nadsonian 'enigma' of Russian culture. As we saw in Chapter 2, Nadson was a Russian poet who declared his Jewishness only when pogroms threatened his rejected people, for him always alien *(chuzhoi)*; for Mandelstam Nadson was the antipodes of his cultural godfather, Chaadaev.[18] Such is the culture of the maternal strata in the narrator's family make-up, the culture of Vilna (the 'Jerusalem of Lithuania') in the 1880s and 'self-immolation' in the populist *Narodnaia volia*. Jewish involvement in *Narodnaia volia* meant a rejection of the alternative – trying to better the lot of Russian Jewry – in favour of working toward a new social order which would benefit Russian and Jew. The choice was not easy, and the required self-sacrifice is described openly by Pavel Akselrod in his *Perezhitoe i peredumannoe* ('Life and Thoughts'). Akselrod believed the Jewish problem insignificant 'in face of the expected era of equality and fraternity' which would follow empowerment of the Russian peasantry, and that was why he dedicated himself to their redemption.[19] In order to be acceptable to the Russian peasantry, many Jews hid their Jewish identity or converted.

The sixth chapter of *Noise of Time* offers a definitive portrait of what it calls in its title 'The Judaic Chaos'. The Jewish family is presented as a band of home-spun philosophers and wanderers making impertinent demands. Mandelstam borrows an ecclesiastical image of the Church when he writes of the synagogue as a 'Jewish ship' split asunder into men's and women's sections, in contrast with the Talmudic image of the Torah as a sea, as when the child's soul in 'Gedali' rocks like a ship on the enchanted waves of Judaism. The discomfiture and dislocation of Judaism are emphasized by the boy's blundering into the women's balcony and his strangely criminal stealth. The ritual is false and meaningless to him.

Here Mandelstam introduces a crucial category of oppositions, that of language. Like the cultural geology of the bookcase, the languages of the father and mother are decisive in the poet's formation: 'The speech of the father and the speech of the mother – does not our language feed throughout all its long life on the confluence of these two, do they not compose its character?' (84). The vocabulary of the mother's Russian may have been poor but 'it had roots and confidence'. It was clear and free from foreignness, whereas 'My father had absolutely no language; his speech was tongue-tie and languagelessness' (85). The father's non-glossia *(bez"iazychie)* is not even Jewish, nor simply a Judaic denial of the Christian Logos, which for John – and from the viewpoint of Mandelstam the philo-*logist* – brought the world into being and out of primeval chaos, and which is identified with the Christ figure who links the divine will and the universe. Mandelstam rejects as entirely unintelligible the non-culture of an autodidact who abandoned the Talmud for Schiller and spoke in the abstractions of Herder, Leibniz and Spinoza. In so doing he rejects the ideal option of civil emancipation sought by the *maskilim* and posits the Jew as Other in negative Hegelian opposition to logocentrism.

Logos, in its derivation from Plato and the Greeks, signifies a rational cosmos, which can be read as a Book and which retains a permanent, unalterable character, in contrast to the Hebraic conception of the divine word as a dynamic system of revelation unfolding in History.[20] This Hellenist notion of Logos would be more suitable for a poet who represents himself as a Book. The *déraciné* poet is the books he has read; his cultural history is his creative biography: 'A *raznochinets* needs no memory – it is enough for him to tell of the books he has read, and his biography is done' (110). Time past engenders a tongue-tied generation of deracinated intellectuals *(raznochintsy)* who must forge out of the noise of time their own pristine language, the euphony of the Russian language and the language of poetry. The tension between Hebraism and Hellenism exercised Mandelstam's mind and language, as it had troubled Heine and Shestov. In Heine's *Self-Portrait* the pain of Jewish identity is inflicted in physical and psychological wounds on a child likewise born at the dying of the century and the dawn of a new age of Revolution and War, events which proved to be of no little import for the poet's destiny. Heine had, like Mandelstam, converted to Lutheranism, the 'admission ticket to European culture', although he was indifferent to formal religion, turning in adversity and defiance to Hebraism. However, Heine's love-hate relationship with Germany and the German language finds little parallel in the life of 'Zinaida's Jewboy', as Mandelstam was known among the symbolist circles of Zinaida Gippius.[21]

Moreover, the Hebraic consciousness of sin is opposed to the Hellenist urge to see things clearly in their essence and beauty. We recall that Matthew Arnold urged resistance to the disabling uneasiness of Zion in 'Hebraism and Hellenism'. If the Revolution signalled the end of St Petersburg, both as city and as culture, then Hellenism afforded Mandelstam the hope for a resurrection of culture through the Word, even if in *O prirode slova* ('The Nature of the Word', 1922) it was Bergson's 'profoundly Judaic mind' which insisted on the 'fan' of immutable human values. Hellenism remained a warm hearth *(ochag)*,[22] the true homeland of the poet, just as Judaism was a non-homeland, a destiny not his (not *svoi*). For Mandelstam, Russia was the bearer of the holy message of Hellenism. Hellenism expressed for him the millennial hope for a 'third renaissance' in Russia, an idea connected with Moscow's identification as a Third Rome and with Russia's spiritual heritage in the Eastern Church.

The father's homeland is the grandparents' wooden house – a further semiotic opposition to the stable stone of St Petersburg's Russian culture. The journey there is a particularly alarming experience. In the grandmother's only Russian word 'Pokushali?' is tasted the bitter and unpalatable flavour of the Jewish cuisine. Communication is impossible and, when left alone in this totally unfamiliar, frightening, stifling Jewish world, the boy urgently wishes to flee, just as the boy in Babel's Childhood stories seeks to escape the constraints of his grandmother's house or his basement home. It is significantly the Russian-tongued mother who rescues him.

The cacophony of Judaic non-culture is particularly evident in the opposition of Jewish and Russian concerts. In the labyrinth of Jewish Dubbeln, for example, with its smell of swaddling clothes (a double image of claustrophobic constriction), the unceasing Jewish cacophony shrieks out its 'mercilessly false brass note' of wandering musicians. The Judaic music is a vagabond, disharmonic non-culture, like the vulgar synagogue service for which tickets must be obtained as if for a concert, a reference to the inauthenticity of the culture of the Jewish *arrivistes* and a rejection of identification with the Ostjuden ('bad' Jews of the *shtetl*). Again, the Riga coastal resort is a country apart, a 'Sahara' of unbelievably pure yellow sand, but even here Lévi-Strauss's 'dual organization' operates. In the Aryan 'clean' half of the territory, German students drink beer to the consoling sounds of Strauss, while on the other side of the boundary a parvenu Jewish orchestra 'strains' at the neurotic and discordant notes of Tchaikovsky's *Symphonie Pathétique:* 'What conviction sounded in those violin voices, softened by Italian docility but still Russian, in the dirty Jewish sewer!' (88).[23] This derogatory reference to the unclean Jewish space should perhaps be understood as the poet's attempt to satirize neurotic Jewish sensibilities and to distance writing self from experiential self in the portrayal of the alienation of a *raznochinets* of the 'Fourth Estate'. In any case, in the following chapter the poet expresses his zeal for the concerts of both Hofmann and Kubelík, and he returns to the cultural framework of the Pavlovsk railway station concerts in a general description of the sanctum of the Petersburg intelligentsia.

Incidentally, the narrator claims categorically never to have heard Yiddish at home, and that he discovered only in later years that 'melodious, always surprised and disappointed, interrogative language with its sharp accents on the weakly stressed syllables' (84), a hardly derogative comment on what the assimilationists contemptuously dubbed the Judeo-German *zhargon*. The description of the Yiddish folklorist and onetime *narodnik* S. An-sky is likewise anything but deprecatory, even if he is a momentary guest at the home of the Karaite doctor Boris Naumovich Sinani,

Table 2:   *Binary oppositions in Mandelstam's 'Noise of Time'* [24]

BOUNDED	NON-BOUNDED
alien *(chuzhoi)*	one's own *(svoi)*
chaos	culture
profane	sacred
abyss	mirage
melancholy	festivity
there (marginality)	here (centrality)
flight	arrival
menace	security
yellow-black	red, yellow
Judaism	Petersburg

a 'Gleb Uspensky out of the Talmud-Torah' (the traditional Jewish elementary school) (107), who plays the Jewish apostle Peter at the Last Supper as against the young Boris Sinani's combination of a Russian shepherd and John the Baptist, whose early death prevented him from taking up his role in the revolutionary apocalypse. The intellectual aesthetics of the Sinani household, with its sacred territories of populism and the 'graven image of Mikhailovsky' (107), formed a lasting impression on Mandelstam, then a self-assured Marxist who made the younger Boris Sinani his mentor, a significant confession considering that by the time of writing the Bolsheviks had repressed the Social-Revolutionaries. An-sky had had to flee, disguised as a priest, abandoning the Jewish heritage he had collected in the Jewish Ethnic Museum and a political future as a Social-Revolutionary deputy. An-sky is revered as a genuine source of Jewish culture, as a 'gentle Psyche afflicted with haemorrhoids', quite unlike the banker Goldberg and his German poetry or the non-culture of Mandelstam's own home, where the unnatural national pride of his Hebrew teacher stirs up revolt in the young boy.

If we now examine the paradigmatic oppositions of *Noise of Time* (see Table 2) it will be observed that, in contrast to the topology of *Red Cavalry*, the bounded territory of Judaism is perceived as unmistakably alien *(chuzhoi)* by the poet who reconstructs a language of being and of writing out of his negation of the Judaic chaos. There is here no wish to return, there is no homeland to which to return, as there is a ruined *shtetl* where the Odessa Jew seeks his kith and kin and to whom he goes in his despair. Yet Mandelstam, who writes from a position of complete assimilation, is not quite the 'self-hating Jew' Maurice Friedberg would have him,[25] despite the poet's frenzied, overinsistent protest against the Judaic chaos. Mandelstam was resisting the impossible demands of Time when he could neither resort to a cultural alternative nor rely upon an ethnic security.

'THE EGYPTIAN STAMP'

In *Egipetskaia marka* ('The Egyptian Stamp'), an experimental prose narrative originally meant to supplement *Noise of Time* and first published in 1928, memory is a sickly Jewish girl who tries to elope, and in Jewish homes reigns a 'melancholy, bewhiskered silence'. The 'centrifugal' velocity of Modernity's post-Einsteinian time and the instability of post-Revolutionary time each threatens the sepulchre of the sacred objects that identify the age: 'The centrifugal force of time has scattered our Viennese chairs and Dutch plates with little blue flowers. Nothing is left. Thirty years have passed like a slow fire. For thirty years a cold white flame has licked at the backs of mirrors, where the bailiff's tags are attached.'[26] Time was no longer to be counted in dynasties and centuries but in the fleeting moments of survival.

'The Egyptian Stamp' is set in the summer of 1917, the summer of Kerensky's 'lemonade' government. The 'Egyptian Stamp' of the title is Parnok, who is modelled on Valentin Parnakh, or Parnac as he sometimes spelt it in emigration. Parnakh was also a Jew and very much like Mandelstam in his small stature and haughty gesture, if we are to judge from a portrait of Parnakh by Picasso. He was an eccentric poet and translator who went abroad and lived in Paris from 1915 until the 1920s,[27] and he had a sister, Sofia, who changed her name from the family surname Parnokh to Parnok, a name that sounds neither Jewish nor Russian. Sofia ran away from her father and eventually converted to Russian Orthodoxy. Once a lover of Marina Tsvetaeva, Sofia spent the same summer as Mandelstam in Koktebel' in 1915. She wrote poetry, as well as a review of Mandelstam's book of poetry

Kamen' ('Stone', 1913),[28] under the transvestite *nom de plume* Andrei
Polianin, just as her brother had taken the almost drag-costume
pseudonym of Valentina Melik-Khaspabova. This might explain
the naming of Mandelstam's anti-hero, and it could be that the
fate of a minor poet suggested the differences of race, gender and
name to Mandelstam when he wrote 'The Egyptian Stamp'. As
previous scholars have pointed out, in 'The Egyptian Stamp ' the
narrator is haunted by fear of being usurped and dispossessed, the
constant anxiety of the Diaspora Jew and an immediate concern
when History dispossesses both the supporters of the *ancien régime*
and many hapless victims, among them the archetypal victims,
the Jews.

The surreal nightmare of homelessness in this story intensifies
the phantasmagoric aura of St Petersburg in the Russian literary
tradition from Pushkin's *Bronze Horseman*, through Gogol's Petersburg Tales to Dostoevsky's *White Nights, The Double, Notes from the
Underground* and *Crime and Punishment.* In one plotline of this
unconventional modernistic piece, Parnok is trying to retrieve his
clothes which have been taken from him in a mysterious manner
(like the coveted overcoat in Gogol's story) and which Mervis
takes to an officer, Captain Krzyzanowski, who is a Gogolian
Nose and a Dostoevskian Goliadkin figure.[29] Mandelstam is
rereading Dostoevsky rereading Gogol rereading Pushkin and
other antecedents, but the performance of Russian literary texts is
also a personal odyssey of a Jew stripped of his identity. If *Noise of
Time* could be poetically autobiographical, then 'The Egyptian
Stamp' is intimately personal. Clarence Brown notes that both
works are obsessively onomastic and toponymic. Both are slant-
eyed in their selection of factual basis, but 'The Egyptian Stamp'
is more Jewish in its references to people and places, in particular
the Jewish quarter of St Petersburg with its private, concealed
references to Mandelstam's family residences and the hunch-
backed watchmaker who recalls Spinoza. Jewish poverty menaces
the narrator on a nightmarish journey that takes him back in time
and space against his will through the plotless story of his life. The
pen that writes the text resists the writing and at one point almost
fails the writer. The writer prays not to be like Parnok but
recognizes his Double in him. To separate himself from his

creation is to become independent of his self, to achieve the distance of a poet looking at himself as a stranger; and it is to resist becoming a non-entity, to resist the Jewish and other alien presences in the story.

The second plot-line involves an attempt by Parnok to save a victim of mob justice from lynching. Clarence Brown has argued for the basis of this plot in an incident from Mandelstam's own life,[30] when he intervened with Feliks Dzerzhinsky, the head of the Cheka, to save a foreign count, an art historian he did not even know, from the hands of the terrorist Bliumkin. Thereafter Mandelstam lived in terror of Bliumkin, this strange man who would raise a loaded pistol at him in public.[31] Mandelstam, suggests Clarence Brown, secretly wants to be a hero, not a victim.

DREYFUS IN MOSCOW

Mandelstam's *Noise of Time* has been called 'simultaneously the culmination of the first phase of his life as a poet – his artistic *rite de passage* – and an esthetic declaration of intellectual maturity.'[32] It is a writing-out of the self which makes an analogy between the personal status of the *raznochinets* and the universal status of the poet. Tiring of the hack work and scenarios which kept him, as they kept Babel,[33] from his real work, Mandelstam insisted, in *Chetvertaia proza* ('Fourth Prose', 1930–31), that the writer's trade, as practised in Europe and particularly in Russia, was 'incompatible with the honourable title of Jew, of which I a.n proud. My blood, burdened with its inheritance from sheep breeders, patriarchs and kings, rebels against the shifty gypsyishness of the writing tribe' (186). Clare Cavanagh understands the 'honorable title of Jew' to be a rejection of cultural apostasy by Russian Jews and a recreation of what Sander Gilman called a Jewish Other 'as a substitute for hatred of the self'. Mandelstam would be rejecting the identity of the poet who accepted the Revolution that had stripped him of cultural identity, and identifying with the alternative construct of the Jew-Poet, in Tsvetaeva's formulation in her *Poema kontsa* ('Poem of the End', 1924), the martyr who does not compromise the writer's calling.[34] Tsvetaeva's poem describes the poet's parting from her lover as they walk through Prague and look down on the Jewish Ghetto, a place which makes her think that it is more worthy to become an eternal Jew because 'life is for converts only / Judases of all faiths'. In this way Tsvetaeva evokes the lies and betrayal around her. She stamps on the paper which gives her the right to live and calls for vengeance for the pogrom victims, understood in a metaphysical sense of doomed non-conformists like the author:

> Ghetto of chosenness! Ravine and rampart.
> Expect no mercy!
> In this most Christian of worlds
> Poets are yids![35]

This invented construct covered the 'hole' of languagelessness and alienation associated with the Judaic chaos in *Noise of Time* and forged a creative personality out of marginality, akin to the 'pariah status' Hannah Arendt accorded Franz Kafka, so that linguistic and generic subversion by a marginal wanderer, who foregrounds the name given him by the State (the crooked 'Mandelstam Street' in a 1935 poem), is an essential condition for genuine art free from ideological conscription.[36]

'Fourth Prose' was an unburdening of self, to paraphrase Clarence Brown, that ended five years of silence as a poet, after a vicious campaign of defamation which began in 1928 with the publication of Mandelstam's revision of two Russian translations of Charles de Coster's *La Légende de Thyl Ulenspiegel,* for which the publishers credited Mandelstam as sole translator. The Mandelstams felt that the press campaign which used as its pretext the charge of plagiarism was their own Dreyfus Affair and that the intention was clearly to destroy Mandelstam's literary fame.[37] It was Nikolai Bukharin who saved Mandelstam by commissioning him to travel to Armenia, then under Soviet rule. The travel writing which Mandelstam brought back, *Journey to Armenia,* was just as much a celebration of Christian Armenia with its pagan nomadic past as it was a negation of Moscow and Moscow's political and literary establishment, while 'Fourth Prose', fourth in a series commencing with *Noise of Time* but also echoing the Fourth Estate of *deraciné* intellectuals, was a personal confession of faith in the Word and a rejection of official Literature and official Authors who sold out to the Soviet system. Mandelstam takes up his 'Jewish staff' and condemns as 'gypsy' tinkering and thievery the compromised commerce of the writers' tribe. Art was a craft, Mandelstam believed, and the poet must speak, not write. The word *(slovo)* was flesh and bread, and the only defence against monstrous Time, which devours the State and the sacred church of Culture alike, as he wrote in *Slovo i kul'tura* ('The Word and Culture', 1922). After the Revolutionary Terror and his own experiences of imprisonment and of flight, Mandelstam was to see post-Revolutionary time as a monstrous beast:

> My animal, my age, who will ever be able
> to look in your eyes?
> Who will ever glue back together the vertebrae
> of two centuries with his blood?[38]

In '1 Ianvaria 1924' ('January 1st, 1924') the poet runs away from the ogre – no longer mythical or playful as in his first book, 'Stone', – and his typological flight, an impossible escape from Time in search of the 'lost word', draws him away from his own door.[39]

FROM THE MIRE OF JUDAISM TO THE LAIR OF THE REVOLUTION

Mandelstam converted to Lutheran Christianity, according to his widow, only to meet the formal entrance requirements of the University of St Petersburg, which practised a percentage discrimination against Jewish candidates, and he later attached no significance to his baptism.[40] Osip Mandelstam confessed to the symbolist poet Vladimir Gippius that he was brought up in indifference to religion at home and at school and that his first religious experiences dated from his juvenile infatuation with Marxism (when he read Kautsky's *Erfurt Program* and attempted *Das Kapital),* but he was converted to religious individualism by reading Ibsen, and then was attracted to the human compassion of Tolstoy and Hauptman. Explaining his complex attitude to the symbolists, Mandelstam sensed in his relationship with Gippius the beginning of a religious sensibility or search that was not in any definable way a commitment to Christianity.[41] There is little evidence of Mandelstam's rejection of his family, even if his father's ideas were, according to Nadezhda Mandelstam, rather eccentric and not easily comprehensible. Aaron Zakharovich Steinberg, an exact contemporary of Mandelstam who knew the poet in Heidelberg in winter 1910, recalls their conversations on philosophy as well as on the Jewish Question and notes that Mandelstam's attitude to the latter was 'not altogether normal'.[42] None of this accounts for the hysterical reaction to Judaism in *Noise of Time* which Mikhail Karpovich, in his memoir of Mandelstam, thought overdone.[43] One can hardly take seriously Sergei Makovsky's account of Mandelstam's mother as the uncultured wife of a vulgar Jewish leather merchant dragging her *Wunderkind* to the editorial offices of *Apollon*,[44] for which Nadezhda Mandelstam can find no better term than 'preposterous'.[45] It is therefore hard to find a biographical explanation for a hostility which does not appear to be grounded in the kind of intense guilt felt by Kafka in his own relationship with his father, of which Kafka spoke in his *Letter to My Father* (1919), although it is interesting that Kafka thought his social and ethnic rootlessness typical of his generation of children of Jews from provincial communities.[46] Why, then, the loud protest at a Judaism that Mandelstam barely knew? The answer, I believe, lies in the aesthetic concept of 'Judaism' in Mandelstam's poetry.

In some of his early poetry the poet spoke of himself as a reed growing out of an evil and muddy pool yearning for acceptance in the 'forbidden' life *outside:*

> I grew out of an evil, slimy pool,
> rustling with a reed pen
> and passionately, languidly, caressingly
> breathing forbidden life.[47]

It would be a matter of conjecture to identify this quagmire with the negatively evaluated closed space of the confining Jewish home, though the poet seems to echo the sinful mire of Psalm 69, 3, and the poet's origin in a 'slimy pool' also recalls Jeremiah's description of the doomed prophet of a fallen people as having fallen into a pit, where he is abused and covered in water

(Lamentations 3, 53–4), a parable of spiritual and national down-fall that fits the semiotic pattern of the Jewish exilic condition outlined in Chapter 1.[48] The ending of the first publication of Mandelstam's poem in the third issue of *Apollon* for 1911 denies the theological meaning ascribed to suffering on the cross of anti-Semitism and looks to some imminent and final victory that will avenge the suffering of the poet / Crucified Jew.[49] The removal of this ending might suggest either the dashing of optimism or a prudence necessitated by changed circumstances.

The contrary impulse is the dominant theme in 'Stone' of seeking to capture the ephemeral joy of everyday living, the ethereal lightness of soaring cathedrals. In Pushkin's address to the poet's imagination in *Eugene Onegin* (VI, xlvi), which summons the qualities of freshness and lightness so appealing to Mandel-stam, we also find the muddy 'pool' *(omut)*. Vladimir Nabokov translates:

> let not a poet's soul grow cold,
> callous, crust-dry,
> and finally be turned to stone
> in the World's deadening intoxication
> in that slough where with you
> I bathe, dear friends![50]

The stinking swamps of Dante's *Inferno* evoked in Mandelstam's *Razgovor o Dante* ('Conversation About Dante'), such as the sinful slough in which the wrathful are bogged down, gurgling their non-glossia in Canto VII, may be more relevant here than Herzen's political interpretation of the pool ('omut') in Pushkin's poem as 'the deep and muddy river of civilized Russia ... a dumb and formless mass of baseness, obsequiousness, bestiality and envy, a formless mass which draws in and engulfs everything ...'[51] Mandelstam's pool ('omut') is associated with both the imprison-ing Jewish past and an eschatological image of Petersburg, but also with the reflected bed in the image of insomnia and nocturnal heaviness in the well-known 'Solominka' (1916). In another poem in 'Stone', 'V ogromnom omute prozrachno i temno' ('In a large pool, transparently and darkly ...', 1910), the muddy pool ('omut') looms larger and more menacing, while the poet's heart, pulled in different directions by his roots and by his wish to break free, alternately sinks to the alluring silt at the bottom and floats effortlessly to the surface. In 'Neutolimye slova ...' ('Unquenchable Words ...', written in a Berlin suburb the same year) the crucified Jesus is the archetypal Jew as well as the poet resisting the gravitational pull of Judaism, visibly impaled on his suffering. Judea turns to heavy stone, while soldiers guard Jesus' stiffening corpse, a corolla ('venchik', also a halo) on a brittle and *alien* stem, a lily sinking in its native pool, whose depth celebrated its law ('Torzhestvovala svoi zakon'), which could be read as the inflexible Law of the Old Testament, as the Christians understood it. The binary pull of the competing cultural systems can thus be seen to organize the imagery of Mandelstam's Judaic themes into positive and negative fields quite early in his poetry, although it is noteworthy that in *Noise of Time* the author no longer fears the danger of sinking back, of dying artistically and spiritually.

There is in the top–bottom opposition an apprehension of the chaos in the Creation story in Genesis but it is also a Dantean vision of the oblivion awaiting the creating artist, the defining polarity of earth's firm support or the bliss of heaven to which he must raise himself. Theologically, the bottomless pit of hell represents also the anxiety and sinfulness of earthly existence and the soul's hope for salvation. Yet the poetic self drawn into the abyss of despair and death is familiar in its Romantic portrayal in Wordsworth's *The Prelude* and *The Excursion* , in Keats's *Endymion* and in Poe's story 'The Pit and the Pendulum', as well as in Baudelaire's *Spleen et idéal*. Gregory Freidin sees the 'pool' poems and 'Unquenchable Words ...' as a coded meditation on Mandelstam's predicament as a Russian Jew which employs two strategies. The first is the symbolist genre of the confession. The second is the Acmeist theme of the large-scale cultural and historiosophic edifice which portrayed the poet's public persona as an outcast but with cultured and honourable points of self-reference.[52]

The poem describing the funeral of the poet's mother, 'Eta noch′ nepopravima ...' ('The Night Is Irremediable', 1916), introduces into the apocalyptic theme of the crucifixion the black

and yellow suns. Kirill Taranovsky has attempted to clear the
clouds obscuring the image of the suns in this poem,[53] and he
finds an obvious interpretation of the yellow sun in the light
illuminating the temple where the mother's funeral is being
held.[54] However, Jewish funerals are not held in synagogues and
since the Destruction of Jerusalem by the Romans there has been
no Jewish Temple. Hence the Jews ('iudei') conducting the burial
rights are both bereft of priesthood and – in the eyes of the
Church – bereft of grace ('Blagodati ne imeia / I sviashchenstva
lisheny'). Mandelstam generally refers to *iudei* rather than *evrei*,
making us think more in scriptural terms than of the suffering
masses of the contemporary Pale. I would suggest that there is
here a montage of the apocalyptic nocturnal sun of New Testament Jerusalem onto the curiously Christian image of the burial
of the Jewish mother under the Judaic yellow sun, which the poet
finds so much more terrifying than the black sun of the Christian
promise of resurrection. The bereaved son awakes from his vision
literally enlightened by the black sun in his cradle, and in this
figurative return to the cradle the poet makes a choice between
the two suns. Apart from the wonderful lightness of Mandelstam's
poem, its miraculous neatness and the distancing of the poet from
a particularly moving personal experience, there is nothing
remarkable in this theological distinction. However, we might
note that the theological oppositions are also spatial: the Jewish
womb descends into the enclosing, perhaps even comforting
tomb, paralleling the cradle which lulls the poet until he wakes to
the new sun 'at the gates of Jerusalem', the sun of guilt and doom,
but also of redemption and passion.

I do not think that the black sun and the yellow sun should be
confused with the black-yellow prayer shawl,[55] but there is a
black-yellow light in another eschatological poem, 'Sredi sviash-
chennikov levitom molodym' ('Among the Priests a Young
Levite', 1917) in *Tristia*.[56] In this poem the ominous yellow sky of
night is a foreboding of the destruction of the Temple, but also of
Jerusalem/Petersburg and the death of Russian Christian culture
in the Revolution. Nadezhda Mandelstam believes that the young
Levite whose warning is unheeded by the elders is none other
than Mandelstam himself.[57] Yet the 'joy of Judea' is the point of

view of doomed Judaism, not of the young Levite who has helped to swathe Jesus in precious linen.

A poem of 1919, 'Vernis' v smesitel'noe lono' ('Return to the Incestuous Gloom'), again posits the choice between the two suns, this time Leah's choice between the 'sun of Ilium' and the oblivion of 'yellow dusk.' Leah will not be Elena (Hellene),[58] but the conclusion of the poem is no longer openly antagonistic to Judea: 'No, you will love a Jew, / Disappear in him – and God be with you'.[59] The 'burden' of Jewish royal blood mentioned here and in 'Fourth Prose' seems as heavy and wearisome as the Judaic references in the early christological poems, but now there is something noble in this option of a poetic identity which bypasses the sordid history of the Jews in Russia and turns to the Levant, where Hellenism first battled with Hebraism.

Later the poet turned to Spain, where Mandelstam in his Voronezh exile discovered a new ancestor, a poet who composed sonnets in prison,[60] possibly Fray Luis de León (1527?–1591), arrested by the Inquisition on a 'Judaizing' charge. Taranovsky suggests Mandelstam must have known Valentin Parnakh's book, *Ispanskie i portugal'skie poety, zhertvy inkvizitsii* ('Spanish and Portuguese Poets, Victims of the Inquisition', 1934).[61] Yet, as Taranovsky points out, Nadezhda Mandelstam's reference to the 'two arrests' of the Spanish poet is not to be found in Parnakh's biographical note on Luis de León. However, it is known that León was denounced twice after his incarceration by the Inquisition, in 1580 and 1582, and that he obtained paper and ink during his four years in prison, where he wrote one of his major works.[62] Mandelstam would have appreciated the famous words attributed to León when he resumed his lectures at the University of Salamanca after his release: he addressed the students waiting to hear of his experiences, 'Dicebamus hesterna die ...'.[63] More interesting is the fact that Parnakh had previously appeared in the guise of Parnok as Mandelstam's Double in 'The Egyptian Stamp', an anti-heroic Jewish poet from whom the authorial voice wishes to be separated. Now, in the thirties, Parnakh's book appeared in Russia with a preface that drew a daring analogy between the plight of the Jewish poets under the Inquisition, who wrote in the language of their Christian oppressors, and the Jews in Tsarist Russia. The Jewish reader under Stalin might not be blamed for failing to reach the ideologically desirable inference that Jews were now fully emancipated and acculturated citizens of a free country. The unwritten analogy between Jews writing in Spanish or Portuguese and Jews writing in Russian (like Mandelstam and Parnakh himself) is even more instructive. The poem selected to represent Luis de León was in fact titled 'Prison':

> For five years lies and envy
> Have kept me here incarcerated.
> But there is consolation in submissiveness
> For the one who has abandoned the world
> And its wicked agitation.
>
> In this miserable house,
> As in a blessed field, he
> Is equal only to God,
> And meditates in strict quietude,
> Neither flattering nor being flattered.[64]

Mandelstam would have appreciated this and would have been struck, too, by Parnakh's comparison of Leone Ebreo's *Elegy about Time* with Ovid's *Tristia*, but he could not be said to want to imitate this scion of the Abarbanel family and he created no counterpart to Heine's Don Isaac Abarbanel in *The Rabbi of Barachach*.

RETURN TO JUDEA

A year after the publication of *Noise of Time*, there appeared a newspaper sketch by Mandelstam in which he discovers the joyful life of the Jews, Ukrainians and Russians of Kiev with much the same enthusiasm that Babel had, in 1916, preached to St Petersburg the virtues and *joie de vivre* of Odessa, of the sunny South which promised Russia's literary messiah and national Maupassant ('Odessa'). Typically, Mandelstam ferrets out the bohemian or underworld elements, but he also takes note of a scene worthy of Chagall in a Jewish prayer house in a basement, where the noisy worshippers are likened to schoolboys in their striped prayer shawls 'za zheltymi, tesnymi partami'.[65] The stuffy confines of Judaism are again associated with an image of childhood, with Time forever locked in immaturity and retardation, with spatial descent and with yellow. The complaints about NEP by the Podol artisan with the sheepish yellow eyes would have aroused sympathy in Isaak Babel's Gedali. Yet Jewish poverty in Kiev – very different, one would think, from Mandelstam's own upbringing as the son of a prosperous leather merchant – is not wholly despicable, for he welcomes the atmosphere of virtuosity and eccentricity in the Jewish crowd.

Of similar interest is another newspaper sketch of the same year, 'Mikhoels', dedicated to the renowned Soviet Yiddish actor. The moving performance of Mikhoels sums up for Mandelstam the earthy, bitter-sweet music of the *shtetl*, not Judaism or *shtetl* life, but a melody that will outlive their imminent destruction. However, Mandelstam never appropriated Yiddish culture as he appropriated the cultures of Western Europe and Hellenism. Yiddish was never the *mamaloshen* ('mother tongue') it was for Babel. If Mandelstam did in some way come closer to his Jewish brethren, as has been suggested, then this was doubtless part of his experience of the pressures not only of cultural but also of personal survival, together with the knowledge that he was named for the biblical Joseph (Osip): 'Joseph, sold into Egyptian bondage, / Could not yearn more acutely'.[66] If the yearning for the contaminated and heavy air of the rejected home permeates the exile into which Joseph has been sold, we should not be surprised to encounter those irremediable guilt-laden wounds in Mandelstam's poetic consciousness. George Steiner, reading the Brown–Merwin translation of the 1916 requiem for the poet's mother, connects the son's rebirth into adult aloneness with a bereavement into an exile from which there is no return, the exile of the modern Diaspora Jewish writer, whose sole homeland is the text, as for generations of Jews in exile the text of the written and oral Law was a homeland.[67] The poet's consciousness breathed the air of exile from early on, before exile became, as Nadezhda Mandelstam testifies so amply, an actual condition of his life and work.

As for Mandelstam's desire to return to the Jewish homeland at least spiritually and poetically, to which Nadezhda Mandelstam claims there is an allusion in the 1931 'Canzone',[68] the poem's interpretation is open to differences of opinion and reading. The poet clearly wants to flee the Hyperborean land of what he terms, in another poem of the same year to which Nadezhda Mandelstam makes reference, hated 'Buddhist' Moscow, and he looks to the Biblical Ararat of the Sabbatical land of Armenia, Judea's younger sister, as Mandelstam calls it in 'Fourth Prose':

> I will abandon the Hyperboreans' land
> In order to feast my eyes on the dénouement of fate,
> I'll say 'salaam' to the chief of the Jews
> For his raspberry caress.[69]

Arguing for a most careful and caring contextual reading of Mandelstam and against scholarly 'keys', Nadezhda Mandelstam links the 'raspberry caress' of the Chief of the Jews with the warm raspberry colour in Rembrandt's *Prodigal Son*. Mandelstam, she explains, is reassessing his destiny and returning, as in the New Testament parable, to his Father, here Judaic and not just Heavenly, to his Davidic descent which was likewise claimed for the Christians' messiah. Through the Zeiss binoculars the poet attains the prophetic foresight of the Psalmist as well as the Dantean vision which reduces distance and time; though Mandelstam could, either alternatively or additionally, be imitating Moses looking towards the Promised Land, which is barred to him, from his vantage point on Mount Nevo ('zren'em napitat''). Mandelstam could get no further south than Ararat, Noah's point of disembarkation, so that Armenia became his own beloved place of refuge and gateway to the culture of the Levant. He received much kindness ('laska') from the local 'Chief of the Jews' Askanaz Artem'evich Mravian, People's Commissar of Foreign Affairs of the Armenian Republic in 1920–1 and Commissar of Education from 1923, who died suddenly in 1929 but not before extending an invitation to Mandelstam to lecture at Erevan University. Mravian's first name cannot but have struck Mandelstam's sense of humour, especially considering the pun on his surname in 'Fourth Prose'. There is a tradition of identifying Armenia with Ashkenaz, one of the seventy nations mentioned in Genesis 10, 3 as a descendant of Japhet, ancestor of the Greeks and Slavs, after the repopulation of the world following the Flood, although in later rabbinical literature and to this day Ashkenaz refers to Germany, origin of much of East European Jewry, hence also a collective epithet for European Jews. The similarity is striking between Jewish and Armenian history in both premedieval and modern periods, and there has been a Jewish presence on Armenian soil since Hellenist times. It was once believed that the lost ten tribes dwelled there. Mandelstam would have been aware of the medieval Christian claim of a Hebrew genealogy for Armenia.

The green of Armenia's lush valleys in Mandelstam's poem recalls the Biblical fable of the fox and the grapes, but it also establishes a prophetic and historical overview which rejects the colourless modernity of Moscow.[70] The raspberry colour is the royal crimson of David, King of Israel, the poet-king, and a christological prefiguration in Christian iconology, but one which suggests a new and positive shade of Judaism.[71] Nevertheless, there seems to be no incontrovertible evidence that Mandelstam might have reevaluated his relationship with the Jewish people and the Zionist cause, as Kafka apparently did. Judaism can be discerned somewhere on Mandelstam's idiosyncratic iconostasis, an iconostasis as strange as that of Mervis in 'The Egyptian Stamp'. Yet Mandelstam's poetic credo enshrined play and freedom within a modernistic fleshing of the word that was christological in its identification of poet and Crucified Jew, but his goddess was classical simplicity. Judaism was not only other *(chuzhoi)*, incompatible, and complexly obscure; it was, in Mandelstam's aesthetics, a non-word. Mandelstam's Christian reception of *Iudeia*, the country of Judas (as distinct from the actual *Iudaizm* of the Jewish masses), may be contrasted with the unorthodox (and non-Orthodox) use of Christian mythology in Babel's portrayal of the dying East European *shtetl* awaiting its messiah. The downward drag of the burden of Judaism depicted in his early poetry could not withstand Mandelstam's Russian and

Christian reception of Hellenism. The negative colour of Judaism could not weigh down – to use Mandelstam's Acmeist adaptation of Hugo's geological and architectural metaphor of writing in *The Hunch-Back of Notre-Dame* - the soaring cathedral of his poetic thought: 'out of heavy weight', he wrote in 'Notre-Dame' (in 'Stone'), 'I too will create the sublime'. Nowhere is there more eloquent expression of this than in *Noise of Time*.

CHAPTER 5

The father, the son and Holy Russia: Boris Pasternak, Hermann Cohen and the religion of 'Doctor Zhivago'

Everything has a second birth.
William Wordsworth, *The Prelude*

AUTOBIOGRAPHY AS SECOND BIRTH

The concept of 'origin' was of special importance to Pasternak. In his book on Pasternak,[1] Lazar Fleishman has stressed that it was a loaded word in the Soviet period, when writers were expected to reject pre-Revolutionary and non-proletarian origins. We will see in the second half of this chapter how Pasternak was concerned in later years to present an original inspiration that reinvented the self in terms of a Russian literary heritage that ran counter to this official discourse. Pasternak rebelled against the Romantic notion of the poet's autobiography as identical with the poet's life, which had been adopted by the Russian symbolists, and wrote of the heart of poetry, instead of the poet's heart.[2] As it was for Rilke in *The Notebooks of Malte Laurids Brigge,* or for Joyce in *A Portrait of the Artist as a Young Man,* the autobiographical form in Boris Pasternak's *Okhrannaia gramota* (*A Safe-Conduct,* 1931) was a self-apprenticeship in poetry which gave an account of poetic origins as well as of poetic language and perception. This was a history of the imagination in James's terms, which gave the history of the poet's mind, like Wordsworth's *Prelude* or like Rilke's *Notebooks.*[3] These were a prelude to the art which would follow, a necessary clearing away of emotional or mental rubble before the poet could tackle a major work – for Rilke the *Duino Elegies*[4] – except that in Pasternak's case there was more than one rebirth and autobiography was to be continually revised in line with changing conditions in Russia and in Pasternak's personal life. After the 1925 Party resolution on literature and the increasing dominance of the hard-line Marxist proletarian writers' association RAPP in literary politics, Pasternak had cause to fear for his artistic freedom. The writing of *A Safe-Conduct* coincided, moreover, with the breakdown of Pasternak's first marriage.

The book was begun in 1926 when Pasternak was engaged in a triangular correspondence with Rilke and Marina Tsvetaeva, whose 'Poem of the End' he read that year, along with Maiakovsky's *Chelovek* ('Man') and Esenin's *Pugachev*.[5] In *A Safe-Conduct* Pasternak created his poetic self in the image of Rilke, but he was understandably hesitant to don the mantle of the Soviet laureate Maiakovsky, whose suicide, after the love boat smashed to smithereens on the rocks of ideological and artistic contradictions, concludes the revised first edition of the book in 1931. The first part of *A Safe-Conduct* appeared in August 1929 in the Leningrad journal *Zvezda*, together with Pasternak's translation from Rilke's 'Requiem', forming a poetic dialogue with Rilke, who had died in December 1926. The appearance of the second and third parts coincided with the Pilniak and Zamiatin affairs and the dissolution of *Lef*, among other non-Proletkul't movements, and current events find cryptic reference in the treatment of Marburg and Maiakovsky.[6] Death, as Boris Thomson seems to suggest,[7] heralded a second birth, and *Vtoroe rozhdenie* ('Second Birth', 1932) was indeed the title of Pasternak's next book of poems.

The title *Okrannaia gramota* refers to an anachronistic and therefore polemical use of a term in the early years of the Revolution for the guarantee of inviolability of valuable private cultural property that might otherwise be plundered or nationalized,[8] suggesting that it was the preservation of his poetry rather than his person that Pasternak had in mind, a secret record that had to be decoded *poetically*.[9] It is a title that, according to Krystyna Pomorska, also refers to the imparting of the Divine Word to the prophet Isaiah for transmission to the people, an idea attributable to Pushkin's famous poem called 'The Prophet' following Lamartine's declaration that a real poet was but a kind of prophet in the Biblical mode.[10] *A Safe-Conduct* demonstrates Pasternak's belief in the mysterious protection guarding his career, evidenced in the providential coincidences of railway timetables, which guided him to the fateful meetings that were to endow him with the gift – in all senses – of poetry.

The first meeting granted to Pasternak on his poetic journey was with Rilke. Pasternak declared that the story of Rilke's genius was to be told by what happened to his readers: 'I am not presenting my recollections in memory of Rilke. On the contrary I myself received them as a gift from him.'[11] Pasternak's discovery of Rilke through the poet's book on his father's shelf and the remembrance of the chance encounter with Rilke himself on an express train in 1900 determine his place in Rilke's poetry, as well as intimating Pasternak's own gift of poetry.[12] Pasternak takes from Proust the idea that the 'world's best creations, those which tell of the most diverse things, in reality describe their own birth'.[13] The apparent disjointedness of narrative connection emphasizes both the fragmentariness of the modern experience and the nature of the creative process, the flux and fluidity of life expressed in the Pasternakian imagery of snowstorms and rain showers, metonymic of the interpenetration of the human and natural world.[14]

Coincidence in both *A Safe-Conduct* and *Doctor Zhivago* is elevated almost into a metaphysical principle. What Pilling calls the 'untimeliness of coincidence' focuses the past and moves it forward into the future. This is not so much 'time regained', as in Proust, but time collapsed. Pilling has traced this idiosyncratic theory of time to Pasternak's 1916 essay 'The Black Goblet', in which he distinguished between 'time' as it turned into 'history' and 'eternity' which is unknowable and belongs to the realm of the lyric poet.[15] Roman Jakobson, on the other hand, in drawing attention to the metonymic language of *A Safe-Conduct*, sees the poet defining his life negatively, by contiguity, and that is why the train journey serves as a useful metaphor for the randomness of connections in which the self is not a genuine agent but an observer.[16] The repeated motif of the train in both *A Safe-Conduct* and *Doctor Zhivago* expresses the idea of an undeveloped person-ality in transit. As Pilling puts it, each journey takes him 'over the barriers' into an unfamiliar world, 'a crossing over into a new faith', not in the strictly theological sense, but a faith in the miraculous benevolence of life.[17]

These brief remarks should make clear why *A Safe-Conduct* cannot be read as a conventional autobiography, but also why it is so revealing in its presentation of self and the idea of the poet. The poet proceeds by negation and crossing-out, self-definition by rejection of what he is not, but he also gives a statement by counterpoint and self-negating observation of his claim to origins in the pre-Revolutionary world of painting and music. Boris Pasternak's childhood is indeed incomprehensible without an understanding, first, of Leonid Pasternak's early association with the *Peredvizhniki*, then of his personal mix of realism and Russian-style post-impressionism.[18] Though his mother gave up a career as an international concert pianist, Boris positively breathed music at home and, as a budding composer, was privileged to know Skriabin. There is also Lermontov, Lermontov's *Demon*. Tolstoy is also there, not least because the great teacher was ever present in the Pasternak household, and not only through Leonid Pasternak's illustrations of *Resurrection* and the final drawing of the dead novelist at the railway station at Astapovo in November 1910, another railway encounter which imprinted itself on Boris Pasternak's impressionable memory. Incidentally, Pasternak was only too aware that Skriabin's neo-Nietzschean influence was at odds with a Tolstoyan outlook. But such contradictions shaped Pasternak's complex personality.

At the same time there is much that Pasternak wrote out of his life, and one example in *A Safe-Conduct* is the Judaic element in the culture of the Pasternak home. Leonid Pasternak was claimed by Bialik as a Jewish national artist, and the reservations and qualifications in Leonid Pasternak's reply to Bialik illuminate the artist's affinity to both Russia and the Jewish national spirit. He explained that he had never left the fold, although his art was unappreciated by the Jewish bourgeoisie, but he had 'grown up, of course, in Russian surroundings, received a Russian education, and developed under the influence of tendencies in the Russian eighteen-eighties, i.e. tendencies towards assimilation, and *with a debt of service to the Russian people*'.[19] Leonid Pasternak defined his understanding of the Jewish national spirit in non-ethnic and non-religious terms in his 1923 monograph on Rembrandt, *Rembrandt i evreistvo v ego tvorchestve* ('Rembrandt and Jewry in his Work'), and he considered it conducive to the new art that would arise in Palestine, which he visited in 1924 on a sketching tour.[20] Leonid Pasternak's book is dated Moscow 1918–20, a time (as mentioned in Chapter 2) when Efros, a staunch critic of Leonid Pasternak, was advocating an avant-garde Jewish aesthetics based on An-sky's rediscovery of folk-art. Leonid Pasternak looks instead to Rembrandt's Calvinist perception of the Jews as a Biblical nation, a people of shepherds and patriarchs, and he senses ideal qualities in Rembrandt's humanization of everyday scenes, a gift he had long admired and tried to emulate. Lazar Fleishman has com-mented on the significance of his father's views on the Jewish spirit for Boris Pasternak's art,[21] and George Gibian has proposed a theory that Boris Pasternak transferred the spiritual and national ideas in the Rembrandt monograph to the Russian people in the novel *Doctor Zhivago*.[22] Gibian's hypothesis is that Boris Pasternak's ideas, embodied in the central themes of *Doctor Zhivago*, drew him into a dialogic confrontation with his father's views and with a Slavophile view of Russia's historical mission and of the special role of Russian literature. Where Leonid Pasternak saw Rembrandt drawing out the spirituality of Old Testament figures, Boris Pasternak, reasons Gibian, substituted the New Testament (a fundamental Christian hermeneutic strategy, by the way) and the inner freedom of Christianity which the Jews had rejected. There is really no inconsistency in the difficulty noted by Gibian of reconciling Pasternak's belief that Christianity overrode nationhood with the moral superiority of Russia as the suffering nation. For Pasternak, as Gibian shows convincingly, the Russian Revolution represented a mystical event parallel with the Gospels, and the poet had a prophetic task (like another converted Jew, Paul) to preach a vision of history associated with Russia's special destiny. I would go further and suggest that this may explain not only the religious ideas of Zhivago, to which I shall shortly return, but also the curious treatment in *A Safe-Conduct* of Hermann Cohen, the famous neo-Kantian, under whom Boris Pasternak studied in 1912.

Cohen's appointment to a full professorship at Marburg in

1876, like Leonid Pasternak's appointment to the Moscow School of Painting and Sculpture, was fairly exceptional. Cohen had strongly denied any double loyalty of German Jewry in his defence of Judaism in 1880 against the historian Treitschke's charge that it was the national religion of an alien race; and he later testified in a lawsuit that Judaism did not discriminate against gentiles, but that, on the contrary, the chosen people were chosen to realize the messianic unity of mankind. We can only guess at the relevance of this for Boris Pasternak's views on nationhood and Russia's messianic mission, which (typically for Christianity) denied the Jews such a role. In 1912 Cohen retired from Marburg to lecture at the Berlin Lehranstalt für die Wissenschaft des Judentums. This involvement in the founding of modern Jewish studies in Germany and Poland marks a decisive step in the reformulation of the Kantian system in order to affirm the truth of Judaism, set out in *Die Religion der Vernunft aus den Quellen des Judentums,* published posthumously in 1919. Cohen's visit to Moscow in 1914 made an impression on Russian Jewry and is said to have dissuaded some from apostasy. Boris Pasternak certainly felt sufficient nostalgia to revisit Marburg in 1923. By then Cohen was dead.

It was Skriabin who, in 1909, advised Boris Pasternak to transfer from the Law Faculty to the Historico-Philological Faculty of Moscow University, where he studied philosophy. At that time the works of Henri Bergson were becoming popular in Russia, while Husserl and the Göttingen school found a militant proponent in the young Gustav Shpet. We know that Pasternak took part in the doctrinal debates of those days because he wrote an attack on the advocate of logical psychologism, Theodor Lipps.[23] The rector of the university, S. N. Trubetskoi, was an active supporter of the Marburg philosophers and he sent his best students to study under Hermann Cohen and Paul Natorp. Pasternak found two aspects of the Marburg school attractive:

First of all it was original. It dug everything over down to the foundations and it built upon clear ground. It did not share the lazy routine of all the *isms* which one can think of, which always cling to their profitable tenth-hand omniscience, are always ignorant, and are for some reason or another always afraid of a review conducted in the free air of our ancient culture. The Marburg school did not suffer from any terminological inertia and it turned back to primary sources, that is, to the authentic signatures left by thought in the history of science. If current philosophy talks about what one writer or another thinks, and current psychology – about how the average man thinks, and if formal logic teaches us how we should think at the baker's in order to get the right change, then the Marburg school was interested in how science has thought in its twenty-five centuries of continuous authorship at the blazing source and origin of the world's discoveries. In such a disposition, authorized, as it were, by history itself, philosophy grew young and wise beyond recognition, and from a problematic discipline it turned into the primordial discipline about problems, which indeed it ought to be.

A second feature of the Marburg school derived directly from the first and consisted in its discriminating and exacting approach to the legacy of history. ... In Marburg they knew history to perfection and never tired of hauling treasure after treasure from the archives of the Italian Renaissance, French and Scottish rationalism and other little-studied schools. In Marburg they looked at history through both Hegelian eyes, that is, in a brilliantly generalised fashion, but at the same time within the exact limits of commonsense plausibility.[24]

Apart from the noteworthy keyword 'original', the insistence on historicism and especially the reference to Hegel in this excerpt from *A Safe-Conduct* is of interest to readers of *Doctor Zhivago*, although Pasternak points out that he does not intend a presentation of Cohen's system. Such a presentation would not suit the era of Stalinism and the First Five-Year Plan; nor would it suit Pasternak's purpose in writing *A Safe-Conduct,* to evoke in figurative language the genesis of his poetic creativity.

Pasternak was registered at Marburg University from 9 May 1912 to 3 August 1912. During that brief span of time he became one of Cohen's promising students and earned an invitation to dinner that Pasternak describes in terms of an invitation to a career in philosophy, an invitation which he rejected.

The chapter on Marburg in *A Safe-Conduct* blends with Pasternak's impressionistic account of his intellectual development and omits the historical and personal forces that were to change his life or were to change the history of Russia. Cohen's presence permeates the streets and cafés of Marburg only as much as

Leonid Pasternak and Tolstoy are mutely present in previous
chapters. He is there in the lecture-room, waving vaguely in the
direction of the Marburg fire-station when he speaks of the
Elysian Fields. However, that is not the same thing as the author
of *Ethics of Pure Will*.

There exists a sketch by Leonid Pasternak of the philosopher
together with his Russian student in a Marburg street, although
this was based on a study done at one of the philosopher's lectures
and we know that the painter was in the habit of planting
members of his family in his portraits. But more revealing for the
difference in attitude it shows towards Jewishness between Cohen
and the Pasternaks is Cohen's reaction to a suggestion by some of
his students that his portrait be commissioned for his seventieth
birthday. Boris Pasternak was given the awkward task of approaching the great man and proposing the commission be given
to his father, whose name was unknown to Cohen. The latter
was, moreover, labouring under the misapprehension that he was
expected to pay for his portrait. Later on, when Cohen finally
agreed, the condition upon which he insisted was that the painter
be Jewish. To this Boris Pasternak responded in a letter home
(18 June 1912):

> something is distasteful to me in all this. He is right: neither I nor you
> are Jews, although we not only voluntarily but also without a shadow of
> martyrdom bear all that this happy circumstance obliges us to (for
> example, the impossibility of my earning a living on the basis of the only
> faculty that is dear to me), and we not only bear it, but I will bear it and
> I consider it unseemly to try to escape it; but in no way is Jewry any
> closer to me for all that.[25]

This frank admission of acceptance of the status of Jew without
commitment to Judaism underlines the rift that would surely have
come between Pasternak and Cohen if another event had not
separated them.

Pasternak's studies in Marburg were interrupted in July by the
visit of the Vysotsky sisters. Pasternak's infatuation with one of the
sisters, Ida Davidovna, ended with her rejecting the prospective,
though as yet prospect-less, suitor. Pasternak's frustration at an
unsatisfying parting led to a mad flight to Berlin by train as an

unwelcome travelling companion of the Vysotskys, followed by his return to Marburg and the rejection on the rebound of Cohen and philosophy. Now Pasternak threw himself into poetry, finding a new lyrical voice released by unrequited love.

The rejection of his marriage proposal was to be such a pivotal event in Pasternak's poetics that he came back time and again to the poem he wrote about it, 'Marburg'.[26] However, this only partly explains Pasternak's revisionism in writing out the Marburg episode in *A Safe-Conduct*, a revisionism taken further in the later, much shorter account in *Avtobiograficheskii ocherk* (*An Essay in Autobiography*, 1956–7). The impetuosity of Pasternak's behaviour should make obvious his temperamental unsuitability for a philosophical career; but, in terms of the structure of *A Safe-Conduct*, it is the traumatic epiphany which brings about the fateful decision, just as lack of perfect pitch and the horrendous discovery of that flaw in Skriabin led to the rejection of musical composition earlier in the book, although these drawbacks need not have been fatal. Indeed, as Christopher Barnes has shown, Pasternak did not give up music until summer 1909,[27] and he had been writing verse since 1909–10. Moreover, Pasternak is virtually silent on his involvement with another woman at this time, his cousin Olga Freidenberg. Their relationship broke off in 1910 and now those two years held them apart. On receiving an unexpected letter from Olga on 28 June Pasternak rushed to Olga's hotel in Frankfurt (another, different mad flight), but Olga found him two years behind her in development, as she wrote to him later the same day.[28] If turning to pure logic had been a way of trying to cure himself of Romanticism, now these two years, years to be crucial to the story of his spiritual birth in his later years, were suddenly discovered to be a wrong turning. Pasternak replied to her letter that he was repudiating philosophy, maths and law in order to return to his true self. In *A Safe-Conduct* it reads as if the new vision which Pasternak gained on his return from the Vysotskys in Berlin was predicated on rejection in love. It would be truer to say that Pasternak needed an emotional jolt to make up his mind about his increasingly ambivalent attitude toward Cohen and philosophy.

Of the towering father-figures which dominate *A Safe-Conduct* –

Rilke, Tolstoy, Skriabin, Cohen and Maiakovsky – all die; only Rilke survives to eternity in the poet's consciousness. Of these potential paternal models, only Cohen lacks any claim to inspiration in both poetry and the Russian spirit. The pilgrimage to Germany was shared with revolutionary Jewish students, who made up a growing proportion of Russian students at German universities after 1905 and who saw Germany as a cultural as well as political haven; yet, for all the historicism of Pasternak's poetic summation of Marburg's picturesque charisma, Pasternak describes himself coming to Marburg in the footsteps of the eighteenth-century Russian philosopher Mikhail Lomonosov, and he comes not so much to the anti-mystical sanctuary of neo-Kantianism as to the shrine of St Elizabeth, a mystical symbol of transcendental values.

Nonetheless, Cohen is described as a 'genius', a term in Pasternak's vocabulary that denotes both high esteem for a hero and recognition of essential truths. We cannot doubt the impact Cohen made on Pasternak, particularly on what Sir Isaiah Berlin once suggested might be Marburg's neo-Kantian sense of unity in Pasternak's poetics, 'induced by the sense of the pervasiveness of cosmic categories ... which integrate all the orders of creation into a single, biologically and physiologically, emotionally and intellectually, interrelated universe'.[29] This was an intellectual climate which influenced the Russian formalists and which, amongst the various trends in European philosophy, in particular the ideas of Bergson, moulded the modernist outlook in poetry and prose. It was Cohen who gave basic neo-Kantian concepts of individual and moral answerability to the Nevel' circle of M. M. Bakhtin, and particularly M. I. Kagan who had studied at Marburg, concepts which they then outgrew but which survived in their terminology. Nils Åke Nilsson has traced Pasternak's idea of the power of poetry as independent of the persona of the poet to the neo-Kantian view of the function of art and noted that it is encountered in the English Imagists of the period; it is found also in Rilke, to whom Pasternak declared his indebtedness in *A Safe-Conduct*.[30] However, the perception of time and space in *A Safe-Conduct* reminds us just as much of Proust, whom Pasternak had started to read but found 'too close'.[31]

Perhaps Boris Pasternak was not so much disillusioned by Cohen as put off by the academic milieu at Marburg, by the 'skoty intellektualizma' (herds of intellectual cattle), as he wrote to his friend Shtikh on 19 July 1912.[32] The tradition of Prussian discipline and academic precision seem obviously at odds with the romantic tendencies of a student who spent much of his time absorbed in the poetry of Verlaine. Pasternak's description of Cohen and neo-Kantianism actually has more affinity in its emphasis on individuality with his father's appreciation of Rembrandt's *Blessing of Jacob* in the Kassel art gallery: the keyword is 'chelovek' (man).[33] Another keyword which is significant in Boris Pasternak's later work is 'radost'' (joy), and it is the human warmth in Rembrandt's renderings of biblical scenes drawn from contemporary Jewish life that attracted Leonid Pasternak to Rembrandt's *Prodigal Son* in the Hermitage, a painting which also drew the attention of Nadezhda Mandelstam in her attempt to interpret Mandelstam's 'Canzone'. In this rendition of the New Testament story, the father expresses in his caress of the son the warmth and tenderness of divine love for the sinful flock, compassion and grace. Leonid Pasternak sees here the quintessence of the moral teaching of Christianity as inherited from Judaism by Jesus, the disciple of Hillel.[34] Rembrandt's Calvinist background endeared him to the Sefardic community in Amsterdam as the bearer of the message of the Bible, and the Pasternaks themselves boasted a Sefardic lineage going back to the famous Bible commentator Isaac Abarbanel (sometimes spelt Abravanel) and the expulsion of the Jews from Spain in 1492. Leonid Pasternak refers to it in a letter of December 1924 to Boris Pasternak, and the genealogy was repeated by Valentin Parnakh in an essay on Russian poetry, with reference to Boris Pasternak.[35] However, the family's obvious assimilation makes the identification with Rembrandt's artistic vision a claim to personal identity in the absence of close ties with Jews and Judaism.

Leonid Osipovich disliked the nouveau-riche Jews of Kissingen, where his wife Rozalia was taking the cure, and much preferred what he considered the truer spirit of Judaism in the Rembrandt collection at Kassel, where he took Boris when he visited his family. It was on that visit to Kissingen that Boris attended Ida

Davidovna's birthday party on July 14, and nothing could point up the fundamental incompatibility between them more than Ida Davidovna's offensive comment that he should live more 'conventionally' (she later married a Kiev banker, clearly more suited to keep her in the style to which she was accustomed).The contrast between the ostentatiously wealthy Jewish bourgeoisie at Kissingen, materialistic and unappreciative of the fine arts (the uncultured 'bad Jew' of the stereotyped Other), and the aesthetic and spiritual vision discernible in Rembrandt's Jewish portraits comes out strongly in Leonid Pasternak's Rembrandt monograph. It seems fair to presume, therefore, that Boris Pasternak would have had little difficulty in choosing between them.

Hermann Cohen's anti-Zionism, as he explained in his letters to Martin Buber, was based on the universalism of the Jews' messianic mission and on his conviction that Jews must stand by Germany, their cultural homeland. If, as Gibian claims, Pasternak in *Doctor Zhivago* transfers the messianic mission to Christianity (which Cohen could not regard as a religion of reason because of its mysticism) and to its spirit in Russian historical destiny, he was in effect rejecting the role-model of Cohen as an alternate father. Moreover, Pasternak's admiration for his own father's achievement, in particular his sense of strict honesty in art and dedication to the ideals of a past epoch, left the poet feeling guilty because he felt that he could never hope to match his father's accomplishments. The writing of *Doctor Zhivago* was dedicated to his father's memory. However, we find in Pasternak's prose several examples of a father's paradigmatic abandonment of his son. In 'Story of a Contraoctave' the art of the father literally cripples the son when the organist, carried away by inspiration, plays octaves on the boy's body. In 'Liuvers' Childhood' one is struck by the coldness of the mother and the father's absence. *Doctor Zhivago* opens with the orphaning of Yuri Zhivago and the suicide of his father who had abandoned him. This would suggest that Boris felt as if he had been rendered impotent by his parents' success. Indeed, the public neuroses which Boris suffered may be due to feelings of inadequacy when faced by his mother's illustrious career and concert performances, while his father's artistic achievement may have proven crippling for his son who tried to imitate him (at one point Boris was drawing and painting in the manner of his father).

Pasternak saw *Doctor Zhivago* as a statement of his whole work, enshrining the idea of the poet as a Hamlet who is chosen and – like Jesus in Gethsemane – prays that the cup might pass him by. The Hamlet figure continues the Russian tradition of the self-questioning, ineffectual intellectual, as well as reminding us of another portrait of the artist, Joyce's Stephen Daedalus in *Ulysses*. Christopher Barnes, a biographer of Pasternak, writes, 'Pasternak's picture of Yuri Zhivago was in fact partly an exercise in self-portrayal, depicting a man who felt at one with nature, art and history, and who saw himself as inheritor of a broad Russian and European culture'.[36] And even if Pasternak did not see himself quite as the voice of social conscience, he does follow Pushkin in his overall concern in *Doctor Zhivago* for the spiritual and more humane values identified with the Russian nation.[37] To Pasternak's way of thinking, these were values antithetical to any attachment to Judaism. The hero of his epic novel, subtitled a 'poema' like Pushkin's *Eugene Onegin,* cannot be thought of otherwise than in the tradition of the Russian realist novel and otherwise than within terms of Pasternak's rather idiosyncratic adoption of the Christian faith.

A few words are first necessary on Boris Pasternak's conversion to Christianity. He is said to have been secretly baptized by his nanny, Akulina Gavrilovna. This was possibly no more than a private fantasy, like his fantasy that he was not his parents' son (a fantasy later transferred to Doctor Zhivago) or his self-imagining as a woman (apparent in 'Liuvers' Childhood').[38] Lazar Fleishman suggests[39] baptism could have been a response to the eviction of Jews from Moscow in March 1891, but this was an edict from which Leonid Pasternak was in any case exempt by virtue of his higher education. The sumptuous decoration of Russian churches and the pageantry of Orthodox ritual deeply impressed the child, and his parents made no objection to his attending church services with Akulina Gavrilovna. Later he was

to go to church 'of his own accord' to listen to the magnificent
Moscow church choirs,[40] and in Berlin he would listen with
rapture to the organ at the Gedächtniskirche, a performance used
in the Hoffmannesque 'Story of a Contraoctave' and described
by Aleksandr Pasternak in his memoirs.

With the telling revision of later years Pasternak was to write to
Jacqueline de Proyart on May 2, 1959:

J'ai été baptisé par ma bonne de prime enfance, mais à cause des
restrictions contre les juifs et surtout dans une famille qui en était
exempte et jouissait d'une certaine distinction acquise par les mérites
artistiques du père, le fait s'était un peu compliqué et restait toujours
mi-secret et intime, objet d'une inspiration rare et exceptionnelle plutôt
que d'une calme habitude. Mais je pense que c'est la source de mon
originalité. Je vivais le plus de ma vie dans la pensée chrétienne dans les
années 1910–1912, où se formaient les racines, les bases principales de
cette originalité, la vision des choses, du monde, de la vie ... [41]

One or two points are particularly remarkable in this confession
of faith. Firstly, Pasternak's Russian Christianity, which became,
at the end of his life's work, after the writing of *Doctor Zhivago*,
so characteristic of his self-image and authorial personality, is
presented as emanating from the most stereotyped images of
Russianness, the nanny who teaches the folk-lore and religious
truth of the popular heritage. As Rijngaila Salys has shown,
Leonid Pasternak was not adverse to prefiguring his son as a
Pushkinian figure and this can be seen in the sketch of him with
the family nanny.[42] Secondly, the clandestine nature of the
baptism would seem inexplicable, given those very restrictions on
Jews which Boris Pasternak mentions and which applied to many
who lacked a baptismal certificate. We recall Leonid Pasternak's
refusal, when accepting his appointment at the Moscow School of
Art, to undergo even nominal conversion to the Russian
Orthodox Church.

The Pasternaks would never have thought of themselves as
wandering Jews, despite Leonid Pasternak's love for cosmopolitan
Odessa, but as thoroughly Muscovite and Russian, sharing the
rituals of the Russian year such as Easter egg painting (immortalized by Leonid Pasternak in a 1916 sketch) with their Russian
Orthodox and assimilated Jewish friends and neighbours. Boris

Pasternak once declared to his friend Aleksandr Shtikh: 'By blood I am a Jew, but in everything else and with that exception I am Russian.'[43] Recording his meetings with Pasternak in Chistopol, where a number of writers were evacuated during the Second World War, Alexander Gladkov quotes him as saying that he was for complete assimilation of the Jews, and that he felt at home in Russian culture, in the Russian literary tradition that was open to Western influence, as in the example of Pushkin: 'I have Jewish blood in my veins, but nothing is more alien to me than Jewish nationalism – except, perhaps, Great-Russian chauvinism.'[44] After the war, following the campaign against Zoshchenko and Akhmatova and against the background of increasing anti-Semitism in the arts, Pasternak brushed off the anti-Semitic attacks because he thought the Jewish problem was best solved by complete assimilation, arguing that Pushkin, who was after all considered the most Russian of poets, refuted racist or ultra-nationalist theories because, according to the legend that he was descended on his mother's side from an African slave, he was a mulatto.[45] This was a time when the Jewish director of the Sovetskii pisatel' publishing house, Levin, was denounced in the press for republishing verse by Pasternak. By coopting Pushkin Pasternak both claimed legitimacy and hinted at the precarious position of a court poet embroiled in intrigues against him; but the advocacy of apostasy was by this time a matter of personal faith, reflected later in *Doctor Zhivago*, not merely a deflection of the voice of the Other. When he met Boris Pasternak in 1945, Sir Isaiah Berlin found a Russian poet who would not be thought of in any other way; he was not embarrassed to speak of his Jewish origin but simply disliked discussing the matter: he wished the Jews to disappear as a people.[46] Olga Ivinskaia remembers Pasternak's ultrasensitivity about his Jewish origins when dictating personal details for an official form; 'when he came to "nationality", he hesitated and then mumbled: "Nationality: mixed – write that down." '[47]

The years 1910 to 1912, to which Pasternak dates his first finding of inspiration in Christianity, were years in which he immersed himself in music and philosophy, in fields which could hardly be said to be in conflict with his parents' ambitions for him. Indeed, it was his mother's hard-earned income from piano lessons that got Pasternak to Marburg. Moreover, 1912 marked both his exposure to Hermann Cohen's class in ethics and the abandonment of philosophy for reasons which have apparently not much to do with the professional difficulties a Jew would face in Russia, as Hermann Cohen had hinted.[48] His parents' affinity with German culture had in fact made them decide to send Boris to the Lutheran school in Moscow, and he was sent to a state school because that afforded at least the chance for a Jew to enter higher education if he got a gold medal. It was only reluctantly that he agreed to register his marriage to his first wife with a rabbi in addition to the civil registry.[49] The only time he attended a Jewish burial, when his mother-in-law died in 1928, he found the rites repugnant.[50]

Guy de Mallac believes that the decisive step was made in the 1930s when Pasternak, who had previously been married to the Jewish painter Evgeniia Lourie, went to live with Zinaida Niko-laevna Neuhaus (née Eremeeva), a Russian Christian.[51] A further 'inspiration' seems to have occurred while Pasternak was fire-watching in Moscow during the Second World War, and Lazar Fleishman has conjectured that Pasternak's embracing of Christianity coincided with a temporary lifting of restrictions on the Orthodox Church during the war against Germany, a war perceived by some at the time as a patriotic struggle of George and the dragon, one of the motifs of *Doctor Zhivago*. There was, argues Fleishman, no question of an alternative other than a religious identification with Russia. Full expression of Pasternak's Christianity is first given only in *Doctor Zhivago*, a novel which Pasternak had been evolving over the years and which polem-icized many of the ideas about identity and poetry which affected him most intimately.[52]

By Christianity Pasternak means the idea of self-sacrifice that informs the religious ideas of Doctor Zhivago. Zhivago's ultimate gift, the giving of one's self to others through loving and poetry, *in imitatione* of the sacrifice of Jesus, is incompatible with Judaism's conception of sacrifice (of money or animals) as a way of coming closer to God, community and national destiny. That is probably why Judaism did not satisfy Boris Pasternak's thirst for mysticism.[53] In contrast to Hermann Cohen's reconciliation of Kantian aesthetics and reason with Judaism, Pasternak's faith excluded any concept of Judaism as a valid ethical or artistic system. In the reinvention of his childhood in the later *Essay in Autobiography*, Pasternak attributes to the proximity of the insulted and injured of Moscow's streets the early compassion he felt for women, as well as for his parents, whom he felt he had to save from the torments of hell by performing some great heroic deed. This origin of the idea of the poet as self-sacrificing hero identifies his concept of sexual and filial love with suffering ('stradanie') and with a mystical christological notion of redemption through art.

DOCTOR ZHIVAGO'S CLOSELY OBSERVED TRAINS

A few examples from *Doctor Zhivago* will suffice to illustrate how the presentation of Jews and Judaism reflects Pasternak's own 'original inspiration' in Russian Christianity, a Christianity informed by the thought of Berdiaev, Fedorov and Shestov, and how the idea of the poet comes to be identified with the Russian national idea in a Tolstoyan epic of history from the 1905 uprising to the dashing of hopes in the Revolution in 1929. The ultimate message of the novel is contained in the spiritual freedom Zhivago carries within him and which he hands down in the memory of the next generation, a message contained in the imagery and metaphors of the novel that run counter to official discourse because they are inspired by a view of history based on Pasternak's understanding of the Gospels, which he understood to initiate the era of History, before which there was only Myth.[54]

The first example features the recurrent leitmotif of the train journey,[55] a leitmotif familar from *A Safe-Conduct*, which brings about the fateful encounter with Misha Gordon in the opening chapter of the novel, 'The Five O'Clock Express'. This chapter introduces us to the key notion of resurrection (at the funeral of Zhivago's mother), and to an anthropomorphized landscape (where the blizzard and the shower are intimate with human existence). Nature marks time by the Russian Orthodox calendar of feast and saints' days, by the Russian agricultural year, by the coming apocalyptic violence of the 1905 Revolution. The un-

frocked priest and ex-Tolstoyan Nikolai Nikolaevich Vedeniapin
is here the spokesman for the logical-ethical view of history,
which he bequeathes to Yuri Zhivago and Misha Gordon. The
time is summer 1903 and the scene a visit to the country by
Nikolai Nikolaevich, accompanied by the boy Yuri Zhivago, who
has been entrusted to his care. Nikolai Nikolaevich makes a
speech on faith and history which introduces 'the two basic ideals
of modern man ... the idea of free personality and the idea of life
as sacrifice'.[56] It is at this crucial point that the express train
appears on the horizon and is stopped by the suicide of Yuri's
father. On the train with his father is Misha Gordon, whom the
dead man had befriended, clearly as a substitute for the son he
had abandoned; it is Misha who thinks of his Jewish identity as
something that cuts him off from the rest of humanity, an obstacle
to the general freedom from existential anxiety.

This freedom came from the feeling that all human lives were
interrelated, a certainty that they flowed into each other – a happy
feeling that all events took place not only on the earth, in which the
dead are buried, but also in some other region which some called the
Kingdom of God, others history, and still others by some other
name. (15)

The inter-relationship of men and the struggle with death, which
constitutes a shared historical experience, prove incompatible
with being a Jew. To underline the point, Misha's thoughts on
Jewish identity and the suicide of Yuri's father coincide with the
appearance of the widow Tiverzina and Yuri's ecstatic prayer for
his mother's soul in a nearby field. The chapter closes with Nika,
the son of a convicted revolutionary terrorist, tasting the freedom
and elation of the Russian natural landscape, which are denied to
the Jew Misha.[57]

In order to emphasize the importance of the negation of
Judaism, the link between Misha and Yuri is cemented when the
former is briefly adopted emotionally by the latter's father. The
Gordons' social position (second-class) in the train, the Gordons'
status in Moscow, and the friendship that will develop between
Misha and Yuri under the influence of Nikolai Nikolaevich all
point to a parallel with Pasternak's own childhood in Moscow, a

parallel which, in its revision of autobiography, bears personal significance for its explicit statement on Judaism as a central thesis of a cosmology that forms the basis for the imagery and ideology of the novel.[58] It will be noted that it is Misha who tells Yuri that it was Komarovsky (the unnamed lawyer on the five o'clock express) who drove Yuri's father to his death. Misha discloses this information at the exact moment when Yuri's discovery of Komarovsky's relationship with Lara shatters his youthful Tolstoyanism after Madame Guishar's attempted suicide. It is that moment which Lara, speaking of Komarovsky as the evil genius of both her life and Zhivago's, later calls 'predestination'.

The second example of what one might call railway-timetable providence is Misha's visit – by train – to the Galician front during the First World War. Misha, who graduated, like Pasternak, in philosophy, plays a dubious role here as a spectator, while Zhivago, now a poet and a doctor, views war with the expert eye of experience and art. Misha happens to meet Zhivago and to be holed up with him in a remote village, just before Zhivago's meeting with Lara, who is serving as a nurse while searching for her missing husband. The thoughts of Zhivago and Gordon on seeing a victim of anti-Semitism in the battle zone (the scene of what An-sky described as the 'Destruction of Galician Jewry') once more come at an important juncture in the ideational and plot development of the novel. Misha's response to what Zhivago sees as the unjustified persecution of the Jews and their perpetual, unnecessary suffering is part of the historical, and therefore artistic, overview (the context is, moreover, a discussion on prose style). Just as Nikolai Nikolaevich saw Jesus bringing to an end the history of nations and liberating man through individualism, his disciple Misha declares that the Jews lost the opportunity to attain spiritual happiness by not accepting the teachings of Jesus. The Jews can end their persecution by accepting their true historical destiny, by accepting Christianity: their leaders should tell them, ' "Don't hold on to your identity. Don't stick together, disperse. Be with all the rest. ... You are the very thing against which you have been turned by the worst and weakest among you" ' (105). This solution to the Jewish Question, which so angered David Ben-

Gurion, is explicitly integral to a philosophy that sees individual fates throughout the novel as contingent on the interrelated human struggle with death – that is, life; that is, art. History, Pasternak told Aleksandr Gladkov, could be described as 'a parallel universe created by mankind in response to an instinctive wish to hold death and non-being at bay. Time and memory – that is, history – are what constitute true immortality, for which the Christian idea of personal life everlasting is a poetic image.'[59]

The ultra-assimilationist position is not unique to Misha's understanding of the teachings of Nikolai Nikolaevich. It is found in the words of Lara, a coincidence that Zhivago underscores, and it is again worth noting the context. Zhivago has settled at Varykino with Tonia and his family but forms a relationship with Lara in the nearby town of Yuriatin. Lara identifies with her social origins in the tenement block of the railway workers, the Tiverzins, and declares that she cannot agree on major issues with Zhivago, a doctor of upper-class origins who hoped to seclude himself from the storm of the Revolution. It was her husband Antipov, alias Strelnikov, who bombarded Yuriatin in order to wrest it from the Whites under Galliulin, a mutual friend of Zhivago and Lara. The coincidences are this time only indirectly predestined by the railway network. Zhivago travels by train from Moscow through the Russian countryside with its imagery of spring floods, and Strelnikov's armoured train overtakes Zhivago's, leading to the fateful encounter of Lara's two lovers.

In the section immediately following Lara's pronouncements on the Revolution, Strelnikov, Galliulin and the Jews, Zhivago rides homewards, hesitant to break with Lara, yet conscious of his betrayal of his wife and family. Easter is approaching and the nightingale repeats its call to awake to resurrection. It is at the intersection which he approaches blindly, wrapped in the ecstasy of love, that he is stopped and conscripted into the Forest Brotherhood, a forced service that separates him from his family and tests his values of loyalty and self-respect. It is loyalty that Lara has been talking about, the loyalty to human compassion which brought Lara to Galliulin's headquarters in intercession for some victim of the White terror. Recalling the pogroms, Lara, the history teacher, remarks:

Incidentally, if you do intellectual work of any kind and live in a town, as we do, half of your friends are bound to be Jews. Yet in times when there are pogroms, when all these terrible, despicable things are done, we don't only feel sorry and indignant and ashamed, we feel wretchedly divided, as if our sympathy came more from the head than from the heart and had an aftertaste of insincerity (250).

What prevents full compassion for the plight of the Jews? The answer is the same that Misha gave to Zhivago after witnessing ill-treatment of an old Jew on the Galician front: the Jews are to blame for not dissolving completely into the rest 'whose religion they founded', for not becoming Christians, whom they, the Jews, have failed to understand!

Of course, it's true that persecution forces them into this futile and disastrous attitude, this shamefaced, self-denying isolation that brings them nothing but misfortune. But I think some of it also comes from a kind of inner senility, a historical, centuries-long weariness (251).

The coincidence with Misha's assimilationist standpoint is too much not to be noticed by Zhivago, who remarks on it. Lara has now taken over as Zhivago's spiritual mentor from Nikolai Nikolaevich, who has sold himself to the Bolsheviks.

In Lara's apartment at Yuriatin Zhivago is made to overhear Sima Tuntseva preach the teachings of Nikolai Nikolaevich, using imagery which applies immediately to Zhivago's relationship with Lara and to the symbolism of resurrection in the novel, particularly the imagery taken from the Easter story. In a markedly modernist way that reminds us of Rilke's treatment of the Gethsemane theme, Passion describes the sufferings of Jesus, but also the compassion for a sinful woman.[60] Sima's abhorrence of the Lenten self-mortification of the flesh reminds us of the earlier rejection of Tolstoyanism in that moment of revelation in Madame Guishar's room. In the Easter liturgy of the Russian Orthodox Church Mary Magdalene prays for repentance for her sinful past so that she might dry the feet of Jesus with her hair. Her hair is compared to Eve's in Paradise, just as Lara compares herself and Zhivago to Adam and Eve in Paradise.

The sacrilegious analogy is further confirmed by the two magpies with their portent of the news that will free Zhivago of his responsibility to Tonia and his legal family. Now Lara will be free to teach Zhivago love through suffering – passion in all senses.

Lara's view of the Revolution in apocalyptic terms merges with Zhivago's artistic and religious vision, now sufficiently mature to take over from the voices of the redundant Nikolai Nikolaevich and of the implied author. Lara is Miriam at the well, she is Mary Magdalene and the rowan tree of the Russian forest, a child spirit nestling in Zhivago's soul, her beauty divinely given in the Transfiguration scene at the end of Chapter 12. Lara represents Russianness (a point also made in George Gibian's essay to which I have referred) and she has more than once been identified with Marina Tsvetaeva, whose relationship with Pasternak has parallels with Lara's relationship with Zhivago, a parallel of interest also because of Tsvetaeva's notion of the 'Jew-Poet' in 'Poem of the End', which, as already mentioned, Pasternak read in 1926.[61] It has also been said that Olga Ivinskaia was in real life an equivalent spiritual force in the cluster of religious ideas in the mind of Zhivago, who has betrayed the dutiful, though unexceptional, Tonia, represented as an archetypal Virgin Mary, immaculately domestic, a Botticelli. However, to see Lara, as some have, as an equivalent to Olga Ivinskaia's role in Pasternak's life would be to distort a plain reading of the novel, though it is remarkable that both Varykino and Peredelkino were threatened idylls of poetic creativity isolated by snow and government hostility, both coincidentally situated on the former Samarin estate (and it was Dmitri Samarin who had got Pasternak interested in going to Marburg).

Lara is bound up with a poetic image of Russianness, as evinced in the folk-song rendered by the sorceress and the Russian chronicle account of the knight cutting the woman's shoulder. The thought is almost inescapable that Pasternak, who made so much effort to stress his Russianness, who wanted to be thought of as having roots deep in the Russian soil, needs Lara as a symbol of the rejection of Judaism and the identification with a christological perception of Nature in characteristically Russian terms. Summing up what Lara is, Zhivago pictures her as the vast expanse of Russia on a spring evening, as representative of life and existence:

And this vast expanse is Russia, his incomparable mother; famed far and wide, martyred, stubborn, extravagant, crazy, irresponsible, adored, Russia with her eternally splendid, and disastrous, and unpredictable adventures (325).

At the end of this almost unbearably sentimental passage Zhivago bursts into tears of repentance out of admiration for Lara's perfection, thus unconsciously bearing witness to what Sima Tuntseva will say a little later about Mary Magdalene and repentance. Even if we forgive Zhivago the ravings of a demented starved lover who has trekked across the snowy wilderness on foot, and even if we forgive the author the ultimate obscurity of his thought, it is impossible to mistake such identification of religious idea with ethnicity.

The way in which the poems of Yuri Zhivago complete the novel and are an essential part of it speaks for an imagery and message which reject Judaism in favour of an 'original' Christian vision of Russia's destiny. 'Original' is a key word for Zhivago, and it is associated with his definition of miracle as original inspiration. There is a strange similarity with Hermann Cohen's neo-Kantian system when God is presented as an ethical idea whose moral law motivates man's mission. Both the immaculate conception and the idea of resurrection are presented in human ethical-logical terms which nevertheless can be known only in poetical language. For Zhivago the revelation of the birth of Jesus is a unique historical moment that can be conceived only as a mystical experience. It has made man god-like and therefore irrevocably and unrepeatably changed the course of human history. That is why the Revolution is not seen as a threat to Christianity, but as an affirmation of its apocalyptic prophecies.

Poetry is the sole means for man to intuit knowledge of that historical reality which is testified to by nature. Metaphors are made literal in order to demystify the supernatural, but also to represent the transcendence of eternal values in the mundane world. The theme of non-recognition of the intersection of fates is tied at the end of the novel to the story of Mary Magdalene, who assumed the resurrected Jesus to be a gardener – a reference to John 20, 10–18. This brings together two organizing groups of imagery which represent the movement of history: the vegetable world, which is contiguous with human existence, and the mechanical metaphor of the railway line, familiar from the allegorical convention of the journey, in Russian literature a convenient vehicle for social criticism, and an expression of historical time and distance. The railway with its tangled and vulnerable network of lines is reminiscent of the chaos of civil war from which Zhivago fled. It signals the intersection of personal and historical fate (for instance, Antipov's decision to go to the front is illumined by the headlight of a locomotive), but it also measures a moral and spiritual relationship with nature and with Russia's destiny. The railway is portentous, as in the 'bad omen' which the accident had for Anna Karenina in Tolstoy's novel when she first met Vronsky, a chance encounter which comes to her mind later when she is on the way to throw herself under a train – though the metaphor of the candle in that episode and the theme of suicide are used rather differently by Pasternak.

Boris Pasternak had an intuitive trust in premonition. The sudden turns in his choice of career in *A Safe-Conduct* are marked by some propitious phrase (Skriabin's or Ida Vysotskaia's) or chance event (such as the chance meeting at a railway station with Rilke in 1900, the recollection of which augurs a poetic vocation in the framing of the narrative). The year 1903 was typical of such turning-points in Boris Pasternak's life. That summer a student was drowned trying to rescue the daughter of friends of the Pasternaks. Coming back home to his summer residence, Leonid Pasternak saw the Goldinger house burning, and thought that it was his family in danger; his hair went grey. On June 7 a passenger train made an emergency halt near Obolenskoe after one of the passengers had fallen to his death, clearly the basis for the suicide of Misha Gordon's father. On August 6 Boris Pasternak suffered a leg injury when he fell from his horse, leaving him with a slight handicap that was, as he put it, to exempt him from combat duty in two world wars. Recalling this disastrous attempt at horseriding, Boris Pasternak's brother Aleksandr commented on Boris Pasternak's 'inordinate passion to accomplish things patently beyond his powers, ludicrously inappropriate to his character and cast of mind'.[62] This, more than anything, sums up Pasternak's characteristic career decisions and the fatalistic view of events in his life. The delirium he experienced as a result of the accident was described by Pasternak on the tenth anniversary of the event as a revelation of rhythm that would henceforth set the tone for his perception of future events.[63] In *An Essay in Autobiography* it is presented as pointing him towards musical composition under Skriabin. August 6 is the Day of Transfiguration in the Orthodox Church and 'Avgust' ('August'), one of the poems of Doctor Zhivago, expresses in concentrated form this favourite idea of transfiguration as an expression of the poet's rebirth.

The death of Zhivago on a stalled tramcar similarly signals the inevitable journey of life towards the final destination of death and, beyond that, to redemption. The providentiality of the journey is marked by miraculous coincidences, here the crossing of Mlle Fleury's path – unknown to either of them – just as he suffers a heart attack. The thought of individuals setting off at different times on parallel courses moves Zhivago to speculate on the possibility of something like a theory of relativity in the sphere of human destiny, but, instead of a coherent presentation, the story moves on to its conclusion and epilogue (which includes another stopped train in Tania's story), before Zhivago's poems achieve a kind of resurrection through art and faith. The year in which Zhivago dies, as Angela Livingstone has pointed out,[64] is 1929, the end of NEP and the transition to the first Five-Year Plan, the year of the Pilniak and Zamiatin affairs and the ascendancy of the proletarian writers' union RAPP. It also precedes the year of Maiakovsky's suicide, associated with a tramcar ride in *A Safe-Conduct.* As Gordon notes, the noble ideals of the Enlightenment have faded in the crude materialism of the Revolution, just as Greece gave way to Rome; however, the unspoken outcome of the parallel is that Christianity will succeed the Revolution as it did Rome.

That final outcome of history is fully consistent with Pasternak's 'original' inspiration in his religious faith. The Revolution swept away the world inhabited by the Pasternaks, the world of

Tolstoy and Skriabin, the world described in *A Safe-Conduct*, and when the Pasternak family went abroad Pasternak remained in Russia to pursue a life of poetry, an art which was by definition to be identified with Russia and which by circumstance separated him from his father and the father-figures who had shaped his path. In *Doctor Zhivago* Pasternak perfected an artistic vision whose native and 'original' Christianity negated both Judaism and identification with the Jewish people. Lazar Fleishman has argued that Pasternak, writing against the background of the anti-Cosmopolitan campaign which foregrounded the Jew's alien status in Russian literature, responded to state anti-Semitism by denying Jewish separatism, but undermined the official discourse by preferring apostasy in Christian faith with its 'true' internationalism rather than to Soviet ideology with its bogus internationalism. While the novel is demonstrably polyphonic – dangerously so for times when only official truths were acceptable and voicing any others could bring disfavour or worse – I would disagree, for the reasons I have already given, that Yuri Zhivago is merely a mute auditor of Lara's views on Jews and Judaism, as Lazar Fleishman concludes.[65] The hope invested in apostasy was a hope that one might be thought of as a Russian poet, and it is as one of the foremost Russian poets of the twentieth century that Boris Pasternak is remembered. Let us not forget that the novel was completed after the murder of six million Jews, when genocide had shown there was no hope of escape in apostasy, and that Pasternak must have been aware that he was speaking as a severed bough. Therefore, insofar as he ever thought of himself as the Prodigal Son in Rembrandt's painting, Pasternak's choice meant a rejection of the old Father in favour of the new.

CHAPTER 6

Ilia Ehrenburg, the eternal chameleon

Forgive me, please forgive me, for
every feast and every day, it's
been my fortune to have more,
twice as many more than you!
And yet if I've had twice your days
there has been room in them for twice
as many fears and injuries.
Who knows which century it was
easier to bear?

Margarita Aliger, *To a Portrait of Lermontov*[1]

WILL THE REAL COMRADE EHRENBURG STAND UP?

When asked what he did during the Terror after the French
Revolution, the abbé Sieyès simply replied, 'I survived.' Com-
menting on Ehrenburg's life, Erik de Mauny has cited this in
order to name Ehrenburg '*the* great survivor on the Soviet literary
scene.'[2] In his Memoirs *Liudi, gody, zhizn'* (*People, Years, Life*, 1961)[3]
Ehrenburg himself feels compelled to answer that nagging question, how he managed to survive when so many of his contemporaries perished. He answers that life for his generation was like
a lottery, not a game of chess. Few would find that answer
satisfactory.

True, survival in the twentieth century is no mean achievement. Ehrenburg was fond of misquoting Descartes, 'I survive,
therefore I think.' Yet Ehrenburg did make conscious decisions:
to return to the Soviet Union, to accept censorship and distortion
of his reports from Spain, to keep silence abroad on the Stalinist

Terror, or to assent to being used as a Soviet propaganda tool during and after the Second World War. Ehrenburg's silences during the persecution of Jewish writers in the anti-Cosmopolitan campaign make him a figure tainted with complicity, if not betrayal, in the eyes of many. Esther Markish, the widow of the executed Yiddish poet, accuses Ehrenburg of a 'shameful role' during the Black Years of Soviet Jewry, that of the *shirmakh* – Russian slang for 'cover':

When thieves rob a victim one of the gang distracts the attention of passers-by. This is the cover. Objectively, Ehrenburg was a cover of this type during ... 1949–1952. While anti-Semitism was approaching the National-Socialist level, Ehrenburg traveled the world stressing his Jewish origins, delivering speeches defending the Stalinist peace policy and denouncing by his very presence on international platforms the 'slanderous allusions' to a so-called anti-Semitic campaign in the USSR.[4]

There were several Ilia Ehrenburgs. There were the fictional Ilia Ehrenburgs in his satirical self-portraits, as in his novel *Julio Jurenito* (1922). Invention alternates with fictionalized truth in *Kniga dlia vzroslykh* ('Book for Adults', 1936). In an 'autobiography' of 1958 he wrote that a writer couldn't easily break the habit of inventing much of his life and hiding behind his fictional characters. There was Paul Jocelyn, a pseudonym taken from Lamartine's epic poem for the *Izvestiia* Paris correspondent, while the poet Ilia Ehrenburg wrote poetry during Stalin's Purges. Later he wrote in his 1958 autobiography that he had never believed in a faith (*vera*) but did believe in *vernost'*, which may be translated as fidelity or truthfulness. A poem about the Spanish Civil War entitled 'Vernost'' (1939), however, speaks for moral ambiguity when we know that devoted communists on the Spanish front line were recalled to Moscow for purging. Ehrenburg speaks of the 'solidarity of comrades', but under whose bullets? At this time Ehrenburg found himself unpublishable because the Molotov–Ribbentrop pact made his anti-fascist position untenable prior to the German invasion of Russia. The collection of poetry called *Vernost'*, which includes a poem about the fate of the Jews, 'Brodiat Rakhili, Khaimy, Lii' ('There Wander Rachels, Haims, Leahs'), could be published only after an unexpected telephone call from Stalin in April 1941 approving publication of *Padenie Parizha* ('The Fall of Paris').

The conflict of mind and heart or the betrayals of marital faithfulness are glossed over in Ehrenburg's Memoirs or described as a bout of 'flu, a typical evasion of the unpleasant necessity to tell the truth, as well as excusing moral incapacitation. A characteristic psychosomatic illness occurred when Ehrenburg was stuck in Paris, accused of being a communist spy and unable to voice his feelings about the Germans in the Soviet press (II, 204).[5] In April 1945, after Aleksandrov's attack on his virulent anti-German stand in *Pravda*, at a time Stalin was looking to the postwar division of Europe into communist and Allied blocs, Ehrenburg feared the worst consequences of falling into disfavour and was struck by severe toothache.[6]

There was the Ilia Ehrenburg who lied beyond the call of duty and the Ilia Ehrenburg who protested against abuses of the system, whether it was the false façade erected by Intourist in the thirties or defence of a student expelled from the Komsomol for support of liberalism in art in the Khrushchev era. The image of Ehrenburg as a defender of liberalism dates from the Thaw, named for his novel of that title which indicated the ending of the winter of Stalinism. As a Deputy in the Supreme Soviet Ehrenburg tried vainly to intervene in individual cases of Gulag prisoners who turned to him in the absence of any legal recourse; they referred him in their letters to what he had written in his novels, and he might have been bitter about his inability to live up to those humanitarian values and to the role of a writer in Russian society.

Then there is the 'Jewish' Ehrenburg who represented pride in a Jewish identity which did not compromise a sense of belonging to Russia. Hitler's invasion of Russia freed him from the gag of silence about Nazi anti-Semitism. The relative liberalism in the arts of 1941, when writers were conscripted to patriotic duty, allowed him to openly identify with the Jewish victims of fascism and to remind his readers that his mother's name was Hannah. Like Vasily Grossman's Viktor Shtrum, Ehrenburg could say that the Nazis had reminded him he was a Jew – as if it had not mattered before! – and he became sensitive to charges of Jewish cowardice in the ranks of the Red Army in a way which suggests defence of his own identity as a Jew and a Russian writer.[7] After Ehrenburg's death the 'Jewish' part of his archive was deposited in Yad Vashem, the Holocaust memorial in Jerusalem. Those papers, devoted to the collection of materials for the banned *Black Book* of Holocaust testimonies, demonstrate Ehrenburg's position as a *Jewish* representative in the eyes of Soviet Jewry after the decimation of any remaining communal or cultural leadership. As for his own management of that position, he championed selected causes which involved clear abuses of local Party power and which could be presented as harmful to the interests of the Central Committee or to the image of the Soviet Union abroad. For example, in the Khrushchev period Ehrenburg was approached with pleas to intervene in a variety of anti-Semitic incidents, from a blood libel in the Caucasus to discrimination in employment or marital problems. Ehrenburg's instructions to his secretary, the wording of his replies or his apparent failure to reply reflect his refusal to become more than an 'address' for Soviet Jewish petitioners.[8] His archives and his published Memoirs are at least consistent in the imitation of a discourse that is correct (another nuance of *vernost'*) while presuming a frame of reference at variance with any plain meaning. A case in point is Ehrenburg's article in *Pravda* on 21 September 1948, which voiced the Kremlin's warning to Soviet Jews that Israel and Zionism were not for them, despite the Soviet recognition of the new Jewish state. The authorities' fear of any articulation of Jewish identity was borne out the next month in the spontaneous welcome Soviet Jews gave to the Israeli delegation headed by Golda Meir, the Israeli consul. The article could be seen as consistent with Ehrenburg's assimilationist views, which denied any bond between Jews of different countries, yet it required some double-thinking to oppose anti-Semitism and at the same time serve the interests of a régime that had embarked on a markedly anti-Jewish policy in the dissolution of remaining Yiddish cultural institutions and the arrest of leading cultural figures.

Babel, whom Ehrenburg regarded during the Purges as far more able than himself to understand what was happening, did manage to compartmentalize his life into his family abroad, his creative self, the distanced narrating 'I' and his Russian lovers, by two of whom he had children;[9] but he never betrayed his moral integrity, even at the end when under torture a 'confession' was extracted from him which he soon retracted, deprecating himself for having in a moment of weakness defamed loyal friends, chief among them Ehrenburg himself, who was implicated as the liaison in Babel's alleged espionage. Or take Pasternak who felt guilty after his telephone call from Stalin about Mandelstam, then under arrest, since Pasternak was a poet who enjoyed the dubious privilege of official recognition though not creative freedom. Pasternak also survived both the Terror (despite refusing to sign public denunciations of Yakir and Tukhachevsky, though his name was included anyway)[10] and later the anti-Cosmopolitan campaign. Pasternak lived to welcome Olga Ivinskaia back from the camps, but he died amid a storm over his unimpeachable non-conformity in publishing *Doctor Zhivago* abroad. Very different is the case of Ilia Ehrenburg, who did not fall into prolonged silence and could not bear remaining unpublished. Helen Muchnic voiced a typical Western response to Ehrenburg's Memoirs when she asked, if Ehrenburg felt able to write not once but twice to Stalin asking to be allowed to go back to Spain, why couldn't he use his influence on behalf of his friends?[11] Of course, refusal to denounce 'enemies of the people', such as his friend and protector Nikolai Bukharin, was either daring or foolhardy, and silence was courageous at a time when opposition was suicidal. However, Ehrenburg issues many disclaimers in his Memoirs, and the excess of disclaimers draws attention to something besides official double-think. What, then, are we to make of his declaration that his Memoirs are a confession box in which the curtain can be both raised and lowered?

A simple answer would be that Soviet censors and Party policy prevented Ehrenburg speaking the full truth about himself and his times in *People, Years, Life*. He was writing on the edge of the permissible and had to make much clear by subtle hints. For example, the prevalence of unashamed anti-Semitism in the Soviet Union was made quite explicit by his referring to Tsarist times when anti-Semitism was still something of which intellectuals were ashamed (1, 56) – a phrase which drew upon him the wrath of the editorial board, including one Jew who was afraid of the taboo subject being raised and who dubbed Ehrenburg a 'Shabbos Goy', one who ought to know what he was supposed to do or not do without being told.[12] Actually, what he was willing to say was only too clear. Ehrenburg was not writing 'for the drawer', or leaving 'unofficial' versions for posterity – apart from Book 7, unpublished at his death, and a suppressed chapter on Nikolai Bukharin, who was active in the same illegal revolutionary organization of school pupils and later became one of the leaders of the Revolution. Arrested by Stalin in 1937, subjected to a show trial and shot, Bukharin was rehabilitated only under Gorbachev's *glasnost*. One reason why Ehrenburg was able to publish in the Soviet Union despite ferocious personal attacks on him by Marxist ideologues and the suspicion attached to one who lived abroad during the thirties would be thanks to the mysterious 'immunity' which he says he was accorded. But after Bukharin's fall his protection – which all could remember from Bukharin's foreword to *Julio Jurenito* – would if anything be detrimental.

However, despite proclaiming artistic freedom as the banner of his Memoirs and the credo of his life's work, the narrator of *People, Years, Life* records his feelings of self-satisfaction at being awarded Stalinist medals. This at the same time as Ehrenburg recalls the fear which gripped Moscow in 1937: listening out for the lift at night, the notice about not flushing books down the toilet (always the reporter's eye for detail). Maybe he really did not understand that the mastermind behind the Terror was Stalin himself, or maybe his plea of 'confusion' is no more than just camouflage. The fact is that he himself notes how sore his hands were after joining in the applause of Stalin at a public rally. The French police certainly had a thick file on Ehrenburg as a suspected Soviet agent, and it would be impossible to draw a line between the despatches of a newspaper correspondent and other services rendered to Moscow.[13]

The truth – if it ever existed in purely unadulterated and absolute form – is far more difficult to unravel. Ehrenburg was writing his Memoirs as a chronicle of his times for a generation which knew little or nothing of the culture which he treasured:

the Decadent poets of the turn of the century, in particular Briusov who had welcomed Ehrenburg's early collections of verse; the avant-garde painters who befriended Ehrenburg in bohemian Paris – Soutine, Modigliani, Rivera and Picasso – whom Khrushchev decided to denigrate. In a country which denied freedom of speech and movement, Ehrenburg's Memoirs were a visa to the West. He wrote of a world before the First World War when you did not need visas to travel. He wrote of how it felt to come from an authoritarian state to a city where *nobody cared what you did*. He wrote of classics of Western literature which were either disparaged or not published in Russia, and which usually could be discussed only in references in hostile critical articles. Ehrenburg was, moreover, the first to be entrusted with even a partial official sanction for the task of resuscitating the dead non-persons; his was the only major account of the Stalin Terror before Nadezhda Mandelstam's memoirs, which were in any case for many years not publishable in Russia. To rewrite the cultural history of a generation required after de-Stalinization the expletion of the personal self. Hence the 'evidence' brought by archival documents of the Tsarist police attesting to the criminality of the young revolutionary, and the many third-person accounts of Ehrenburg by others or the seemingly impartial recording of conversations in which Ehrenburg took part, not to mention numerous reflections on *Julio Jurenito* which is itself a problematic fictionalization of self. In *People, Years, Life* Ehrenburg declared that, although much is made up in the biography of the self-mocking fictional 'Ehrenburg', his views are frequently true reflections of his own former self (1, 65). Such distancing or negating devices nevertheless cleverly conceal Ehrenburg's actual beliefs or thoughts and we shall probably never know which is Ehrenburg and which 'Ehrenburg'.

One might also ask whether sincerity is broached when Ehrenburg complains that Pasternak – whom he lauds as one of Russia's greatest lyrical poets – allowed his novel *Doctor Zhivago* to be used by enemies of the USSR and that in it Pasternak had not told the official truth about the Revolution (1, 256). The correspondence Ehrenburg conducted with his publishers and with Khrushchev shows a wily and slippery negotiator for compromise who plays the devil's advocate. What will our enemies think? How will Party policy be served? But in this paperchase duel Ehrenburg is not willing to be killed like Pushkin. Ehrenburg must appear to be telling the truth, when all know that he is not allowed to tell all the truth; he must play the game, but all know that the rules are dishonest ones.

The figure of the double-faced Janus is one of many projections of the self in Ehrenburg's Memoirs; but, like many such figures, it is qualified by the semantic adjustment of historical 'accuracy': 'Janus had two faces, not because he was two-faced as is often said, no, he was wise: one of his faces was turned towards the past, the other towards the future' (1, 47). As for the past, Ehrenburg enjoys selective amnesia: 'Forgetfulness was sometimes dictated by the instinct of self-preservation' (1, 46) because it was impossible to go on weighed down by memory. The only thing that can pragmatically be done – apart from suicide, of which many cases are recorded in the Memoirs – is to prefer wisdom to despair. Opportunism? Certainly a self-professing cynic would not lose sleep over moral qualms. Ehrenburg himself believed it was the only way to get published, which meant to survive as a writer and to stake a claim for liberalization. The tactics of negotiated compromise are perhaps the sole alternative to silence, when one must be silent about the most important things and when freedom is relative: the *Daily Express* reporter in Spain also had his reports expurgated or rejected. Yet the many distortions and partial truths are not motivated exclusively by political exigency.

Ehrenburg has after all still to defend himself against the implicit charge of the anti-Cosmopolitan campaign directed mainly against Jewish writers and artists who were allegedly subverting Russian culture. For his life was genuinely cosmopolitan. He kept a mistress, Paris, while loving his legally native Moscow. He believed truth was to be found in literature, not in Marxist textbooks, and he was unequivocally a westernizer. In the Memoirs he portrays himself as taking a stand against all forms of monolithism in society and art, despite the fact that in 1932 his novel *Vtoroi den'* ('The Second Day') described the industrialization of the nation with the enthusiasm of an observer of the

Second Day of Creation, with the awe appropriate to the building of a new order undaunted by the human cost, something which did not make it easier to publish the novel in Moscow, where it appeared with cuts.[14]

One reason Ehrenburg committed himself to the Soviet cause at the beginning of the thirties was his disgust at the syndicalism of Western and particularly American capital which, in his view, was destroying Europe and causing untold human misery. However, more decisive in the thirties was what was happening in Germany, and Ehrenburg passionately opposed fascism, whether by organizing left-wing European writers or by covering the Spanish Civil War and later the Soviet war front. From the first pages of the Memoirs, Ehrenburg imposes on his narrative the perspective of both Stalinism and fascism. This is not just because many of those whom he describes were to end up in concentration camps, and not just because the narration does not proceed chronologically. After the signing of the Molotov–Ribbentrop agreement, it was explained to him that it was expedient for Jews to keep their views to themselves. After the war, Zhdanov's campaign against Akhmatova and Zoshchenko spelt a warning for independent-minded writers and served notice that the relative relaxation of wartime was at an end. Ehrenburg, who had naively thought the Purges would not return, witnessed the aftermath of the extermination of the Jews, but now found that his hatred of the Germans brought him into disfavour. The Jewish Anti-Fascist Committee, in which he had been active alongside Vasily Grossman, Perets Markish and Itsik Feffer, was disbanded. The type for the *Black Book* was broken up. Mikhoels was murdered. Markish, Feffer and other leading Yiddish writers were arrested, later to be executed. Worse was to come when the 'Doctors' Plot' was unveiled and Ehrenburg was asked to sign a letter asking for the Jews of the Soviet Union to be exiled to Kazakhstan. He was the only one, besides Viniamin Kaverin, Mark Raizin and General Yakov Kreizer, who refused to sign; and he wrote a letter to Stalin explaining in his usual casuistic fashion that persecution of the Jews would not serve Soviet interests abroad and would encourage the Jews' sense of separate identity.[15]

So it is not surprising that Ehrenburg takes great pains to define national identity as resulting from a geographical accident with no racial implication, but neverthless having important cultural characteristics. He defined his own culture as Russian and, like Marshak, Mandelstam and Pasternak, he appropriates Russian texts in the text of his biography. Chronology follows Russian Time, with its hiatus in the Revolution (though it lacks the radical rewriting of the calendar that followed the French Revolution). Ehrenburg prefaces his life with the allegorical paradigm of Chekhov's short story 'The Duel', which Chekhov began the same month Ehrenburg was born. The hero Laevsky is sick of life but life cannot be relived: 'If it had been possible to bring back the days and years, he would have replaced the falsehood in them by truth, idleness by work, boredom by joy ...' (cited by Ehrenburg, I, 51.) His enemy is von Koren, who would exterminate him (*sic*) in line with progress and the principle of natural selection. Chekhov describes the pursuit of truth which proceeds two steps forward, one back, and Ehrenburg too dreams of a boat which might one day sail to the real truth. Ehrenburg comments on both the story and his life: 'I have met many von Korens in my lifetime, I have often lost my way, made mistakes, and, like Laevsky, I have grieved for a dim star which I had cast out of the sky; like Laevsky, I have admired the oarsmen battling against the high waves' (I, 52).

Ehrenburg is pulled by the power of the past in his pursuit of truth, and pleads consistency of heart even if he changed his skin as many times as his suits (elsewhere he speaks of beliefs as shoes which can be worn in until they are comfortable and discarded when worn out). The date of his birth, 14 January 1891, is significant not just because, like the birthdays of Osip Mandelstam and Boris Pasternak, it heralds the end of the nineteenth century, the end of humane values and culture. It is the day when Chekhov writes to his sister about the unbearable atmosphere of biting attacks and petty criticism against him while he was eulogized in the most tasteless manner (very much Ehrenburg's situation at the time of writing his Memoirs). Ehrenburg might well feel nostalgia for what he describes in the opening passages of his Memoirs as the slow, humane and cultured pace of nineteenth-century Time. Ehrenburg invokes his desire as a child to rip the clock off the wall, an anarchic act of destruction but one which desperately attempts to symbolically stop Time. It was not just the rapid pace of modern life which made dangerous or impossible the preservation of memory and correspondence in the twentieth century. Time was out of joint.

Apart from making obligatory obeisance to Lenin and Gorky by citing them when making judgements on famous writers, Ehrenburg makes a stand against monolithic concepts of the State and of culture, fulfilling the moral role of the Russian writer and particularly the Pushkinian image of the poet charged with a prophetic mission. Like other Soviet Jews, Ehrenburg claims the status of Russian writer through the performance of texts in order to slant ethnic biography and literary ontogenesis. He co-opts Chekhov and echoes Belinsky when he asserts that the Russian language itself enshrines the principle of freedom in its euphony and rhythm. Eternal truths are typically enshrined in Russian proverbs, though like many popular sayings which Ehrenburg adopts they are often twisted out of context into a special, more oblique meaning.

Ehrenburg had seen the pogroms in Kiev after the Revolution and narrowly escaped death at the hands of an anti-Semitic White officer; he was saved by a Jew serving in the White Army. Abroad, he was denigrated as a Jew and was also deemed a traitor by Russian émigrés because he had left Russia on a Soviet passport. He describes the Revolution as a Sphinx, an ambiguous application of an ambiguous figure for his own ambivalence. So in reinventing his life Ehrenburg must prove his loyalty to the Soviet system (notwithstanding his own 'errors' and the 'betrayals' of Stalinism) and to Russian culture, while defending himself against anti-Semitism, which, as will be seen, is the overriding definition of his Jewishness: as he declared in a radio broadcast on his seventieth birthday, he was a Jew as long as there were anti-Semites. This may fit Sartre's definition of a Jew whom others regard as such, but it does not make him one bit more 'authentic'. On the contrary, we will see that Ehrenburg's self-definition springs from his earlier Christian mystical beliefs and experience of pogroms, as well as his attempt to sustain identity as a Russian writer.

There is little that is genuinely Jewish in Ehrenburg's background. The impression which Ehrenburg gives is of a youthful revolt against the bourgeois world of his father, of ideological commitment to the revolutionary cause after discovering the miserable poverty of workers at the brewery where his father worked as manager. Ehrenburg claims membership in the heritage of Russian literature and defies the anti-Semitic strain in it which would bar him. In his 'Book for Adults' Ehrenburg raised the question of his alleged inability as a Jew to understand Russian literature and wrote that this only made him double his efforts in his 'forbidden love' for Russia. In *People, Years, Life* he prefaces the chapter on his family (to whom he barely returns during the Memoirs) with the case of the nineteenth-century Russian poet Fet, who wrote against Nihilists and Jews (Ehrenburg counts as both) but who discovered before he died that his father was a Hamburg Jew. Ehrenburg suggests that Fet wanted to conceal this secret when he ordered that the letter which bore the information be buried with him. To be buried with one's secret is not to bury the secret. After the Revolution the grave and the letter were exhumed. As Ehrenburg knew, Stalinism and Nazism held a man responsible for his grandparents, not just his parents, and it did not help to cry vehemently that the apple had rolled far from the tree.

Born in Kiev but brought up from the age of five in Moscow – where only privileged Jews were allowed to reside – Ehrenburg relates that his mother came from a devout Jewish family and that she remembered the Day of Judgement in heaven and the pogroms on earth. Ilia's father belonged to the first generation of assimilated Jews who 'broke out of the ghetto' and studied in a Russian school. Of his uncles Ilia identifies with Lev, who wrote poetry, translated Heine (a significant choice!) and ran a travelling circus. Ilia clearly enjoys the scandalous effect of the posters put up in Kharkov advertising Ehrenburg's Circus, just as he likes telling us that once in Paris he was mistaken for another uncle, Boris, wanted for embezzlement. Ehrenburg would have us believe that even as a child he vacillated in his views, but at the same time he notes the proximity of Tolstoy, who once visited the brewery which his father managed: the idealistic resistance to evil would be a recurrent theme in his life.

There remains, in fact, little residual Judaism in the house apart from the mother's vague 'traditions' and 'superstitions', fasting on the Day of Atonement and the memorial candle on the anniversary of her mother-in-law's death. These 'memories' of Judaism are typically illegible, as indecipherable as Mandelstam's 'Judaic Chaos'. The mother is a sickly creature who suffers from a lung ailment. The role-model which she impresses on her son is the example of the Familiant boys, who declaim Pushkin. What Judaism there is to rebel against is to be found (as in Marshak's memoir) in the maternal grandfather's house where the Jewish Sabbath is kept with all its prohibitions.[16] Mention of the Judaic 'prohibitions' is contextualized with a summer stay in a dacha at Boiarka when the boy's pranks were punished by locking him in the coal shed. Stripping naked, the boy rolled on the floor and frightened the kitchenmaid out of her wits when she opened the door to find the devil standing in front of her. More than once Ilia plays the devil, though not a malevolent one, he assures us, and at school he dreamt of being not Lermontov but Lermontov's Demon. His decision to burn down the dacha is yet another example of the desire to break out of the moral and physical boundaries of 'Jewishness'. It could be that this devilry explains his delinquent behaviour, or rather the display of delinquency, and a chronic perversity in refusing to get his lessons right in his dealings with Authority.

Ehrenburg writes that his father disapproved of Jews who converted to Russian Orthodoxy, and from an early age he realized that he should never be ashamed of his origins. Unlike the Soviet Jew of the 1930s whose son came home from school (presumably after hearing some jibe) unable to believe that his father and his mother were Jews, he knew at the age of eight that being a Jew meant discrimination and pogroms. The only way of beating the *numerus clausus* was to get top marks and excel in maths and Russian literature. Ehrenburg explains that he was brought up in Moscow (not in the Pale) and played with Russian (not Jewish) children; his language was Russian (not the Yiddish which his parents spoke when keeping secrets from him). Yet, while disclaiming any affinity with Judaism or Jewry, while negating a Jewish language (he denies he knew Yiddish in the chapter on Perets Markish), Ehrenburg puts forward his candidacy as a symbolic victim of anti-Semitism: 'I understood the word "Jew" in a special way: I belong to those who may be legitimately insulted. This seemed to me unfair and at the same time natural' (I, 56). The Jews were supposed to have crucified Jesus, but Ehrenburg's uncle told him that Jesus was a Jew. His nanny (like Pasternak's) taught him about Jesus, but he rebelled against the Christian teaching of turning the other cheek. When he first went to the *gimnaziia* one of the boys abused him with an anti-Semitic ditty. 'Without stopping to think I hit him in the face. Soon we made friends. No one insulted me again' (I, 56). Immediately following this incident Ehrenburg clears the entire Russian intelligentsia of any trace of anti-Semitism, for which the blame is unequivocally laid at the door of the Tsarist autocracy. Yet the hope is admittedly illusory that the Dreyfus Affair and the filthy anti-Semitism in his native Kiev would be rendered anachronistic by revolution and modernity; Ehrenburg's Memoirs will have to record the virulence of anti-Semitism in the twentieth century.

On the surface, the meaning of 'Jew' is restricted to the idea of martyr, in the Christian sense. Deep down Ehrenburg identifies with the fate of the Jewish people in the pogroms and the Holocaust, partly because the Russian writer traditionally speaks for the victim and partly because his identity as a Russian writer is challenged by anti-Semitism. A clue to this conundrum is supplied by Ehrenburg himself when he describes his friendship with the Polish poet Julian Tuwim (1894–1953).

In Tuwim Ehrenburg found a kindred spirit, a poet who wrote in Polish and satirized both the nationalists who attacked him for polluting Polish letters and his fellow Jews, the Zionists. Jewish themes, when they appeared in his poetry, were often born of self-hatred. In the Holocaust Tuwim regained a sense of belonging to the Jewish people, and in 1944 in his New York exile he wrote a brief essay 'We, the Polish Jews', which serves Ehrenburg as his text not only for the chapter on Tuwim, but for his general readjustment of identity after the Holocaust.[17] Tuwim wrote the essay on the first anniversary of the Warsaw Ghetto Uprising, when it was apparent that Poland would emerge from the war but not necessarily would its Jews. As the horrendous truth of the Final Solution began to emerge Tuwim stopped writing his major work *Kwiaty polskie* ('Polish Flowers') and fell silent, probing his guilt-ridden emotions about being an assimilated Polish Jew faced with the fate of European Jewry when the world stood silent. He could not change his feeling that he was a Pole born in Poland and speaking the Polish language, who wrote in Polish, breathed Poland in exile, and looked forward to returning to Poland. The essay assumes an imagined dialogue with Tuwim's Polish detractors, and explains the logical contradiction of claiming to be a Pole and a Jew by the definition of blood – not the racist definition, but the blood of martyrdom: 'There are two kinds of blood: blood in the veins and blood from the veins.'[18] The first kind is the racist definition which plunged Europe into destruction; the second is the blood which flows from the veins of the Jews (not 'Jewish blood', insists Tuwim) into a new River Jordan of baptismal blood. Tuwim is seeking readmission into Jewish peoplehood but in Christian terms of a Church based on blood-sacrifice. The Order of the Jew 'Doloris Causa' is the self-deluding dream of a poet unable to resolve the contradiction between the fate of his Polish pen and his Jewish mother. He envisions a monument to the Holocaust which will be a new crucifix, a Golgotha, a monument to the Jews' eternal Jeremiad.

As it happened, Tuwim's essay and the martyrdom of the Jews were to be suppressed for many years in the Polish national consciousness. Communist policy in the USSR, and in the Eastern Bloc which it controlled, denied the Jewish identity of the victims of the Holocaust and played down the role of Jewish partisans and of Jews in the Red Army. Stalin wanted no rivals to his hero worship, and the stereotype of the Jewish coward who chickened out of fighting was more virulent than the facts about the numbers of Jewish partisans and Red Army heroes. This was precisely the point which moved Ehrenburg, who wrote only in Russian and claimed identity as a Russian writer, to take up

Tuwim's idiosyncratic appeal in his infamous *Pravda* article and in his Memoirs as if it were a feasible platform for the assimilated Russian Jew. It was all the more attractive for Ehrenburg since its language was entirely non-Jewish and Christian.

The chapter on Tuwim in Ehrenburg's Memoirs is informed by this slanted view of the assimilated Russian Jew. It opens with a paean of love for the Polish poet, a bitter satirist of the bourgeoisie who frequented Warsaw's cafés (presumably this reminds Ehrenburg of his beloved bohemian Paris). Tuwim is presented as a Pushkinian figure having affinities with Lermontov, Blok and Maiakovsky. His love for Poland – and, of course, also for Russia – would indeed seem unqualified if it were not for the anti-Semitic nature of the attacks on Tuwim. Not surprisingly, Ehrenburg does not quote his own observations of Polish anti-Semitism in *Viza vremeni* ('Visa of Time', 1929) which he described as beating the Jews with a wet towel.

In a previous chapter devoted to the fate of Marina Tsvetaeva, Ehrenburg had quoted her words in 'Poem of the End' – with passing reference to the Italian Jewish painter Modigliani – that all poets are 'yids' (I, 245), applying this definition of the poet as Other (in the same tradition as Pushkin's negroid lips) to an archetypal 'ghetto' of the Russian poet that serves as an epitaph for Tsvetaeva herself. Here, however, Ehrenburg surreptitiously reascribes Tsvetaeva's identification of poet and Jew to the ghettoes of the Holocaust and his own self-image as a martyred poet, whose Jewishness, in the spirit of Tsvetaeva's line, is a definition of the poet.

THE ROAD TO DAMASCUS

Casting himself in the role of Doubting Thomas, Ehrenburg draws attention away from a phase in his life in Paris before the First World War which he does not deny or apparently regret: his conversion to Catholicism and his decision to become a Benedictine monk. This was a decision he did not carry out, Anatol Goldberg believes, because he was living with a Russian student, Ekaterina (Katia) Schmidt, by whom he had a daughter, Irina, in 1911.[19] Ehrenburg abandoned Trotsky in Vienna because of the harsh things that the latter said about poetry, and he returned in 1910 to the bohemian freedom of Paris cafés (so different from strict Party discipline), to the Closerie des Lilas and later the famous Rotonde, where the penniless Ehrenburg 'sat out' endless cups of coffee with Picasso, Rivera, Modigliani, Soutine, Apollinaire and other creators of the new art. But it was not possible to live without belief in some kind of church. Ehrenburg looked for a faith which would explain the root of evil in the world and be more compatible with poetry than Bolshevism. The Memoirs lovingly record the young man's passion for French and Spanish medieval poetry, which he translated into Russian and which he imitated in his own verse; he had fallen in love with the madonnas of the Renaissance on his travels to Belgium and Italy. His spiritual teacher was the French poet François Jammes, who once expressed the desire to go to heaven with the little donkeys of his native Pyrenees: 'His Catholicism was free of both asceticism and bigotry' (1, 109). Another poet who served as a role model here was the Jew Max Jacob, who was baptized as a devout Catholic with Picasso as a godfather of rather dubious piety. Ehrenburg notes that Max Jacob ended his days as a Jew in a Nazi concentration camp.

Ehrenburg had become disenamoured of the Bolsheviks soon after coming to Paris. Participating in an illegal organization and publishing an underground magazine in Russia matched a schoolboy's sense of adventurous, though somewhat foolish, heroism. Abroad, the squabbles between Bolsheviks and Mensheviks detracted from what Ehrenburg called paradoxically in his Memoirs the romanticism of a clear-headed unromantic radicalism that would sweep away injustice. After spending time in a Russian prison, Ehrenburg was sent abroad by his parents. They had wanted him to study in Germany, where many secular Jewish intellectuals and revolutionaries attended university, but Ehrenburg chose Paris, the City of Light, the City of Art. Ehrenburg dutifully attended revolutionary meetings where he could be with other Russians and in his Memoirs dutifully reports his meeting with Lenin; but the vituperous *enfant terrible* also abused Lenin in a short-lived magazine he produced in Paris.[20] If Jammes helped Ehrenburg reconcile pantheism with Christianity and helped him reconcile both the Renaissance and his new love for Paris with being an émigré Russian, it was Léon Bloy who helped him reconcile his new faith with his identity as a self-hating Jew. A French biographer, Ewa Bérard, comments, 'Le serein bonheur d'exister partagé avec Jammes cède la place à une révolte enragée contre le monde bourgeois, l'amour s'efface devant la haine, les prières reculent devant les visions apocalyptiques.'[21] Bérard thinks it very probable that one of the books by Bloy which Ehrenburg read was *Le Salut par les Juifs* (1892). Bloy claimed that his credo had nothing to do with anti-Semitism, but in fact he gave it theological, even mystical, credence when he depicted the Jews as the embodiment of absolute evil who alone bore a cross in a world of moral apathy and bourgeois conformism. The eternal damnation of the Jews guaranteed the health of mankind. 'L'histoire des juifs barre l'histoire du genre humain comme une digue barre un fleuve, pour en élever le niveau.' In their unrivalled ignominy there was hidden, believed Bloy, some 'mystère infiniment adorable'.[22]

There is one poem of this period which deals with Ehrenburg's feelings about his Jewish origins. The undated poem 'Evreiskomu narodu' ('To the Jewish People') appeared in Ehrenburg's collection of verse *Ia zhivu* ('I Live', 1911). The cover of the book by V. Ravich portrayed a mock-tombstone, and overriding the pagan sensuousness of the poems to Dionysus, Pan and Apollo is a sense of the irrevocable end and a joyful reunion with mother earth. In 'Rossii' ('To Russia') the poet's feelings of weariness and decay are relieved by the sight of earthy peasants who have joined the city workers in a tavern, or by the thought of villages and fields. Foreign exile makes the poet want to cry over Russia and his unavoidable fate. It is the sight of an Orthodox church that cheers him – rather like the way in which Orthodox churches appear in fellow-Parisian Chagall's Vitebsk scenes of this period to locate iconically the artist's distance from Russia as well as from Jewish life, and his nostalgic but ultimately painful feelings for them. Elsewhere in this collection the poet expresses at-one-ment with the serenity of the Russian countryside, or prayerful ecstasy over the first blade of vernal grass. Unlike Chagall, however, the poet senses security in his religious faith. The Jewish mob mocking Jesus on his last journey in one poem are addressed as 'you', and the poet finds inspiration when he is hurt by the contemporary world. It is therefore with a Christian sense of martyrdom and a belief in the redeeming power of the blood of the crucifixion that the poet addresses the Jews, and he does so as an outsider. Like Pasternak in *Doctor Zhivago*, Ehrenburg shares the fundamental Christian view of the Jews as fossilized by history: they have forgotten their God and their native language (*rodnoi iazyk*). Shunned by the whole world, they wander in poverty and misery, earning their stereotyped image as greedy traders and shopkeepers, a pariah nation that breeds feeble freaks and is doomed to die. The poet speaks to the unwanted Jews in the condescending familiar second person singular (*ty*) and tells them to go back to their native fields of Jerusalem, where at least they might die in their own land:

> You are not needed here; persecuted strangers
> Assemble your enfeebled children,
> Go away to the native fields of Jerusalem,
> Where you knew happiness in your youth.
> You will see abandoned furrows,
> And once more you will push the rusted plough.
> Perhaps there under the olive branches
> You will rest from centuries of torment.
> And if you have to die soon,
> Then don't die here, among foreign fields,
> But there, where you saw other sights,
> Where you knew happiness in your youth.[23]

Ewa Bérard believes the poem was influenced by the Beilis trial of 1911 and that it suggests dormant thoughts of the Jews' national destiny;[24] but even if the adoption of self-hating stereotypes was ironic, the last lines of the poem would throw in doubt both identification with the persecuted people and any prophecy of their future rebirth in the agricultural resettlement of the Land of Israel, then being undertaken by Zionist pioneers. Significantly, the poem is followed by 'Parizh' ('Paris') and 'Vozvrat' ('Return') which end the collection. Paris, the city of licentious living, is alien (*chuzhoi*), while the final poem is distinctly eschatological in its view of the end of the City and the end of Time. The Return is to the earth – the mystical *Russian* earth. This confused mixture of Slavophilic Christian mysticism (reminiscent of *pochvenstvo*) with symbolist anti-urbanism, this mixture of themes and positions from the pagan to the Catholic, was noticed at the time by another Jew troubled by the end of Time and of the City. 'The sharp Parisian pang of melancholy', wrote Osip Mandelstam in a review of *Oduvanchiki* ('Dandelions', Paris, 1912), 'dissolves into a hopeless "Levantine" infatuation with Russian nature.'[25]

In another of the few poems that relate to Jewry, in 'Dandelions', Ehrenburg declares:

> Jews, beyond my strength it is to live with you,
> Estranged, hating you,
> In wanderings long and weary
> I come to you, every time ...
> ... I am poisoned by Jewish blood,
> And somewhere in the murky depths
> Of my wandering soul
> I feel a filial love for you.
> And in times of sorrow and despondency,
> I feel that I am a Jew![26]

The heavy burden of being a Wandering Jew, which poisons the blood, and the contradictory love of the Prodigal Son are Christianized conceptions of Jewishness as a cross which is both a curse and a blessing, not so different from Mandelstam's contrary impulse of repulsion and return. Very likely one explanation for such reawakened feelings of identity is the renewed manifestations of anti-Semitism like the Beilis trial, which does not let the poet forget his origins and his inescapable fate as a double alien in France.

Briusov called Ehrenburg 'a schoolboy émigré', but it was not schoolboy prankishness which made Ehrenburg translate Jammes together with Ekaterina Schmidt. Ehrenburg was recognized by the St Petersburg literary world, and his identification with Russianness was now of both flesh and spirit (though it was a Jewess, Elizaveta Polonskaia, who introduced Ehrenburg to Blok and to poetry). It is perhaps worth noting that the satirical poem

'Ballada ob Isake Zil'bersone' ('Ballad about Isak Zilberson') is datelined Eze, 1916,[27] the French village near Nice where Ehrenburg had lived with Katia till she took up with Tikhon Sorokin. Ehrenburg probably could not keep her on his meagre literary earnings, the stipend sent from their parents in Russia and his dreams of medieval troubadors. The humorous ballad depicts a shlemiel, the archetypal Yiddish anti-hero, who fails in life and, like Y. L. Perets's 'Bontshe the Silent', cannot answer God when dead. The themes of anti-Semitism at school, unreciprocated love and the figure of the hapless conscript look forward to Lazik Roitshvanets and suggest autobiographical concerns; but the self-image as a failure is an artistic pose, like so many such projections in Ehrenburg's writing, to cover the void within.

Ehrenburg's confusion of beliefs at this time was bound to end in a nervous breakdown. A commission to cover the Western Front from the Petersburg *Birzhevskie vedomosti* ('Stock Exchange News', a newspaper that despite its name published the leading poets and writers of the day) gave him respite from a spiritual and emotional dead-end: he threw himself into the passionate defence of pacifism after witnessing the horrors of the First World War and later published his sketches in *Lik voiny* ('The Face of War', 1922). Ehrenburg's sketches attracted attention at the time for their virulent pacifism.[28] The war is a cup of suffering that will cleanse the sins of a sick society, a new Calvary; but this eschatological vision of the new technological Armageddon also bitterly satirizes the warmongers and speaks for an internationalist solidarity of man – Ehrenburg was upset particularly by the French treatment of Russian soldiers and of the colonial Senegal troops. The war was to make him lose his faith,[29] and the book ends on a Jobian note akin to the questioning of Divine justice in a long parable of 1916, *Povest' o zhizni nekoi Naden'ki*, which turns into hate, not love of God.[30] The senseless cruelty of war was to be a recurrent theme of First World War poetry and fiction, and one can compare Isaak Babel's contempt for Honour and Patriotism in his reworking of a book of war sketches by Gaston Vidal, 'Na pole chesti' ('On the Field of Honour', 1920); but, unlike Babel, Ehrenburg organizes his anecdotal episodes into a picture of overwhelming and universal despair.

The February Revolution rallied Ehrenburg and many others to the Russian embassy in Paris. However, the emotional return to Russia was marred by the pandemonium that met Ehrenburg on his arrival. In *Julio Jurenito* Ehrenburg later depicted himself reading poetry in cafés, dining and enjoying a partiality for skirts, in a word unable to find any one truth in the Revolution with which he could identify. In his Memoirs Ehrenburg recalls the general confusion and his own disorientation, though his was by his own account not so different from the average Russian intellectual's position (1, 232). Katia was living with her father 'who refused even to hear my name: on top of all my other crimes, I was a Jew' (1, 230). This is yet another example of the projection of the self-hating Jew disassociated from self, an image which conveniently distances a problematic identity. The Bolsheviks were identified by their enemies as Jews, the Revolution being seen as an apocalyptic phase in the conspiracy of the Elders of Zion; on the other hand, for Soviet Russian readers of Ehrenburg's Memoirs the Russian Revolution is supposed to be seen as truly Russian, but breaking with all forms of religion. To insinuate his loss of faith Ehrenburg uses the story of how his daughter Irina asked to go to the Kazan cathedral, where Ehrenburg 'disobeyed' his daughter in refusing to kneel down in prayer, scandalizing the other worshippers (1, 230–1). In this way, Ehrenburg can have us infer some kind of break with his past, but without coming out for or against the Bolsheviks at a crucial moment in any Soviet biography.

Ehrenburg rejected Blok's article 'The Intelligentsia and the Revolution', and after the Brest peace treaty and the repression of the opposition press in June 1918 Ehrenburg criticized Blok's sanctification of the Revolution in *The Twelve*. Writing in the newspaper *Vozrozhdenie*, Ehrenburg mocked those poets who justified the Revolution as a sacred cross, just as they had embraced the First World War as a holy cause. Instead, Ehrenburg attacked Lenin's seizure of power as an act of violence which crucified Russia.[31] In his poem 'Molitva o Rossii' ('Prayer for Russia', 1918) he prayed for the victims as well as the perpetrators. He prayed 'for our native land',

For our fields, deserted and cold,
For our hearts bereft of love,
For those who cannot pray,
For those who strangle little children,
For those who sing sad little songs,
For those who go about with knives and daggers ...

Let her atone with feverish toil
For these infernal years,
That she may taste another joy
Of repentance and toil!
O Lord, forgive
One who has gone astray on her mysterious path.
May the golden sun rise again,
The white churches, their azure tops,
Pious Russia!

For Russia
To the Lord of the world we pray.[32]

Voloshin wrote in a contemporary review that Ehrenburg's poetry was built on the two ideas of Church and Fatherland, ideas that had 'not long ago become so dirtied and compromised that the intelligentsia had rejected them.' No one, continued Voloshin, expressed love for Russia more passionately than this apostate Jew ('Iudei, otoshedshii ot iudeistva') who was born with no rights in that Fatherland under the Tsars and had spent a decade in demoralizing exile, flirting with Catholicism and not accepting Russian Orthodoxy. The fact that a Jew was considered to have no right to voice such sentiments made him, in Voloshin's view, more worthy than his detractors.[33] Ehrenburg was to make much of this 'prohibited' love for Russia.

In autumn 1918 Ehrenburg fled Moscow after being held hostage by the Bolsheviks. However, in November 1918 his mother passed away in Poltava, still occupied by the Germans. After arriving late for his mother's funeral, Ehrenburg joined the wave south to emigration, hoping, he wrote to Voloshin, to preserve Russia inside himself. In his native Kiev, capital of the Ukraine which was for a short while independent, Ehrenburg, in Nadezhda Mandelstam's words, took refuge in irony and detachment. But his mother's death had made him think of mortality as a triumph or justification of life.[34] A letter preserved in private archives confides Ehrenburg's thoughts under the impact of bereavement and civil war: he was turning to quietude and reconciliation. 'Even my rhythm is becoming slower and straighter. That's dangerous; it could be death. My sacred "no" is weakening.'[35] This was, however, to be a brief interlude in the consistent scepticism which characterizes Ehrenburg's life and his self-image in *Julio Jurenito*, not so different, perhaps, from the 'necessary heresy' of Evgenii Zamiatin, who declared himself to be no longer a Bolshevik when Bolshevism became dogma after the Revolution.[36]

When the Reds took Kiev in February 1919 Ehrenburg found a job working with juvenile delinquents in one of the mushrooming Soviet institutions. The political interregnum in the Ukrainian capital saw the astounding creativity of the Yiddish modernists grouped around *Eygns* and Dovid Bergelson. In the modern art workshop of Aleksandra Ekster, Ehrenburg met his second wife, Liuba, who worked alongside Nadezhda Khazina, the future spouse of Osip Mandelstam. Nadezhda Mandelstam recalls in her memoirs how Ehrenburg chastised her for her juvenile response to Maiakovsky's poem about the officers who were thrown into the Moika. Death stalked the streets, armed men killed at whim and Ehrenburg thought no poet should be lighthearted about it.[37] Ehrenburg had first welcomed the Whites, but must have had doubts about his hopes for a new Russia considering the resurgence of the call 'Beat the Jews and Save Russia'. At the time he declared that Jewish blood had had no remedial effect on Russian soil, but the pogroms had actually strengthened the Jews' love for Russia.[38] In *People, Years, Life* Ehrenburg places the pogroms in the context of Perets Markish's modernist dirge, 'The Heap', for the victims at Horoditsh, as well as in the perspective of Babi Yar, the ravine in Kiev where the Nazis murdered thousands of Jews. While trying to depersonalize the experience, Ehrenburg mocks the brutality and greed of the perpetrators and ascribes their ferocity to despair (1, 299–300). In a story published in 1928, 'Staryi skorniak' ('The Old Furrier'), Ehrenburg depicts the *pogromshchik's* desire to revenge the destruction of his village and his demented fury at the Jew's religious acceptance of 'sweet' death.

In the bloodiest massacres to hit East European Jewry before the Holocaust Ehrenburg could not, however, be a neutral bystander. In the terror that reigned in Kiev, Jews were beaten and killed as supporters of Bolshevism. Yet it was the Bolsheviks whose 'virus', Ehrenburg wrote, had contaminated the Russian soul with the godless freedom of Ivan Karamazov's nihilism. Vasily Shulgin, who had earlier denounced the Beilis trial, challenged the Jews to learn the lesson and repent Marxist belief in the class war. Ehrenburg's reply[39] was that his love for Russia was a difficult and sometimes humiliating apprenticeship, but he had not lost either his faith or love: the Tsarist tricolour gave him the security of Russian culture and the Jew's only homeland. This was, to be sure, a perverse love that endangered both identity and existence, and before leaving Kiev Ehrenburg sought to give it some sort of philosophical reasoning: his faith was sustained by the sacred 'no' which was the people of Israel's 'salt' and which constituted their self-destructive mission. Ehrenburg was inspired by the French Jewish poet André Spire's *Poèmes juifs*, a collection of verse published in October 1919 which was written under the impact of the Russian pogroms and the Dreyfus Affair that pushed Spire toward Zionism and a defiant Jewish pride. He had been encouraged by Charles Péguy, but then found himself rebutted, a useful parallel with Ehrenburg's situation in Russian poetry and with Ehrenburg's own sources in French Catholicism. Spire looked to poetry as a prayer that was nourished by love for one's native land, and we can identify here the idea later developed by Ehrenburg of the mission of the Jews. In fact, Ehrenburg translated Spire into Russian and wrote an article about him in 1919 with the significant title 'Sviatoe "net" ' ('The Sacred "No" ').[40]

Together with Mandelstam, the Ehrenburgs fled to the Crimea, where they sheltered in Voloshin's villa at Koktebel'. From there they managed to get to Menshevik Georgia on a barge. On the boat to Theodosia Ehrenburg had narrowly escaped being thrown overboard by a Jew-hating Cossack; Liuba had almost died of typhus at Koktebel' for want of a syringe and alcohol. In the Crimea Mandelstam had been picked up by Wrangel's security agents; in Georgia he was arrested as a double agent. These perils and the uncertain future after the defeat of Denikin may have pressed Ehrenburg's decision to go back to Soviet Russia. In 1922 he was to write that Mandelstam had persuaded him to return and face History and monstrous Time. Entrusted with sealed documents, Ehrenburg braved bandits and partisans searching for Commissars and Jews and returned to Moscow as a Soviet envoy accompanied by the Mandelstam brothers, only to be arrested shortly afterwards by the Cheka as a suspected agent of Wrangel! Bukharin saved him from death and Meyerhold gave him a new lease of life working for youth theatre. However, by February 1921 Meyerhold, a foremost figure of the avant-garde, had been forced to relinquish his position. In March 1921, again thanks to the intervention of Bukharin, the Ehrenburgs left Russia on Soviet passports – among the first of many intellectuals who left Russia in this way. As a writer he could only write as a Russian, but to write freely he needed liberty and clean paper. Neither commodity was available in large quantities in Moscow. A collection of poems published in Riga and entitled *Razdum'ia* ('Meditations', 1921), written in Koktebel' and Moscow, sum up his feelings about Russia in the wake of the pogroms and the Civil War. This is his farewell to Russia, to the pointless wandering among the ravines where the bodies of massacred children lay. Here new meaning is given to the mystical notion of the Russian earth: Ehrenburg's mother and also the pogrom victims are buried in the fertile black loam. Russian earth is now alien terriory, a dead-end space. He rips off his monastic robes, tearing his skin, and declares:

> I renounce, thrice renounce
> Everything I lived yesterday
> ... I accept your cross, unbelief
> In order to again and again crave!
> I kneel and kiss the black earth.
> Oh how brief are the hours of existence!
> My mother, frail bright soul,
> You are mine! You are mine! You are mine![41]

This poem has been taken as Ehrenburg's profession of atheism, but we should note that he later characterized craving as preferable to believing, and it is this unquenchable thirst of scepticism which Ehrenburg had characterized as the Jewish contribution to civilization. It is the cross of unbelief that he must carry after Russian earth can no longer accommodate both his love for Russia and his mortality as a bereaved Jew. He was born in the world of yesterday, so he cannot learn the new language of the Revolution and cannot master its difficult ordinances. He portrays himself dying on the threshold of the new era in which his words will be an indecipherable epitaph for future generations. Despite the hysterical tones, the choice is clear. After the revelation of Golgotha at the new Sinai of the Revolution, Ehrenburg flees the Barbarians in the fiery East and sets his face toward the dawning West, though – as he kept saying – love of the West was not to be regarded as unfaithfulness to Russia. Yet not all connection had been lost with the past and with his former self:

> Having betrayed the dead god, I shall never forget
> His difficult and childish names.[42]

In his book *Zoo, or Letters Not About Love*, the formalist critic Viktor Shklovsky, who also lived through the pogroms in Kiev in autumn 1918, dubbed Ehrenburg Pavel Savlovich, 'A Saul who had failed to become Paul', referring to the conversion of the Christian apostle on the road to Damascus and implying that whenever Ehrenburg embraced a new creed – as when he forsook Catholicism for Constructivism – he never really renounced his previous beliefs. 'It was because of the cold,' wrote Shklovsky, 'that Peter renounced Christ. The night air was fresh, and he drew near to the fire, but by the fire there was public opinion, the servants asked Peter about Christ, and Peter renounced him ... It's a good job that Jesus was not crucified in Russia: the climate is severe with thick blizzards ...' (cited by Ehrenburg, 1, 394). 'On the Road to Damascus' was in fact a title Ehrenburg had used in Kiev for a 1919 newspaper attack on the Bolsheviks' Jesuitic justification of the means by the ends, in which he called for Russia to see the light and turn away from Smerdiakov's amoral 'all is permissible'. Anatol Goldberg comments that Ehrenburg 'was drawn to various beliefs, but always dreaded and resisted total conversion ... He wanted both to be free and to belong. But for all his attachment to Russia, it was only in the West that he could be a free Soviet writer.'[43] Ehrenburg himself adopted the 'Paul son of Saul' label and uses it in his Memoirs when he describes Russian émigré life in Berlin, where he lived after he was deported from France as a Bolshevik propagandist.

Ehrenburg's dual position meant that he could publish (as long as it was possible) in the West and in the Soviet Union: he contributed to both the émigré journal *Novaia russkaia kniga*, edited by Iashchenko, and the Soviet fellow-traveller *Krasnaia nov'*, edited by Voronsky. In his Memoirs Ehrenburg sums up his position as not being unusual in the plurality of beliefs and non-beliefs which then proliferated among writers in Russia and abroad:

> in each of my books I 'dissociated' myself from myself. It was precisely at this time that Victor Shklovsky called me 'Paul, son of Saul'. Coming from him, this did not sound malicious. In life he did what nearly all his contemporaries did; that is, he changed his opinions and judgements more than once, though he did this without bitterness and even with a certain bravado; only his eyes were sad, as they had probably been from birth (I, 393).

Those sad eyes are a coded epithet for the Jew, and Shklovsky serves as an example of the Jew who suffered in Russia but cannot live happily abroad among a hostile émigré community, a mediator of European culture in Russia who cannot write freely inside Russia. Shklovsky – associated with the formalist circle repressed under Stalin and forced to recant – is presented by Ehrenburg, who often projects aspects of himself onto others, as someone who never renounced anything in order to get closer to the fire (in Shklovsky's parable of Peter) and endured feeling cold.

AU-DESSUS DE LA MÊLÉE

'Au-dessus de la mêlée' was Ehrenburg's programmatic title for his non-partisan defence of Soviet poets who were seen by émigré critics as traitors to Russia, but naturally Ehrenburg was tarred with the same brush.[44] Ehrenburg liked to receive visitors in Berlin's Prager Diele café, later back in the Paris Rotonde, and bask in his public image of a Bohemian writer, a world-weary cynic, a Catholic-Jew of no faith – just some of several masks which Ehrenburg cultivated. Not to state any firm belief or clear position created an ambiguity particularly suited to the mannered style of the modernistic narrative at which Shklovsky himself excelled, a narrative which was constructed out of fragments and digressions, an apparently plotless story in which the authorial self is disturbingly absent. The individual is divided, missing the wholeness of the hero of the nineteenth-century novel which he nevertheless despises. The intersubjective centre of narration observes the self from outside as the Little Man, the Charlie Chaplin lost in the modern metropolis; the self as Other coalesces with the alienated Intellectual, the Judas-Jew, in the rapid swirl of confused and dramatic events of war and revolutions. Short staccato sentences imitate the breathlessness of telegrammatic Time.

During his Catholic phase Ilia Ehrenburg had, under the influence of Léon Bloy, come to see the pogroms as part of a Divine plan of redemption through evil. The discussion of the Jewish Question and the modern civilization responsible for it in *Neobychainye pokhozhdeniia Khulio Khurenito i ego uchenikov* ... ('The Extraordinary Adventures of Julio Jurenito and his Disciples', 1922) suggests a similar apocalyptic scheme in which the author satirizes himself as Jew and as Russian émigré. The book's full title is 'The Extraordinary Adventures of Julio Jurenito and his Disciples – Monsieur Delhaie, Karl Schmidt, Mister Cool, Aleksei Tishin, Ercole Bambucci, Ilia Ehrenburg and Aysha the Negro – in Days of Peace, War and Revolution, in Paris, Mexico, Rome and Senegal, in Kineshma, Moscow and other Places, as well as Various Reflections by the Master on Pipe-Smoking, Death, Love, Freedom, Chess, the Tribe of Judah, Constructivism and Many Other Matters'. Its publication in 1922 marks Ehrenburg's shift to prose, and the book is meant to sum up everything Ehrenburg thought about his times prior to his return to the West. Julio Jurenito is a demonic figure, a provocateur, who aims to destroy the world by exacerbating existing evils, and in doing so puts everything to the acid test of lethal satire that was to prove prophetic of Hiroshima and Auschwitz. Actually, Jurenito simply takes to their logical extreme Ehrenburg's observations of the well-oiled machine of war on the Western Front by encouraging the evil genius of Mr Cool, who can buy anything with money.

Jurenito is also an alter ego, who died on 12 March 1921, when the real-life Ehrenburg abandoned Russia. Jurenito follows the itinerary of Ehrenburg's own biography as well as some of his fantasy journeys. Further evidence that Jurenito represents Ehrenburg's 'second soul' is the fact that the model for Julio Jurenito is the painter Diego Rivera, who was close to Ehrenburg in his prewar Paris days, and who once almost killed him during a psychopathological fit. Diego Rivera also appears in the book as a friend of Jurenito and a 'witness' to his coming.

Jurenito appears to Ehrenburg in 1913 on the eve of the First World War, the first calamity in the global apocalypse, in the Rotonde, the forum of all nations, and he proceeds to assemble disciples from each nation. He appears naked, accompanied by a breastless female companion, but then his tail and horns prove illusory. The narrator describes that evening in a phrase of particular relevance to Ehrenburg's biography (or biographical self-invention) as his 'road to Damascus'. In a scene reminiscent of the opening of Bulgakov's later reworking of the Faust legend in *Master and Margarita,* Ehrenburg's Master mocks the idea of good and evil, of morality and the meaning of life; the only 'reality' is to be found in the pipe which he smokes.[45] A Mexican anarchist, Jurenito is baptized in the name of belief and disbelief in Catholicism among the great painters: Julio–Maria–Diego–Pablo–Angelina. The appearance of Jurenito in Europe is explained by the level of amorality. Jurenito explains to Mister Cool that belief is as rare in Europe as a pretty virgin or an honest minister:

Your faith is cowardly, it is shaded with doubt and irony, a boyish curiosity and a merchant's anxious calculation when buying goods. ... Your unbelief is no braver than your belief which drags along behind it superstition, repentance a half-hour before death, the books of Steiner and constant hanging around the door of the insurance company.[46]

Atheists, then, are not sincere in their unbelief, and therefore the unquestioning faith of the negro Aisha is a formidable weapon in Jurenito's hands.

Jurenito is little more than a satirical device who can be
dropped whenever necessary, a true devil's advocate; yet Ehrenburg's cynical and lighthearted treatment of what clearly does
matter to him both underscores the moral decay of Europe and
exposes the ambiguity of his unbelief. Jurenito's and his own
pipe-smoking, Shklovsky suggested, are meant to suggest philosophical detachment. Ehrenburg's typical strategy is the denial of
rumours and the negation of slander, leaving the impression of a
shadow-boxer who is himself a shadow.

Crossing the border from decadent European civilization into
revolutionary Russia, Jurenito discovers an inverted anarchic
world[47] where he can hatch more plans and negate them. In a
rehash of the 'Legend of the Grand Inquisitor' from Dostoevsky's
novel *The Brothers Karamazov* (a scene also used by Zamiatin in his
satirical dystopia *We)*, Jurenito chats with Lenin, the unnamed
'captain on the bridge' of the Russian Revolution, and hears him
defend the need for suppression of liberty and justify executions
in the name of the future happiness of mankind. However, the
retreat from War Communism into NEP disappoints Jurenito,
who finds the new normalcy of neo-capitalist Russia not so
different from the West. His death leaves his disciples to work
things out for themselves. But 'Ehrenburg' goes back to the West
where he can retain what Bukharin called his 'nihilistic hooli-
ganism'.[48] That is, I believe, because unlike Jurenito, the Jew
'Ehrenburg' is the archetypal Outsider in Europe.[49]

The shock and disbelief which meet the master's announce-
ment of invitations to watch the spectacle of the actual genocide
(*sic*!) of the Jewish tribe is one way of exposing the world's silence
about the bloody massacres of 1918–19 and the never-ending
persecution of the Jews. Most ridiculous of all is the outburst of
Aleksei Spiridonovich Tishin, the muddleheaded Russian émigré
intellectual, who protests that such things as pogroms could not
happen in the twentieth century and that he could not support
such a proclamation as one who had read Merezhkovsky! The
Master promises that the twentieth century will be a merry one
without any moral scruples, and that readers of Merezhkovsky
will be among supporters of the pogrom. Anti-Semitism is deep-
rooted, he relates, going back to the Egyptians who appeased the

earth with Jewish blood in a drought year. The Italians believed the earth shook because of the Jews and buried them alive. Now the earth must be sprinkled again with Jewish blood because it is the world's great remedy. Jurenito demonstrates the difference of the Jew from the rest of humanity in order to explain the persistence of hatred for the Jews, who are different by blood and should be regarded as either arsonists or saviours; the Jew is always the sectarian child who betrays its parents by inventing subversive new faiths: Christianity and now Communism. The world, explains Jurenito, is split between those who say yes and those who say no. As he asks each member of this peculiar League of Nations to choose between 'yes' and 'no', they instinctively move away from the Jew. 'Ehrenburg' finds himself cast out as a scapegoat, but alone unequivocally chooses 'no' because the Jew is the eternal cynic and heretic. There is a time, in the words of Ecclesiastes, to gather stones and a time to cast stones, and the Jew 'Ehrenburg' insists on throwing stones, that is he insists on an anarchic or nihilistic freedom.

Ehrenburg's former (or present) beliefs are reflected when we are told that Jewish blood has been spilt through the ages as a scapegoat sacrifice. This caricature of Léon Bloy's credo ends with the Master kissing 'Ehrenburg' on the forehead, and it is not clear whether this is a Judas kiss or the kiss of the Grand Inquisitor. But it remains quite clear that the Jew is supposed to carry the world's cross of anti-Semitism. Whereas Jews had believed throughout their medieval persecutions that their suffering was a Divine rebuke and anticipated the End of Time (*kets hayamin*) which would bring universal messianic redemption, Ehrenburg apparently continued to believe that the suffering of the Jews was a religious mystery, which explained why pogroms continued after the Revolution which had brought neither redemption nor the end of History. In one of the stories in *Nepravdopodobnye istorii* ('Unlikely Stories', 1922) a Russian officer believes in the Protocols of the Elders of Zion, unaware of the Bolshevik Revolution. 'Shifs-karta' ('The Steamship Ticket'), in *Shest' povestei o legkikh kontsakh* ('Six Tales about Easy Endings', 1922), which depicts quite accurately the requisition of a synagogue by the *Evsektsiia* and the destruction of Jewish life under the Bolsheviks, ends with the martyrdom of an old Jew in a pogrom against the background of a mystical apocalypse. The story was illustrated by El Lissitzky with a modernist montage (see Figure 9, p. 67) composed of a black hand and a gravestone inscription superimposed on a Talmudic plan of the Temple, a Star of David and the Hamburg–New York steamship line, thus drawing upon and subverting Jewish images of national identity and disaster (the destruction of Jerusalem and the pogroms), while suggesting death and emigration as expressive of the fate of Russian Jewry. Professor Chimen Abramsky points out that Lissitzky did this collage in Berlin when he was undecided whether or not to return to the Soviet Union.[50] However, Alan Birnholz suggests that the inverted typography on the binding of Ehrenburg's book and the cover design suggest an element of playful jocularity.[51] Lissitzky and Ehrenburg were both active in bridging Russia and modernist Western art in their editing of *Veshch'* in Berlin, an attempt to influence Russia with constructivist ideas and an attempt to ease the blockade of the Soviet Union on the cultural front.

   Though it is a grotesque fantasy of what being a Jew really means, the role described by Julio Jurenito of the Jew who breaks his head against the wall of dogma and convention (the metaphor is Dostoevsky's in *Notes from the Underground*) in order to constantly question the established order of things, this vital source of scepticism and sacred 'no', akin to Zamiatin's 'necessary heresy', fits Ehrenburg's definitive views on the Jews in a brief essay of 1925, 'Lozhka degtia' ('A Spoonful of Tar'). Ehrenburg takes for his title the Russian proverb that a spoonful of tar will spoil a barrel of mead, but typically subverts the meaning of the proverb by claiming the opposite, that figurative tar – scepticism and dissent – improves the taste. For all the contradictoriness and confusion of his ideas, Ehrenburg's logic dictated that the Jew could live only in exile, for only in the Diaspora did he fulfil his role among the nations. Here Ehrenburg resisted the Zionist argument that the only way to end persecution of the Jews was to settle them in their own homeland and to restore them to the normal status of a territorial nation-state. For Ehrenburg Jewish 'separatism' – one of the chief arguments of the anti-Semites –

was itself racist, but more importantly it eliminated the Jew's role as a heretic. Ehrenburg often quoted the German writer Ernst Toller's remark, 'To say "I am proud of being a Jew" is as ridiculous as saying "I am proud of having brown eyes." '.[52] Yet while saying that national identity did not matter, he tried to create a philosophy out of the fact that it did.

Ehrenburg characterized the Jew in 'A Spoonful of Tar' as a subversive influence who guaranteed freedom because he was gnawed by doubts and could not believe in blind faith. This was a definition of the Jew-Poet, except that this was by implication a self-definition of the non-Jewish Jew. The examples cited by Ehrenburg of Babel and Pasternak are both significant and, as we have seen, problematic. Ehrenburg's model is a Spanish-Jewish poet, Santob de Carrión (Rabbi Shem-Tov ibn Ardutiel), who was born at the end of the thirteenth century in the Castilian town of Soria and died some time after 1345. Ehrenburg would have been attracted by the combination in Santob de Carrión of accommodation with the ruling power and a sharp polemical subversion of conventional Christian topoi, notably the rose among thorns, which comes to symbolize the claimed legitimacy and moral authority of the self-deprecating Jew-Poet against the background of deteriorating relations of Jews and Christians in northern Spain prior to the Expulsion of 1492. Ehrenburg would have also been sympathetic to the sceptical voice that scourged the materialism of this world, its 'avid commitment to mundane experience and existential doubt, its religious reticence and ethical relativism, and its pragmatic but probing approach to reality and survival'.[53] However, there is in Ehrenburg's account little of the real Santob de Carrión.[54] Asked by King Pedro the Cruel to soothe his insomnia, the Jew advised him in a book of quatrains that everything is transitory, just as the moon begins to wane as soon as it is full. The King countered that truth from the mouth of a Jew was like wine in rotten barrels. To this Ehrenburg has Santob de Carrión reply that the world was divided into those who drank wine and those with dry lips: ' "What is better? Andalusian wine or thirsty lips? Fool! The taste of the most wonderful wine is soon forgotten, but unquenched thirst lasts." '[55] The Jew prefers exile from Eden because freedom is preferable to happiness. Ehrenburg seems again to be drawing on Dostoevsky's underground man, and he cites André Spire to support the Romantic idea of the Wandering Jew for whom scepticism and criticism are conditions of his existence (although Spire, as mentioned above, had come to a different conclusion, the Zionist solution). Just as Jurenito divided the world into yes-men and Jews who voiced the everlasting 'no', Ehrenburg argues that it is better to thirst for truth than to believe. This fantasy of the Jew as no-sayer subverts the discourse of anti-Semitism, particularly the conspiracy theory and Dostoevsky's charge in his famous essay in *Diary of a Writer* that the Jew is both the same as everyone else and different. The difference of the Jew does not threaten Holy Russia, but it is a necessary spoonful of tar in a barrel of mead.

If the Wandering Jews appeared to Ehrenburg as the 'insulted and injured' of humanity, this was not just a defence mechanism of an assimilated Jew but also a means of differentiation from the non-assimilated and 'non-cultured' mass of Jews in Eastern Europe, the Ostjuden. Commissioned by the Soviet fellow-traveller journal *Krasnaia nov'*, Ehrenburg's 'Visa of Time' is a travelogue of Poland and Eastern Europe which seems to have escaped the attention of most commentators and in which Ehrenburg describes the Jewish world as an outsider with Christian mystical leanings. This commission, like other examples of *sotsial'nyi zakaz* of this period of increasing dominance by the Proletkul't, was an opportunity offered to writers to prove their allegiance to the Bolsheviks, and Ehrenburg accepted without hesitation because it was a way out of the impasse of emigration and also a means to reclaim a cultural homeland: the original journal publication provides eloquent testimony to a self-hating Jew's display of differentiation from the Ostjude and his zeal in proselytizing for Russian culture and the Soviet régime.[56] In the chapters of the book version devoted to the Jews of Poland, Ehrenburg views Hasidism as a mystical movement like that of the Franciscans, which began – in line with Ehrenburg's concept of necessary heresy and the botanical analogy of natural decay – as a revolution which decayed into dogma and betrayed its ideals of 'happiness, love and humanitarianism'. The comparison with the Franciscans also brings Ehrenburg to compare Hasidism with

Dostoevsky's description of the mystic Zosima. He presents the uncorrupted tsadik as a kind of Russian holy fool (as is Santob de Carrión in the 'Legend of Rabbi Shem Tov and King Pedro the Cruel'), just as Francis of Assisi and Father Zosima are the standard by which Ehrenburg retrospectively measures the stature of Jammes in his Memoirs (although Jammes was neither Francis of Assisi or Father Zosima). The notion of spiritual ascent through descent which Ehrenburg underscores derives from the Cabbala, but Ehrenburg's reading of it is Dostoevskian. Indeed, the comparison of the legends about the Kotsker rebbe with the philosophy of Dostoevsky seems incredible. Yet though he was an assimilated Jew proselytizing for Russian culture, who had grown up in Moscow and who lived in France, at a distance from any Jewish community but close to many Jews in the avant-garde, Ehrenburg had now come face to face with authentic and unashamed Judaism. The emotional and cultural shock must have surprised Ehrenburg, as it had earlier deeply affected in different ways Jiří Langer and Isaak Babel. In the Bratslav Hasidim Ehrenburg found a correspondence to his lost faith in messianism, both communist and Christian. In Yosele Skverno-vitser he found a village dreamer, a poet and leader of poor workers, a hidden mystic – the *lamed vavnik* of Jewish folk-lore – who combined for Ehrenburg the amalgam of love for man and the mystical inspiration of the Ba'al Shem Tov, the founder of Hasidism. The Bratslav Hasidim are the most messianic of Jewish sects and Ehrenburg was familiar with the tales and sayings of their dead rebbe, Nakhman of Bratslav, from Martin Buber's well-known German translation and adaptation.[57]

LAZIK'S TIN WHISTLE

Such a view of East European Jewry also permeates an entire novel devoted to a Jewish picaresque hero whose misadventures recollect those of Voltaire's Candide as the scathing satire reduces everything to absurdity. *Burnaia zhizn' Lazika Roitshvanetsa* ('The Stormy Life of Lazik Roitshvanets', 1928) relates how a poor Jewish tailor from Gomel tries to adapt to the new Bolshevik régime, tries always to keep in step with the times but constantly falls foul of the authorities. Lazik is a shlemiel type familiar from Yiddish literature, but the Yiddishisms and Hasidic stories are largely stylized or invented. Lazik adapts Talmudic *pilpul* (academic, hair-splitting argument) to Marxist dialectics, showing up the absurdity of communist demagoguery and the ridiculous miscarriages of justice which cost life and liberty.[58] In fact the book is fundamentally hostile to both Judaism and Communism.

Lazik's troubles start with an inadvertent sigh and a denunciation puts him in prison. Finding his home, trade, and shirts requisitioned in his absence he sets off on his wanderings, determined to join them if he cannot beat them. Lazik is a born survivor: 'it's no use losing hope', he says, 'that's as bad as suddenly dying twenty years before your time'.[59] In order to earn a crust of bread and a slice of sausage he learns to mimic any official language and beguile his listeners with a mouthful of verbiage to convince them he loyally 'belongs'. He becomes a candidate member of the Party in Kiev, a bureaucrat administrator of non-existent rabbits in Moscow, then a Proletarian critic. All this is good fun, and mimicry exposes the nonsense of the system, but reduction to the absurd is subversively applied to all ideologies and societies, from Communism in Russia to Capitalism in the West, from the Christian missionaries in London's East End to Zionism in Mandatory Palestine. Nothing is sacred and there is nothing left in which to believe except the dignity of sinful man and the struggle for individuality.

Ehrenburg's Christian mystical views show through his readings, or rather misreadings, of Jewish texts such as the Talmud and Hasidic stories. The Jew is the quintessential wanderer who, try as he might, cannot help brooding over what he is supposed not to brood about, the perennial disturber of the peace who must ask questions.[60] In a Berlin prison Lazik claims as his ancestor another luckless tailor (like him, named for Lazarus) who was made to run naked around Rome for the pleasure of the Pope and the salvation of the Jewish community. As in Sholem Asch's story 'The Carnival Legend' (mentioned in my earlier discussion of crucifixion stories in Chapter 2), Jesus takes the martyr's place out of identification with the Jew as the eternal victim of crucifixion, persecuted as crucifier of the Christian god.

Jesus saves the collapsing tailor, who is, in Ehrenburg's version, doomed to die because of the corruption by the Church of Jesus' teachings. Jesus is here Yoshua – the Jewish Jesus – the saviour of the poor who dreamed of complete happiness and justice. Here the blasphemous Russian Jewish tailor is elaborating the idea that as long as Jesus was a poor carpenter's son his utopian dreams were divine, but as soon as the Church deified him he became mere household furniture:

There seem to be a hundred Roitshvantses crucified every day, and nobody even protests. But what of that laughter of children, what of those loaves of golden bread on the tables of the poor? Oh, all that, of course is ridiculous fantasy. Silence, crass Roitshvanets! No point in philosophizing![61]

This too serves in an underhand way to square Ehrenburg's own disappointment in a utopian messianism and elaborate his views on the necessity of the Jew in a Dostoevskian scheme of things.

Lazik may have cheated the system, but he does not think himself guilty of deceiving anyone. Yet he is punished everywhere for what he has not done. This might also be said of Ehrenburg's own supposed treachery. At the time of writing the book Ehrenburg was contemplating his return to Russia. He had published a number of novels exposing the West as a false paradise in which people were exploited by wealthy tycoons and international manufacturing corporations. The reasons which Lazik gives for his own decision to return home to his native Gomel may have been a sounding out of Ehrenburg's own thinking. Lazik ends up in Mandatory Palestine and finds it a country like any other, except that, to his great disillusionment, it is Jews who are dealing the blows to his body, by now an 'overstamped passport'. The soil of the holy Land, he feels, is not his own. True to Ehrenburg's conception of the Jew who is an alien everywhere, Roitshvanets negates the Zionist claim to 'normalize' the status of the Jews by returning them to their ancestral homeland. Having been disabused of the possibility of even daily existence, let alone an Eldorado, and having suffered beyond endurance, Roitshvanets now wants to return to Gomel, 'our native land' and to 'die at home'.

As he lies dying at Rachel's Tomb (reminding us of Sholem Asch's union of Rachel with Mary), he tells the guardian of the holy site a story about a Hasidic tsadik who told his disciples that Hell was preferable to a false Paradise or a Heaven made for angels. In this parable Lazik has the tsadik assert that it is not possible to rise without first falling. Ehrenburg's peculiarly Dostoevskian adaptation of Buber's reinterpretation of the classic Hasidic tales seems to be saying that the insulted and injured of this world are blessed *because* they never rise and never attain any mystical truths, but only express common humanity and suffering. Lazik ends his life and the book with the well-known tale of the Ba'al Shem Tov, which Ehrenburg later said he heard in a Paris café from the Yiddish novelist Varshavski and which delighted Perets Markish, who told Ehrenburg this was applicable to the role of the poet (I, 456). The story tells of the boy who blows his whistle on the Day of Atonement and arouses God's mercy when He sits in judgement. The beatific smile on the lips of Ehrenburg's own Bontshe the Silent resembles the smile of the child who blew the whistle in Ehrenburg's version of the Ba'al Shem Tov story and recalls the pogrom victims in 'The Steamship Ticket' and 'The Old Furrier'; this smile stands for compassion amidst futility and indifference, and though this misses the point of the original tale, it makes a clear equation between the Jew as crucified victim forced to run naked around Rome and his cousin the Good Soldier Švejk.

The book was welcomed by Jewish readers as Ehrenburg's declaration of identity as a Jewish writer, but the Soviet authorities reacted coolly to the book's scathing attacks on the corruption and bureaucracy of the totalitarian Soviet system. At a reception during the First Soviet Writers' Congress in 1934 attended by several Politburo members, Ehrenburg feigned surprise when Lazar Kaganovich protested against the 'nationalist' Jewish content of the book (II, 38); as the last Jew left in the Politburo he was clearly embarrassed by suggestions in the book that anti-Semitism still existed in Russia.

At the end of his career, writing in *People, Years, Life*, Ehrenburg explained that he had not included 'Lazik' in his Collected Works because the Nazi genocide of millions of Laziks had made a satirical stereotype tasteless and obscene. Ehrenburg does not say in his Memoirs that the Zamiatin and Pilniak affairs of 1929 rendered impossible the publication of this sort of satire in the Soviet Union. Indeed, 'The Stormy Life of Lazik Roitshvanets' was published in the Soviet Union only in 1991. A more plausible reason is that the many Jewish references in the book would be embarrassing when Ehrenburg was emphasizing his own distance from anything ethnically Jewish and manoeuvring his way into publication by the Soviet authorities in order to win their acceptance of his role as 'our correspondent' abroad, a roaming cultural ambassador to French intellectuals. He had himself used the traditional anti-Semitic stereotypes from both Tsarist times and the NEP period of the world Jewish conspiracy, the smell of Jewish money, the Jew's sexual perversion and treachery in his novel *Edinyi front* ('United Front', written in 1929) which was part of a series of exposés of Western capitalism between 1928 and 1932, including one novel that brought him a libel suit by the Czech shoe king Batá. Ehrenburg's disillusion with the West and his exposure of the ugly face of Capitalism was bound to ingratiate the author with the Soviet authorities, but it was no doubt a sober appraisal of the prospects of an émigré Russian writer in a declining West during the Depression and the rise of Fascism, on the one hand, and the tightening constraints on individual freedom in Stalin's increasingly isolationist Russia under forced collectivization and industrialization, on the other.

Ehrenburg's self-identification after the Holocaust can be seen as a refinement of his former notion of the Jew as bearer of the world's cross. Tuwim's essay spoke of Jewish blood that flowed *from*, not in, the veins; Tuwim's crucified Jew fitted Ehrenburg's general conception,[62] and he could now fuse Tsvetaeva's identification of poet and Jew with his identification as a *Russian* writer with Jewish victims of anti-Semitism, just as Evtushenko, in his poem 'Babi Yar', was to merge poet and Anne Frank, and identify fully with Dreyfus and with the pogrom victims, writing that in the eyes of anti-Semites he is a Jew.

Hope betrayed

The call for revenge against the Nazis in Ehrenburg's countless
press reports from the front and leaflets distributed among Soviet
troops is couched in a rhetoric of patriotic defence of the Motherland. There can be little doubt that Ehrenburg's 'forbidden' love
for Russia was sincere, but this was also the only strategy available
to Jewish witnesses of the Holocaust when no public statements
could be made inside the Soviet Union about the Final Solution
and when, as Ehrenburg knew, anti-Semitism was rife among
those very troops whose sympathy Ehrenburg wished to enlist.[1]
Moreover, many inhabitants of the German-occupied areas of
the Soviet Union, until recently citizens of the world's first
socialist society, were openly collaborating with the Nazis and did
not hide their pleasure at the destruction of the Jews. A similar
strategy is deployed in Vasily Grossman's *Zhizn' i sud'ba* (*Life and
Fate*, 1960; first published abroad in 1980).[2] Grossman's novel will
afford a last example of 'double-voicing' in the discourse of the
Soviet Jew writing in Russian, after it had become clear that
emancipation and revolution had not given the Jews equal status;
on the contrary, the Holocaust brought home to the Jews their
alien identity and awakened pain at their lost heritage. While not
attempting a full study of Grossman, this concluding chapter
offers a case illustrative of the textual strategies employed by the
four writers who have been at the centre of our discussion and an
epilogue (in all senses of the word) that is both chronological and,
as far as hopes for a cultural identity in the Soviet period go,
apparently final.

Grossman and Ehrenburg were among the first to collect
testimonies to the Final Solution after the Red Army liberated

the Ukraine and Belorussia. Their immediate response is indicative of their reassessment of identity, their sense of collective destiny and their strategies in resisting anti-Semitism, in particular Ehrenburg's persistent attempts to have the heroism of Jewish combatants recognized, and the appeal of both writers to a largely biased readership. In his 1944 poem 'Babi Yar', Ehrenburg comes as an alienated, urbanized outsider to his native Kiev, but he reidentifies with the Jewish dead, the archetypal coded destiny of the Jewish people, now given a new and final meaning:

> What good words and pen,
> When this stone lies on my heart,
> When I carry like a forced labourer
> Someone else's memory?
> ... now every pit is familiar,
> And every pit is now my home.[3]

When Evtushenko's poem 'Babi Yar' raised a storm of criticism for its condemnation of prevalent Russian anti-Semitism in 1961, it was compared unfavourably with Ehrenburg's earlier poem of the same title, which did not make the 'mistake' of naming the victims as Jews, though in another poem of 1944, 'V eto getto liudi ne pridut ...' ('People will not come to this ghetto ...'), Ehrenburg identified the victims by their star. Ehrenburg defended Evtushenko and was himself attacked.

If Ehrenburg had, in his 1940 poem 'Brodiat Rakhili, Khaimy, Lii' ('There wander Rachels, Hannahs, Leahs') 'remembered' he was a Jew and his mother was called Hannah, Margarita Aliger in 'Tvoia pobeda' ('Your Victory', 1945) declares she has not forgotten she is a Jew and is proud of her Jewish heritage. Her attitude is less fatalistic than that of Ehrenburg and Grossman. In 'Kak ubivali moiu babku?' ('How Did they Kill my Grandma?', published 1964), on the other hand, Boris Slutsky describes the heroic death of his grandmother at the hands of the Germans from the loyal Soviet perspective of the martyr's call for revenge by the Red Army in which the Jewish poet served, and the poem records the Russian neighbours' admiration for the grandmother's defiance.

Similarly, Anatoli Rybakov's novel *Tiazhelyi pesok* (*Heavy Sand*, 1979) presents the Holocaust through the narration of a sixty-year-old chatterbox who protests loudly that he is married to a Russian woman, could be considered a Jew only by Nazi racial laws and, although his family could claim German descent and roots in Switzerland, Soviet Russia is his homeland. The obedient anti-Zionist stand, with its denunciations of Jewish religion, can be compared with the 'official discourse' adopted by Ehrenburg; yet the novel presents the Holocaust as a Jewish experience, albeit shared with the Soviet nation, and presents its account of Jewish revolt and partisan resistance as an untold tale. The heavy sand of the title is the sand that has obliterated the grave of the narrator's father, and it is a quotation from Job 6, 2–3, which speaks of the words of grief being swallowed up by oblivion, a clear reference to Soviet repression of Jewish memory of the Holocaust. The ending of the novel, in which an improbable memorial to the victims of Nazism is unveiled, voices a plea to correct the lack of memorial for the victims of the Holocaust, and, like Evtushenko's protest in his poem 'Babi Yar', it is a protest against both repression of memory and anti-Semitism. The Hebrew inscription (a sure sign of wishful thinking!) is not a translation of the Soviet formula that erases the Jewish identity of the victims under the general heading of 'communists' or 'civilians', but a quotation from Joel 4, 21, where God says 'I shall not excuse the shedding of their blood', which appears in the Sabbath prayer, according to the Ashkenazic rite, commemorating the martyred victims of the Crusaders in the Rhineland, a fundamentally Jewish text which reinscribes collective memory and identity. By telling his Russian interlocutor that the translation is 'exact' the narrator is telling us there is a hidden discourse that rereads the 'official discourse' in its own terms. The family saga of Jacob and Rachel points to a Jewish historical paradigm beginning with the Patriarchs, though the martyrology of Dina Ivanovskaia is Christian in its iconology of a crucifixion of a tortured saint. Ever the loyal Soviet citizen who has 'forgotten Yiddish', the narrator nevertheless cannot be sure (i.e. refuses to confirm Party propaganda) whether Dina's last song was some Jewish, Ukrainian or Russian song or the International!

Russian forests and medieval legend, love-trysts and mystical yearnings, as well as the bombed-out ruins of Stalingrad and the bleak vistas of concentration camps, form the backdrop of Grossman's novel *Life and Fate* and place it well and truly in a Russian literary convention. The spirit of Prince Igor shines under the moonlight prior to the epic Stalingrad offensive, and Darensky muses on the fate of Russia and the Russian language. His Russianness, in contrast to the false Russianness of Krymov's investigator, is spontaneous when he protests at maltreatment of a wounded German prisoner. Place is literary. Kazan, for example, is characterized by its belonging to the Russian literary tradition: it is the city of Derzhavin, Aksakov, Tolstoy and Gorky – and, for good measure, Lenin. Grossman wrote relatively little on Jewish themes, though his Civil War story 'V gorode Berdicheve' ('In the Town of Berdichev', 1934) deals with a poor Jewish family, the Magazaniks, who foster a pregnant Russian commissar before she abandons her baby, fired by the same revolutionary enthusiasm as had inspired the now outlawed Jewish socialist movement, the Bund. However, even this risky reference to Jewish political aspirations and the description of resignation to pogroms and requisitions are outweighed by affirmation of Red victory. A chapter on the fate of the Jews in *Vse techet* (*Forever Flowing*, 1963, published posthumously abroad in 1970) forms part of a broader canvas of the destiny of Russia. Just as Ehrenburg liked to cite Chekhov's support of Zola for his defence of Dreyfus in the name of a Russian writer, Grossman portrays the Holocaust as a danger to that same humane liberal Russian tradition. When by summer 1942 the Germans and their allies had achieved control of much of Europe and North Africa, 'The time had come for National Socialism to realize its cruellest designs against human life and freedom. ... Adolf Hitler and the Party leadership had decided upon the final destruction of the Jewish nation' (195). Anti-Semitism is the logical result of totalitarianism and therefore it is a danger to human freedom.[4] Moreover, in a lengthy exposition of anti-Semitism in Book 2, Chapter 31, the narrator, now speaking in his own voice, sees Jewish history as exemplary: anti-Semitism proves the litmus-paper of freedom.

Such a conclusion is borne out by the analogy drawn between Soviet and Nazi totalitarianism. The novel opens in a German concentration camp, but the 'correct' narrative voice does not disguise the falsity of the claim that sending 'saboteurs' or potential dissidents to the camps was an innovation of the Nazis, as if the Soviet Gulag did not already perform that function. Another example is the representation of politically correct Communist Party voices, such as Mostovskoi, whom the author allows to be contradicted by ideological opponents – a religious believer, an émigré Menshevik, Vlasovites, and the Grand Inquisitor himself, Obersturmbannführer Liss. The most pathetic case is that of Tolia's father Abarchuk, who remains a convinced supporter of the Communist Party even when a prisoner of the Gulag. Krymov, brought straight from Stalingrad to the Lubianka, cannot believe he is now an 'Enemy of the People'. In Bakhtinian terms almost all discourse in the novel is given in quotation marks; while essentially parodic, double-voicing in the character zones refracts the author's intentions in the internal dialogization of languages of the novel.[5]

Grossman positions complementary episodes in strategic parallels to make clear the identity of totalitarianism, whether Nazi or Bolshevik, and he dramatizes contradictions in Party ideology to subvert the discourse of Soviet propaganda, the only permissible discourse. The *apparatchiki* of the totalitarian state, such as Getmanov, do not let personal emotion or anything human hinder the obsessive witch-hunt, and he even subjects a child to suspicion for doodling on a portrait of Stalin. Novikov admires the commissar's power and his ability to twist any situation according to the current Party line, for example his insistence on the promotion of a Russian officer instead of a Kalmyk or Jew. The Kalmyk represents a Tolstoyan ideal of the freedom of the steppe, while the Jew is forced by Hitler or Stalin to serve the same totalitarian state which is persecuting his brethren. Russian patriotism serves the call to arms and Jewish patronyms become suspect, something incomprehensible to Viktor Shtrum who at the same time knows that his Tatar friend Karimov does not shun affinity with his people and has hopes of seeing his family again, whereas he barely knows two words of Yiddish and will never see his mother again.

As an air force squadron prepares to be redeployed at Stalingrad, an incident is played out between the unpopular Commissar Berman and the Jewish airman Korol which exposes the 'double-voicing' of the discourse of the Other. The incident makes fun of Solomatin's prejudice that a Jew could not behave heroically like a Russian, as well as serving as a defence mechanism against this commonly held anti-Semitic stereotype. Solomatin is spokesman for the popular image of the Jews as cunning operators in league with each other who manoeuvre themselves into administrative positions. As the squadron prepares for one of the most momentous and decisive battles in Russian history, Solomatin taunts Korol, who is embarrassed about his Jewishness, that he wants to be sent to fight for Berdichev, 'your very own Jewish capital' (167). What is more fascinating than the documentation of Korol's proud defence against the charge of Jewish separatism and cowardice is the way the 'correct' ideological discourse is handled by Berman, the overzealous commissar, who must display his conscientious loyalty to the Party line. What might be passed off as a joke must not be allowed to be interpreted as complicity with Jewish separatism, a serious ideological error when the Jews were supposed to deny any ethnic identity beyond their ostensible 'autonomous territory' of Birobidjan and to accede to the lie that the 'friendship of the Soviet peoples' countermanded any affinity Jews might have had among themselves. The Jew must prove himself more loyal than Stalin. So Berman has to explain that Korol had 'failed to overcome his nationalist prejudices and that his behavior evinced a contempt for the friendship of peoples' (169). The look that Berman gives Korol is a tacit coded message that makes him uncomfortable. Having ostentatiously reprimanded the 'true' culprit, the victim of anti-Semitism, for his anti-Soviet behaviour in not repressing his Jewish identity, Berman goes on to reprieve Korol from punishment and instead to undertake his ideological education so that he will grow out of his '*shtetl* mentality' and appreciate the ideals of revolution and democracy! This is not the end of the story, for what happened gives grist to Solomatin's belief in the Jewish conspiracy: 'You see, Lenia, it's always like that. They stand up for each other all right

– but on the sly. If it had been you or Vania Skotnoi you'd have ended up in a penal colony' (170).

This cautionary tale parallels a similar jibe by a criminal prisoner at Rubin who refuses to put him on the sick list. When Rubin is brutally murdered, Abarchuk, who had been quick to condemn Rubin in his heart, is one of those who lies in his bunk without doing anything to prevent the murder or help the victim. The episode at the air-base, however, has more personal meaning, since Grossman was born in Berdichev, one of the largest centres of Jewish population and now behind enemy lines; nearly all the Jewish population were shot. Grossman's mother had stayed behind to look after a niece in Berdichev and was killed. Grossman identified with Tuwim's definition of the Jew 'Doloris Causa' to the point of obsession,[6] and the painful awareness of his own mother's fate must have spurred Grossman's identification with the Jewish people. When the author's imagination follows Sofia Levinton and the little boy David into the gas chamber, in a most extraordinary depiction of Madonna and Child, Grossmann is following his mother's last steps to her death with the other Jews of Berdichev shot by the Nazis. The letter from a mother left behind in the Ghetto is a moving document which speaks with warmth for the humanity of the victims and their determination to cling to their humanity to the last. Victor Shtrum's mother must unlearn the lessons of Soviet propaganda:

That morning I was reminded of what I'd forgotten during the years of the Soviet régime – that I was a Jew. (81)

... ever since the time of the Tsars I've associated anti-Semitism with the jingoism of people from the Union of Michael the Archangel. But now I've seen that the people who shout most loudly about delivering Russia from the Jews are the ones who cringe like lackeys before the Germans, ready to betray their country for thirty pieces of German silver. (82)

So the Revolution did not eradicate anti-Semitism after all, nor are the *intelligentsia* immune. The message of the mother to her son, or Grossman's reconstruction of his mother's message to him as a Russian writer,[7] is that Marxism did not change people, that humanity can be found where least expected, in individuals, and not in class solidarity. The last belongings which Shtrum's mother chooses to pack include works by Pushkin, Maupassant and Chekhov as well as some family photos, and this cultural heritage is Grossman's sole inheritance in his attempt to cope with the unimaginable horror of the total destruction of his people.

Grossman had been one of the first to bear witness to the liberated concentration camps, collaborating with Ehrenburg on the ill-fated *Black Book*. Like Ehrenburg and Grossman, Sofia Osipovna Levinton comes as a Westernized intellectual to the unfamiliar homeland of the Jews and Grossman confines himself in his imagination with her in the sealed cattle-car, attuning his ear to Yiddish and to poverty. Heine, observes one of the passengers, was not of much use to the Jewish people when German savages rounded them up like cattle (198), although it was Heine who symbolized the baptismal entry-ticket into Western culture and his romantic verse lives on elsewhere in the novel.

A similar discovery is made through the naive eyes of David, who is sent to his grandmother's in Kiev and discovers a Jewish world unknown to him, a world of family warmth, personal identity and collective destiny. The image of the goat in his Russian story-book (rather than the traditional Jewish goat in the allegorical Passover song *Khad Gadya*), and the sight of a ritual slaughter confirm his instinctive knowledge of the inevitability of the coming mass murder. Shortly afterwards, the Jews are sent to their death like cattle. Grossman emphasizes that the same hate-campaigns used by Stalin to elicit obedience during the extermination of the kulaks and the 'Trotskyite-Bukharinite' victims of the Purges were now used by Hitler in the very same areas to prepare for the extermination of Ukrainian and Belorussian Jewry. In both cases the victims themselves obey and actually make possible the maintenance of the camp system. Grossman, himself a prize-winning novelist whose writings had served the Party, wonders at the ability of Jewish intellectuals to justify what was happening to them, or of peasant poets to praise the system that destroyed millions. Grossman attributes the phenomenon of mass obedience in the twentieth century to the dependence of totalitarian ideologies on state terror not merely as a means to an end but as an object of worship, as well as to an instinct for self-preservation when the world is divided up into the Good and the Bad, the living and the dead. That is a reason for the conspiracy of silence after the Holocaust and after Stalinism, a silence which Grossman is breaking in his novel. He knows only too well that Russia's unpreparedness for war resulted partly from the murder of its best generals and soldiers in the Purges and the blind trust in Hitler. The war had raised hopes in the circles of Sokolov and Viktor Shtrum of postwar freedom of the press and freedom of speech, and they speak openly of the Purges. Yet to describe those delusions when they had been so cruelly dashed during and after the war required a rare act of courage in resistance to self-censorship.

One of the figures representing the alter ego of the author is the brilliant physicist Viktor Shtrum, one of several Jews in the novel who have married Russians or come from a mixed marriage and whose Jewish identity has hitherto been submerged. Shtrum is portrayed as a spiritual and intellectual child of his time, a time characterized as wolf-like by Mandelstam, the poet whose blood cannot be made wolf-like (267). It is when Viktor summons the courage to speak his mind freely at the Sokolovs' that he finds the inner conviction of his beliefs and makes the scientific breakthrough which he sought. Later, when Russian chauvinists with Party approval denounce Einstein, Shtrum's theories circulate in Moscow laboratories like Mandelstam's banned verse (Book 2, Chapter 27). Apart from the example of the fate of the arrested poet, the reference to Mandelstam is significant for the light it sheds on Grossman's own literary identity as a Jew who had paid the price of cultural and ideological apostasy. When Shtrum is threatened with a Dreyfus affair and he again speaks up against racial discrimination and for freedom of thought it is his mother, the Holocaust martyr, who inspires him. Her letter to him is in his inside pocket when he decides not to attend the meeting at which he is expected to recant. He has reverted to the identity of a *shtetl* Jew and adopts the status of a pariah. However, when he unexpectedly receives a phone call from Stalin he does not behave much better than Pasternak when the poet was called up by Stalin and given the chance to defend Mandelstam. Then Shtrum signs a letter condemning the innocent doctors Levin and Pletnev, accused of murdering Gorky, just as Grossman signed a letter condemning his fellow Jews for complicity in the 'Doctors' Plot', perhaps in the vain hope of disassociating himself from the 'Bad Jews' and exonerating the Jewish people from collective guilt.[8] Shtrum discovers all the feelings of cowardice, pangs of conscience, vanity and remorse that were familiar to Grossman in his corresponding field of literature. Grossman predates the symptoms of the anti-Cosmopolitan campaign to wartime, no doubt thinking of his own victimization over his novel *Za pravoe delo* ('For the Just Cause', 1952). Indeed, one of Victor's colleagues is called Gurevich, one of the coded epithets for literary critics of Jewish descent who were attacked in the press. One of the expressions used by his colleagues to coerce him into signing is that he is a 'real Russian', so that in signing he also suppresses his identity as Jew and compromises his intellectual honesty: a form of self-negation which closely resembles that required of Ehrenburg and Grossman. The letter also condemns such figures as Isaak Babel, by then a non-person sentenced to 'ten years without right of correspondence', i.e. execution, which makes clear the dilemma facing the Soviet Jewish writer. Moreover, the trumped-up charges implicated doctors in Gorky's death, thus hinting both at the Doctors' Plot and the alleged Jewish threat to Russian literature. The real heroes seem to be Ikonnikov who refuses to build a gas chamber and Chepyzin who refuses to work on the Atom bomb.

The authority of the novel derives not from its witness-account of the unconventional heroism and illicit individualism of the Russian soldier at Stalingrad but, as in *War and Peace*, to which frequent reference is made, from its moral message in the Russian literary tradition. Stalingrad represents the destiny of freedom in the balance. Grossman sees in the victory at Stalingrad the turn to an openly Russian nationalist state and the seeds of the Black Years to follow. After describing the megalomaniac minds of Hitler and Stalin the 'official' narrative voice asserts,

This awakening of national consciousness can be related to the tasks facing the State during the war and the years after the war: the struggle for national sovereignty and the affirmation of what is truly Russian, truly Soviet, in every area of life. (665)

Grossman was writing for publication, not the drawer; but even in the Thaw, on the eve of the publication of *One Day in the Life of Ivan Denisovich*, it was not permissible for the author to expose the forced lie of the discourse of the Other, to bring the skeletons out of the cupboard, when the skeletons were still taboo after the Holocaust. What remained of Jewish culture after the destruction by the Nazis and the Sovietization of annexed territories had been further reduced by the 'anti-Cosmopolitan' campaign, the dissolution of the Jewish Anti-Fascist committee, the closure of Yiddish publications and institutions, the murder of Solomon Mikhoels and the arrest of leading Yiddish writers, several of whom were executed. Just before Stalin's death the 'Doctors' Plot' had raised the possibility of deportation of the Jewish population of the USSR. The limited relaxation on Yiddish literature and Jewish communal life under Khrushchev was superficial and did not undo Stalin's completion of the destruction wrought by Hitler. The unprecedented arrest of Grossman's novel by the KGB was therefore clearly meant to gag expression of the betrayed hope of the Revolution's most loyal supporters. So we can see in conclusion that for many like Grossman apparent ideological apostasy and complete acculturation met with the dimming of any hope of acceptance as a Russian writer. After the 'Stalinist night' Grossman comes back to a premodernist model of the Russian writer driven by a moral imperative, one which defines as a Russian ideal the adoption of freedom and democracy and rejects Russian chauvinism as a value of state. The Jew's fate in the gas chamber is the end result of a chauvinist ideology that bases moral or biological superiority on racial and ethnic distinction. Grossman champions Chekhov's humanitarianism and has Darensky accuse a fellow-officer of disgracing the Russian people by beating a German prisoner. The irony is that the Jew's 'forbidden love' for Russia was still unacceptable when different sectors of Russian society engaged in the post-communist debate over Russia's political future and national identity pointed to this very fact as proof of the alien identity of Grossman.[9]

After the defeat of Hitler and the death of Stalin the lesson of Jewish experience is not encouraging:

> The Warsaw Rising, the uprisings at Treblinka and Sobibor, the various mutinies of *brenners* [corpse-burners in the camps], were all born of hopelessness. But then utter hopelessness engenders not only resistance and uprisings but also a yearning to be executed as quickly as possible. (215)

The question Grossman is asking is whether human nature has been changed by totalitarianism – in which case there is no hope for the future – or whether the few sparks of resistance such as the Warsaw Ghetto Uprising, which were born of both hope and hopelessness, testify to something indubitable in the human spirit against which the violence of totalitarianism is powerless: 'Man's innate yearning for freedom can be suppressed but never destroyed. ... This conclusion holds out hope for our time, hope for the future' (216).

Obedience to totalitarian ideology, Grossman never tires of telling us, could not win a war against fascism. What counts is the individual who does not yield the right to his individual peculiarities, his right to be different. In Stalingrad the soldiers suffer the common fate of Russia under bombardment, a fate that cuts through differences of class, ethnicity and belief, an uncontrollable fate of grief and despair that somehow does not dampen a desperate conviction in the freedom of the human spirit. One could not find a more fitting concluding statement to a study of Jews writing in Russian who faced one of the most daunting periods in human history. Babel could not have written had he not held hope for a better future, but he did not live to see the Holocaust and not all of what he wrote in the years of Stalinist Terror has come down to us. Like Babel, Ehrenburg believed in basic notions of human dignity and freedom, even if his scepticism made his professed beliefs doubtful and even if his methods of survival and apparent willingness to compromise smack of an opportunism that made a virtue of necessity.

Mandelstam and Pasternak, in their separate ways, never renounced faith in Russian culture, which was the hope by which they lived. Vasily Grossman may be a final instance of their dilemma, but he also shows how the generation of the Holocaust differs from the generation of the Revolution in the lessons they have learned from History.

Notes

PREFACE

1 Lev Kopelev, *The Education of a True Believer*, translated by Gary Kern (New York: Harper & Row, 1980), 121. Emphasis in the original.

2 A. Flegon and Iu. Naumov, *Russkii antisemitizm i evrei: Sbornik* (London: Flegon Press, 1968), 161.

3 Lev Kopelev comes to the same conclusion in *The Education of a True Believer*, a typical autobiography of an assimilated Jew in the years from the Revolution to Stalinism, whose faith in the Party may have been shaken, but not his faith in Russianness. Some of the false expectations and mutual misunderstandings of Israelis and new immigrants are summarized in Dmitri Segal, 'Russian Aliyah and Israeli Culture', in *The Soviet Man in an Open Society*, ed. Tamar Horowitz (Lanham MD: University Press of America, 1989), 247–9. The clash of cultures and languages has opened a new satirical genre of which a hilarious example is the Russian-language magazine *Beseder?*, which parodies Communist Party discourse and Israeli politics, but which provides many indications of social adaptation, self-image and cultural stereotyping (Narspy Zilberg, 'In-Group Humor of Immigrants from the Former Soviet Union to Israel', *Israeli Social Science Review*, 10, 1 [1995]: 1–22). See also Naomi Shepherd, *Russians in Israel* (New York: Simon & Schuster, 1993).

4 Shafarevich was strangely echoed in Fridrikh Gorenshtein's epic novel *Psalom* (1986), a prophetic vision of the Jewish Anti-Christ's punishment of Russia (see Harriet Murav's discussion of the place of this novel in the debate of rival national myths opened up by *perestroika*, 'A Curse on Russia: Gorenstein's Anti-*Psalom* and the Critics', *Russian Review*, 52, 2 [1993]: 213–27). On Shafarevich's 'Russophobia' see Zoia Krakhmal'nikova, 'Russophobia, Anti-Semitism and Christianity: Some Remarks on an Anti-Russian Idea', *Religion, State and Society* (formerly *Religion in Communist Lands*) 20, 1 (1992): 7–28, and the response by the late Mikhail Agursky in

the same issue, 'Fundamentalist Christian Anti-anti-Semitism in Modern Russia', *Religion, State and Society*, 20, 1 (1992): 51–5. For a polemical defence against the charge that emigrants were ungrateful to Russia or were stabbing her in the back see Simon Markish, 'O evreiskoi nenavisti k Rossii', *22*, 38 (1984): 209–18. This is a reply to Zinaida Shakhovskaia, 'Evrei i Rossii', *Vestnik russkogo khristianskogo dvizheniia*, 141 (May 1984). On the rise of Russophilism among the intelligentsia see Vladimir Shlapentokh, *Soviet Intellectuals and Political Power: The Post-Stalin Era* (Princeton University Press, 1990), a book written before the rise of Zhirinovsky in the 1993 elections.

5 See for example, on the Russian literary context of the Hebrew poetical revival, Hamutal Bar-Yosef, 'Kh. N. Bialik i russkaia poeziia', *Ariel* (Russian edition), 3 (1990): 24–49; 'Romanticism and Decadence in the Literature of the Hebrew Revival', *Comparative Literature*, 46, 2 (1994): 146–81.

6 *Bialik* (London: Peter Halban, 1988), 50. Aberbach points to the influence in particular of Pushkin, Lermontov and Heine, as well as the Russian-Jewish poet Semyon Frug, and suggests the novels of Turgenev were an important model for the moral authority of art (48–9). The following chapter will explore in more detail the symbiosis and tension between Russian time and the Jewish calendar, between the Russian or Ukrainian landscape and Jewish territory.

7 See Dan Almagor, 'Hakoakh haamiti hu koakh hamilim', *Yedi'ot akhronot (musaf shev'a yamim)*, 13 December 1991, 24.

8 A pioneering study of Jews in the 'second wave' of Russian culture in emigration between the world wars is *Evrei v kul'ture russkogo zarubezh'ia: sbornik statei, publikatsii, memuarov i esse*, ed. Mikhail Parkhomovskii, 1 (Jerusalem: Published by the compiler, 1993).

9 *The Fall* (New York: Harper and Row, 1976), 17.

10 Grigory Svirsky, *Hostages: The Personal Testimony of a Soviet Jew* (London: Bodley Head, 1976), 300.

11 Translated as 'The Wandering Jew', *Glas: New Russian Writing*, 6 (1993): 127–35.

12 Some materials towards such a cultural history may be found in Benjamin Pinkus, *The Soviet Government and the Jews: A Documented Study* (Cambridge: Cambridge University Press, 1984). For a *samizdat* survey of writing by Soviet Jews in Russian on Jewish themes see 'Merran', 'Deformatsiia dushi: Evreiskaia tema v sovetskoi literature', *Vremia i my*, 64 (1982): 147–165.

13 The terms 'Russian-Jewish', 'Russian Jewish', 'Russian-language Jewish' or 'Russian literature by Jews' reflect both the changing perspectives over the years and the *Weltanschauung* of the commenta-

tors; see V. Lvov-Rogachevsky, *Russko-evreiskaya literatura* (Moscow: Gosudarstvennoe izdatel'stvo, 1922); I. A. Kleinman, 'Evrei v noveishei russkoi literature', *Evreiskii vestnik* (Leningrad, 1928): 163–6; Joshua Kunitz, *Russian Literature and the Jew* (New York: Columbia University Press, 1929); M. Slonim, 'Pisateli-evrei v sovetskoi literature', *Evreiskii mir* 2 (1944): 146–64; G. Aronson, 'Evrei v russkoi literature, kritike, zhurnalistike i obshchestvennoi zhizni', in *Kniga o russkom evreistve, 1917–1967* (New York: Yoseloff, 1968), 361–99. Mikhail Vainshtein, in his non-academic collection of prefaces to his editions of Jewish authors, *A list'ia snova zeleneiut: stranitsy evreiskoi russkoiazychnoi literatury* (Jerusalem: 'Kakhol-lavan', 1988), does not distinguish between thematic Jewish material and content, ignores the Yiddish context and prefers the vague categories of Freedom and Individuality in the 'Jewish Tragedy'. For Simon Markish the cases of Babel, Ehrenburg and Grossman are 'examples' of Russian–Jewish attitudes to 'Jewish civilisation' discussed in his essays cited below and translated into Hebrew as *Shalosh dugmaot* (Tel-Aviv: Hakibuts hameukhad, 1994). Jews in the theatre suffered the fate of both the avant-garde (Meyerhold, for example) and Jewish culture (Mikhoels, for example). On Jewish contributions to drama see Béatrice Picon-Vallin, *Le Théâtre juif soviétique pendant les années vingt* (Lausanne: L'Age d'Homme, 1973) and V. Levintina, *Russkii teatr i evrei* (Jerusalem: Biblioteka Aliia, 1989). On the post-Stalin period see *Jewish Culture and Identity in the Soviet Union*, ed. Ya'akov Ro'i and Avi Beker (New York: New York University Press, 1990). For a pioneering anthology of essays and fiction examining the status of the Jew in Russia see *Jews and Strangers*, a special issue of *Glas: New Russian Writing*, 6 (1993).

14 Elaine Feinstein, *Three Russian Poets* (Manchester: Carcanet, 1979), 10, 26.

15 Cited ibid., 11.

16 *Post-War Russian Poetry*, ed. Daniel Weissbort (Harmondsworth: Penguin, 1974), 112–13.

17 *Nightingale Fever: Russian Poets in Revolution* (New York: Knopf, 1981), 5–17.

18 Cited ibid., 229.

19 Donald Fanger, 'Conflicting Imperatives in the Model of the Russian Writer: The Case of Tertz/Siniavsky', in *Literature and History: Theoretical Problems and Russian Case Studies*, ed. Gary Saul Morson (Stanford University Press, 1986), 111–24. For examples of the Russian writer's moral imperative see George J. Gutsche, *Moral Apostasy in Russian Literature* (Dekalb IL.: Northern Illinois Press, 1986).

20 Gregory Freidin, 'By the Walls of Church and State: Literature's Authority in Russia's Modern Tradition', *Russian Review*, 52, 2 (1993): 149–65. Freidin's stimulating discussion invokes Michel Foucault's post-Nietzschean idea of the disappearance of the author in his seminal essay 'What is an Author?' Freidin takes issue with Sir Isaiah Berlin's presentation of the Russian intelligentsia of the 1840s as idealistic élitists who saw themselves as sacred vessels, conscious of their social mission and sincere, though perhaps naive ('The Birth of the Russian Intelligentsia', *Russian Thinkers* [London: The Hogarth Press, 1978], 114–35). Sir Isaiah does point out that Russian intellectuals were driven to obsessive mysticism only later, by police repression.

I. BURNING EMBERS

1 Gershon Shaked, *The Shadows Within: Essays on Modern Jewish Writers* (Philadelphia: Jewish Publication Society of America, 1987), 3–21.

2 Wilson, *The Wound and the Bow* (London: Methuen, 1961), 259.

3 On literary stereotypes of the Jew in Russia see David I. Goldstein, *Dostoyevsky and the Jews* (Austin: University of Texas Press, 1981); Felix Dreizin, *The Russian Soul and the Jew: Essays in Literary Ethnocriticism* (Lanham MD: University Press of America, 1990); J. Kunitz, *Russian Literature and the Jew* (New York: Columbia University Press, 1929). On the Soviet period see Maurice Friedberg's 'Jewish Themes in Soviet Russian Literature' and 'Jewish Contributions to Soviet Literature', in *The Jews in Soviet Russia since 1917*, 3rd edition (Oxford University Press, 1978), 197–216 and 217–25 respectively. B. Gorev's 1917 brochure 'Russkaia literatura i evrei' is a post-Revolutionary view of this taboo subject revised in V. Lvov-Rogachevsky, *Russko-evreiskaia literatura* (Moscow: Gosudarstvennoe izdatel'stvo, 1922), 3–29; translated as 'Russian Literature and the Jews,' in V. Lvov-Roga-chevsky, *A History of Russian Jewish Literature*, ed. and translated by Arthur Levin (Ann Arbor: Ardis, 1979), 13–31. On the theme and image of the Jews in Stalinist Russian and Yiddish literature, see Bernard Choseed, 'The Soviet Jew in Literature', *Jewish Social Studies*, 11, 3 (July 1949), an article written before the execution of Yiddish writers in 1952 and before Khruschchev's exposure of Stalin's crimes; a revised version appears as 'Jews in Soviet Literature', in *Through the Glass of Soviet Literature: Views of Russian Society*, ed. E. J. Simmonds (New York: Columbia University Press, 1953), 110–58. A treatment of the post-Stalinist era is given in Jakub Blum and Vera Rich, *The Image of the Jew in Soviet Literature: The Post-Stalin Period* (New York: Ktav, 1984).

4 See Jacob S. Raisin, *The Haskalah Movement in Russia* (Philadelphia:

The Jewish Publication Society of America, 1913); Louis Greenberg, *The Jews in Russia: The Struggle for Emancipation* (New York: Schocken Books, 1976).

5 See Alexander Orbach, *New Voices of Russian Jewry: A Study of the Russian-Jewish Press in the Era of the Great Reforms, 1860–1871* (Leiden: Brill, 1980); Yehuda Slutsky, *Ha'itonut hayehudit-rusit bemeah ha-19* (Jerusalem: Mosad Bialik, 1970); Moshe Perlmann, '*Razsvet*, 1860–1861: The Origins of the Russian-Jewish Press', *Jewish Social Studies*, 24 (1962): 162–82; Simon Markish, '*Voskhod* – glavnyi zhurnal russkogo evreistva', *Cahiers du Monde Russe et Soviétique*, 28, 2 (1987): 173–82.

6 *The Jews of Odessa: A Cultural History, 1794–1881* (Stanford University Press, 1985). On Odessa as a centre of Jewish culture in Hebrew see Ezra Spicehandler, 'Odessa as a Literary Center of Hebrew Literature', in *The Great Transition: The Recovery of the Lost Centers of Modern Hebrew Literature,* ed. Glenda Abramson and Tudor Parfitt (Totowa NJ: Rowman & Allanheld, 1985), 75–90; Steven J. Zipperstein, ' "Assimilation", *Haskalah* and Odessa Jewry', ibid., 91–8. See also Patricia Herlihy, *Odessa: A History, 1794–1914* (Cambridge MA: Harvard University Press, 1991).

7 See V. Lvov-Rogachevsky, *A History of Russian Jewish Literature,* ed. and translated by Arthur Levin (Ann Arbor: Ardis, 1979); Gregor Aronson, 'Jews in Russian Literary and Political Life', in *Russian Jewry, 1860–1917,* ed. J. Frumkin (New York: Yoseloff, 1966), 253–99. Simon Markish, 'Osip Rabinovich', *Cahiers du Monde Russe et Soviétique,* 21, 1 (1980): 5–30; 21, 2 (1980): 135–8; Simon Markish, 'A propos de l'histoire et de la littérature juive d'expression russe', *Cahiers du Monde Russe et Soviétique,* 26, 2 (1985): 139–52.

8 *Ocherki proshlogo* (St Petersburg, 1875), 206.

9 Sander L. Gilman, *Jewish Self-Hatred: Anti-Semitism and the Hidden Language of the Jews* (Baltimore: Johns Hopkins University Press, 1986), 2. See also Borukh Kurzweil, 'Sinat-'atsmo besifrut hayehudim', in his *Sifrutanu hekhadashah – hemshekh o mahafekhah?* (Jerusalem: Schocken, 1971), 331–401. Earlier Hannah Arendt applied Max Weber's term 'pariah' to Heinrich Heine, seeing him as a true Jewish voice who claimed the inner freedom of the Other, but she wrote when the Jew had been outlawed in Europe and her own displaced status testified to the collapse of Enlightenment ideals of human freedom and emancipation ('The Jew as Pariah: A Hidden Tradition', in *The Jew as Pariah: Jewish Identity and Politics in the Modern Age* [New York: Grove, 1978], 67–91).

10 Shmuel Ettinger, 'The Position of Jews in Soviet Culture: A Historical Survey', in *Jews in Soviet Culture,* ed. Jack Miller (New Brunswick: Transaction Books, 1984), 5.

11 Paul Mendes-Flohr, *Divided Passions: Jewish Intellectuals and the Experience of Modernity* (Detroit: Wayne State University Press, 1991), 67.

12 When the Jews migrated to the big cities they had to pretend that they had forgotten Yiddish, prompting Franz Kafka to remind his Prague Jewish audience that they knew more Yiddish than they thought (John Cuddihy, *The Ordeal of Civility: Freud, Marx, Lévi-Strauss and the Jewish Struggle with Modernity* [New York: Basic Books, 1974], 228). It is tempting to apply this, as John Cuddihy does, to Chernikhovsky, Babel and Mandelstam, and it is true that a secular book, worse a Russian book, would be a sign of apostasy in the *shtetl*; but it seems to me that Cuddihy's model of urbanization applies more to German-Jewish and American-Jewish prewar acculturation which Cuddihy sees as an invasion of the 'Protestant' space of the modern *Gesellschaft* (230–1). Historically, Jews were *inorodtsy* (of alien birth) in Russia and before the Revolution they were to a large extent prevented from assimilating in the large cities by decrees and regulations.

13 Michael Stanislawski, *For Whom Do I Toil? Judah Leib Gordon and the Crisis of Russian Jewry* (New York: Oxford University Press, 1988), 50–1. 'Be a man' was the advice of King David on his deathbed to his son Solomon (1 Kings, 2, 1). To be a *mentsh* was the directive of generations of Jewish parents, similar to the rabbis' homiletic exegesis of Exodus 2, 12 when Moses saw that there was no man and killed the Egyptian or, in the same spirit, the first-century sage Hillel's counsel, 'in a place where there is no man, be a man' (Ethics of the Fathers, 2, 6).

14 Jonathan Frankel, *Prophecy and Politics: Socialism, Nationalism and the Russian Jews, 1882–1917* (Cambridge University Press, 1981). See also Stephen M. Berk's study of the response of Jewish intellectuals to the 1881 pogroms, *Year of Crisis, Year of Hope: Russian Jewry and the Pogroms of 1881–1882* (Westport CT: Greenwood Press, 1985). Michael Aronson has adduced evidence, contrary to popular opinion, that the pogroms were not organized or sponsored by the government (*Troubled Waters: The Origins of the 1881 Anti-Jewish Pogroms in Russia* [Pittsburgh: University of Pittsburgh Press, 1990]).

15 Michael Stanislavski, 'Jewish Apostasy in Russia: A Tentative Typology', in *Jewish Apostasy in the Modern World*, ed. Todd M. Endelman (New York: Holmes & Meier, 1987), 189–205. A *melamed* is a Hebrew Bible tutor, typically in some forsaken *shtetl* school or in a private home.

16 See Robert J. Brym, *The Jewish Intelligentsia and Russian Marxism: A Sociological Study of Intellectual Radicalism and Ideological Divergence* (London: Macmillan, 1978); Eli Lederhandler, *The Road to Modern*

Jewish Politics: Political Tradition and Political Reconstruction in the Jewish Community of Tsarist Russia (Oxford University Press, 1989); Erich E. Haberer, *Jews and Revolution in Nineteenth-Century Russia* (Cambridge University Press, 1995).

17 For an account of the conference see Emmanuel S. Goldsmith, *Architects of Yiddishism at the Beginning of the Twentieth Century: A Study in Jewish Cultural History* (Rutherford: Fairleigh Dickinson University Press, 1976), 185–221. See also Régine Robin, *L'Amour du yiddish: Ecriture juive et sentiment de la langue (1830–1930)* (Paris: Sorbier, 1984), 89–129.

18 The generalization is not strictly accurate, since there had long been primers in Hebrew. Hebrew poetry, as well as philosophical or polemical works, had been produced continually in the various countries of dispersion. Hebrew was also the language of many *Haskalah* publications which, along with books of Russian poetry, were read clandestinely by *yeshiva* students and drew them away from tradition. The leading modern Hebrew poet Khaim Nakhman Bialik, for example, made his first steps towards secularity and literature through the Hebrew as well as Russian books he found in the Volozhin *yeshiva*.

19 See Il'ia Serman, 'Spory 1908 goda o russko-evreiskoi literature i posleoktiabr'skoe desiatiletie', *Cahiers du Monde Russe et Soviétique*, 26, 2 (1985): 167–74.

20 See Alice Nakhimovsky, 'Vladimir Jabotinsky, Russian Writer', *Modern Judaism* (May 1987): 151–73.

21 'O "evreiakh i russkoi literature"', in *Fel'otony* (St Petersburg: Izdatel'stvo Dvizheniia Kherut, 1913), 40–8.

22 'S. An-sky and the Paradigm of Return', in *The Uses of Tradition: Jewish Continuity in the Modern Era*, ed. J. Wertheimer (New York and Jerusalem: Jewish Theological Seminary/ Cambridge MA: Harvard University Press, 1992), 243–260.

23 On An-sky's expedition and last years see Abraham Rechtman, 'The Jewish Ethnographical Expedition', in *Tracing An-sky: Jewish Collections from the State Ethnographic Museum in St Petersburg*, ed. Mariëlla Beukers and Renée Waale (Zwolle: Uitgeverij Waanders, 1992), 12–15; and David G. Roskies, 'Introduction', in S. An-sky, *The Dybbuk and Other Writings* (New York: Schocken, 1992), xi–xxxvi.

24 David Aberbach, *Realism, Caricature, and Bias: The Fiction of Mendele Mocher Sefarim* (London: Littman Library of Jewish Civilization, 1993).

25 Simon Dubnov, *Nationalism and History: Essays on Old and New Judaism* (Philadelphia: Jewish Publication Society of America, 1958). See Sophie Dubnov-Erlich, *The Life and Works of S. M. Dubnov: Diaspora*

Nationalism and Jewish History (Bloomington: Indiana University Press, 1990).

26 The 'Correspondence Between Two Corners' first appeared as a booklet in Petersburg in 1921 and it is included in the standard edition of Ivanov's collected works, *Sobranie sochinenii* (Brussels, 1979), III, 383–415. Martin Buber found the exchange sufficiently significant to publish a German translation in 1926. An English translation can be found in the September 1948 issue of *Partisan Review*.

27 'In the Russian World of Letters', *Menorah Journal*, 12 (1926): 302–5. In a similar attempt to sketch a model of identity, this time from the standpoint of Russian Jewish émigrés who had had to flee the Nazi occupation of France, I. Kisin cites Gershenzon's insistence on freedom from cultural or philosophical identification in the 'Correspondence Between Two Corners' as an example of the 'revolt' of the Russian Jewish intellectual against history ('Razmyshleniia o russkom evreistve i ego literature', *Evreiskii mir*, 2 [New York, 1944]: 164–72). Ehrenburg also gave favourable mention to Gershenzon in his memoirs, *People, Years, Life*.

28 Mark Slonim, 'Pisateli-evrei v sovetskoi literature', *Evreiskii mir*, 2 (1944): 146–64. Much the same conclusion is reached by Gregor Aronson, 'Jews in Russian Literary and Political Life', in *Russian Jewry, 1860–1917*, ed. J. Frumkin (New York: Yoseloff, 1966), 283–84. Several Russian-Jewish writers, including Mark Aldanov, Yulii Aikhenvald, Semyon Yushkevich, Nikolai Minsky and Sasha Cherny, went into emigration after the October Revolution. The nationalistic poet Semyon Frug had died in 1916; Andrei Sobol remained pessimistic about the attitude of Russian intellectuals toward Jews until his suicide in 1926; David Aizman died in 1922.

29 Eisig Silberschlag, *Saul Tchernichowsky: Poet of Revolt* (Ithaca: Cornell University Press, 1968), 97–8. Hebrew thought had never been uninfluenced by the Greeks, but the Rabbis warned vociferously against straying into those alien fields; Yehuda Halevi, the foremost Hebrew poet in medieval Spain, warned 'Let not the wisdom of the Greeks beguile you; it bears no fruit but only flowers' (Silberschlag, *Saul Tchernichowsky*, 42). Yehuda Halevi was himself not unfamiliar with Greek philosophy, but in Chernikhovsky's generation new interest in Greek literature had been opened up by Berdichevsky's circulation of Nietzschean ideas.

30 See Alan L. Mintz, *Hurban: Responses to Catastrophe in Hebrew Literature* (New York: Columbia University Press, 1984); David G. Roskies, *Against the Apocalypse: Responses to Catastrophe in Modern Jewish Culture* (Cambridge MA: Harvard University Press, 1984).

31 Lotman, *Universe of the Mind: A Semiotic Theory of Culture* (Bloomington: Indiana University Press, 1990), 131.

32 Lotman, *Struktura khudozhestvennogo teksta* (Moscow: Iskusstvo, 1970), 265–79.

33 Sicher, 'Binary Oppositions and Spatial Representation: Towards an Applied Semiotics', *Semiotica*, 60, 3–4 (1986): 211–24.

34 The spatial opposition of holy/profane in primitive cultures has been explored by Mircea Eliade in his seminal *The Myth of the Eternal Return* (Princeton University Press, 1965). An interesting example of the functionality of spatial boundaries in Judaism is the law governing the Paschal sacrifice, which must be eaten whole and within domestic boundaries. As a commemoration of the coming into being of the Jewish people and their exodus from Egypt, it is barred both to alien gentiles and to apostates, both categories of outsiders who are excluded because they have *alienated* themselves from the ways of God (the medieval commentator Rabbi Solomon Yitskhaki – commonly known by his acronym as Rashi – in his interpretation of Exodus 12, 43 citing the midrashic compilation, Mekhilta Piskha chapter 15). Incidentally, Jews in Russia were fond of pointing out that the numerical value of 'SSSR' in the mystical system of Gematria was equivalent to that of Egypt! On the Nietzschean aspects of the metaphor of breaking out see S. G. Shoham, *Salvation through the Gutters: Deviance and Transcendance* (Washington: Hemisphere Publishing Company, 1979). Shoham speaks of the lure of social deviance in terms of an analogy of the trauma of birth and the Cabbalistic 'breaking of the vessels'. One of the examples is 'breaking the covenant to confirm it', though we should be careful not to confuse the heresy of the Frankists with the ideological breakout of modern apostates, whether they be self-hating Jews, Zionists (as was Bialik) or devoted revolutionaries. Shalom Kremer has described a similar breaking of boundaries in the failed heroes of I. D. Berkowitz, who burst out of the confines of the Jewish *shtetl* into the big world outside or who emigrated to America, but could find no remedy for their spiritual anguish (*Realizm veshvirato* [Tel-Aviv: Massada, 1968], 73–83).

35 On Bialik's imagery see Dov Sadan, *Avnei hagader* (Tel-Aviv, 1970). Adi Tsemakh has shown the importance of Bialik's childhood memories for an understanding of his writing, pointing out that the tension of the two worlds, Jewish and gentile, is marked by the wall that divides the *yeshiva* from the enchanted flowering garden and water-spring, two symbols of his childhood. The closed garden of sinful temptation and forbidden gentile love in this story, which recalls the one in Song of Songs 4, 12, is an underlying motif of

Bialik's poetry (*Halavi hamistater: 'iyunim beyitsirato shel kh. n. bialik* [Jerusalem: Kiryat sefer, 1966]), 68–78.

36 For a description of the publications after the Revolution see *Jewish Publications in the Soviet Union, 1917–1960*, ed. Ch. Shmeruk (Jerusalem: Historical Society of Israel, 1961); Ch. Shmeruk, 'Yiddish Literature in the USSR', in *The Jews in Soviet Russia since 1917*, ed. Lionel Kochan, 3rd edition (Oxford University Press, 1978), 242–80; Benjamin Pinkus, *The Jews of the Soviet Union: The History of a National Minority* (Cambridge University Press, 1988). The dilemma facing the Jew is summed up succinctly by Chimen Abramsky in an inaugural lecture at University College, London, *War, Revolution and the Jewish Dilemma* (London, 1975).

37 David E. Fishman, 'Preserving Tradition in the Land of Revolution: The Religious Leadership of Soviet Jewry, 1917–1930', in *The Uses of Tradition: Jewish Continuity in the Modern Era*, ed. J. Wertheimer (New York and Jerusalem: Jewish Theological Seminary/ Cambridge MA: Harvard University Press, 1992), 85–118.

38 A. Estrin, 'Revoliutsiia v evreiskom mestechke', *Zhizn'*, 1 (1924): 313–29.

39 See the anthology of accounts, documents and martyrologies relating to the illegal Zionist pioneers active in Soviet Russia, *Hekhaluts berusiya* (Tel-Aviv: Hapo'el hatsa'ir, 1932).

40 Translated by Pearl Grodzensky in *Voices Within the Ark*, ed. Howard Schwartz and Anthony Rudolf (New York: Avon Books, 1980), 122.

41 On Hebrew in the USSR see Yehoshua Gilbo'a, *Leshon 'omedet 'al nafshah: tarbut 'ivrit bevrit-hamo'atsot* (Tel-Aviv: Sifriyat hapo'alim, 1973) and his 'Hebrew Literature in the USSR', in *The Jews in Soviet Russia since 1917*, ed. Kochan, 226–41. A memoir of the situation of the Hebrew writers during and immediately after the Revolution has been written by Ben-Tsion Dinur, one of the group allowed to leave the Soviet Union in 1921: *Bimey milkhamah vemahafekhah* (Jerusalem: Mosad Bialik, 1960). On those who remained and believed in a Hebrew Communism see Ruth Karton-Blum, 'Hebrew Communist Literature in Soviet Russia', in *The Great Transition: The Recovery of the Lost Centers of Modern Hebrew Literature*, ed. Glenda Abramson and Tudor Parfitt (Totowa NJ: Rowman & Allanheld, 1985), 104–9. The linguistic and cultural schizophrenia of the Soviet Hebrew writer is treated fully in Gilbo'a's *Oktobraim 'ivriim* (Tel-Aviv, 1974). For a survey of the reflection of the Revolution in Hebrew literature see Nurit Guvrin, 'Mahafekhat oktober berei hasifrut ha'ivrit', in her *Maftekhot* (Tel-Aviv: Hakibuts hameukhad, 1978), 78–119. A remarkable case is that of Tsvi Preigerzon, who wrote short stories in the manner of Babel and Bergelson, and who survived imprisonment

from 1949 to 1965, gaining posthumous recognition in Israel in the gap between Hazaz and Agnon. See Hagit Halperin, 'A Hebrew Writer in the Soviet Union: The Case of Zvi Preigerzon', *Jews in Eastern Europe*, 1 [20], (1993): 5–14; Lili Baazova, 'Tsvi Preigerzon, 1900–1969: Ocherk zhizni i tvorchestva', *Tel'-Aviv zhurnal*, 3 (1993): 38–9.

42 Der Nister was the pseudonym of Pinkhas Kahanovich and it is a Kabbalist term meaning the 'hidden one'. I have followed the reading of this story by Chone Shmeruk, ' "Under a Fence": Tribulations of a Soviet Yiddish Symbolist', in *The Field of Yiddish: Studies in Language, Folklore and Literature (Second Collection)*, ed. U. Weinreich (London: Mouton, 1965), 263–87. A taste of the bitter dilemma of the Soviet Yiddish modernists can be obtained from Irving Howe and Eliezer Greenberg's anthology, *Ashes out of Hope: Fiction by Soviet-Yiddish Writers* (New York: Schocken, 1977), which includes an English translation of 'Under a Fence'.

43 A. Lezhnev, *Sovremenniki* (Moscow: Krug, 1927), 95–118. See Efim Etkind, 'O poeticheskom "importe" i, v chastnosti, o evreiskoi intonatsii v russkoi poezii dvadsatykh godov', *Cahiers du Monde Russe et Soviétique*, 26, 2 (1985): 193–217. In the post-Revolutionary period, of course, non-standard and dialect language was ideologically justified as characterizing proletarian speech, and the playful use of Odessisms by Bagritsky or Babel was not yet out of place in the demographical and cultural flux. A partial parallel might be Chicano speech in American poetry. However, unlike the linguistic interference of French in early nineteenth-century Russian literature, when French and Gallicisms were productive in the Russian cultural polysystem and served as legitimate markers of cultural status, Yiddish was used as a macaronic device by some Soviet Jewish poets to refer to a doomed culture. A different and more ambivalent example is the poetess Elizaveta Polonskaia, like Lev Lunts a member of the Serapion Brotherhood, who celebrated the romanticism of the Revolution in her Russian verse. Yet in her collection *Upriamyi kalendar'* Polonskaia suddenly bursts into Yiddish when she finds herself recognized by a half-blind old woman in the *alien* crowd who addresses her in the words: 'And though you have forgotten both faith and kin, /A id iz imer a id! / My blood sings in your veins and sings in an alien voice' (quoted in Slonim, 'Pisateli-evrei v sovetskoi literature', 151). The poetess cannot evade the ethnic markers of her sad eyes and her blood or the fact that the Russian language in her blood is *alien* ('*chuzhoi*'). Another example is 'Kol Nidre', a poem by the Imagist Matvei Roizman (1896–1973), who introduces the Hebrew words of the Day of Atonement prayer

to identify with the Marranos in a martyrology of the pogrom victims. I will return to the discussion of linguistic interference and the native:alien opposition in Chapter 3 below.

44 I. Babel, *Sochineniia* (Moscow: Khudozhestvennaia literatura, 1990), 11, 362. The *Bnei 'akiva* (Sons of Akiva) are the youth movement of the religious Zionist party Po'el mizrakhi; considering their ideological orientation and the persecution of Zionist activity in the Soviet Union the reference is surprising, and Babel may really have meant Rabbi Akiva himself, the famous sage of Talmudic times.

45 See Zvi Gitelman, *Jewish Nationality and Soviet Politics: The Jewish Sections of the CPSU, 1917–1930* (Princeton University Press, 1972).

46 The original ending may be found in I. Babel, *Detstvo i drugie rasskazy* (Jerusalem: Biblioteka Aliia, 1979), 57.

47 *Evreiskii al'manakh: khudozhestvennyi i literaturno-kriticheskii sbornik*, ed. B. Kaufman and I. A. Kleinman (Petrograd-Moscow: 'Petrograd', 1923), 27–43.

48 An archival MS of a letter to Gorky from 1922 reveals Lunts's concern that in the eyes of Russians he could not be a writer because he was a Jew and that they did not understand he was trying to do something different from other Russian writers. Cited by M. Vainshtein in his afterword to his own privately published edition of Lev Lunts, *Rodina i drugie proizvedeniia* (1981), 318. Lunts had excelled in his accomplished performance at university where he mastered European and Russian literature, which he studied under the formalist critic Boris Eikhenbaum, but once again we see that this mastery of cultural texts did not give confidence in identity formation. It is interesting to note that when Viniamin Kaverin uses Yiddish in the underworld slang of the gangsters in *Konets khaza* ('End of the Gang', 1926), it is differentiated from the narrator's Russian.

49 'O natsional'nom vospitanii', *Fel'otony* (St Petersburg: Izdatel'stvo Dvizheniia Kherut, 1913), 12–13.

50 Ibid., 40.

51 Of course, this is from the viewpoint of the official discourse; see further examples in Lotman, *Universe of the Mind*, 131–3.

52 The Soviet semioticians Yuri Lotman and Boris Uspensky have in fact shown how the space of the West was perceived as being diabolical, left-handed and inside-out in binary opposition to Holy Russia. See 'Binary Models in the Dynamics of Russian Culture', in *The Semiotics of Russian Cultural History*, ed. A. D. Nakhimovsky and A. S. Nakhimovsky (Ithaca: Cornell University Press, 1985), 30–66.

53 See particularly on the notion of boundary and on geographical space Iu. M. Lotman, *Universe of the Mind*. As pointed out by Frederik Barth, boundaries are not necessarily territorial and are significant

in defining ethnic and cultural identities of social groups ('Introduction', in *Ethnic Groups and Boundaries: The Social Organization of Culture Difference*, ed. Frederik Barth [London: Allen and Unwin, 1970], 9–38).

54 Nadson,   *Polnoe sobranie stikhotvorenii* (Moscow: Sovetskii pisatel', 1962), 284.

55 'Encounter: Russians and Jews in the Short Stories of David Aizman', *Cahiers du Monde Russe et Soviétique*, 26, 2 (1985): 175.

56 Jerome Bruner, 'Life as Narrative', *Social Research*, 54, 1 (1987): 11–32.

57 Ibid., 17.

58 *Metaphors of the Self: The Meaning of Autobiography* (Princeton University Press, 1972), 125.

59 Louis Renza, 'The Veto of the Imagination: A Theory of Autobiography', in *Autobiography: Essays Theoretical and Critical*, ed. James Olney (Princeton University Press, 1980), 295. A dissident view is that of Janet Varner Gunn, who emphasizes the reading, not the writing, of self, and its display, rather than its concealment (*Autobiography: Towards a Poetics of Experience* [Philadelphia: University of Pennsylvania Press, 1982]).

60 Paul de Man, 'Autobiography as De-Facement', in his *Rhetoric of Romanticism* (New York: Columbia University Press, 1984), 67–81.

61 The genre of the 'pseudo-autobiography' or fictionalized childhood in Russian literature from the 1850s to 1920s is described in a book by Andrew S. Wachtel, *The Battle of Childhood: Creation of a Russian Myth* (Stanford University Press, 1990). Among the topoi of this genre discussed by Wachtel was the end of childhood with the loss of the mother or the move from the country estate to the city; these topoi could hardly be felt by Jewish modernist writers to be identifiable with their own childhood. On the relevance of the poet's myth of self to modern Russian poetry see Svetlana Boym, *Death in Quotation Marks: Cultural Myths of the Modern Poet* (Cambridge MA: Harvard University Press, 1991). For a discussion of the problematics of autobiographical writing see Jane Gary Harris, 'Autobiographical Theory and the Problem of Esthetic Coherence in Mandelstam's *Noise of Time*', *Essays in Poetics*, 9, 2 (1984): 33–66; and Jane Gary Harris, 'Diversity of Discourse: Autobiographical Statements in Theory and Praxis', in *Autobiographical Statements in Twentieth-Century Russian Literature*, ed. Jane Gary Harris (Princeton University Press, 1990), 3–35. I will be returning to some of these questions in Chapters 4 and 5, but since I am dealing with the *poetic* creation of self (and not the biographical identification of the author with the writing persona) I have not limited myself to generically autobiographical texts. The relevant issues in such texts are dealt with in James

Olney, *Metaphors of Self: The Meaning of Autobiography* (Princeton University Press, 1972); Paul Eakin, *Fictions in Autobiography: Studies in the Art of Self-Invention* (Princeton University Press, 1988); Robert Elbaz, *The Changing Nature of the Self: A Critical Study of the Autobiographic Discourse* (Iowa: University of Iowa Press, 1987).

62 The extent to which any Jewish connection is erased is illustrated in a typical Soviet biography of Marshak by B. Galanov, *S. Ia. Marshak: zhizn' i tvorchestvo* (Moscow: Detskaia literatura, 1965). A sample of the Zionist corpus of Marshak's poetry has been republished in *Na odnoi volne: evreiskie motivy v russkoi poezii*, ed. Tamar Dolzhanskaia (Jerusalem: Biblioteka Aliia, 1974), 125–35.

2. MODERNIST RESPONSES TO WAR AND REVOLUTION: THE JEWISH JESUS

1 David G. Roskies, *Against the Apocalypse: Responses to Catastrophe in Modern Jewish Culture* (Cambridge MA.: Harvard University Press, 1984).
2 An English version of the story of the Ten Martyrs may be found in Raphael Patai, *Gates to the Old City: A Book of Jewish Legends* (New York: Avon Books, 1980), 358–70. The story has passed into the Day of Atonement liturgy in the 'Eleh ezkera' prayer.
3 *Fictional Transfigurations of Jesus* (Princeton University Press, 1972).
4 See Paul Fussell, *The Great War and Memory* (New York: Oxford University Press, 1975), 117–20.
5 Cited in David Perkins, *A History of Modern Poetry from the 1890s to the High Modernist Mode* (Cambridge MA: Harvard University Press, 1976), 283–84.
6 See D. J. R. Bruckner, Seymour Chwast, and Steven Heller, *Art Against War: 400 Years of Protest in Art* (New York: Abbeville, 1984).
7 See Ziva Amishai-Maisels, 'The Jewish Jesus', *Journal of Jewish Art*, 9 (1982), 84–104.
8 *Depiction and Interpretation: The Influence of the Holocaust on the Visual Arts* (Oxford: Pergamon, 1993), 178–9.
9 See Ernest Namenyi, *The Essence of Jewish Art* (New York: Yosselof, 1960).
10 Avram Kampf, *Jewish Experience in the Art of the Twentieth Century* (South Hadley MA: Bergin & Garvey, 1984), 12.
11 Ibid., 203.
12 Ziva Amishai-Maisels, 'Chagall's Jewish In-Jokes', *Journal of Jewish Art*, 5 (1978): 76–93.
13 Cited in Ziva Amishai-Maisels, *Depiction and Interpretation*, 185. Maisels interprets *Calvary* on one level as a response to the Beilis trial

which reverses the blood-libel – it is the Jewish child who bleeds (*Depiction and Interpretation*, 179).

14 See Mira Friedman, 'Icon Painting and Russian Popular Art as Sources of Some Works by Chagall', *Journal of Jewish Art*, 5 (1978): 94–107.

15 The modernists argued that God had broken the terms of the Covenant, whereas in Jewish tradition it was God who accused Israel of breaking the Covenant; indeed, the Fast of the 17th of Tammuz, to which reference was made in the previous chapter, also commemorated the Breaking of the Tablets by Moses on discovering the sin of the Golden Calf. In the modern Jewish experience of catastrophe, not even Rabbi Levi-Yitskhak of Berdichev or other disputants with God who invoked the terms of the Covenant went as far as the modernists in breaking the Covenant in life and in their texts, a further resonance of breaking-out and breakdown that is also a breakage of text. See Roskies, *Against the Apocalypse*.

16 Efros, 'Lampa Aladina', *Evreiskii mir*, 1 (Moscow, 1918): 297–310. For a discussion of Efros and his views on Jewish modernism see Nicoletta Misler, 'The Future in Search of its Past: Nation, Ethnos, Tradition and the Avant-Garde in Russian Jewish Art Criticism', in *Tradition and Revolution: The Jewish Renaissance in Russian Avant-Garde Art, 1912–1928*, ed. Ruth Apter-Gabriel, 2nd edition (Jerusalem: Israel Museum, 1988), 143–54.

17 Obviously things are far less clear-cut than this might suggest: artistic works by Jews were influenced by the wide spectrum of competing trends in modernism, the Christian language of Western art and Renaissance conventions, Marxism and assimilation, the pull of centre versus periphery, folk-art versus internationalism, Paris versus Russia. Also, since Jews could not always obtain residence rights to enter art school in St Petersburg before the Revolution, Yehuda Pen's art school in Vitebsk was a first opportunity for several Jews, including Chagall, to become artists before they outgrew the provincial Jewish world. For detailed accounts see Avram Kampf, *Jewish Experience in the Art of the Twentieth Century*, 15–47; Seth L. Wolitz, 'The Jewish National Art Renaissance in Russia', in Apter-Gabriel, *Tradition and Revolution*, 21–42; John E. Bowlt, 'From the Pale of Settlement to the Reconstruction of the World', ibid., 43–60; Mirjam Rajner, 'The Awakening of Jewish National Art in Russia', *Jewish Art*, 16–17 (1990–91): 98–121.

18 For a fuller discussion of Sholem Asch's ecumenism see Goldie Morgentaler, 'The Foreskin of the Heart: Ecumenism in Sholem Asch's Christian Trilogy', *Prooftexts*, 8, 2 (1988): 219–44.

19 Roskies, *Against the Apocalypse*, 263–5.

20 The personal crisis of the officer-poet bears comparison, despite the Zionist resolution of the plot, with the internal conflict of the Jewish intellectual in Babel's *Red Cavalry*. Dalia Dromi, a doctoral student at UCLA, has drawn my attention to another work by Meiri, 'Rabi yeshu me-tsfat' ('Rabbi Jesus from Sefad'), as well as to Agnon's 'Niflaot shamash bet hamidrash' ('The Wonders of the Studyhouse Beadle'); the ironic use of Jesus as a Jewish victim bears comparison with Babel's use of a Jewish Jesus in 'At St Valentine's Church' referred to later in this chapter.

21 See Roskies, *Against the Apocalypse, passim.*

22 Roskies, *Against the Apocalypse,* 267–74. See Greenberg's 'In malkhus fun tselem' ('In the Kingdom of the Cross'), *Albatross* (Berlin), 3–4 (1923): 15–24.

23 *Gezamlte verk,* II, 431–3; reproduced in Roskies, *Against the Apocalypse,* 265.

24 Ruth R. Wisse, *A Little Love in Big Manhattan* (Cambridge MA: Harvard University Press, 1988), 96.

25 Cited ibid., 112.

26 Translated as 'The Mound' in *The Literature of Destruction: Jewish Responses to Catastrophe,* ed. David G. Roskies (Philadelphia: Jewish Publication Society, 1988), 364.

27 Seth Wolitz, 'A Yiddish Modernist Dirge: *Di Kupe* of Perets Markish', *Modern Jewish Studies,* Annual VI (1987), 56–72.

28 'Pirkei mahafekhah', *Hatekufah* 22 (1924): 69–97.

29 Maurice Friedberg, 'Yiddish Folklore Motifs in Isaac Babel's *Konarmija*', in *American Contributions to the 8th International Congress of Slavists, Zagreb-Ljubljana, 1978,* ed. Victor Terras, II (Columbus OH: Slavica, 1978), 192–203.

30 Hasidic leader, wrongly translated as 'rabbi' in most translations of Babel's stories.

31 Babel's wartime 1920 diary has been published in Isaak Babel, *Sochineniia* (Moscow: Khudozhestvennaia literatura, 1990). I, 362–435. The published date of June for this and other entries is almost certainly incorrect and I have corrected to July (see Chapter 3, note 51 below).

32 Meir Bosak, 'Hamodel hahistori le "ben harebi" shel babel', *Ma'ariv,* 20 November 1987, Literary Supplement, 3.

33 *The Street* (New York: Schocken, 1985), 73.

34 Isaak Babel, *Detstvo i drugie rasskazy* (Jerusalem: Biblioteka Aliia, 1979), 186–7.

35 Isaak Babel, *Sochineniia* (Moscow: Khudozhestvennaia literatura, 1990), I, 404.

36 Aleksandr Flaker, 'Babel' i pol'skoe sakral'noe iskusstvo', *Russian*

Literature, 32 (1987), 29–38. See also Efraim Sicher, 'The Road to a Red Calvary: Myth and Mythology in the Works of Isaak Babel of the 1920s', *Slavonic and East European Review*, 60, 4 (1982), 528–46.

37 In her drunken lust a Russian peasant woman crushes the angel Alfred and then refuses to forgive Jesus for her life of incessant sex and pregnancy. This story, incidentally, bears a remarkable likeness to a similar tale by Boccaccio in the *Decameron* about a lover masquerading as an angel who is forced to flee and leave his wings behind.

38 Babel, *Detstvo i drugie rasskazy*, 120.

39 Ziva Amishai-Maisels, 'Chagall's Jewish In-Jokes', *Journal of Jewish Art*, 5 (1978): 76–93. The portrayal of the body of Jesus by many Renaissance painters was less prudish than we tend to think, and Leo Steinberg has offered a theological justification for the frank depiction of the earthly incarnation of the Christian messiah in *The Sexuality of Christ in Renaissance Art and in Modern Oblivion* (New York: Pantheon Books, 1983). For a survey of the treatment of Jesus by Buber and other modern Jewish authors see Hermann Adler, 'Das Christus Bild im Lichter Jüdischer Autoren', *Symbolen: Jahrbuch für Symbol Forschung*, 2 (1961): 41–62.

40 Zsuzsa Hetényi, 'Bibleiskie motivy v *Konarmii* Babelia', *Studia Slavica Hungarica*, 27 (1981): 229–40.

41 Ibid. Cf. Zsuzsa Hetényi, 'Eskadronnaja dama, vozvedennaia v madonnu', *Studia Slavica Hungarica*, 31 (1985): 161–69.

42 The carnival or circus theme in Rybak and Chagall comes to mind again here, and the Purimspiel source among others has been noted in Chagall's case (Ziva Amishai-Maisels, 'Chagall and the Jewish Revival: Center or Periphery?', in Apter-Gabriel [ed.], *Tradition and Revolution*, 75) as well as the general influence of the *comeddia del l'arte* and Evreinov's innovations in the theatre. See Avram Kampf, 'Art and Stage Design: The Jewish Theatres of Moscow in the Early Twenties', in Apter-Gabriel (ed.), *Tradition and Revolution*, 125–42. Carnivalization in Bakhtin's thinking explains inversion of language and authority, but the carnival freedom celebrated by the Cossacks in Rybak's Pogrom series mocks the idea.

43 Marc Chagall, *Chagall on Chagall* (Israeli edition, Tel-Aviv: Steimatzky's, 1979), 102. By contrast 'Self-Portrait at the Easel' (done in Vitebsk, 1914) does not bear any such self-referential inscription, though 'Jew in Red' (1915, when Chagall was prevented by the war from returning to Paris) is inscribed with the verses from Genesis telling of God's command to Abraham 'Get thee from thy country, from thy native land and from thy father's house to the land I will show you' and also Jacob's hearkening to his parents' advice to flee

Esau and seek a bride abroad. The pogroms have evidently drained the Jew's blood to his beard and the Biblical verses call on the painter to leave Russia with his bride. See the interpretive account of Chagall's complex identity conflict in this period by Ziva Amishai-Maisels, 'Chagall and the Jewish Revival: Center or Periphery?', in Apter-Gabriel (ed.), *Tradition and Revolution*, 71–100. Chagall's autobiographical *My Life* is scarcely reliable, since it was written in 1922 when Chagall turned his back on Russia and looked to Europe after being denied the recognition he felt he deserved. The murals Chagall did prior to his departure for Moscow's Jewish Chamber Theatre, however, demonstrate the aesthetic ideals he would have liked to dictate to the new Yiddish theatre, in which he depicts himself being introduced like a Holy Infant by Efros. This was an expression of an aesthetic steeped in Jewish tradition and it did not lack a scorn for the Christian world: a circumcision scene suggests that cultural or artistic apostates (like Lissitzky, whom Chagall considered a traitor because of his defection to Malevich and Suprematism) ought to return to the fold (Ziva Amishai-Maisels, 'Chagall's Murals for the State Jewish Chamber Theatre', in *Chagall – Dreams and Drama: Early Russian Works and Murals for the Jewish Theatre*, ed. Ruth Apter-Gabriel [Jerusalem: Israel Museum, 1993], 21–39).

44 Alan Birnholz, 'El Lissitzky', doctoral thesis, Yale University, 1973, 242. Kampf strongly disagrees with this interpretation (*Jewish Experience in the Art of the Twentieth Century*, 208). See chapter 6 below on Lissitzky's collaboration with Ehrenburg and Ehrenburg's assessment of his situation and the pogrom experience.

45 K. Michael Hays, 'Photomontage and its Audience: El Lissitzky Meets Berlin Dada', in *The Avant-Garde Frontier: Russia Meets the West, 1910–1930*, ed. Gail Harrison Roman and Virginia Hagelstein Marquardt (Gainesville FA: University of Florida Press, 1992), 169–95. Hays nevertheless makes some important points about Lissitzky and his self-portrait in the context and intertext of the encounter between the Russian avant-garde and the West. We should not forget, however, that Lissitzky was an engineer by training and an architect, and that there is also a Jewish context in the work Lissitzky did with Chagall and other book illustrators in Kiev, a major Jewish avant-garde centre, which spearheaded the revolution in Russia typography, blending elements of the *lubok* and Jewish folk-motifs (Camilla Gray, *The Russian Experiment in Art, 1863–1922* [London: Thames and Hudson, 1971], 253–4).

46 Birnholz, 'El Lissitzky and the Jewish Tradition', *Studio International*, 186 (October 1973), cited in Kampf, *Jewish Experience in the Art of the Twentieth Century*, 46.

47 Haia Friedberg, 'Lissitzky's *Had Gadya*', *Jewish Art*, 12–13 (1986–7): 292–303, cited in Ruth Apter-Gabriel, 'El Lissitzky's Jewish Works', in Apter-Gabriel (ed.), *Tradition and Revolution*, 113.

48 The idea of replacing 'Bei zhidov' with 'Bei belykh' was suggested to Lissitzky by Ilia Ehrenburg, according to the Russian Jewish artist Boris Aronson (cited in Kampf, *Jewish Experience in the Art of the Twentieth Century*, 46).

49 'Kladbishche v Kozine', *Detstvo i drugie rasskazy*, 158. Elijah may prefigure the rebbe's son of the same name who turns revolutionary.

50 Roskies, *Against the Apocalypse*, 265.

3.　THE JEWISHNESS OF BABEL

1 S. Markish, 'Russko-evreiskaia literatura i Isaak Babel'', in Isaak Babel, *Detstvo i drugie rasskazy*, 319–45; English translation, 'The Example of Isaac Babel', *Commentary*, 64, 5 (1977): 36–45.

2 M. Lazarev, 'Zadachi i znachenie russko-evreiskoi bellestriki', *Voskhod*, 5–6 (1885): 28–42.

3 Paustovsky, *Naedin'e s osen'iu* (Moscow: Sovetskii pisatel', 1966), 142–3.

4 See V. Veshnev, 'Poeziia banditizma', *Molodaia gvardiia*, 7–8 (1924): 276; A. Lezhnev, *Literaturnye budni* (Moscow: Krug, 1929), 266, 267, 269; A. Lezhnev, *Sovremenniki: Literaturno-kriticheskie ocherki* (Moscow: Krug, 1927), 124–7.

5 A. Kaun, 'Babel: Voice of New Russia', *Menorah Journal* (November 1928): 400–1.

6 C. Fadiman, 'The Jew on Horseback', *Menorah Journal* (February 1927): 102. The Jew on horseback had in fact been associated with apostasy since Talmudic times, though through the ages Jewish generals and devout Hasidim had made excellent horsemen.

7 J. Kunitz, *Russian Literature and the Jew* (New York, 1929), 190, note 5.

8 For a comparison of Yushkevich and Babel, see Walenty Cukierman, 'Isaak Babel: Jewish Heroes and their Background', *Yiddish*, 2, 4 (1977): 18–19. Others who had described Odessa's underworld and its racy slang, a mixture of Yiddish, Russian and Ukrainian, include L. Kornman ('Karmen') and the St Petersburg journalist E. Doroshevich.

9 'Avtobiografiia', *Detstvo i drugie rasskazy*, compiled with notes by Efraim Sicher (Jerusalem: Biblioteka Aliia, 1979), 7. Babel's stories will be cited from the complete and uncensored versions in this edition in my own translation (page references will be given in brackets). A second volume, *Peterburg 1918*, ed. E. Sicher (Ann Arbor: Ardis, 1989), includes the rest of the prose. The more recent Soviet two-volume edition *Sochineniia* (Moscow: Khudozhestvennaia litera-

tura, 1990) contains most, though not all, of the surviving corpus and restores some passages, but retains many Stalinist excisions and editorial changes without comment.

10 'Odessa', *Peterburg 1918*, 15–18; *Sochineniia*, I, 62–5.

11 Babel claimed to have worked for the Cheka in his 1924 'Autobiography', but Nathalie Babel says that her mother told her this was pure fabrication ('Introduction', in Isaac Babel, *The Lonely Years: Unpublished Stories and Private Correspondence, 1925–1939* [New York: Farrar & Straus, 1964], xiv). There is, however, some circumstantial evidence that Babel worked for the Cheka, at least in the capacity of translator; many Jews joined the Cheka out of feelings of vengeance for the *ancien régime* and would have felt that the narrator of 'The Journey' who dons the robes of majesty (the Tsar's dressing-gown) has turned the tables on the former persecutors of the Jews. The Cheka agent Borovoi in 'Froim Grach' is probably exceptional in voicing regret for the past when the last of the Odessa gangsters is eliminated.

12 Transcript of remarks made in Moscow, September 1933, after a second trip to Europe (IMLI fond 83, opis' 1, edinitsa khraneniia 6). Part of the remarks was published in 'Na Zapade', *Vecherniaia Moskva*, 16 September 1933.

13 Letter of 20 October 1928, in *The Lonely Years*, 106. His sister had also left Russia in 1925 to live with her husband in Brussels and was followed by Babel's mother. Meanwhile, from 1925 until 1928, Babel continued a relationship with the future wife of Vsevolod Ivanov, Tamara Ivanovna Kashirna, who bore him a son, Mikhail. In 1934 Babel finally settled down with Antonina Nikolaevna Pirozhkova, an engineer on the Moscow Metro project, by whom he had a daughter, Lidia.

14 Conversation with Babel's sister, Meri Shaposhnikova, in Brussels, in Judith Stora-Sandor, *Isaac Babel: l'homme et l'oeuvre* (Paris: Klincksieck, 1968), 18–20.

15 See Chapter 1.

16 Babel, quoted in Ia. Eidel'man, 'Mendele Moikher-Sforim: Na torzhestvennom zasedanii v Dome soiuzov', *Literaturnaia gazeta*, 5 March 1936, 6.

17 *Bliuzhdaiushchie zvezdy* (Moscow: Kinopechat', 1926). Republished in Babel, *Sochineniia*, II, 447–94.

18 *Izbrannye proizvedeniia*, trans. S. Hecht, ed. I. Babel (Moscow-Leningrad: Zemlia i fabrika, 1926–27).

19 O. Ronen, 'I. E. Babel'', *Kratkaia evreiskaia entsiklopediia*, 1 (Jerusalem: Keter, 1976), 272.

20 Stora Sandor, 19.

21 *Ogni* (Kiev), 9 February 1913, 3–4. The story is reprinted in *Detstvo i drugie rasskazy*, 11–14 and in *Sochineniia*, 1, 34–6.

22 Nathalie Babel, 'Introduction', in Babel, *The Lonely Years*, xvi-xvii.

23 According to a file in the Leningrad Historical Archives, cited in I. Livshits, 'Protiv tendentsiioznykh istolkovanii tvorchestva i biografii I. E. Babelia', *Voprosy literaturovedeniia i iazykoznaniia* (Kharkov), 2 (1965): 222–5.

24 'Tri chasa dnia', in *Peterburg 1918*, 199–201.

25 'Dvorets materinstva', *Peterburg 1918*, 50. The full texts of Babel's contributions to *Novaia zhizn'* can be found in *Peterburg 1918*, 41–85, and in *Sochineniia*, 1, 154–96.

26 *Vecherniaia gazeta*, 16 March 1918, subtitled 'Iz tsikla *Gershele*' ('From the Hershele Cycle'). A version of the Yiddish source may be found in *Hershele Ostropoler, der velt berihmter vittsling* (New York: Hebrew Publishing Company, n.d.), 65–6.

27 'Rabbi', *Detstvo i drugie rasskazy*, 135. It is not known whether Babel continued with the Hershele stories, but he did think of Hershele when watching the Hasidim pray in a Dubno synagogue (Diary entry for 23 July 1920, *Sochineniia*, 1, 385).

28 The practice is not so different from Chagall's 'translation' of Yiddish jokes and idioms discussed by Ziva Avishai-Maisels (see note 12 to Chapter 2 and the remarks on linguistic interference in Chapter 1).

29 Konstantin Paustovsky, *Vremia bol'shikh ozhidanii* (Moscow, 1960), 151–2.

30 There is no evidence that the Babel family were harmed by the violent outbreaks of 1904–5, and it is denied by Nathalie Babel, *The Lonely Years*, xiv–xv.

31 Michael Gold, 'A Love Letter from France', *New Masses*, 13 August 1935. This article was translated into Russian in *Literaturnyi Leningrad*, 14 September 1935, 1.

32 Letter of 9 October 1935, *The Lonely Years*, 290.

33 Letter of 9 October 1935 to A.G. Slonim, *Sochineniia*, 1, 347–8.

34 Letter of 15 December 1928, *The Lonely Years*, 112.

35 *Zakat* (Moscow: Krug, 1928), 95. The reference to Jesus is missing in other editions.

36 Ibid., 96. The midrash on Ecclesiastes (Kohelet raba) says something similar about the cyclicity of sunset and sunrise.

37 See Chone Shmeruk, 'Yiddish Literature in the USSR', in *The Jews in Soviet Russia since 1917*, ed. Lionel Kochan, 3rd edition (Oxford University Press, 1978), 242–280. Little attention has been paid to the thematic parallels with Perets Markish's 'Brothers', Moshe Kulbak's *Zelmenyaner* or Bergelson's 'Civil War' in his 'Stormy Days'. Indeed, these works attracted similar criticisms of a 'non-Marxist' standpoint levelled at Babel's *Red Cavalry*.

38 I. Babel, *Dertseylungen* (Kiev: Kultur-lige, 1925). There is no indication that this is a translation and Babel may have had a hand in this Yiddish publication of his stories. D. Feldman's translation appeared the same year in Kharkov, followed by Gitl Mayzl's in the Warsaw *Literarishe bleter*.

39 A rare example of Babel's signature of a public anti-Trotskyite denunciation is 'Lozh', predatel'stsvo i smerdiakovshchina', *Literaturnaia gazeta*, 26 January 1937, 4.

40 For instance, Patricia Carden in *The Art of Isaac Babel* (Ithaca: Cornell University Press, 1972) barely mentions Babel's Jewish background except to quote from Judith Stora-Sandor's book *Isaac Babel: l'homme et l'oeuvre*, which has very little on Judaism. James E. Falen in *Isaac Babel: Russian Master of the Short Story* (Knoxville: University of Tennessee Press, 1974) and in his thesis (University of Pennsylvania, 1970) quotes the Hagada as his only 'East European' source, and claims Nietzsche and the Classics as literary sources or parallels. See on this problem Efraim Sicher, 'Babel's Jewish Roots', *Jewish Quarterly*, 3 (1977): 25–7.

41 F. Levin, *Babel': Ocherk tvorchestva* (Moscow, 1972), 139.

42 G. A. Belaia, E. A. Dobrenko and I. A. Esaulov, *'Konarmiia' Isaaka Babelia* (Moscow: Rossiiskii universitet, 1993), 5.

43 Ibid., 37.

44 This is Roskies's conclusion about the 'coding' of Hebrew in the Yiddish of Sholom Aleichem (Roskies, *Against the Apocalypse*, 163–82). The relations between the languages of Jewish culture in Russia are illuminated by the discussion on contact between cultural systems in Itamar Even-Zohar, *Papers in Historical Poetics* (Tel-Aviv: Porter Institute for Poetics and Semiotics, Tel-Aviv University, 1978), especially 14–20.

45 See Ziva Shamir, '"Hadalut srikah bearuvah": mimush vehakhazah shel idiomatikah idit beshirat kh. n. bialik', *Hasifrut*, 3–4 (1986): 211–19. For further examples of linguistic interference in Babel see Sicher, *Style and Structure in the Prose of Isaak Babel* (Columbus OH: Slavica, 1986). 71–81.

46 Michel Serres, *L'Interférence* (Paris: Editions de Minuit, 1972), 157; cited in Murray Baumgarten, *City Scriptures: Modern Jewish Writing* (Cambridge MA: Harvard University Press, 1982), 154. Baumgarten gives Gedali as an example of a cultural cross-reference that negates the discourse of the Revolution and points to moral irony in Gedali's going to the synagogue to pray, thus confirming the Judaic version of messianism (154–5).

47 A. B. Murphy, 'The Style of Isaac Babel', *Slavonic and East European Review*, 44 (1966): 366–8.

48 See Efraim Sicher, 'The Road to a Red Calvary: Myth and

Mythology in the Works of Isaak Babel of the 1920s', *Slavonic and East European Review*, 60, 4 (1982), 528–46.

49 For an account of the hostilities between the Bolsheviks and Poland see Norman Davies, *White Eagle, Red Star: The Polish–Soviet War, 1919–20* (London: Macdonald, 1972).

50 See 'Rytsari tsivilizatsii' ('Knights of Civilization'), *Krasnyi Kavalerist*, 14 August 1920 and 'Nedobitye ubiitsy' ('Unvanquished Killers'), *Krasnyi Kavalerist*, 17 September 1920. Reprinted in *Sochineniia*, I, 203–6. An English translation can be found in Efraim Sicher, 'The "Jewish Cossack": Isaac Babel in the First Red Cavalry', *Studies in Contemporary Jewry*, 4 (1988): 127–33.

51 The manuscripts of the Diary and of the drafts for the *Red Cavalry* stories are kept in the private collection of Babel's widow Antonina Nikolaevna Pirozhkova in Moscow. The Diary entries run from 3 July 1920 to 6 July 1920, followed by a break from pages 69 to 88, which are missing from the manuscript; the Diary continues from 11 July 1920 to 15 September 1920, covering most of Babel's stay in the First Red Cavalry. The Diary was published in full after many difficulties for the first time in *Sochineniia*, I, 362–435. This publication and other commentators read 'June' for the first entries, which must be a mistake, because, as Norman Davies points out, Zhitomir had not yet been taken on 3 June ('Isaak Babel's *Konarmiia* stories and the Polish-Soviet War', *Modern Language Review*, 67, 4 [1972]: 847); in any case, the first entry was evidently written on a Saturday, which makes it without a doubt 3 July 1920. I have given the correct dates throughout. I have previously discussed the Diary in 'The "Jewish Cossack": Isaak Babel' in the First Red Cavalry', 113–34, An English translation of the Diary by H. T. Willetts is available in Isaac Babel, *1920 Diary*, ed. Carol Avins (New Haven: Yale University Press, 1995); the translations in this chapter are my own.

52 Partly published in *Literaturnoe nasledstvo* LXXIV (Moscow: Akademiia nauk, 1965), 490–9. I refer to the complete manuscripts in the collection of Antonina Pirozhkova.

53 In 1938 Babel avowed that the stories were based directly on the Diary, much of which he claimed to have lost and supplemented from memory of the events (transcript of an address to young writers from the national republics, 30 December 1938, in the archives of A. N. Tolstoi, Institut Mirovoi Literatury i Iskusstva, fond 43, opis' 1, edinitsa khraneniia 944, 2b, l. 33). I. Smirin has discussed the transfer of Diary material to the stories in his 'Na puti k *Konarmii:* Literaturnye iskaniia Babelia', *Literaturnoe nasledstvo*, LXXIV, 467–82.

54 See Furmanov's diaries in his *Sobranie sochinenii*, IV (Moscow, 1961),

and L. K. Kuvanova, 'Furmanov i Babel'', *Literaturnoe nasledstvo*
LXXIV, 500–12.

55 The Russian original appears in Smirin, 'Na puti k *Konarmii:*
Literaturnye iskaniia Babelia', *Literaturnoe nasledstvo* LXXIV, 467–82.

56 *Jewish Chronicle*, 16 July 1920, 11–12. It goes without saying that the
outrages of summer 1920 pale in comparison with the unspeakable
horrors of 1918–19 committed by Petliura's forces, including the
Zhitomir pogroms of January 1919, after the suppression of the
local Soviet, and of March 1919, after a brief Bolshevik occupation.
The retreating Petliura forces also carried out atrocities in areas
of Eastern Galicia not under Bolshevik occupation in August-
September 1920 (L. Motzkin, *Les Pogromes en Ukraine sous les gouverne-
ments ukrainiens, 1917–1920* [Paris: Comité des délégations juives,
1927], 82–9; cf. appendices 17, 36, 45, 46). See also I. Cherikover, *Di
ukrainer pogromen in yor 1919* (New York: YIVO 1965), and *Antisemitizm
i pogromy na Ukraine, 1917–1918* (Berlin: Ostjudisches Historisches
Archiv, 1923); I. Shekhtman, *Pogromy Dobrovol'cheskoi armii na Ukraine:
K istorii antisemitizma na Ukraine v 1919–1920 gody* (Berlin: Ostjudisches
Historisches Archiv, 1932).

57 For corroboration of Babel's account see the memoirs of Holocaust
survivors from Hoszcza in B. Ayalon-Baranik and A. Yaron-
Kricmar, *Hoshtsh: Sefer zikaron* (Tel-Aviv: Irgun yotsei hoshtsh, 1957),
25–9.

58 'The Destruction of Galicia', in *The Literature of Destruction: Jewish
Responses to Catastrophe*, ed. David G. Roskies (Philadelphia: Jewish
Publication Society, 1988), 225. An-sky's testimony is relevant here
also because of the examples of Jewish medical officers who
repressed their identity and did not react to anti-Semitic incidents,
as well as of Jewish conscripts who surreptitiously aided the victims
of their Cossack comrades-in-arms. A Jewish medical officer serving
in the Tsarist army also evoked the Destruction of Jerusalem when
he saw Husiatyn razed to the ground by Russian troops in 1916
(Gershon Levin, *In velt krig* [Warsaw, 1923]). These texts and the vast
literary tradition of which they form a part are discussed in Roskies,
Against the Apocalypse.

59 A contemporary observer of the massacres in the Ukraine also
compared them in scale and location to those committed by
Khmelnitsky, and concluded that there was little left of the hopes of
the *maskilim* for an enlightened attitude to the Jews (Shimon
Bernfeld, *Sefer hadema'ot* [Berlin: Eshkol, 1923], 74–7).

60 First Cavalry recruits included former soldiers in Denikin's army,
responsible for massacres in the Ukraine, and Budyonny is alleged
to have permitted his cavalry to organize several pogroms in the

provinces of Ekaterinoslav and Volhynia, notably at Korsun, the Cossacks declaring they must 'beat the Jews and save Russia' (*Jewish Chronicle*, 23 July 1920, 15). Bolsheviks were reported responsible for rape and the brutal murder of women and children at Brody (*Jewish Chronicle*, 27 August 1920, 10–11), though it is not always easy to establish responsibility in view of the charges and counter-charges of Polish and Soviet war propaganda. After Budyonny had received orders from Tukhachevsky to transfer to the front against Wrangel, First Cavalry troops carried out pogroms (designated as such in Soviet sources) during the march to the Dnieper. Budyonny arrested two brigadiers of the Sixth Cavalry Division whose chief of staff was responsible, and a purge was carried out (Norman Davies, *White Eagle, Red Star*, 232). Relevant archival material may be found in Piotr S. Wandycz, *Soviet–Polish Relations, 1917–1921* (Cambridge MA: Harvard University Press, 1969). Sergei Shtern cites an order by Budyonny of 20 October 1920: 'We must take the Crimea come what may, and we will take it, in order to begin the life of peace. The German Baron is making desperate efforts to stay in the Crimea but he will not succeed. Traitors to the revolution are helping him – the Jews and bourgeois. But a decisive blow from our glorious cavalry will suffice and the traitors will be wiped out. Stand firm and have no mercy. The Crimea will be ours' (*V ogne grazhdanskoi voiny* [Paris: Russkoe knigoizdatel'stvo Ia. Povoloskaia, 1922], 187).

61 Trotsky confirms the existence of this common misconception *(My Life* [New York: Charles Scribner's Sons, 1930], 361).

62 Isaac Babel, *You Must Know Everything: Stories, 1915–1937*, translated by Max Hayward (New York: Farar, Straus & Giroux, 1969), 131–2. The word *Jude* is German, not Yiddish, which can be explained by the fact that many assimilated Jews preferred German to Yiddish. In the Diary Babel records a number of such phrases, including one very similar to the one uttered by Shulmeister, but directed at himself (Diary, 23 July), so that this scene could be a projection of Babel's own fear of penetration of his mask, as well as of his guilt about the shooting of prisoners, bringing together his moral and Jewish identity.

63 Mosher's real name was Lt.-Col. Merian C. Cooper and he came from Florida, not New York. See K. M. Murray, *Wings Over Poland* (New York: Appleton, 1932); J. B. Cynk, *History of the Polish Air Force, 1918–1968* (Reading: Osprey Publishing, 1972)

64 In some of the conversations which Babel had with local Jewish youth he displayed open admiration for the Zionist pioneers and did not hide his identity. This is according to the memoirs of Akiva

Govrin, 'Vstrechi s I. Babelem', serialized in *Nasha strana* between 8 March 1974 and 5 April 1974; a Hebrew translation appeared as 'Pegishot 'im Yitskhak Babel', *Moznayim* 38, 1–2 (1973–4): 42–9. In the Diary entry for 26 August 1920 Babel mentions being shown around Sokal' by a local Zionist, and he had probably had experience of the Zionist movement in Odessa before the Revolution (as mentioned above).

65 S. M. Budyonny, 'Babizm Babelia iz *Krasnoi novi*', *Oktiabr'*, 3 (1924): 196–7. Babel countered in a letter to the editor in the next issue of *Oktiabr'* that his descriptions of the First Cavalry were essentially authentic, and cited a letter from First Cavalry veteran S. Melnikov. Melnikov had been surprised to find himself described along with Timoshenko, commander of the Sixth Division, in one of Babel's stories ('Melnikov and Timoshenko', later retitled 'Story of a Horse' and 'Continuation of Story of a Horse'; the heroes were also renamed, as were other real personages in *Red Cavalry*). Melnikov thanked Babel for his story, but pointed out that he had never resigned from the Party as stated in the story, though it was true that Timoshenko had abused his power and taken his white steed. Melnikov also noted there were 'negative features' of Budyonny's army which the author did not mention, such as the looting in Równe (archive of *Krasnaia nov'*, Rossiiskii Gosudarstvennyi Arkhiv Literatury i Iskusstva, fond 602, opis' 1, edinitsa khraneniia 1718). See also Melnikov's later memoir, 'Pervaia konnaia', *Krasnaia niva*, 6 (1930): 6–7. In 1928 Gorky entered into debate with Budyonny over the absence of communists and the masses in Babel's stories, and the question of ideological commitment is one that dogged the treatment of Babel in the Soviet press ever after. A former doctor in the First Cavalry made a relevant point about the transcendence of art when he attested to the fundamental truth portrayed in *Red Cavalry*: 'Babel saw more than we. What can one do if in a certain sense all of us, witnesses and participants in Budyonny's campaigns, remember "after Babel"?' (I. Kassirskii, 'Nikto puti proidennogo', *Znanie – sila*, 6 [1967]: 12–14). Needless to say, Babel's portrait of Budyonny's First Cavalry and of Budyonny himself was hardly flattering, at a time when songs and popular legend, as well as literary publications such as Aseev's 1923 poem *Budyonny*, were already establishing the Cossack commander's reputation as an epic hero. Unfortunately, evaluation of the fictional picture has been obscured by criticism of Babel for historical 'discrepancies', such as the confusion of the rivers Słucz and Zbrucz or the impossible deployment of forces in 'Crossing the Zbrucz' (see Norman Davies, 'Isaak Babel's *Konarmiia* Stories and the Polish–Soviet War', 845–57).

66 The 'ship' and 'waves' presumably refer to the 'sea' of the Talmud in the commonplace Jewish idiom.

67 The 'shy star' recalls a reference to lechery in a 1908 poem by Bialik, 'Be'erev hakayits' ('Summer Evening'), while in his well-known poem 'Hamatmid' ('The Talmud Student') the twinkling stars evoke a lyrical world of nature outside which both describes and undermines the student's situation amid the rotted Talmuds, memories of lost youth and longing for the Messiah. As already noted in Chapter 1, there is a common theme of breaking out of the dying Jewish world and the pull of a lyrical eroticism likewise pulls the narrator toward the gentile world. Babel could have expected his Jewish readers to be acquainted with Bialik's verse and with his pre-Revolutionary lecturing and publishing activities in Odessa. Bialik prayed at the Brody Synagogue, frequented by Babel's father (as Babel remembered in his Diary), and it is very likely this would have been a personal memory for Babel himself.

68 'Reshimot', *Bereshit*, 1 (1926): 15–38. Babel authorized these translations personally. See Y. A. Gilbo'a, *Oktobraim 'ivriim* (Tel Aviv: Sifriyat hapo'alim, 1974) and also above p. 23.

69 Efraim Sicher, *Style and Structure in the Prose of Isaak Babel* (Columbus OH: Slavica, 1986), 87–9.

70 Zvi Gitelman compares Babel with Shlomo Ya'akov Nepomnia-shchii, who had served in the Cheka and in the Red Army during the Soviet-Polish War, having earlier studied in *yeshivas* and worked for the Zionist movement (*Jewish Nationality and Soviet Politics: The Jewish Sections of the CPSU, 1917–1930* [Princeton University Press, 1972], 283–4). Gitelman cites private correspondence in which Nepomniashchii evokes the conflicts reflected in this passage, and confides how difficult it was to break with the past and to reconcile Hebrew and Judaism with communist ideology: 'I will say, in Gordon's words, "I am a slave to Hebrew forever." No-one will be able to uproot "khumash-and-Rashi" from my soul. I gave my best years to these old writings.' Giving back the Torah on Mount Sinai, he knows he will be naked without it but looks forward to the new Genesis (letter to David Charney of 1925, cited in Zvi Gitelman, *A Century of Ambivalence: The Jews of Russia and the Soviet Union, 1881 to the Present* [New York: Viking, 1990], 115). The similarity to Ilia Bratslavsky is remarkable, as is the resonance of the imagery of returning the covenant and expectation of a new genesis discussed in the previous chapter.

71 The surviving chapters are reprinted in *Peterburg 1918*, 165–77.

72 *Peterburg 1918*, 181–5; *Sochineniia*, II, 224–8.

73 The manuscript of 'The Jewess' appears in *Peterburg 1918*, 202–12.

74 See for example V. Arkhipov, 'Uroki', *Neva*, 6 (1958): 187–99.

75 See L. Livshits, 'Materialy k tvorcheskoi biografii Isaaka Babelia', *Voprosy literatury*, 4 (1964): 110–35.

76 James Falen, *Isaac Babel: Russian Master of the Short Story* (Knoxville: University of Tennessee Press, 1974), 132–59.

77 Patricia Carden, *The Art of Isaac Babel* (Ithaca: Cornell University Press, 1972), 128. Carol Luplow's monograph, *Isaac Babel's Red Cavalry* (Ann Arbor: Ardis, 1982), recognizes the complexity of Babel's narratorial vision and the contradiction of Liutov's romanticism, but like other Western studies on Babel it is hampered by a restricted historical perspective.

78 This judgement of Babel is in my view more relevant to the American Jewish intellectual. It has been repeated by David G. Roskies, who defines Babel's aim in the Diary as being to 'purge' his 'rabbinic sensibilities' so as to 'transmute the horror into a higher level of reality' and through the artistic creation of Liutov to raise his 'conversion to the Cossack code of violence to a choice of universal significance', a response to Jewish catastrophe that assimilated the literary type of the *ba'ale-guf*, the Benia Kriks, to the murderous standards of modernity (*Against the Apocalypse*, 159–62). Taken at its face value this false assumption about Babel's 'self-hate' would seem to contradict Babel's urgent awareness of the historical significance of what he witnessed in Galicia and Volhynia. Indeed, Roskies himself discusses the Diary earlier in his book in connection with An-sky's wartime diary, 'Destruction of Galician Jewry', which inspired the Warsaw ghetto diarists. See also Arkady Lvov, 'Babel the Jew', *Commentary*, 75 (March 1983): 40–9.

79 Lionel Trilling, 'Introduction', in Isaac Babel, *Collected Stories* (Harmondsworth: Penguin, 1974), 16–17. Trilling believes there is violence inherent in the creative act of the artist as he breaks through to vision outside the cave of the Platonic myth. That act of violence in the intellectual effort to break free is surely less applicable to the voyeuristic standpoint of Babel's intellectual narrator who is forced to watch the violence of others, sometimes against his own people.

80 For a discussion of Babel's insatiable curiosity as it affects the narratorial standpoint see Efraim Sicher, 'Isaak Babel: Voyeur of the Short Story', *Stand*, 23, 2 (1982): 54–8.

4. THE 'COLOUR' OF JUDAISM: OSIP MANDELSTAN'S *NOISE OF TIME*

1 Efraim Sicher, *Style and Structure in the Prose of Isaak Babel* (Columbus OH: Slavica, 1986), 46–50. In what follows I have used my

preliminary discussion of synaesthesia in Mandelstam's prose and poetry in 'The "Color" of Judaism: Timespace Oppositions in the Synaesthesia of Osip Mandel'shtam's *Shum vremeni*', in *Aspects of Modern Russian and Czech Literature*, ed. A. B. McMillin (Columbus, OH: Slavica Press, 1989), 31–54.

2　See Ada Steinberg, *Word and Music in the Novels of Andrey Bely* (Cambridge: Cambridge University Press, 1982), 203–36. Bely analysed colour symbolism in his *Masterstvo Gogolia* (1934); compare Jacques Catteau's application of the principles of Kandinsky's *Spiritual in Art* to Dostoevsky in *La Création littéraire chez Dostoievski* (Paris: Institut d'études slaves, 1978), 511–23.

3　Osip Mandelstam wrote satirically: 'Miauknul kon' i kot zarzhal – / Kazak evreiu podrazhal'. Literally, 'The horse meowed and the cat neighed / The Cossack imitated the Jew.' ('Pavlu Vasil'evu', in Osip Mandelstam, *Sobranie sochinenii*, revised edition [New York: Inter-Language Literary Associates, 1967], I, 297). There is a pun on meowed/grew flabby and neighed/got infected. This epigram was written for a poet of Cossack extraction, Pavel Nikolaevich Vasil'ev (1910–37), and dates from the late 1920s. The Jew is, of course, Isaak Babel, who is introduced in Mandelstam's *Egipetskaia marka* ('The Egyptian Stamp'): 'Vot Babel': lisii podborodok i lapki ochkov'. *Sobranie sochinenii*, revised edition (New York: Inter-Language Literary Associates, 1971), II, 21. Clarence Brown translates this as 'Here is Babel: the fox chin and pawlike glasses' (*The Prose of Osip Mandelstam*, translated by Clarence Brown [San Francisco: North Point Press, 1986], 146. By contrast, the description of Yosif Utkin is appropriate to our discussion of his verse in Chapter 1: 'A certain Jew, probably a Komsomol member' ('Odin evrei, dolzhno byt' komsomolets...') (*Sobranie sochinenii*, I, 296).

4　Nadezhda Mandelstam, *Hope Abandoned*, translated by Max Hayward (Harmondsworth: Penguin Books, 1976), 71–2.

5　Nils Åke Nilsson, 'Osip Mandel'shtam and his Poetry', in *Major Soviet Writers: Essays in Criticism*, ed. by E. J. Brown (Oxford University Press, 1973), 171. Recent studies of Mandelstam that emerged after *glasnost'* include *Zhizn' i tvorchestvo O. E. Mandel'shtama*, ed. S. S. Averintsev *et al* (Voronezh: Izdatel'stvo Voronezhskogo universiteta, 1990); Benedikt Sarnov, *Zalozhnik vechnosti: sluchai Mandel'shtama* (Moscow: Knizhnaia palata, 1990). In English there are Clarence Brown, *Mandelstam* (Cambridge University Press, 1973) and Jane Gary Harris, *Osip Mandelstam* (Boston: G. K. Hall, 1988).

6　Sicher, *Style and Structure*, 87–8. See also Joe Andrew, 'Structure and Style in the Short Story: Babel's "My First Goose"', *Modern Language Review*, 70 (1975): 366–79.

7 Nadezhda Mandelstam, *Hope Against Hope,* translated by Max Hayward (Harmondsworth: Penguin Books, 1975), 289.

8 Mandelstam, *The Noise of Time: The Prose of Osip Mandelstam,* translated by Clarence Brown (San Francisco: North Point Press, 1986), 109. All further references to this edition will be given in brackets.

9 Jane Gary Harris, 'Autobiography and History: Osip Mandelstam's *Noise of Time*', in *Autobiographical Statements in Twentieth-Century Russian Literature,* ed. Jane Gary Harris (Princeton University Press, 1990), 100.

10 See Victor Terras, 'Time Philosophy of Osip Mandel'shtam', *Slavonic and East European Review,* 47 (1969): 344–54, and Gregory Freidin, 'The Whisper of History and the Noise of Time in the Writings of Osip Mandel'shtam', *Russian Review,* 37 (1978): 421–37.

11 Vladimir Nabokov's poetic autobiography *Speak Memory* also speaks of being born with the death of the nineteenth century, but from a different perspective: 'The cradle rocks above an abyss and common sense tells us that our existence is but a brief cradle of light between two eternities of darkness' (*Speak Memory* [New York: Putnam's Sons, 1966], 19). However, both exploit the modernist techniques of recovery of time and the representation of individual consciousness under the fragmenting impact of the upheavals of history in Woolf, Joyce or Proust, discussed by Erich Auerbach in *Mimesis* (New York: Doubleday, 1957): 463–88. See also Jane Gary Harris, 'An Inquiry into the Function of the Autobiographic Mode: Joyce, Mandelstam, Schulz', in *American Contributions to the Ninth International Congress of Slavists (Kiev 1983),* ed. Paul Debreczeny, II (Columbus OH: Slavica, 1983), 201–21.

12 The Jewish prayer shawl *(talit)* is usually worn by married males during morning services and it betokens a post-confirmation membership in the Jewish community. The Bible prescribes a four-cornered fringed garment containing the purplish-blue dye of the shellfish *murex brandaris,* now only remembered in the symbolic black stripes of modern prayer shawls, which are generally woollen, though they may be made of silk and might be discoloured yellow by age and by a repellent memory.

13 Kirill Taranovsky, *Essays on Mandel'shtam* (Cambridge MA: Harvard University Press, 1976), 57–59. The mythopoeic modelling of Petersburg in Mandelstam should be seen in the context of both a response to Bely's symbolist contribution to the mythicizing of the city and the demise of the imperial capital after the Revolution. See also Ann Lisa Crone, 'Echoes of Nietzsche and Mallarmé in Mandel'stam's Metapoetic "Petersburg"', *Russian Literature,* 30 (1991):

405–30; and S. G. Shindin, 'Gorod v khudozhestvennom mire Mandel'shtama: Prostranstvennyi aspekt', *Russian Literature,* 30 (1991): 481–500.

14 'Dve lish' kraski v mire ne poblekli: / V zheltoi – zavist', v krasnoi – neterpen'e' ('Kantsona', in Osip Mandelstam, *Sobranie sochinenii,* 1, 168).

15 Even in *Judenrein* Finland the Jewish smell of money sticks to the Russified merchants the Sharikovs, descendants of Jewish *kantonisty.* Finland is presented as a world apart, clean and cosy, where the family have a dacha (their approved social status symbol); yet Finland's humiliated national right to self-determination does not bring to the poet's mind the demeaning situation of the Jews in the Pale of Settlement.

16 How far we have come from Bialik's bookcase (in 'Before the Bookcase') and from his Hebrew verse which broke with the discourse of the Haskalah and rocked the grandfather's bookcase in 'And if the Angel Should Ask'!

17 See S. Solovev's intriguing colour codes for various Russian writers, 'Tsvet, chislo i russkaia slovesnost'', *Znanie – sila,* 1 (1971): 54–6.

18 See Claire Cavanagh, 'Synthetic Nationality: Mandel'shtam and Chaadaev', *Slavic Review,* 49, 4 (1990): 597–610. On Mandelstam and Chaadaev see also Carol Avins, *Border Crossings: The West and Russian Identity in Soviet Literature, 1917–1934* (Berkeley: University of California Press, 1983), 17–27.

19 Louis Greenberg, *The Jews in Russia: The Struggle for Emancipation* (New York: Schocken, 1976), 1, 148.

20 Harold Fisch, *Jerusalem and Albion: The Hebraic Factor in Seventeenth-Century Literature* (London: Routledge Kegan Paul, 1964), 67. Other aspects of these issues have been discussed in Moses Hess's classic *Rome and Jerusalem* and by Paul Eidelberg in his *Jerusalem versus Athens* (Lanham MD: University Press of America, 1983).

21 Nadezhda Mandelstam, *Hope Abandoned,* 41.

22 On the opposition of the Hellenist *hearth* to the Hebraic non-culture see Taranovsky, *Essays on Mandel'shtam,* 50. On Mandelstam's understanding of Hellenism and of its relation to Christian art see Ryszard Przybylski, *An Essay on the Poetry of Osip Mandelstam: God's Grateful Guest* (Ann Arbor: Ardis, 1987), 45–78. See also Leon Burnett's comparison of the respective appropriation of Greek culture by Mandelstam and Keats, 'Heirs of Eternity: An Essay on the Poetry of Keats and Mandel'shtam', *Modern Language Review,* 76, 2 (1981): 396–419. The appropriation of another's word, the making *svoi* of another culture, is, in Mandelstam's case, a homecoming of a poetic Odysseus to Hellas, not to Judea.

23 In the parodic 'Zhil Aleksandr Gertsovich' (1931) Mandelstam mocks the Jewish musician who turns out Schubert 'like a clean diamond':

> On Shuberta naverchival,
> Kak chistyi brilliant.

In playing with his patronym, the poet sugests this 'son of a heart' is also a son of a bitch. But the poem ends more equivocally, in resignation,

> Vse, Aleksandr Serdtsevich,
> Zavercheno davno...
> Bros', Aleksandr Skvertsevich,
> Chego tam, vse ravno... *(Sobranie sochinenii,* 1, 163.)

See Nadezhda Mandelstam, *Hope Against Hope,* 210–11. Maurice Friedberg gives this as an example of flight from Judaism and compares a poem by Tuwim on the Chagallian theme of a fiddler on the roof ('Jewish Contributions to Soviet Literature', in *The Jews in Soviet Russia since 1917,* ed. Lionel Kochan, 3rd edition [Oxford University Press, 1978], 223).

24 A thorough semantic analysis of Mandelstam's lexicon has been undertaken by Iu. Levin in his 'O nekotorykh chertakh plana soderzhaniia v poeticheskikh tekstakh: Materialy k izucheniiu poetiki O. Mandel'shtama', *International Journal of Slavic Linguistics and Poetics,* 12 (1969): 106–64. The semantic fields and binary oppositions are infinitely complicated by Mandelstam's subtextual allusions and intertextual references, as many scholars have shown.

25 Maurice Friedberg, 'The Jewish Search in Russian Literature', *Prooftexts,* 4, 1 (1984): 96. However, Leon Yudkin asserts that the negative portrayal of Judaism in *Noise of Time* does not in any way obscure the poet's recognition that it is his source *(Jewish Writing and Identity in the Twentieth Century* [London: Croom Helm, 1982], 65). In *Defenses of the Imagination* (Philadelphia: Jewish Publication Society of America, 1977, 25–46), Robert Alter speaks of 'hyperacculturation' as the response of Mandelstam, as well as of Babel, to the malaise of a stigmatized cultural and ethnic minority. See also Arthur A. Cohen's interesting, though ultimately speculative, *Osip Emilievich Mandelstam: An Essay in Antiphon* (Ann Arbor: Ardis, 1974). A somewhat tendentious polemic on the 'Jewishness' of Mandelstam's poetry can be found in Maia Kaganskaia, 'Osip Mandel'shtam – poet iudeiskii', *Sion,* 20 (1977): 174–95; and T. Kamneva, 'O stat'e M. Kaganskoi', *22,* 1 (1978): 218–23. A scholarly and commendably clear overview can be found in Kathryn Brown, 'Order and Chaos: Religious Issues in the Works of Osip Mandelstam', *Menorah: Australian Journal of Jewish Studies,* 2, 1 (1988): 28–41. Brown distinguishes between Mandelstam's formal conversion to Christianity

and his mythological thinking about cultural concepts of Christianity in a social model of order and chaos. Donald Rayfield has also written about this in 'The Flight from Chaos', *European Judaism*, 6 (Winter 1971–2): 37–43.

26 'The Egyptian Stamp', in *The Noise of Time: The Prose of Osip Mandelstam*, ed. and translated by Clarence Brown (San Francisco: North Point Press, 1986), 133.

27 Parnakh made a minor career writing about dance and introduced jazz to the Russian public. He even invented a dance. See *Russkii Berlin, 1921–1923*, ed. Lazar Fleishman, R. Hughes and O. Raevsky-Hughes (Paris: YMCA Press, 1983), 312–13; and A. Bakhrakh, *Po pamiati, po zapisiam* (Paris, 1979), 166–70. Parnakh also wrote articles for American-Jewish and French magazines about contemporary Russian poets, including Pasternak and Mandelstam himself.

28 *Severnye zapiski*, 4–5 (1916): 242–3. See Diana L. Burgin, *Sophia Parnok: The Life and Work of Russia's Sappho* (New York University Press, 1994).

29 For a discussion of the literary lineage of 'The Egyptian Stamp' see Clarence Brown, 'Introduction', in his edition of *The Noise of Time: The Prose of Osip Mandelstam* (San Francisco: North Point Press, 1986), 37–55; and see also Daphne West, *Mandelstam: The Egyptian Stamp* (Birmingham, England: Birmingham University, 1980). Scholars associated with the Moscow-Tartu school of semiotics, Iu. Levin, Dmitri Segal, R. Timenchik, V. N. Toporov and T. V. Tsivian, have written about the inter-referentiality of Mandelstam's writings and have given 'The Egyptian Stamp' as an example of a polyphonic dialogue of Mandelstam with Akhmatova as well as his literary forefathers (see their joint publication, 'Russkaia semanticheskaia poetika kak potentsial'naia kul'turnaia paradigma', *Russian Literature*, 7–8 [1974]: 47–82). They also point to the resonance of Akhmatova's *Beg vremeni* ('Flight of Time') in the title of Mandelstam's *Shum vremeni*. On the breaking up of semantic space in 'The Egyptian Stamp' see Dmitri Segal, 'Voprosy poeticheskoi organizatsii semantiki v proze Mandel'shtama', in *Russian Poetics*, ed. T. Eekman and D. S. Worth (Columbus OH: Slavica, 1983): 325–52.

30 Brown, 'Introduction', 50–1.

31 Nadezhda Mandelstam, *Hope Against Hope*, 120–8.

32 Jane Gary Harris, 'Introduction: The Impulse and the Text', in Osip Mandelstam, *The Complete Critical Prose and Letters*, ed. Jane Gary Harris (Ann Arbor: Ardis, 1979), 4. See also Jane Gary Harris, 'Mandel'shtam's Aesthetic Performance', *Canadian-American Slavic Studies*, 19, 4 (1985): 426–42; Charles Isenberg, *Substantial Proofs of Being: Osip Mandelstam's Literary Prose* (Columbus OH: Slavica, 1987).

33 Babel advised Mandelstam to drop translation work and helped him

get work at the VUFKU film studios in Kiev (letter to his father of February-March 1929 in the archives of Mandelstam's younger brother Evgenii, published in *Novyi mir*, 10 [1987]: 201–2). Babel had some experience editing and revising filmscripts in order to earn money and gain time for his own work, which was becoming increasingly difficult to publish.

34 Clare Cavanagh, 'The Poetics of Jewishness: Mandelstam, Dante and the "Honorable Calling of Jew"', *Slavic and East European Journal*, 35, 3 (1991): 321. See also Clare Cavanagh, *Osip Mandelstam and the Modernist Creation of Tradition* (Princeton University Press, 1994).

35 Marina Tsvetaeva, *Sochineniia*, 1 (Moscow: Khudozhestvennaia literatura, 1984), 389. Tsvetaeva's phrase 'Poets are yids' was adopted by Ehrenburg, as we will see in Chapter 6, and has become almost commonplace in discussions of the Russian poet as martyr.

36 Cavanagh, 'The Poetics of Jewishness', 323–30.

37 Dmitri Segal has located further comments by Mandelstam on this affair concealed in a foreword to a translation he did from Bernard Lecache, in which he identifies the French Dreyfusards with antiquated feudalism and sees French-Jewish writers as a cultural bridge of assimilation in the spirit of Mandelstam's ideas on Hellenism and Hebraism ('Eshche odin neizvestnyi tekst Mandel'shtama?', *Slavica Hierosolymitana*, 3 [1978]: 174–192). See also the poet's letter to his wife of 24 February 1930, *Sobranie sochinenii*, III, 259.

38 Mandelstam, 'The Age', *Selected Poems*, translated by Clarence Brown and W. S. Merwin (Harmondsworth: Penguin Books, 1977), 69.

> Vek moi, zver' moi, kto sumeet
> Zaglianut' v tvoi zrachki
> I svoeiu krov'iu skleit
> Dvukh stoletii pozvonki? *(Sobranie sochinenii*, 1, 102).

39 Mandelstam's poetic image of Kerensky as a crucified Jesus figure and his writings in the Social-Revolutionary press in the cold famine winter of 1917–18 negated the conventional Bolshevik propaganda image of the Revolution as a springtime renewal. A poem of May 1918, 'Sumerki svobody' ('Twilight of Freedom') is more complex – see Dmitri Segal, '"Sumerki svobody": Mandel'shtam i russkaia ezhednevnaia pechat' 1917–1918 godov', *Druzhba narodov*, 1 (1991): 243–47; a fuller version previously appeared in the Paris journal *Minuvshee*, 3 (1987). Segal connects the motif of a cold spring with Mandelstam's theme of the dying of Petropolis and another image of a spring disaster, the image of ice in *The Egyptian Stamp*. See also Nils Åke Nilsson, *Art, Society, Revolution, 1917–1921* (Stockholm: Almqvist, 1979).

40 Personal communication to Nikita Struve cited in his *Ossip Mandelstam* (Paris: Institut d'études slaves, 1982), 101. However, Struve

argues that there are grounds to suppose Mandelstam converted out of faith, and cites four poems of 1910 with overt christological themes as part of his claim for an inherently Christian art in Mandelstam's poetry (see especially *Ossip Mandelstam*, 97–146).

41 Letter from Paris to Gippius, 27 April 1908 in *Kamen'*, ed. L. Ginzburg, A. Mets, S. Vasilenko and Iu. Freidin (Leningrad: Nauka, 1990), 204.

42 Clarence Brown, *Mandelstam* (Cambridge University Press, 1973), 46. When asked about his namesake, the famous ophthalmologist, Mandelstam claimed to have no interest in his kinsfolk; but Nadezhda Mandelstam gives a rather different impression of Mandelstam's meeting with the same famous namesake at Terioki at about the same period. Mandelstam was interested to discover his genealogy, including a rabbinical line, in the family tree of the wife of a Yalta watchmaker, though this was in later years, during the New Economic Plan (NEP), when 'a hundred flowers were still in bloom, but the scythe was already being sharpened' *(Hope Abandoned*, 573–7). In a later poem of 1935 (as mentioned above) Mandelstam related to his own name both as immortalized in a street named for him and as the sewer which was associated with Jewish filth in *Noise of Time*.

43 Ibid., 32–4.

44 Ibid., 43–4.

45 *Hope Against Hope*, 210.

46 Evgenii Mandelstam has testified about his brother's relationship with his father. Mandelstam for a long time took little interest in his father's spiritual or intellectual background as a failed *maskil* who had not been able to finish his studies in Berlin for want of money. But in later years there was a rapprochement, and Osip Mandelstam exchanged ideas with his father and took home the philosophical treatise which his father had written in German ('Osip Mandel'shtam: poslednie tvorcheskie gody', *Novyi mir*, 10 [1987]: 202). This accommodation with his father coincided with the deterioration in conditions for writers and his own 'Dreyfus Affair' at the end of the twenties. A letter of 12 December 1936 shows Mandelstam's warm feelings for his father and his nostalgia in the adversity of exile and ill health for his parental home (*Novyi mir*, 10 [1987]: 206).

47 Translated by R. H. Morrison, *Poems from Mandelstam* (Rutherford NJ: Associated University Presses, 1990), 64–5:

> Iz omuta zlogo i viazkogo
> Ia vyros, trostinkoi shursha,
> I strastno, i tomno, i laskovo
> Zapretnoiu zhizn'iu dysha.
> (Mandelstam, *Sobranie sochinenii*, 1, 10).

48 Omry Ronen traced the Judaic theme back to these early poems in 'Mandelshtam, Osip Emilyevich', *Encyclopedia Judaica Yearbook 1973* (Jerusalem: Keter, 1973), 294; and *Introduction to Mandelstam* (Jerusalem, 1983). Ronen connects the autobiographical conflict in 'Iz omuta zlogo i viazkogo...' with Tiutchev's 'rodimyi khaos' in his 'O chem ty voesh', vetr nochnoi...', a reference which looks foward to Mandelstam's own Judaic chaos. Taranovsky identifies the source of Mandelstam's use of Pascal's *roseau pensant* in another poem by Tiutchev, 'Pevuchest' est' v morskikh volnakh', and points out that Mandelstam's *omut* ironically opposes Tiutchev's *more (Essays on Mandel'shtam, 52)*. See also Iu. M. Lotman's review of Taranovsky's book, 'Semantika konteksta i podteksta v poezii Mandel'shtama', *International Journal of Slavic Linguistics and Poetics*, 29 (1985): 133–42. A detailed comparison of Mandelstam and Tiutchev which throws much light on their concepts of empty space, freedom, disharmony and chaos is to be found in E. Toddes, 'Mandel'shtam i Tiutchev', *International Journal of Slavic Linguistics and Poetics*, 17 (1974): 59–85.

49   Ni sladosti v pytke ne vedaiu
                   Ni smysla ia v nei ne ishchu;
                   No blizkoi, poslednei pobedoiu,
                   Byt' mozhet, za vse otomshchu.
                   (Sobranie sochinenii, I, 409).

50 Aleksandr Pushkin, *Eugene Onegin: A Novel in Verse,* revised edition (London: Routlege & Kegan Paul, 1975), I, 248.
                   Ne dai ostyt' dushe poeta,
                   Ozhestochit'sia, ocherstvet',
                   I nakonets okamenet'
                   V mertviashchem upoen'e sveta,
                   V sem omute, gde s vami ia
                   Kupaius', milye druz'ia!

Walter Arndt in his translation renders *omut* as 'that vile quicksand' (Alexander Pushkin, *Eugene Onegin: A Novel in Verse,* revised edition [New York: Dutton, 1963], 160).

51 'On the Development of Revolutionary Ideas in Russia', in *Russian Views of Pushkin,* ed. D. J. Richards and C. R. S. Cockrell (Oxford: William Meeuws, 1976), 23.

52 Gregory Freidin, *Coat of Many Colors: Osip Mandelstam and his Mythologies of Self-Presentation* (Berkeley: University of California Press, 1987), 48. Freidin reads the pool as a mirror which transmutes the poetic self into aesthetic material (50), a self-disliking image of a St Petersburg snob (52). For Freidin 'Neutolimye slova' is a 'most telling account of frustration stemming from a divided loyalty' between Judaism and Christianity, Law and Grace, based on Paul's

Epistle to the Galatians and later developed by Augustine. Mandelstam, argues Freidin, would doubtless have read at the Tenishev School the seventeenth-century sermon on this subject by Metropolitan Hilarion, *Slovo o zakone i blagodati* (302 note). The original publication of 1915 reads 'Neumolimye slova...'

53 Taranovsky, *Essays on Mandel'shtam*, 150–2. On the sun in Mandelstam's imagery and especially the associations with yellow Petersburg see Steven Broyde, *Osip Mandelstam and his Age* (Cambridge MA: Harvard University Press, 1975), 76–102. Compare 'Chernoe solntse' in Mandelstam, *Sobranie sochinenii*, III, 404–11, and also the poem 'Kak etikh pokryval i etogo ubora...' (1915–16), where the day/night and passion/Passion themes are more complex and the black sun rises for the mother: 'I dlia materi vliublennoi / Solntse chernoe vzoidet'. In another poem, 'Kogda v teploi nochi zamiraet' (1918), the burial of the nocturnal sun in Petersburg is connected with the national apocalypse, for the destruction of Judea, deaf to prophecy, prefigures the fate of Petersburg. Apart from Nerval's black sun of Melancholia, there is a connection with Mandelstam's black sun of Phaedra which goes back to Mandelstam's 1915 essay on Pushkin and Skriabin, where he warns that Judea might seize the opportunity of the struggle of Hellenism with Rome to turn back Time and put an end to Christianity and to Art: 'Hellas must be saved from Rome. If Rome wins, it won't be Rome winning but Judaism. Judaism always stood behind Rome's back and only awaits its moment to triumph with the terrible unnatural move. History will reverse the direction of Time – the black sun of Phaedra' (Mandelstam, *Sobranie sochinenii* [Paris: YMCA Press, 1981], IV, 100.) The nocturnal sun of Pushkin's burial in a cathedral may throw light on the poem about the burial of the poet's mother (although Nadezhda Mandelstam has reservations about this in *Hope Abandoned*, 131–2). See on the Phaedra and Night Sun theme in Freidin, *Coat of Many Colors*, 56–83.

54 Taranovsky, *Essays on Mandel'shtam*, 54–5.

55 In his extensive discussion of the blacks, yellows and black-yellow proper of Mandelstam's Judaic theme, Taranovsky points out that the hostile and unhealthy black-yellow colour of the Imperial standard in 'Dvortsovaia ploshchad'' (1915) shares the eschatological allusions associated with Petersburg *(Essays on Mandel'shtam*, 57), and we might notice also the phrase 'V chernom omute stolitsy' that belongs to the same dark *omut* in which are depicted the colour and space of Judaism.

56 Mandelstam, *Sobranie sochinenii*, I, 70.

57 Nadezhda Mandelstam, *Hope Abandoned*, 134. The poem's dedication to A.V. Kartashev, the former Minister of Religions in the Provi-

sional Government and an Orthodox theologian, is adduced by
Freidin as evidence for a reading of the poem casting Russia in the
role of the blind Jews who did not accept Jesus as the messiah. The
priests according to Freidin's interpretation are the theosophian
symbolists Bely, Ivanov and V.V. Gippius. Per Bodin thinks the
poem also refers to another Joseph, Joseph of Arimathaea, vener-
ated in the Russian Orthodox Easter liturgy, who was arrested like
Kartashev for his religious beliefs, and concludes that the poem
marks a turning point in Mandelstam's acceptance of Christianity
and rejection of Judaism ('Understanding the Signs: An Analysis of
Osip Mandel'shtam's Poem "Sredi sveshchennikov" ', *Scando-Slavica*,
31 [1985]: 31–9).

58 Nadezhda Mandelstam identifies herself as the woman whom
Mandelstam is addressing in this poem, who chooses a Jew and joins
with him as his bride; she considered this an expression of Osip
Mandelstam's characteristic desire to have her merge with him
completely. The poet was not originally certain to whom the poem
was directed; then it seemed to him that Nadezhda Mandelstam
would come to him in the manner of Lot's daughters *(Hope
Abandoned*, 267), a manner which suggests not the unloved Leah but
the nocturnal Jewish *succuba*, Lilit. On the merging of the Biblical
Leah with the incestuous daughters of Lot see Taranovsky, *Essays on
Mandel'shtam*, 59–64 and Freidin, *Coat of Many Colors*, 124–53.
Compare also the preceding poems in *Tristia*, 'V khrustal'nom
omute kakaia krutizna!' (1919, a variation on the 'evil pool' theme),
and 'Sestry – tiazhest' i nezhnost'...' (1920, where the sisters might
conceivably be Leah and Rachel, who incestuously shared the same
husband). Both poems make the familiar Mandelstamian juxtaposition of heaviness and lightness – of stone and of air – a central
aesthetic and spiritual opposition in his architectural poem building.

59 'Net, ty poliubish' iudeia, / Ischeznesh' v nem – i Bog s toboi'
(Sobranie sochinenii, 1, 77). The last phrase could be read alternately as
blessing or curse.

60 Nadezhda Mandelstam, *Hope Abandoned*, 562–4. A letter to his father
of 12 December 1936 mentions Mandelstam's interest in 'Spanish
poets', whom he has been reading in the library *(Novyi mir*, 10 [1987]:
206), but they are not named and there is no reason to suppose that
they were Jews or Marranos.

61 Taranovsky, *Essays on Mandel'shtam*, 154 n. 21.

62 Edward Burman, *The Inquisition: The Hammer of Heresy* (Wellingbor-
ough: Aquarian Press, 1984), 145–6. On Luis de León see Aubrey
Bell, *Luis de León: A Study of the Spanish Renaissance* (Oxford University
Press, 1925). Bell rejects the myth of León as a 'monk in ecstasy' and

portrays him as a key figure of the Spanish Renaissance, one of whose achievements was to restore the authority of the Hebrew Bible in his translation of the Song of Songs and to revive the spirit of Hebraism.

63 Parnakh, *Ispanskie i portugal'skie poety, zhertvy inkvizitsii* (Moscow-Leningrad: Academia, 1934), 59. Parnakh had previously published a French version of this book, *L'Inquisition* (Paris: Rieder, 1930).

64 Parnakh, 60. I have translated from Parnakh's Russian simply to emphasize the aptness of the poem to Mandelstam's situation, surrounded by lies and envy.

65 'Kiev' (1926), in Mandelstam, *Sobranie sochinenii*, III, 6. A letter to his father of February-March 1929, however, describes Kiev as *chuzhoi gorod* (an 'alien city'), where there was nothing apart from a Russian newspaper (*Novyi mir*, 10 [1987]: 201–2).

66 'Iosif, prodannyi v Egipet, / Ne mog sil'nee toskovat'!' (Mandelstam, 'Otravlen khleb i vozdukh vypit...', *Sobranie sochinenii*, I, 34). Joseph fits the archetypal poet-Jesus figure sinking in his pool prefigured in the spatial modelling of spiritual as well as physical ascent and descent in Genesis: brought *down* by his brothers into the snake-infested pit, he is later *raised* from the 'pit' in the Egyptian jail by Pharaoh. We have already had occasion to comment on the association of constriction with the Cabbalistic concept of 'Egypt'. Jeremiah also uses the image of a pool of water (as mentioned p. 130 above), and we find in Isaiah 24, 17–18 a similar association of falling into a pit with national disaster.

67 George Steiner, 'Our Homeland the Text', *Salmagundi*, 46 (1985): 4–25.

68 Nadezhda Mandelstam, *Hope Abandoned*, 613–23.

69   Ia pokinu krai giperboreev,
    Chtoby zren'em napitat' sud'by razviazku,
    Ia skazhu 'seliam' nachal'niku evreev
    Za ego malinovuiu lasku.
    (Mandelstam, 'Kantsona', *Sobranie sochinenii*, I, 168).

The Arabic greeting *salaam* might not be out of place, considering the affection by some Zionist leaders of Arab dress and manners. The exact meaning of the alternative Hebrew *selah* which Nadezhda Mandelstam gives in her version is obscure, but as part of the song of the Levites in the Temple it may suggest a return to the 'Young Levite' motif. A more important question is the identity of the 'nachal'nik evreev' (note *evrei* and not *iudei)*. Mandelstam may have been thinking of Herbert Samuel, British High Commissioner of Mandatory Palestine (1920–5), and of the Fourth Aliyah, the mass immigration from Eastern and Central Europe. Taranovsky understands the references here and in 'Skazhi mne, chertezhnik pustyni...' ('Tell Me, Draftsman of the Desert', 1933) to be to the Jewish pioneers conquering the desert and, despite the lack of interest in the draftsman's 'Judaic concerns' in the latter poem, he finds evidence for Mandelstam's 'new interest in the fate and destiny of the Jewish people' *(Essays on Mandel'shtam,* 66–7). Heine, too, had dreamt of a pastoral life in Arabian sands (letter of 14 April 1822 to Christian Sethe), but here there is much scepticism in Mandelstam's poetic metaphor of building on shifting sands, an expression of Judaic instability and childish delusion in line with his aesthetic geology. The sterile sands, like those of the Judaic Sahara at Riga in *Noise of Time* and at Petersburg's *Peski* in 'The Egyptian Stamp', recall the allegory in Canto XIV of Dante's *Inferno* and hence suggest further criticism of Judea.

70 Jennifer Baines, *Mandel'shtam: The Later Poetry* (Cambridge University Press, 1976), 32–5. On the referentiality of the poet and his Time in the Armenia poems see Peter Zeeman, 'Reference and Interpretation, with Examples from Osip Mandelstam', *Russian Literature*, 18, 3 (1985): 257–98.

71 Compare the raspberry waistcoats of Babel's Odessa Jewish gangsters, though one is also worn by Savitskii in *Red Cavalry*.

5. THE FATHER, THE SON AND HOLY RUSSIA: BORIS PASTERNAK, HERMANN COHEN AND THE RELIGION OF DOCTOR ZHIVAGO

1 *Boris Pasternak: The Poet and His Politics* (Cambridge MA: Harvard University Press, 1990).

2 Donald Davie, 'Introduction', in *Pasternak: Modern Judgements*, ed. Donald Davie and Angela Livingstone (London: Macmillan, 1969), 2.

3 See Inger Gilbert, 'Text into Origin: Apprenticeship of Joyce as Artificer, Rilke as Prodigal Son', *Comparative Literature Studies*, 26, 4 (1989), 304–23.

4 John Pilling, *Autobiography and Imagination: Studies in Self-Scrutiny* (London: Routledge Kegan Paul, 1981), 4–7.

5 Pasternak writing in the journal *Chitatel' i pisatel'* in 1928, quoted in Boris Pasternak, *Ob iskusstve* (Moscow: Iskusstvo, 1990), 368.

6 Fleishman, *The Poet and his Politics*, 158–60.

7 Boris Thomson, *The Premature Revolution: Russian Literature and Society, 1917–1946* (London: Weidenfeld and Nicolson, 1972), 268–9.

8 Fleishman, *The Poet and his Politics*, 158.

9 Pilling, *Autobiography and Imagination*, 51–2.

10 Krystyna Pomorska, *Themes and Variations in Pasternak's Poetics* (Lisse:

Peter de Ridder Press, 1975), 64. See the discussion of the Russian model of the Poet in the Preface to the present book. A different view can be found in Serafima Roll, 'The Force of Creative Negation: The Author in Boris Pasternak's *Safe-Conduct*', *Canadian Slavonic Papers*, 34, 1–1 (1992): 79–96. Roll argues that the ideas of Death and Sacrifice in *A Safe-Conduct* are associated with the negation of the author, in the manner described by Barthes and Foucault, whereas I am arguing that Pasternak's 'rebirth' reinvents pre-Revolutionary models of the Poet, albeit in a modernist mode. See also Serafima Roll, 'Writing One's Self: Boris Pasternak's Autobiography *Ochrannaia gramota*', *Russian Literature*, 26 (1989): 407–16.

11 Boris Pasternak, *The Voice of Prose: Early Prose and Autobiography*, ed. Christopher Barnes, 1 (New York: Grove Press, 1986), 30.

12 When, in *Noise of Time*, Osip Mandelstam unearthed the textual geology of his parents' bookcase, the poet similarly saw his own intertextual genealogy in German and Russian lyricism in preference to the Judaic Chaos. See Chapter 4 above on Mandelstam's account of himself as a *raznochinets* through the books he has read.

13 Pilling, *Autobiography and Imagination*, 53. Pilling urges us not to attach too much importance to the influence of Rilke, apart from the way in which external things illuminate internal feelings.

14 *Autobiography and Imagination*, 54–5.

15 Ibid., 57.

16 Roman Jakobson, 'Randbemerkungen zur Prosa des Dichters Pasternak', *Slavische Rundschau*, 8 (1935); translated as 'Marginal Notes on the Prose of the Poet Pasternak', in *Pasternak: Modern Judgements*, ed. Donald Davie and Angela Livingstone (London: Macmillan, 1969), 135–51.

17 *Autobiography and Imagination*, 57–62.

18 Guy de Mallac, *Boris Pasternak: His Life and Art* (Norman: University of Oklahoma Press, 1981), 18–31.

19 Letter to Khaim Nakhman Bialik of February 1923 (apparently unsent), *Slavica Hierosolymitana*, 1 (1977): 307. Emphasis in the original.

20 In conversations with the present author in 1979, Boris Pasternak's sisters Lydia and Josephine vigorously denied that the family had any leanings toward Zionism; but Fleishman adduces evidence that the artist had some sympathy for the Zionist cause during his Berlin days, though this was no more a political commitment than his approval of the Revolution in Russia which removed the Tsarist order (*The Poet and his Politics*, 16).

21 Lazar Fleishman, 'K publikatsii pis'ma L. O. Pasternaka k Bialiku', *Slavica Hierosolymitana*, 1 (1977): 309–16.

22 George Gibian, '*Doctor Zhivago*, Russia and Leonid Pasternak's *Rembrandt*', in *The Russian Novel from Pushkin to Pasternak*, ed. John Garrard (New Haven: Yale University Press, 1983), 203–23. A Russian version appeared as 'Leonid Pasternak i Boris Pasternak: Polemika ottsa i syna', *Voprosy literatury*, 9 (1988): 104–29. This issue of the leading journal of literary criticism contained and itself generated a vicious debate over Pasternak's 'national identity'; see the discussion of this debate in the context of Russian intellectual anti-Semitism in Felix Dreizin, *The Russian Soul and the Jew: Essays in Literary Ethnocentrism* (Lanham MD: University Press of America, 1990), 147–51.

23 Mallac, *Boris Pasternak: His Life and Art*, 55.

24 Pasternak, *The Voice of Prose*, 40–1.

25 Cited in Evgenii B. Pasternak, *Materialy dlia biografii* (Moscow: Sovetskii pisatel', 1989), 157.

26 See Victor Erlich, 'Introduction: Categories of Passion', in *Pasternak: A Collection of Critical Essays*, ed. Victor Erlich (Englewood Cliffs: Prentice-Hall), 1978, 10–18 and S. Schwarzband, 'Pasternak's *Marburg*: On the Evolution of Poetic Structure,' *Scottish Slavonic Review*, 8 (1987): 57–74. Lazar Fleishman discusses the Marburg episode at length and shows how the variants of the poem 'Marburg' document the change in attitude toward Cohen (*Boris Pasternak v dvadtsatye gody* [Munich: Wilhelm Fink, 1980], 232–51).

27 Christopher Barnes, *Boris Pasternak: A Literary Biography, Volume One: 1890–1928* (Cambridge University Press, 1989), 81–9.

28 Boris Pasternak, *Perepiska s Ol'goi Freidenberg*, ed. Elliott Mossman (New York: Harcourt Brace Jovanovich, 1980). Translated in *The Correspondence of Boris Pasternak and Olga Freidenberg, 1910–1954*, ed. Elliott Mossman (New York: Harcourt Brace Jovanovich, 1982). Pasternak's long correspondence with Olga Freidenberg is revealing and frank; he termed it an 'epistolatory *contredanse*' and it continued over the many years when Olga Freidenberg fell under ideological suspicion during the Stalin years. It has since been published in Russia in *Perepiska Borisa Pasternaka* (Moscow: Khudozhestvennaia literatura, 1990).

29 Isaiah Berlin, 'The Energy of Pasternak', in *Pasternak: A Collection of Critical Essays*, 40.

30 Nils Åke Nilsson, 'Life as Ecstasy and Sacrifice: Two Poems by Boris Pasternak', in *Pasternak: A Collection of Critical Essays*, 63–4. Barnes writes that the 'whole aesthetics of creativity set out [in *A Safe-Conduct*] showed a broad implicit kinship with the Austrian poet, and

especially with his quasi-autobiographical *Malte Laurids Brigge'* (Barnes, *Boris Pasternak: A Literary Biography*, 1, 397). While at work on the first part of *A Safe-Conduct* Pasternak had been translating two requiems by Rilke, 'Für eine Freundin' and 'Für Wolf Graf von Kalckreuth', both dealing with the theme of the death of the artist which very much concerned Pasternak (Barnes, *Boris Pasternak: A Literary Biography*, 1, 397–8).

31 Letter to Vladimir Pozner of 1929, cited in Barnes, *Boris Pasternak: A Literary Biography*, 1, 410 note. The Proustian view of time past also had an affinity with Mandelstam's *Noise of Time*, and it was precisely at the time of writing *A Safe-Conduct* that Pasternak grew close to Mandelstam. The interweaving of philosophy and literature makes us think also of T. S. Eliot, who had planned to study at Marburg and wrote his Harvard thesis on Bradley; in *The Waste Land* the sentient intrasubjectivity of the poetic voice and its identification not with an identifiable persona, but with the objects and voices around it suggest, for all the difference in language and temperament, an affinity with the perception of time and space in *A Safe-Conduct*.

32 Cited in Evgenii Pasternak, *Materialy dlia biografii*, 163.

33 The theme of the paper which Pasternak presented at Cohen's seminar was indeed the Nietzschean 'I' and 'true subjectivity' in the legal framework of the State. He wrote to his parents that he was working on the idea of man as subject of Law *(Materialy dlia biografii*, 159–60). V.V. Ivanov has commented on Pasternak's use of Cohen's neo-Kantian vocabulary, such as 'postupki', and the presence in poems written during and after the Marburg period (for instance, 'Poema o blizhnei') of a dialogism with Cohen's discussion of the Biblical commandment to love one's neighbour as oneself (unpublished remarks at the Fifth International Bakhtin Conference, Manchester University, July 1991). Cohen's neo-Kantian vocabulary enjoyed dissemination among Russian philosophers and together with the ideas of Martin Buber left their mark on the Bakhtin circle (for a useful discussion of the latter connection see Katerina Clark and Michael Holquist, *Mikhail Bakhtin* [Cambridge MA: Harvard University Press, 1984], 63–94).

34 L. O. Pasternak, *Rembrandt i evreistvo v ego tvorchestve* (Berlin: S. L. Salzmann Verlag, 1923), 72–7.

35 Fleishman speculates that the story of the Abarbanel family had particular significance for the Pasternaks after the Revolution, when the family was separated by political borders. Isaac Abarbanel's eldest son Yehudah fled to Naples, but was forced to abandon his son, later baptized in Portugal. The story was told by Yehuda Abarbanel – writing as Leone Ebreo – in a Hebrew elegy, 'Elegy

about Time' (1503), which was translated, as noted in the previous chapter, by Valentin Parnakh himself *(The Poet and his Politics,* 18–19). If the parallel has implications, I believe it is not for Boris Pasternak's story about being baptized, as Fleishman suggests, but for the lessons of Spanish Jewish poets for their descendents in Russia, as I have indicated Parnakh was trying to convey in his public presentation of both Spanish Jewish poets and contemporaries such as Mandelstam and Pasternak (see Chapter 4 above).

36 Barnes, *Boris Pasternak: A Literary Biography,* I, 2.
37 Dmitri Segal, 'Evreiskaia tema u Borisa Pasternaka', *Narod i zemlia,* 7 (1988): 189.
38 Barnes, *Boris Pasternak: A Literary Biography* I, 13, 16.
39 Lazar Fleishman, 'K publikatsii pis'ma L. O. Pasternaka k Bialiku', *Slavica Hierosolymitana,* I (1977): 309–16.
40 Barnes, *Boris Pasternak: A Literary Biography* , I, 27.
41 Cited in Jacqueline Proyart, 'Predislovie', in Boris Pasternak, *Sochineniia,* I (Ann Arbor: University of Michigan Press, 1961), xi.
42 Lecture at the Centenary Pasternak conference, Oxford, 1990. Salys has written on the biographical and aesthetic aspects of Boris Pasternak's attitude to his father as a role-model in 'Boris Pasternak on Leonid Pasternak and the Critics: Two Early Texts', *Russian Language Journal,* 42 (1988): 147–8.
43 Letter of 21 December 1917, cited in Barnes, *Boris Pasternak: A Literary Biography* , I, 28.
44 Gladkov, *Meetings with Pasternak* (London: Collins and Harvill, 1977), 73.
45 Ibid., 134.
46 Isaiah Berlin, *Personal Impressions* (London: Hogarth Press, 1980), 179.
47 Olga Ivinskaia, *A Captive of Time: My Years with Pasternak* (London, 1979), 149.
48 Evgenii Pasternak, *Boris Pasternak: Materialy dlia biografii,* 163.
49 Fleishman, *The Poet and his Politics,* 19.
50 Letter to Olga Freidenberg of 16 November 1928, in *The Correspondence of Boris Pasternak and Olga Freidenberg, 1910–1954,* 115.
51 Guy de Mallac, *Boris Pasternak: His Life and Art,* 331.
52 Fleishman, *The Poet and His Politics,* 259–67.
53 Judith Stora, 'Pasternak et le judaïsme', *Cahiers du Monde Russe et Soviétique,* 9, 3–4 (1968): 353–64. Human self-sacrifice is sanctioned only in extreme situations where the sole alternative is to commit a heinous crime such as incest, idolatry or murder.
54 Pasternak cited in Gladkov, *Meetings,* 134. For a discussion of metaphors of history in *War and Peace* and *Doctor Zhivago* see Nicola

Chiaromonte, *The Paradox of History* (revised edition, Philadelphia: Pennsylvania State University Press, 1985) and Elliott Mossman, 'Metaphors of History in *War and Peace* and *Doctor Zhivago*', in *Literature and History: Theoretical Problems and Russian Case Studies*, ed. Gary Saul Morson (Stanford University Press, 1986), 247–62.

55 See Roger Anderson, 'The Railroad in *Doktor Zhivago*', *Slavic and East European Journal*, 31, 4 (1987): 503–19. David Bethea has linked this motif with the Apocalyptic horse in his *The Shape of Apocalypse in Modern Russian Fiction* (Princeton, 1989), 243–56.

56 Boris Pasternak, *Doctor Zhivago*, translated by Max Hayward and Manya Harari (New York: New American Library, 1960), 13. Further references to this edition will be given in brackets.

57 For a christological interpretation of this scene see Mary F. Rowland and Paul Rowland, *Pasternak's Doctor Zhivago* (Carbondale: South Illinois University Press, 1967), 35–43.

58 In a letter to Olga Freidenberg of 13 October 1946, Boris Pasternak called *Doctor Zhivago* an attempt to 'square accounts' with Judaism *(The Correspondence of Boris Pasternak and Olga Freidenberg*, 254–5).

59 Gladkov, *Meetings*, 134.

60 Pasternak regarded the Bible as Mankind's handbook ('tetrad'), but in the sense that it was read by succeeding generations. More important to him than its ethical commands and theological doctrines was a vaguer notion of human compassion, as when Zhivago finds the White conscript whom he inadvertently killed to be bearing an amulet with the same Psalm 91 as the dead Red telegraphist.

61 K.M. Polivanov, 'Marina Tsvetaeva v romane Borisa Pasternaka *Doktor Zhivago*', *devisu* 0 (1992) (pilot issue): 52–8; a shorter version had previously appeared in *Nezavisimaia gazeta*, 9 October 1992.

62 Aleksandr Pasternak, *A Vanished Present*, ed. Ann Pasternak Slater (Ithaca: Cornell University Press, 1984), 70. Aleksandr Pasternak notes that this and other misfortunes at Obolenskoe in 1903 also put an end to an unfinished masterpiece of his father's which might have changed Leonid Pasternak's career.

63 Letter to A. L. Shtikh 6 August 1913, cited in Barnes, *Boris Pasternak: A Literary Biography*, 1, 49. Lazar Fleishman has commented on this transfiguration in *The Poet and his Politics*, 13. Fleishman deems it highly unlikely Pasternak could have been a pupil of Skriabin (ibid., 21).

64 Angela Livingstone, *Boris Pasternak: Doctor Zhivago* (Cambridge University Press, 1989), 38. For other parallels between the events of the novel and Pasternak's own situation both in 1929, when he was writing *A Safe-Conduct*, and at the time of writing *Doctor Zhivago*, during the postwar Zhdanovism, see Fleishman, *The Poet and his Politics*, 267–72.

65 *The Poet and his Politics*, 264–6.

6. ILIA EHRENBURG, THE ETERNAL CHAMELEON

1 Translated by Elaine Feinstein in her edited collection, *Three Russian Poets* (Manchester: Carcanet, 1979), 26.

2 'Postscript', in Anatol Goldberg, *Ilya Ehrenburg: Writing, Politics and the Art of Survival* (London: Weidenfeld and Nicolson, 1984), 278–9. Emphasis in the original. Goldberg's book is filled with warm empathy for Ehrenburg; it was written by an émigré Jew from Russia who broadcast in the BBC Russian Service and who died before completing his book, which retains several uncorrected errors and inaccuracies. Early Soviet studies of Ehrenburg were generally ideologically hostile, as was N. Tereshchenko's *Sovremennyi nigilist: Belletristika I. Erenburga* (Leningrad: Priboi, 1925). The opening up of archival material allowed Aleksandr Rubashkin in his *Il'ia Erenburg: Put' pisatelia* (Leningrad: Sovetskii pisatel', 1990) to considerably expand the treatment given in his earlier *Publitsistika Il'i Erenburga protiv voiny i fashizma* (Leningrad, 1965) but even *glasnost'* did not allow him to give more than a gloss on the Jewish chapters in Ehrenburg's life and other sensitive issues. Recent Western biographies include Michael Klimenko, *Ehrenburg: An Attempt at a Literary Portrait* (Bern/ Frankfurt-am-Main/New York: Peter Lang, 1990); Julian Laychuk, *Ilya Ehrenburg: An Idealist in an Age of Realism* (Bern/Frankfurt-am-Main/New York: Peter Lang, 1991); Ewa Bérard, *La Vie tumultueuse d'Ilya Ehrenbourg: Juif, Russe et Soviétique* (Paris: Ramsay, 1991); Lilly Marcou, *Ilya Ehrenbourg* (Paris: Plon, 1992).Victor Erlich's brief discussion, 'The Turnings of Ilya Ehrenburg', in his *Modernism and Revolution: Russian Literature in Transition* (Cambridge, MA: Harvard University Press, 1994), 237–54, appeared after the completion of this book, and it barely mentions the Jewish side of Ehrenburg's life.

3 A copiously illustrated and annotated edition of all seven books of the Memoirs, which restores cuts and unpublished chapters, was compiled by Ehrenburg's daughter Irina and the literary scholar B. Frezinskii at the end of the Soviet period, *Liudi, gody, zhizn': vospominaniia*, revised and supplemented edition, three volumes (Moscow: Sovetskii pisatel', 1990). All page references will be to this edition and will be given in brackets, with the volume number in Roman numerals. An English translation from the original Soviet edition was *Men, Years – Life* of which the first volume came out as *People and Life*, reissued as *Childhood and Youth, 1891–1917*, with the second volume *First Years of Revolution, 1918–1921*, translated by Anna Bostock and Yvonne Kapp (London: MacGibbon & Kee, 1962); volume III *Truce, 1921–1933* and volume IV, *Eve of War*, were translated by Tatania Shebunina with Yvonne Kapp (London: MacGibbon & Kee, 1963); reissued in one volume as *Memoirs: 1921–1941* (New York: Grosset and Dunlap,

1966); volume v appeared as *The War, 1941–1945* (London: Mac-gibbon & Kee, 1964) and volume vi as *Post-War Years, 1945–1954*, translated by Tatiana Shebunina and Yvonne Kapp (London: MacGibbon & Kee, 1966). The story of how Ehrenburg struggled to have his memoirs published is told in the revised Soviet edition and in Goldberg, *Ilya Ehrenburg* 268–77 and appendices.

4   Esther Markish, *Le Long Retour* (Paris: Robert Laffont, 1974), 286–7; translated in Ewa Bérard-Zarzycka, 'Ilya Erenburg in Stalin's Post-War Russia', *Soviet Jewish Affairs*, 17, 1 (1987): 43. Bérard defends Ehrenburg as having no alternative, citing the words of his secretary Elena Zonina during those years, 'He had everything to lose and nothing to gain' ('Ilya Ehrenburg', 43); see also Bérard's *La Vie tumultueuse d'Ilya Ehrenbourg*, 186–7. Lilly Marcou believes this was the only possible strategy of both self-preservation and assistance to those who could still be saved (*Ilya Ehrenbourg*, 269). Ehrenburg gives his account of what he calls the most difficult days of his life in *Liudy, gody, zhizn'*, iii, 95–105. He explains that he did not want to provide material for anti-Soviet propaganda abroad and did not guess at the full truth about Stalin, even when he appealed (successfully) for his own situation to be clarified in a direct letter to Stalin in spring 1949 after his articles stopped appearing and he feared imminent arrest. On the basis of careful study of the archives of the Jewish Anti-Fascist Committee, Shimon Redlich accepts as substantially true Ehren-burg's claim that he had no part in the trial and execution of Jewish writers and attributes his survival to protective circles of friends in high places and his strategic value for Soviet propaganda ('Hapan hayehudi shel ilya erenburg: be'akevot khomer khadash al hamil-khamah vehashoah', *Yalkut moreshet leti'ud ve'iyun* 53 [1992]: 187–92).

5   Ehrenburg's daughter Irina testifies to several weeks of bed-ridden depression (cited Marcou, *Ilya Ehrenbourg*, 188)

6   Testimony of Feliks Davidovich Itskov, Yad Vashem archives, Jerusalem (P-21/V-1). In his Memoirs, Ehrenburg tells his side of the story (ii, 383–5) with no little pride in the warm letters he received from front-line soldiers who were concerned he had not appeared in print (one even sent him a Napoleonic rifle!).

7   Typical is a letter from one Aleksandr Gitovich to Ehrenburg in 1942 expressing pride in seeing Jewish names on military honours lists, to which Ehrenburg responded with a discussion of accusations about the 'alien' identity of some poets (*Voprosy literatury*, 1 [1993]: 272–3).

8   Ehrenburg's correspondence with Soviet Jews during the collection of material for the Black Book and in the postwar years can be found in the Yad Vashem archives in Jerusalem. A collection of these documents has been published by Mordecai Altshuler, Yits-

khak Arad and Shmuel Krakowski, *Sovetskie evrei pishut Il'e Erenburgu, 1943–1966* (Jerusalem: Yad Vashem/Hebrew University Centre for Research and Documentation of East European Jewry, 1993). Ehrenburg had already become an 'address' for Soviet troops because of his newspaper articles, and as one of the first to document the Holocaust he quickly became an 'address' for Soviet and displaced Jews, too (see Redlich, 'Hapan hayehudi …' and appendices). Mordecai Altshuler sketches Ehrenburg's public statements on Jewish victims of the Holocaust and his complex relations with other members of the Jewish Anti-Fascist Committee in 'Erenburg i evrei: Nabrosok portreta', in *Sovetskie evrei pishut Il'e Erenburgu*, 9–105.

9 Antonina Pirozhkova did try to learn Yiddish and Babel did take her to see Mikhoels's unforgettable performances in Yiddish, but he went alone to visit his Odessa relatives and was not at home when her relatives came.

10 Fleishman, *Boris Pasternak: The Poet and his Politics*, 211–13. Fleishman gives extensive coverage of Pasternak's apparently inconsistent behaviour during these years.

11 *Russian Writers: Notes and Essays* (New York: Random House, 1971), 343–53. Muchnic seems not to have realized what it meant for Ehrenburg to be forced to participate as a spectator in the show trial of Bukharin and other 'Trotskyites'. For Ehrenburg the Terror presented a cruel dilemma: to speak out abroad was to risk the safety of his daughter and family in Moscow and to make dangerous or impossible his return to his cultural homeland in Russia. See Bérard, *La Vie tumultueuse d'Ilya Ehrenbourg*, 195–222.

12 B. Sarnov, 'U vremeni v plenu', in Ehrenburg, *Liudi, gody, zhizn'*, I, 30.

13 Lilly Marcou cites French police files on Ehrenburg and discusses them in her book. By 1939 the French government seemed to believe Ehrenburg had direct access to the Kremlin when they needed planes, while in 1940 the security forces (at that time paranoiacally anti-communist) were convinced Ehrenburg was involved in an insane Soviet conspiracy (Marcou, *Ilya Ehrenbourg*, 191–2).

14 Mark Amusin reads the novel as signalling the end of Ehrenburg's 'internal exile' through the death of the individualist intellectual Volodia Saforov ('Dve emigratsii Il'i Erenburga', in *Evrei v kul'ture russkogo zarubezh'ia: sobranie statei, publikatsii, memuarov i esse*, I, ed. Mikhail Parkhomovskii [Jerusalem: published by the editor, 1992], 97–115).

15 An English translation of the letter is given in Goldberg, *Ilya Ehrenburg*, 281–2. The text reproduced by Sarnov in 'U vremeni v plenu' is incomplete, but the Russian original is reprinted in

Altshuler, 'Erenburg i evrei', 80–1. On Ehrenburg's activities in the Stalinist period see Ewa Bérard-Zarzycka, 'Ilya Erenburg in Stalin's Post-War Russia', *Soviet Jewish Affairs*, 17, 1 (1987): 31–48. On the Jewish Anti-Fascist Committee see Shimon Redlich, *Propaganda and Nationalism in Wartime Russia: The Jewish Anti-Fascist Committee in the USSR, 1941–1948* (Boulder, Colorado: East European Quarterly, 1982) and Hebrew revised and supplemented edition *Tkhiya 'al tanai: hava'ad hayehudi haanti-fashisti hasovieti – 'aliyato veshkiyato* (Beer-Sheva: Ben-Gurion University Press/Hakibuts hameukhad, 1990); additional information can be found in Shimon Redlich, 'Rehabilitation of the Jewish Anti-Fascist Committee: Report no. 7', *Soviet Jewish Affairs*, 20, 2–3 (1990): 85–98.

16 In his earlier autobiographies Ehrenburg related somewhat differently to his Jewishness, while loudly exonerating the Russian people and particularly the intelligentsia from complicity in the pogroms. He distanced himself in *Kniga dlia vzroslykh* ('Book for Adults', 1935) from his grandfather's Judaism, described as *chuzhoi mir* – an alien world – in which he was always doing the wrong thing, while in the Russian world he was alienated as a Jew. However, in a 1922 version of his autobiography he remembers visiting his maternal uncle in Kiev 'every spring' – that is, for the Passover feast – and 'imitating' his uncle at prayer.

17 Tuwim's essay was published in Polish in 1944 in émigré Polish newspapers in the West and in the USSR, as well as in an anthology published by the Warsaw Jewish Historical Commission in 1947, *Pieśń ujdzie cało*, ed. Michał M. Borwicz, XXXVI, 197–202. An English translation appears in Madeline G. Levine, 'Julian Tuwim: "We, The Polish Jews..." ', *The Polish Review*, 17, 4 (1972): 82–9.

18 Levine, 85. Tuwim reestablished contact with Ehrenburg in the expectation of victory by the Red Army; see correspondence in Tuwim, *Listy do przyjaciół-pisarzy* (Warsaw: Czytelnik, 1979), 269–72.

19 Goldberg, *Ilya Ehrenburg*, 28–9.

20 Ibid., 24–5.

21 Ewa Bérard-Zarzycka, 'Ilya Ehrenbourg: Juif, Russe et Européen, 1891–1928', *Cahiers du Monde Russe et Soviétique*, 26, 2 (1985): 221.

22 Bloy, *Le Salut par les Juifs*, cited in Bérard, 'Ilya Ehrenbourg: Juif, Russe et Européen', 221. John Coombes has found Bloy's writings saturated in a castration complex and also argues that they anticipate the absolutist discourse of fascist racism ('Léon Bloy: Language, Reason and Violence', *French Studies*, 42, 3–4 [1985]: 443–57). For the context of Bloy's writing see Richard Griffiths, *The Reactionary Revolution: The Catholic Revival in French Literature, 1870–1914* (London: Constable, 1966).

23 Ehrenburg, *Ia zhivu: Stikhi* (St Petersburg, 1911), 52.

24 Bérard, 'Ilya Ehrenbourg: Juif, Russe et Européen': 221–2. A more qualified statement can be found in her *La Vie tumultueuse d'Ilya Ehrenbourg*, 45–6. Laychuk also omits the last lines and interprets Zionist sympathies into the poem without any further evidence (Laychuk, *Ilya Ehrenburg*, 27–8).

25 'I. Erenburg, *Oduvanchiki*', *Giperborei*, 3 (December 1912): 30.

26 Ehrenburg, *Staryi skorniak i drugie proizvedeniia*, ed. M. Vainshtein, 1 (privately published, Israel, 1983), 342.

27 'Ballada ob Isake Zil'bersone', *Evreiskii mir*, 1 (Moscow 1918): 215–19. For the avant-garde Jewish context of this publication see Chapter 2.

28 Julian L. Laychuk, 'Ilya Ehrenburg: Early Apostle of Pacifism', *Soviet Jewish Affairs*, 5, 2 (1975): 40–7. See also Laychuk, *Ilya Ehrenburg*, 32–52.

29 *Lik voiny* (Sofia: Rossiisko-bolgarskoe knigoizdatel'stvo, 1922), 11.

30 See Laychuk, 'Ilya Ehrenburg: Early Apostle of Pacifism', 44. Voloshin wrote of *Stikhi o kanunakh* and the *Povest'* that these books were soaked in both Christian symbolism and the Judaic spirit, and compared them to Lamentations (cited *Sobranie sochinenii* , 1, 591–2).

31 It is 'we' who crucified Russia in 'Sudnii den'' ('The Day of Judgement', 1918) and the poet writes as a Russian who must share that guilt, not as a Crucified Jew.

32 Erenburg, *Sobranie sochinenii* (Moscow: Khudozhestvennaia literatura, 1990), 1, 70–1.

33 Voloshin, 'Poeziia i revoliutsiia: Aleksandr Blok i Il'ia Erenburg', *Kamena*, 2 (1919): 10–28; cited in *Sobranie sochinenii* (Moscow: Khudo-zhestvennaia literatura, 1990), 1, 596

34 *Hope Abandoned*, t28–30

35 Letter of November 1918 to Vera Merkurova, cited in Bérard, 'Ilya Ehrenbourg: Juif, Russe, Européen', 224.

36 See Zamiatin, 'On Literature, Revolution, Entropy and Other Matters' (1923), in *A Soviet Heretic: Essays by Yevgeny Zamyatin*, ed. Mirra Ginzburg (Chicago University Press, 1970), 107–8

37 *Hope against Hope*, 127.

38 'Evreiskaia krov'', *Kievskaia zhizn'*, 2 October 1919.

39 'O chem dumaet "zhid"?' *Kievskaia zhizn'*, 22 October 1919. See on Ehrenburg's articles of 1919 D. Feldman, 'I. G. Erenburg: Stat'i 1919 goda', *devisu* o (pilot issue, 1992): 5–11.

40 Simon Markish, 'Tri primera', *Vestnik evreiskoi kul'tury*, 4 [7] (1990): 46. See also Bérard, *La Vie tumultueuse*, 79–82.

41 *Razdum'ia* (Riga, 1921), 5.

42 Ibid., 15.

43 Goldberg, *Ilya Ehrenburg*, 53.

44 *Russkii Berlin*, ed. Lazar Fleishman, R. Hughes and Olga Raevskaia-

Hughes (Paris: YMCA Press, 1983), 134–54. One thinks of Babel, who later boasted he was boycotted by the émigré community in Paris as a Cheka agent.

45 Ehrenburg returns to the quasi-demonic, quasi-mystical theme of pipes in his book of stories, *Trinadsat' trubok* ('Thirteen Pipes'), which also has a blasphemous 'Jewish' chapter.

46 I quote from the 1927 first Soviet edition of the novel reprinted in *Neobychainye pokhozhdeniia Khulio Khurenito* (Moscow: Moskovskii rabochii, 1991), 35.

47 Carol Avins applies the Bakhtinian notion of the 'carnival' (taken from Menippean satire) to Ehrenburg's inversion of up–down relations in revolutionary Russia in her brief survey of the novel and its critical reception in her book *Border Crossings: The West and Russian Identity in Soviet Literature, 1917–1934* (Berkeley: University of California Press, 1983), 123–31. Avins dismisses the identity of Eternal Jew as peripheral to Ehrenburg's novel, and she classifies its author as an 'unaligned traveller'.

48 Nikolai Bukharin, 'Predislovie', in Ehrenburg, *Khulio Khurenito*, 16.

49 In an article dating from pre-*glasnost'* days, Boris Paramonov identified Julio Jurenito with Anti-Christ as Nietzsche portrayed him in his essay of that title describing the Jew's pariah status in Western culture, a concept Ehrenburg would have absorbed from that archetypal Russified Jew Lev Shestov ('Portret evreia: Erenburg', *Zvezda*, 1 [1991]: 132–50). The publication of this tendentious essay blends in with a post-Soviet discourse which legitimizes exposure of the Jew's 'true' identity, in this case a literal reading of Julio Jurenito's discourse as a monophonic, non-ironic confession and a key to the Jew-Ehrenburg's faithless and provocative role. Simon Markish has already pointed out in an essay that dates from *perestroika* how untrue is this racist characterization of the Jew, and has noted that there is sufficient basis in Western intellectual history for the Outsider to make it unnecesary to look for a source in Nietzsche ('Tri primera', 42–3).

50 Chimen Abramsky, 'Yiddish Book Illustrations in Russia: 1916–1923', in Apter-Gabriel (ed.), *Tradition and Revolution*, 65–6; cf. Ruth Apter-Gabriel, 'El Lissitzky's Jewish Works', 101–25.

51 'El. Lissitzky', doctoral thesis, Yale University, 1973, 242. See Chapter 2 above.

52 Goldberg, *Ilya Ehrenburg*, 122.

53 T. A. Perry, 'Introduction', in *The Moral Proverbs of Santob de Carrión: Jewish Wisdom in Christian Spain*, ed. T. A. Perry (Princeton University Press, 1987), 5.

54 The image of wine from the lower branches of the vine in the *Moral*

Proverbs serves to reinforce the parable of the rose among thorns and to justify the status of the Jewish poet, while the poet's vindication of the 'No' is found in the rather different context of the negative answer given by his lady love when asked if she loves another. Ehrenburg's manipulation of Jewish sources, which has none of Sholom Aleichem's humorous mischief in Tevye's misquoting of Scripture, is found also in the classic Talmudic dispute over the finding of the lost prayer shawl in 'The Stormy Life of Lazik Roitshvanets' and the wayfarers' prayer for rain in *People, Years, Life.* Simon Markish suggests Ehrenburg was generally ignorant of Jewish sources, but knew some in translation, such as Frug's Berlin edition of Bialik's *Sefer haagadah* ('Tri primera', 46–7).

55 Ehrenburg, *Sobranie sochinenii* (Moscow: Khudozhestvennaia literatura, 1991), IV, 552. Ehrenburg retold Santob de Carrión's 'Advice' to King Pedro in his obituary speech for the leading Yiddish actor and member of the Jewish Anti-Fascist Committee Solomon Mikhoels, murdered by the NKVD (speech of 24 May 1948 at the State Jewish Theatre in Moscow, translated in Ewa Bérard, 'Ilia Ehrenburg in Stalin's Post-War Russia': 36–8). In his Memoirs Ehrenburg again cites Santob de Carrión when he describes Perets Markish as a 'poet of thirsty lips' (I, 458), a revealing identification with Jewish victims of Stalin. Ehrenburg's poem 'Rabbi Shem Tov and Pedro the Cruel', included in his Collected Works, is another version of the same legend which is topical for its noting the solace gained by the cruel despot after executing the dissident Jew-Poet who asked disturbing questions (Ehrenburg, *Sobranie sochinenii* [Moscow: Khudozhestvennaia literatura, 1967], IX, 777–8). The citation of a Jewish poet writing in Spain is significant for the parallel with the Jew writing in Russia, a parallel made explicit in Valentin Parnakh's introduction to his edition of Jewish poets writing in Spanish and Portuguese mentioned in Chapter 4 above. Isaak Babel, by contrast, refers to a better-known figure, Yehuda Halevi, in his story 'The Journey' as an ironic expression of frustrated ideals; this Hebrew poet of the Golden Age in Muslim Spain found himself in the West while his heart was in the East, but he was killed, as legend has it, by an Arab horseman at the portals of Jerusalem. Heine had also claimed the heritage of Yehuda Halevi as an ideal symbiosis of Hebrew and Arabic culture that predated persecution and social instability, though he is also a martyr. But, as Sander Gilman remarks, Heine's parallel with the troubadors and his introduction of a Jewish shlemiel hero expose the shifting sands on which he stakes his identity as poet (*Jewish Self-Hatred*, 184). The same might be said of Ehrenburg, except that the image of the unaccepted

persecuted Jew was an important facet of poetic identity. For both Mandelstam and Ehrenburg, however, Heine's legitimization of the Poet-Jew was likely to have been less important than Heine's reception in Russian literature as the classic Romantic poet.

56 Bérard, *La Vie tumultueuse d'Ilya Ehrenbourg*, 145. Bérard reports that in Warsaw at the end of 1927 Ehrenburg was flouting his identity as a 'Jew of the Soviet faith', which, she finds, fits in with the Polish poet Alexander Wat's formulation of Ehrenburg's 'double sense, double language, double faith'.

57 An English translation of Ehrenburg's sketch appears as 'The Tsadik', in *A Golden Treasury of Jewish Literature*, ed. L. Schwarz (London, 1937), 156–8.

58 In correspondence to Elizaveta Polonskaia of 1927, Ehrenburg described the book as an entirely Talmudic approach to the times (Bérard, 'Ilya Ehrenbourg: Juif, Russe, Européen': 235).

59 *The Stormy Life of Laz Roitshvantz*, translated by Alec Brown (London: Elek Books, 1965), 79. The book was first published in Paris, 1928, and the translation is made from the Petropolis edition (Berlin, 1929). That edition has been republished as *Burnaia zhizn' Lazika Roitshvanetsa: Roman* (Moscow: Sovetskii pisatel', 1991).

60 The Kotsker rebbe's saying that the world's existence was justified by a single sigh and his telling an anxious petitioner that brooding was quite all right were perhaps familiar to Lazik Roitshvanets. In the 1927 story 'V Protochnom pereulike' Ehrenburg also uses the apocryphal legend of the Kotsker rebbe's blasphemous behaviour when he extinguished a candle on a holy day after a prolonged period of self-immolation and exclaimed 'There is no Judge and no Judgement'; this cry of atheistic despair would suit the declarations of blasphemy in Ehrenburg's works which conceal a lost faith prior to a new-found theology.

61 *The Stormy Life of Laz Roitshvantz*, 155–6.

62 See Chapter 2 above for a discussion of the crucifixion in Jewish artistic representation of the pogroms. The use of the crucifixion in art of the Holocaust and post-Holocaust period is surveyed in Ziva Amishai-Maisels, *Depiction and Interpretation: The Influence of the Holocaust on the Visual Arts* (Oxford: Pergamon, 1993), 178–97.

EPILOGUE: HOPE BETRAYED

1 A number of Soviet Jewish writers were familiar with Nazi atrocities from accounts by refugees who had sought asylum in territories annexed by the Soviet Union after the Molotov–Ribbentrop pact, but they were prevented from speaking out. A rare instance of

hinting at the fate of East European Jewry is to be found in the critic Leonid Grossman's article on Lermontov, prepared before the German invasion, which draws parallels with the Velizh blood-libel and thereby provides yet another case-study of conscription of a Russian literary figure and desired cultural values to provide a hidden text (Peter Scotto, 'Censorship, Reading and Interpretation: A Case Study from the Soviet Union', *PMLA* 109, 1 [1994]: 61–70). Ehrenburg was a well-informed journalist and knew of Nazi persecution of the Jews from his stay in occupied Paris and his journey through Germany back to Russia.

2   Grossman, *Zhizn' i sud'ba* (Moscow: Knizhnaia palata, 1988), based on a surviving authorial manuscript, supersedes the first Soviet publication in the magazine *Oktiabr'* earlier the same year. Quotations refer to Robert Chandler's translation, *Life and Fate* (London: Collins Harvill, 1985), from an edited version of a manuscript smuggled to the West by the dissident writer Vladimir Voinovich. On Grossman see S. Lipkin, *Stalingrad Vasiliia Grossmana* (Ann Arbor: Ardis, 1986); S. Markish, 'Primer Vasiliia Grossmana' in his edition of Grossman, *Na evreiskie temy* (Jerusalem: Sifriyat Aliia, 1985), II, 341–532; abridged English version: 'A Russian Writer's Jewish Fate', *Commentary*, 81, 4 (1986): 29–47.

3   Ehrenburg, *Stikhotvoreniia* (Moscow: Khudozhestvennaia literatura, 1977), 187.

4   As is well known, the Wannsee conference which sealed the fate of European Jewry took place in January 1942, but measures against the Jews had already been taken soon after the Germans entered Poland and other occupied countries, something that prior to the German invasion of Russia the Soviet press hid from the Jewish population (some of whom were shortly to fall victim to the Germans themselves).

5   Mikhail Bakhtin, 'Discourse in the Novel', in *The Dialogic Imagination*, ed. by Michael Holquist; translated by Caryl Emerson and Michael Holquist (Austin: University of Texas Press, 1981), 324. The surreptitious insertion of subversive voices did not start with this novel, in the view of at least one scholar, although this novel goes much further in representing non-orthodoxy; see Frank Ellis, 'Vasilii Grossman: The Genesis of Heresy, 1937–1941', *Modern Language Review* 85, 3 (1990): 653–66; see also John Garrard, 'Stepson in the Motherland: The Architectonics of Vasilii Grossman's *Zhizn' i sud'ba*', *Slavic Review*, 50, 2 (1991): 336–46.

6   As witnessed by Natalia Roskina cited in Markish, 'Primer Vasiliia Grossmana', 383.

7   The novel was originally dedicated to the author's mother, and in

fact Grossman had penned his dead mother a letter in 1961 which reads in part, 'When I die you will live in the book I have dedicated to you and whose fate is like yours' (cited by V. Kardin, in his afterword to the novel, 'Prodolzhenie sud'by', in V. Grossman, *Zhizn' i sud'ba* [Moscow: Knizhnaia palata, 1988], 816). The manuscript which was smuggled to the West carried no dedication.

8 On the alleged medical murder of Gorky by Levin and Pletnev as background to the 'Doctors' Plot' see Yakov L. Rapoport, *Na rubezhe dvukh epokh: Delo vrachei 1953 goda* (Moscow: Kniga, 1988), 14–15. The significance of the 'Doctors' Plot' does not escape Vera Sherer, the Jewish doctor, in a humanitarian plea against Stalinism in Ehrenburg's *The Thaw*, and Ehrenburg may likewise (though more subtly) have been projecting onto his heroine his own moral conscience.

9 On the hostility to Grossman see John Garrard, 'A Conflict of Visions: Vasilii Grossman and the Russian Idea', in *The Search for Self-Definition in Russian Literature*, ed. Ewa M. Thompson (Houston: Rice University Press, 1991), 57–75.

Index

CAMBRIDGE STUDIES IN RUSSIAN LITERATURE

General editor MALCOLM JONES

Editorial board: ANTHONY CROSS, CARYL EMERSON, HENRY GIFFORD, BARBARA HELDT, G.S. SMITH, VICTOR TERRAS

In the same series

Novy Mir
EDITH ROGOVIN FRANKEL

The enigma of Gogol
RICHARD PEACE

Three Russian writers and the irrational
T. R. N. EDWARDS

Words and music in the novels of Andrey Bely
ADA STEINBERG

The Russian revolutionary novel
RICHARD FREEBORN

Poets of modern Russia
PETER FRANCE

Andrey Bely
J. D. ELSWORTH

Nikolay Novikov
W. GARETH JONES

Vladimir Nabokov
DAVID RAMPTON

Portraits of early Russian liberals
DEREK OFFORD

Marina Tsvetaeva
SIMON KARLINSKY

Bulgakov's last decade
J. A. E. CURTIS

Velimir Khlebnikov
RAYMOND COOKE

Dostoyevsky and the process of literary creation
JACQUES CATTEAU

The poetic imagination of Vyacheslav Ivanov
PAMELA DAVIDSON

Joseph Brodsky
VALENTINA POLUKHINA

Petrushka – the Russian carnival puppet theatre
CATRIONA KELLY

Turgenev
FRANK FRIDEBERG SEELEY

From the idyll to the novel: Karamzin's sentimentalist prose
GITTA HAMMARBERG

The Brothers Karamazov *and the poetics of memory*
DIANE OENNING THOMPSON

Andrei Platonov
THOMAS SEIFRID

Nabokov's early fiction
JULIAN W. CONNOLLY

Iurii Trifonov
DAVID GILLESPIE

Mikhail Zoshchenko
LINDA HART SCATTON

Andrei Bitov
ELLEN CHANCES

Nikolai Zabolotsky
DARRA GOLDSTEIN

Nietzsche and Soviet Culture
edited by BERNICE GLATZER ROSENTHAL

Wagner and Russia
ROSAMUND BARTLETT

*Russian Literature and Empire: Conquest of the Caucasus
from Pushkin to Tolstoy*
SUSAN LAYTON